Dilemmas
of
Political Participation

Edited by

Robert T. Golembiewski
UNIVERSITY OF GEORGIA

J. Malcolm Moore
EASTERN KENTUCKY UNIVERSITY

Dilemmas o

Jack Rabin

AUBURN UNIVERSITY AT MONTGOMERY

olitical Participation,

Issues for Thought
and
Simulations for Action

PRENTICE-HALL, INC., *Englewood Cliffs, New Jersey*

Library of Congress Cataloging in Publication Data

GOLEMBIEWSKI, ROBERT T   comp.
   Dilemmas of political participation

   Includes bibliographical references.
   1. Political participation—United States—
Addresses, essays, lectures. 2. Political science—
Simulation methods. I. Moore, J. Malcolm, joint
comp. II. Rabin, Jack, joint comp.
III. Title.
JK2274.A3G64   320'.01'84   72-10248
ISBN   0-13-214262-7

Dilemmas of Political Participation

Issues for Thought and Simulations for Action

Robert T. Golembiewski / J. Malcolm Moore / Jack Rabin

Copyright © 1973 by Prentice-Hall, Inc., Englewood Cliffs, New Jersey

Printed in the United States of America

10   9   8   7   6   5   4   3   2   1

PRENTICE-HALL INTERNATIONAL, INC., *London*
PRENTICE-HALL OF AUSTRALIA, PTY. LTD., *Sydney*
PRENTICE-HALL OF CANADA, LTD., *Toronto*
PRENTICE-HALL OF INDIA PRIVATE LIMITED, *New Delhi*
PRENTICE-HALL OF JAPAN, INC., *Tokyo*

Contents

part two

The Institutional Setting
for Participation
93

part five

Games Students Can Play
321

Preface

This book is about political participation and, consistently, it is one of the products of a participative effort by numerous teachers and students of an introductory course in American Government. The goal was one of high impact—to heighten the mutual educational experience for both teacher and student. For the teaching staff, this volume is one reflection of the effort to make the experience as valuable and as engaging as possible —personally and professionally. For the students, this volume is one reflection of the effort to encourage more involvement in the learning process, to urge them to deal with skills as well as concepts.

This book about participation is, by design, a product of an unusually broad range of inputs. The inputs of the teaching staff are easier to identify. Six of the selections below were written expressly for this volume by some of those who taught in Political Science 101 over the years 1968–71. Other teachers in POL 101 variously contributed to the four simulations which constitute a major part of this book, contributions both to design and especially to running the simulations in the classroom.

The inputs of POL 101 students are not so easy to identify, but they are there nonetheless. Several thousand students pretested various readings and variations of the four simulations. Who was teacher and who was student varied even more than normal during this extensive pretesting. Basically, their reactions told us when we had a viable vehicle for adding impact and interest to the basic offering in American Government.

Time and fortune have scattered the group whose work is reflected in this volume, both teachers and students. There are some good times underlying the pages below, and some trying ones as well. We hope both the good and the trying times will have contributed to a better educational experience for those who use this volume.

Dilemmas
of
Political Participation

part one

Perspectives on an Expanding Political Participation

Characteristics and Causes

Patterns of today's political participation are best likened to a kaleidoscope. The patterns can be eye-catching, complex, shifting, and changing from one perspective. From another perspective, it often seems as if the same old things are being done by the same people through the same institutions for political participation. An Archie Bunker is likely to see more turbulent change and instability. His son-in-law, Meathead Mike, is likely to be more impressed by stability and continuity, or even reactionary or repressive tendencies. And both will be correct, up to a point.

That is to say, we are in the early stages of redefining what "political participation" means, of testing expanded notions of who can participate politically and of how they can seek to influence public policy. At this stage, the old and the new notions coexist more or less uncomfortably, and their resolution is still doubtful. A new synthesis, an expanded concept of political participation, may evolve. Or an escalation of differences may continue, with increasingly sharp lines being drawn between those who wish to maintain a traditional definition of political participation and those who desire to innovate and experiment with new forms.

This chapter begins sketching political participation as in-process, as a changing blend of what has been, what is, and what may come to be. The immediate focus is on the characteristics and causes of more or less innovative forms of political participation. Following chapters will emphasize more traditional institutions and concepts that have influenced political participation, and which continue to do so.

3

Throughout the book, two points should be kept in mind. First, the underlying definition of "political participation" is a simple one. Political participation deals with the concepts, ideas, attitudes, and institutions that guide or determine how the development and implementing of public policy are variously influenced. This broad target is approached from two perspectives. One perspective emphasizes "should"—an ideal concept of who should influence public policy, how they should participate, and when they should. The second perspective emphasizes "is"—who actually does influence public policy, when they influence it, and how.

The interaction between should and is, between what is considered legitimate and how various people actually behave, is a critical one. Right now, in simplified terms, some people are behaving in ways and at times that do not fit traditional notions of who should participate in influencing public policy, and when and how. Life is more or less uncomfortable while the adjustment process goes on. Many resolutions are possible. Thus the ideal definition of political participation could be expanded. Or the challenging behaviors could be repressed and the innovators variously hindered. Either way, it is a challenging time to be alive.

Second, no one seems to have a monopoly on truth or virtue in this confrontation of new behavior and older concept. There are crazies in the camps of both innovators and reactionaries. There are whites intent on putting the torch to those who even mildly seek to make participation more meaningful for the previously excluded, that is, as there are whites seeking some new blend of participants with meaningful access to influence on public policy. Similarly, blacks may act responsibly in seeking an expanded concept of political participation. In other cases, blacks may tenaciously support even very dubious soul brothers in their own variation of an earlier theme: If you're white, you're right.

The panorama of the New Participation is so engaging that it is easy to forget what is at stake. New political alliances may be developing. Or perhaps even a revolution may occur via the evolution of novel ways to participate in politics at uniquely intense levels. Or we may be viewing a grotesque game of follow-the-leader, of a few crazies who took advantage of the freakish cresting of range of social, political, and economic factors to trigger new forms of political participation that had little lasting support. These factors include: unprecedentedly large number of adolescents and young adults anxious to make a mark in a world they did not create; unparalleled prosperity and leisure for a burgeoning proportion of the population; widening awareness of the decay of central cities and of the pollution of our physical environment; the simultaneous economic demands of the Vietnam war and of massive social programs; and truly huge increases in the number of college students who overwhelmed the capacities of educational institutions, at least initially. Experiments in participation that seemed reasonable under the full impact of these conditions, consequently, may appear increasingly precious or even absurd if the conditions above are unique to a few brief years.

If we are not clearly experiencing a revolution in the form and intensity of political participation, it is certainly not for lack of attention or interest. Journalists fill the pages of their newspapers, or the screens of our video-tubes, with the results of much contemporary political participation. No imagination is needed to make the stories colorful. Take your pick. The indomitable Red Bear, a 284-pound Tuscarora Indian, leads the Iroquois Confederation in the quest for "Red Power." The equally indomitable and bulky Reverend Billy Joe Hargis finds audiences again eager to hear the nation's problems attributed to another kind of Red power. And President Nixon's memorable journey to China suggests yet another Red power, to influence the chances for peace and to provide new markets for our goods. It is all great theater, both revolutionary and reactionary.

Nor is variety lacking in the New Participants. Some participate to change the status quo; others participate to conserve it; and a few seek to destroy institutions as we know them. Most participate through legitimate means, and their participation is accepted by their fellow citizens because it follows expected patterns. Others resort to illegitimate or unusual means. These means sometimes include violence, and other times delicately tiptoe on that fine line between making a critical point in a forceful way and posing a real threat to the common good, as that is variously defined. Finally, there is a new and vigorous participation by citizens who, by law or by custom, had been excluded as participants. Sometimes with a vengeance that reveals past frustrations, these new participants have recently begun to engage in political activity, and to seek changes in the status quo. These newcomers are frequently treated as illegitimate participants, even when their methods are totally within the boundaries considered legitimate for participants of longer experience.

Some examples suggest the range of the New Participants. Everyone knows about the recent reappearance of Woman's Lib, of course, and the universities are still vibrating in the aftermath of tumultuous student concerns. The catalog goes on and on. Inmates in prison, by law, are nonparticipants. They nonetheless riot, kidnap and hold guards as hostages, and negotiate their demands for changes in public policies concerning prison administration. They participate, even as that means innovating new ways to be heard, or taking risks with older if hazardous techniques. Welfare mothers stage sit-downs in the dingy offices of local agencies, as well as on the majestic granite steps of federal agencies in Washington. They are sometimes successful, sometimes not, in gaining their demands for greater support. What is new is that they seek welfare boldly as a right, not humbly as a privilege. It makes a world of difference, of course. Similarly, civilian review boards have been established to evaluate citizen complaints about the overzealous use of force by police, often the local guardians of the status quo. These illustrations suggest that new participants and new forms of participation can and do produce different governmental responses and reactions.

Part one samples the New Participation, and suggests some of its sources. A number of readings below chart the characteristics and causes of today's patterns of participation. For openers, Bennett M. Berger provides broad perspective on perhaps the major source of fuel for today's new and intense political participation in his "The New Stage of American Man: Almost Endless Adolescence." Biological adolescence lasts a few years, Berger explains, but "technological, economic and social developments conspire to prolong the dependence of the young for 10 or 15 years." The point applies in two senses. Education tends to last longer for each individual; and uniquely large numbers of individuals are involved. This a new phenomenon of the 1960s, and one not easily adapted to.

The nation's schools are the prime repositories of Berger's new and rapidly growing mass of almost endless adolescents. The schools variously maintain large numbers of those who are old enough, sometimes skilled enough, and even willing enough to engage in productive employment, but who are not yet needed. From an important perspective, Berger argues, colleges especially are unique warehouses for aging and improving and storing young citizens until they will not become a glut on the job market. No wonder college-aged citizens often are restless and seek causes or, alternatively, opt for apathetic subjugation to "the system." They have plenty of time to develop both reactions.

With biological adolescence and social-technological adolescence at such growing odds, something had to give. One basic change has been the more intense and common involvement of young citizens in political activity. Reflecting this change and perhaps characteristic of the lessons learned in the 1960s, the right to vote in federal elections has recently been extended to all 18-year-olds.

Long before the law caught up with the spirit of the times, however, many young citizens were taking their own approaches to political participation. Consistent with Berger's analysis, these citizens often were the sons and daughters of the well-to-do, and they reflected every conceivable degree of rejection of their affluent backgrounds. Diana Oughton touched all the bases, from her birth into established rural wealth to her death when a Weatherman bomb factory exploded in New York. In a set of Pulitzer Prize winning news stories, Lucinda Franks and Thomas Powers trace Diana's evolution from unexceptional college coed to dedicated revolutionary in "Making of a Terrorist."

What happened to Diana Oughton is in many senses personal and unique, but the tragedy has its broader implications as well. Ideally, one Diana is too much for her parents and perhaps for herself. But how many Dianas can a society encourage or create, practically, without undermining its own institutions and perhaps even deserving to have them undermined? Or consider the greater loss, Diana's herculean efforts to have an impact on the people and world around her. These efforts she saw frustrated at every turn, perhaps especially in the ultimate instant of the explosion of the bomb that she may have seen as her last hope.

If Diana's tragedy is generalizable to any appreciable degree, there is reason to be alarmed. For there are many other Dianas (and Dans) who support many other causes in less extreme ways than the bombing to which she apparently felt herself driven. And frustration of their need to succeed may encourage these other Dianas to more extreme tactics or, perhaps even worse, to a despair that no tactic is worthwhile because no tactic seems to work.

Whatever else, there are many contemporary training grounds for other Diana Oughtons. Several additional readings direct attention to other major recent explosions of demands for greater participation. Frustration of these demands may lead to personal and societal tragedy, if Diana Oughton's life and death have any broader meaning.

Gerda Lerner focuses attention on one such participative explosion, on the drive by women for equal treatment in "Women's Rights and American Feminism." The drive includes much political theater, as when some women shed their bras as an act of freedom and defiance rather than as an act of love. The hoopla may highlight or obscure the essential thrust of the movement, but essential thrust there is. Lerner's careful historical survey seeks the essential forces that induce today's renewed emphasis on American feminism, which "embraces all aspects of the emancipation of American women, that is, any struggle designed to evaluate their status, socially, politically, economically, and in respect to their self-concepts." Today's Women's Lib, then, is a continuation-in-depth of the earlier successful but narrow attempts to secure women's suffrage and other legal rights.

Similarly, blacks have begun to expand their desires to meaningfully participate, what with a number of pressing legal issues now more or less settled by years of work on civil rights and voting. Innovations are in order to make up for extended deprivation, and some innovations there have been. For example, in many rural areas in the south, blacks were traditionally prevented from participating in politics and, relatedly, were denied public services. In the most ironic cases, they were taxed while denied both services and participation in seeking them. Reliance on a traditional local governmental unit, the incorporated town, can help to overcome some common obstacles facing rural blacks. Carlyle C. Douglas' "Incorporation: A New Tactic for Saving Black Areas" explains both the principle and the practice of securing meaningful control over governmental services for blacks via incorporation of previously unincorporated rural areas.

Other tactics to secure more effective participation for the disadvantaged —the badly educated, the poor, those on welfare, the black—have been innovated in urban settings. Charles E. Silberman, in "The Revolt Against Welfare Colonialism," describes one such successful effort to overcome, or at least to variously counteract, urban apathy. Urban apathy was a reasonable adaptation to the perceived historical uselessness of fighting city hall, of the lack of attitudes and institutions that permitted effective influence on public policy. But the times are a changin', at least in South Chicago. Silberman describes how an organizer-without-portfolio was brought into a local community to help generate participation, and to gradually release control as the local community came to recognize and use its own resources. The vehicle was the establishment of The Woodlawn Organization. The selection illustrates how previous have-nots can participate more meaningfully in a kind of urban social warfare, employing novel tactics. The development of The Woodlawn Organization reflects but one special application of the consistent philosophy of Saul Alinsky, whose motto might be: Can Organize, Will Travel. Silberman describes that philosophy in these terms:

> The essential difference between Alinsky and his enemies is that Alinsky really believes in democracy: he really believes that the helpless, the poor, the badly-educated can solve their own problems if given the chance and the means; he really believes that the poor and the uneducated, no less than the rich and the educated, have the right to decide how their lives should be run and what services should be offered to them, instead of being ministered to like children.

The New Participation does not mean that individualism is dead, be it noted. Some kinds of participation may be solitary, even as they are reactions to massive problems. Consider a new kind of response to environmental pollution, that of the phantom ecologist guerilla. Industrialization has produced astounding conveniences in this country, we all know, as well as huge ecological problems. When industrial pollution kills a fisherman's favorite river, what can one man do? Many of us would get mad, but few get even. The Fox got mad, and then he started to get even. The story of this contemporary righter-of-wrongs-as-he-sees-them is sketched in "Go Fox/Stop Pollution."

The basic dilemma of the New Participation, however, lies in the fact that these new demands for what people want often strain available resources. This is the case even when everyone is agreed about what is good and proper and is willing to do what needs doing. Neither agreement nor willingness may exist, however, and sometimes both are lacking.

Defenders of things-as-they-were do not react indifferently to the changes which have been accomplished and proposed all around them. As the Fox does deter pollution, and as new creations such as The Woodlawn Organization effectively assert their claim for services previously denied or unavailable, so also do they generate new demands for resources. And if the total pool of resources is not increasing fast enough, some people and groups are going to feel deprived, whether relatively or actually. Priorities also will often be at loggerheads. For example, readers of this book may see the need for better highways, more effective sewage disposal, and so on. The new participants may have very different priorities. Perhaps rhetorical questions will drive home this point more quickly than other devices. Who needs a highway, if he cannot afford a car? Who needs a sewer, if he cannot afford indoor plumbing? Who needs an airport, if he has no place to go and no money to buy a ticket? Who needs police, if he has nothing worth stealing? Why have a fire department, if he has nothing worth saving? Do you need military forces, if you own little worth protecting?

The implied conclusion only requires stating. Broader participation in politics undoubtedly means broader distribution of the goods, services, status, and honor which government can confer. This threatens a reduction in the individual shares for long-term political participants, and also implies counter-reaction to new claims for participation. The point is clear in Michael M.

Schneider's "Middle America: Study in Frustration." Schneider, a skilled tradesman, intends to speak for 60–70 million people, the "white working class" and others such as small entrepreneurs and shopkeepers. Schneider writes out of a compassion for efforts to extend the good things to broader ranges of Americans, but he also reflects a sense of desperation for the plight of the Middle American he intends to represent.

Compassion and desperation are on a potential collision course, Schneider notes. His kind of people are being torn apart. Upper-middle-class America urges that he and his kind have compassion for those previously deprived. But that compassion, Schneider reports, has a way of being taken out of the hide of the white working class. A Middle American ends up feeling herniated. "He feels that he is supporting the poor," Schneider notes, "and that the welfare and city budgets come off his back."

Hence all is not necessarily for the best in this most participative of all political worlds.

1

Bennett M. Berger

The New Stage of American Man: Almost Endless Adolescence

When I was an undergraduate 20 years ago, I was chairman of one of the radical student groups at my college and an active official in the regional intercollegiate association of that group. I marched in my share of picket lines, published an article attacking my college president for anti-Semitism, was sung to by the sirens of the local Communist party and even, in a burst of creativity, wrote what in this age of instant classics I suppose qualifies as a classic militant's love song. I called it, "You and I and the Mimeograph Machine" and dedicated it to all the youthful romances born amidst the technology of moral protest.

Later, when I got older and became a sociologist, I resisted becoming a "political sociologist," by which in this context I mean what a lot of the militants mean: a former activist who traded his credentials as a conscious moral and political agent in exchange for the rewards of expertise about political behavior. Though the remarks about student militance which follow may be analytic, I yield nothing to the young in the way of moral credentials.

In trying to throw some sociological light on the nature and character of student unrest, I am not going to comfort the militants by saying that students protest because this is a racist, plastic society or because the curriculum is irrelevant or because the university has sold its soul to the military-industrial complex or because the university is a machine in which students are treated as raw material—when, indeed, their uptight teachers take time from their research to treat them as anything at all. On the other hand, I am not going to comfort their critics by saying that students rebel for kicks or because their upbringing was too permissive or because they are filled with a seething self-hatred or because they are symbolically murdering their fathers in a recurrent ritual melodrama of generational conflict.

What I will try to do is show how certain conditions generic to the direction of our present societal development have helped to bring about the present situation among youth and in the universities. I will also hazard a prediction as to the effects of these conditions during the next decade. An understanding of the problem will not make the solution any easier, for knowledge is not power, but it can at least arm us against panaceas.

· · ·

The problem of student unrest is rooted in the prolongation of adolescence in industrialized countries. But it should be understood that "adolescence" is only minimally a biological category; there are only a very few years between the onset of puberty and the achievement of the growth and strength it takes to do a man's or woman's work. As we know, however, culture has a habit of violating nature. Proto-adolescent behavior now begins even before puberty (which itself is occurring earlier) with the action—and the orientation—we call "preadolescent," while at the other end, technological, economic and social developments conspire to prolong the dependence of the young, to exclude them from many of the privileges and responsibilities of adult life, and therefore to *juvenilize** them.

The casual evidence in support of this deep institutionalization of adolescence is diffuse and quite remarkable. It includes such spectacles as 6-foot, 200-pound "boys" who in another time and place might be founders of dynasties and world-conquerers (like Alexander of Macedon) cavorting on the fraternity house lawn hurling orange peels and bags of water at each other, while tolerant local police, who chucklingly *approve*, direct traffic around the battlefield. It includes the preservation of child-like cadence and intonation in voices otherwise physically mature. It in-

---

*"Juvenilize": a verb I have devised to describe a process through which "child-ish" behavior is induced or prolonged in persons who, in terms of their organic development, are capable of participating in adult affairs. If the process exists, there ought to be a verb to describe it.

cludes the common—and growing—practice (even in official university documents) of opposing the word "student" to the word "adult"—as if students were by definition not adults, even as the median age of university students rises with the increase of the graduate student population.

Adolescence, then, is not the relatively fleeting "transitional stage" of textbook and popular lore but a substantial segment of life which may last 15 or 20 years, and if the meaning of adolescence is extended only slightly, it can last longer than that. I have in mind the age-graded norms and restrictions in those professions which require long years of advanced training, and in which the system of sponsorship makes the advancement of one's career dependent upon being somebody's "boy" perhaps well on toward one's middle-age—a fact not uncharacteristic of university faculties.

Much of the discussion of "youth culture" in recent years reflects the prolongation of adolescence, since it is not surprising that a period of life which may last from age 12 to age 35 might develop its own cultural style, its own traditions and its own sources of motivation, satisfaction—and dissatisfaction. There is thus an enormous stratum of persons caught in the tension between their experience of peak physical strength and sexual energy on the one hand, and their public definition as culturally "immature" on the other.

This tension is exacerbated by a contradictory tendency: while modern industrial conditions promote juvenilization and the prolongation of dependence, they also create an "older," more experienced youthful cohort. They have more and earlier experience with sex and drugs; they are far better educated than their parents were; urban life sophisticates them more quickly; television brings into their homes worlds of experience that would otherwise remain alien to them. Young people, then, are faced not only with the ambiguity of the adolescent role itself and its prolongation but with forces and conditions that, at least in some ways, make for *earlier* maturity. The youthful population is a potentially explosive stratum because this society is ill-equipped to accommodate it within the status system.

Erik Erikson's well-known theory of the "psycho-social moratorium" of adolescence takes the facts of adolescent prolongation and transforms them into a triumph of civilization. By emphasizing the increased time provided for young persons to postpone commitments, to try on social roles and to play the game called "the search for identity," Erikson suggests that the moratorium on lasting adult responsibilities contributes to the development and elaboration of personal individuality. I have no wish to quarrel with Erikson's general thesis here; I have done so elsewhere. Instead, I want to emphasize a fact that is seemingly contradictory to Erikson's observations about the moratorium on adult commitments. Namely, there have actually been increasing and clearly documented pressures on young people for earlier and earlier occupational planning and choice. "Benjamin," ask that famous Graduate's parents repeatedly, "what are you going to *do?*" And the question is echoed by millions of prosperous American parents who, despite their affluence, cannot assure the future economic position of their heirs.

Logically, of course, prolonged identity play and early occupational choice cannot be encouraged at the same time; the fact is, they are. And like other ambiguous values (and most moral values are ambiguous, or can be made so), this pair permit different groups of youngsters to rationalize or justify the kinds of adaptations that differing circumstances in fact constrain them to make. The public attention generated by protesting youth in recent years (hippies, the New Left, black militants) obscures the fact that the majority of young people are still apparently able to tolerate the tensions of prolonged adolescence, to adjust to the adolescent role (primarily, student), to take some satisfaction from the gains it provides in irresponsibility (i.e., "freedom") and to sail smoothly through high school into college where they choose the majors, get the grades and eventually the certifications for the occupations which they want, which want them and which higher education is equipped to provide them— degrees in education, business, engineering, dentistry and so on.

For others, however, the search for identity (quote, unquote) functions as a substitute for an occupational orientation; it gives them something "serious" to do while coping with their problems of sex, education, family and career. In college most of these people tend to major in the humanities or social sciences (particularly sociology) where they may take 10 years or more between the time they enter as freshmen, drop out, return, graduate and go on to pursue graduate degrees or give up on them entirely. I will return to this matter, but for the moment I want to make two general points: (1) that the contradictions create understandable tensions in the young and feed their appetite to discover "hypocrisy" in their elders; (2) that this condition is largely beyond the control of the universities; it is generated by the exigencies of a "post-industrial" society which uses institutions of higher education as warehouses for the temporary storage of a population it knows not what else to do with.

The situation has become critical over the past 10 years because the enormous numbers of the young (even small percentages of which yield formidable numbers of troops for worthy causes) and their concentration (in schools and cities) have promoted easy communication and a sense of group solidarity among them. Numbers, concentration and communication regarding common grievances have made increasingly viable, in almost precisely the way in which Karl Marx described the development of class consciousness among workers, the creation and maintenance of "deviant subcultures" of youth.

This youthful population is "available" for recruitment to moral causes because their marginal, ambiguous position in the social structure renders them sensitive to moral inconsistencies (note their talent for perceiving "hypocrisy"), because the major framework of their experience ("education") emphasizes "ideal" aspects of the culture and because their exclusion from adult responsibilities means that they are generally unrestrained by the institutional ties and commitments which normally function as a brake upon purely moral feeling; they also have the time for it.

The two great public issues of the decade (the Vietnam war and the rights of despised minorities) have been especially suited to enlist the militant predispositions of the young precisely because these issues are clearly moral issues. To take a strong "position" on these issues requires no great *expertise* or familiarity with arcane facts. And the moral fervor involved in taking such a position nicely reflects our traditional age-graded culture to the extent that it identifies virtue with "idealism," unspoiledness and innocence, precisely the qualities adults like to associate with the young.

It is almost as if the young, in the unconscious division of labor which occurs in all societies, were delegated the role of "moral organ" of society—what with all the grown-ups being too busy running the bureaucracies of the world (with their inevitable compromises, deals, gives and takes) to concern themselves with "ideals." This even makes a sort of good structural sense because the unanchored character of the young (that is, their relative unfetteredness to family, community and career) fits them to perform their "ideal" functions—in the same sense and for the same reason that Plato denied normal family life to his philosopher-kings and the Roman Catholic Church denies it to their priests.

It is the combination of moral sensitivity and alienation that accounts both for the extreme juvenophile postures of moral critics like Edgar Friedenberg, Paul Goodman and John Seeley (which sometimes reach the belief that the young are simply better people than the old or middle-aged, and hence even a belief in juvenocracy) and the fear of and hostility toward militant youth by writers epitomized by Lewis Feuer in his new book on student movements. In the latter view, the idealism of the young becomes corrupt, violent, terroristic and destructive precisely because, alienated, detached from institutions, youth are not "responsible"—that is, not accountable for the consequences of their moral zealotry upon the groups and organizations affected by it.

So one is tempted to say that society may just have to accept youth's irresponsibility if it values their moral contributions. But evidence suggests that adult society is in general sympathetic neither to their moral proddings nor toward granting the young any greater responsibility in public affairs. Research by English sociologist Frank Musgrove clearly documents that adults are unwilling to grant real responsibilities any earlier to the young, and there is good reason to believe the same is true in the United States, as is suggested by the repeated failures of the movement to lower the voting age to 18. And as for the "idealism" of youth, when it goes beyond the innocent virtues of praising honesty, being loyal, true and brave and helping old ladies across the street, to serious moral involvements promoting their own group interests ("student power") or those of the domestic or "third world" dispossessed, the shine of their "idealism" is likely to tarnish rather quickly.

Moreover, the moral activism of youth *is* sometimes vulnerable to attack on several counts. The "morality" of a political action, for example, is weakened when it has a self-congratulatory character (and the tendency to produce a holier-than-thou vanity in the actor). It also loses something when it does not involve substantial risk of personal interests or freedom (as it unambiguously *does* with the young only in the case of draft resisters). In the end, along with the society's prolongation of adolescence and encouragement of "the search for identity," continuing praise of the young for their "idealism" (except when it becomes serious) and continuing appeals to them to behave "responsibly"—in the face of repeated refusal to grant them real responsibilities (except in war)—are understandable as parts of the cultural armory supporting the process of juvenilization.

Colleges, universities and their environs are the places apparently designated by society as the primary locations where this armory is to be expended. It is clear that the schools, particularly institutions of higher learning, are increasingly being asked by society to perform a kind of holding operation for it. The major propaganda campaign to encourage students not to drop out of high school is significant less for the jobs which staying that last year or two in high school will qualify one for than it is for the reduced pressure it creates on labor markets unable to absorb unskilled 16- and 17-year-olds. The military institutions, through the draft, help store (and train) much of the working-class young, and the colleges and universities prepare many of the heirs of the middle classes for careers in business, the professions and the semiprofessions. But higher education also gets the lion's share of the identity seekers: those sensitive children of the affluent, less interested in preparing themselves for occupations which the universities are competent to prepare them for than in transcending or trading in the stigmata of their bourgeois backgrounds (work ethic, money-grubbing, status-seeking) for a more "meaningful" life.

It is these students who are heavily represented among the student activists and among whom the cry for "relevance" is heard most insistently. Does it seem odd that this cry should be coming from those students who are *least* interested in the curricula whose relevance is palpable, at least with respect to occupations? Not if one observes that many of these students are, in a sense, classically "intellectuals"—that is, oriented toward statuses or positions for which the universities (as well as other major institutions) have seldom been able or competent to provide certification.

The statuses such students want are those to which one appoints oneself or which one drifts into: artist, critic, writer, intellectual, journalist, revolutionist, philosopher. And these statuses have been undermined for two generations or more by technical and bureaucratic élites whose training has become increasingly specialized and "scientific." In this context the cry for relevance is a protest against technical, value-neutral education whose product (salable skills or the posture of uncommitment) contributes nothing to the search by these students for "identity" and "meaningful experience."

Adding final insult to the injury of the threatened replacement of traditional humanistic intellectuals by technical élites is the ironic transformation of some of their traditional curricula (social sciences particularly) into instruments useful to the "power structure" or "the establishment" in pursuing its own ends. It makes no sense to call a curriculum "irrelevant" and then to turn right around and accuse its chief practitioners of "selling out"; the powerful do not squander their money so easily. The ironic point, then, is not that these curricula are "irrelevant" but that they are far *too* relevant to the support of interests to which the left is opposed.

The villains here are the methodological orthodoxies of the social sciences: their commitment to objectivity, detachment and the "separation" between facts and values. In the view of radical students, these orthodoxies rationalize the official diffidence of social scientists regarding the social consequences of their research, a diffidence which (conveniently—and profitably—for social scientists, goes the argument) promotes the interests of the established and the powerful. This is far from the whole truth, of course. There is plenty of research, supported by establishments, whose results offer the establishment little comfort. But like other "nonpartisan" or value-neutral practices and procedures, the methodological orthodoxies of the social sciences do tend in general to support established interests, simply because the powerful, in command of greater resources and facilities, are better able to make use of "facts" than the weak, and because avoidance of ideological controversy tends to perpetuate the inequities of the status quo.

But the demands for a more activist and "committed" social science and for social scientists to function as advocates for oppressed and subordinated groups may not be the best way of correcting the inequities. A thorough *doctrinal* politicization of social science in the university is likely to mean the total loss of whatever little insulation remains against the ideological controversies rending the larger society; and the probable result would be that the university, instead of being more liberal than the society as a whole, would more accurately reflect the still-burgeoning reactionary mood of the country.

For students who tend to be "around" a university for a long time —the 10-year period mentioned earlier is not uncommon—the university tends to become a kind of "home territory," the place where they really live. They experience the university less as an élite training institution than as a political community in which "members" have a kind of quasi-"citizenship" which, if one believes in democratic process, means a right to a legitimate political voice in its government.*

This conception of the university is quite discrepant with the conception held by most faculty members and administrators. To most faculty members the university is the élite training institution to which students who are both willing and able come to absorb intellectual disciplines—"ologies"—taught by skilled and certified professionals whose competences are defined by and limited to those certifications. But which way one sees the university—as a political community or as an élite training institution—is not purely a matter of ideological preference.

The fact seems to be that where training and certification and performance in politically neutral skills are clearest, the more conservative view is virtually unchallenged. This is true not only for dentistry and mathematics but for athletics, too. Presumably many militant blacks are not for any kind of a quota system with respect to varsity teams, and presumably football players in the huddle do not demand a voice in the decisions that shape their lives. But where what one's education confers upon one is a smattering of "high culture" or "civilized manners" or the detached sensibility and ethics of a science whose benefits, like other wealth, are not equitably distributed—in short, where the main result of liberal education is *Weltanschauung*—it indeed has "political" consequences.

These consequences were not controversial so long as the culture of

---

*Much remains to be clarified about the nature of "membership" in academic communities. So much cant has gone down in the name of "community" that I often feel about this word much like that Nazi who has gone down in history as having said, "When I hear the word 'culture,' I reach for my revolver."

the university was fairly homogeneous and so long as the "aliens" it admitted were eager to absorb that culture. They have become controversial in recent years because the democratization of higher education has revealed the "class" character of academic culture and because of the appearance on the campus of students who do not share and/or do not aspire to that culture. These newcomers have arrived in sufficiently large numbers to mount a serious challenge to the hegemony of traditional academic culture.

Despite their many differences, the new militant "ethnic" students and their supporters among "white radicals," "street people," hippies and other young people on the left have in common their anti-academicism, which is the campus version of the anti-establishment outlook. This is true notwithstanding the fact that the academy has been the most liberal sector of establishment thought and the most sympathetic to at least some of the aspirations of dissident students. Partly, of course, their hostility to the academy is rooted in the fact that the university is where they're at, the institutional location in which they have to work through their prolonged adolescence and the problems associated with it. But beyond this, there is real conflict between the traditional criteria of academic performance and what dissident students demand from academic life.

Research suggests that most of the white radical students have grown up in a milieu where "intellectual" matters were discussed, where books were probably present in their homes, where middleclass manners and style were their birthright, and where, therefore, they learned how to "talk"—that is, where they developed the sort of verbal facility enabling them to do well enough in high school and to seem like promising "college material" if only because they look and sound much like college students have always looked and sounded. With the ascendence of the view that everybody has a right to a higher education (along with the fact that there's no place else to send well-born adolescents), most of them wind up in colleges and universities.

Some of them, despite their verbal facility, are not really bright; many others, despite their ability to get good college grades, strongly resist "conforming" to many of the requirements for professional certification which they demean as mere "socialization." Confronted by academic demands for rigor in their thinking, for sufficient discipline to master a systematic body of knowledge, for evidence that they can maintain a line of logical thinking beyond one or two propositions, and bring evidence systematically to bear upon a problem, many of them are found seriously wanting—some because they are not bright enough, others because they think it a point of honor to resist the intellectual demands made on them.

When their numbers are large enough to enable them to turn to each other for mutual support, it is not surprising that they should collectively turn against the system of criteria which derogates them and, in a manner not unanalogous to the "reaction formation" of slum delinquents who develop a subculture in opposition to middle-class school norms which judge them inadequate, develop an anti-academic viewpoint which defines abstraction, logical order, detachment, objectivity and systematic thinking as the cognitive armory of a repressive society, productive of alienation, personal rigidity and truncated capacity for feeling.

Preoccupied as most of these students are with "identity problems" and moral protest, it is again not surprising that many of them should be less interested in the mastery of academic disciplines, even if they have the ability, than in pursuing what they are likely to call "gut-issues" or nitty-gritty. The kinds of problems they apparently are interested in studying can be inferred from the examination of almost any "Free University" brochure, and what these add up to is a sort of extension division for the underground: practical, topical "rap sessions" on Vietnam, civil rights, encounter groups, pottery, psychedelics, macrobiotics, Eastern religion, rock music and so on.

In the conflict with the established interests of science and scholarship in the university, radical students do win significant victories. New courses do get approved; experimental curricula do get tried out; students do get appointed to important committees; greater weight is attached to teaching in the appointment and promotion of faculty members. But large numbers of these radical students, exhausted by conflict and depressed by negative criticism, drop out of school. In dropping out, however, they do not immediately disappear into the labor market. They tend to remain in the university community, employed occasionally or part time in dead-end jobs, living in furnished rooms or communal houses near the university, and most important for my purposes here, still participating in the marginal student culture which they know so well.

Their participation in this culture is made possible to some extent by the fact that their youth protects them from the degrading consequences of being poor and having no regular or "approved" status in the community. Part of the age-grading system which postpones adulthood is the temporary protection of the young against the stigmata which, for older people, are normally attached to poverty. But over time, this group of "nonstudents" can be regarded as downward mobile, and thereby hangs an interesting prospect.

The United States has no major tradition of large-scale downward mobility. The only major image of intergenerational decline is associated with decadent aristocratic families in ruined Southern mansions. Given the general tendency for downwardly mobile groups to resent the system which derogates them, and given the fact that the channels of upward mobility today are largely through higher education, the hostility to the university of these radical, middle-class "nonstudents" is probably maintained even after they leave it. The irony is that in dropping out, the hippie and New Left children of the middle classes provide opportunity for the upward mobility of the new black and other ambitious "disadvantaged" students.

The blacks and other ethnic militants are presently using higher education in a manner different from that in which their predecessors from the lower class used it. For earlier ethnics, the university served as a channel of mobility for *individuals* from the talented poor: today, it is sought as a means of collective mobility. There are two aspects to this movement. There is the emphasis on ethnic studies programs designed to provide the members of the respective ethnic groups with a sense of pride in their history and culture, and there are the demands that the university play a more active role in ameliorating suffering in the ghettos, not merely through programs of research which exploit the cooperation of ghetto residents without helping them measurably, but by taking the university off the campus, bringing it to them, in their terms, on their turf, for their own purposes.

In the struggle to achieve the ends of the militants, black and white, the traditional university is very vulnerable because the militants have great leverage. Just as the blacks can conceivably turn the urban core into a guerrilla battleground, militant students can bring the universities to the proverbial grinding halt. Continual rallies, classroom disruptions, picket lines, building seizures, student intimidation and general paranoia (to say nothing of the almost continual meetings by faculty and administration committees to cope with the crises and the continual corridor and coffee room gossip by knots of faculty members) can bring the teaching and other academic functions of the university to a virtual standstill.

This prospect raises seriously for the first time the question of whether the traditional university, as we know it, is an expendable institution. And another question, as well: Is it possible that a decision has been made somewhere that it is better to risk the destruction of the university by confining the unrest to the campus than to allow it to spill over into more critical institutions? Pickets, sit-ins, building seizures and non-negotiable demands are one thing on the campuses. Imagine them at C.B.S. on Madison Avenue: no TV until S.D.S. gets equal time; at the Stock Exchange: the ticker tape does not roll until corporation X gets rid of its South African holdings; at the headquarters of the Bank of America: no depositors get through the doors until interest-free loans are made to renovate the ghettos. There would be machine guns in the streets in no time at all!

In 1969, despite the tear gas and the National Guard, it is still hard to imagine tanks and machine guns used against student radicals so long as their militance is confined to the campus. Because if they do close the universities down, exactly who would miss them? The most practical functions the university performs and its activities which are most directly relevant to the national economy (engineering, science, law, medicine, etc.) could be transferred to the private sector. The beginnings of such a transfer are apparent already in the educational functions carried on by private foundations, institutes and industrial corporations.

And if the departments of English and history and political science and sociology and art and so on closed tight shut tomorrow, who would miss them? Aside from the implication of some social science departments in the military-industrial complex, the studies in humanities and social science departments are civilized luxuries with very few sources of government or business support. The student radicals have little sympathy for them and there is probably even less sympathy for them among the students' severest critics. These days, even conservative legislators, in the same breath that they denounce student militance, will quickly add, "Of course, this doesn't mean that there isn't plenty wrong with the university; there is." And if the student revolution can be bought off by substituting Bob Dylan for Dylan Thomas, McLuhan for Freud, Marcuse for Plato, rock for Bach, black culture for Greek culture, rap sessions for formal examinations, how many will care? Who needs high culture anyway? For the radicals it's an instrument of class oppression, and their oppressors, at least in America, have never been too keen on it anyway, except as a tax dodge.

Short of machine guns in the streets and outright revolution, what one can expect to see over the next decade in academic life is greater adaptation by the university to the new kinds of students it must serve and to the new publics whose anticipated support or hostility it must take into account in its planning. By the new students I mean ghetto youth, middle-class white radicals and the identity seekers. By the new publics I mean those millions of citizens whose taxes support the great state universities but who never thought of the university as "theirs" until its politicization encouraged ambitious politicians to call this fact to their attention. Having once been reminded (by Governor Reagan and others), the voters are not likely to forget it soon.

If it comes about, this adaptation is likely to occur in a manner not dissimilar to that in which the major political parties have adapted to third-party movements in the larger political community: by isolating the *most* radical through the adoption of some of their programs and demands, while at the same time adopting severe and punitive policies toward the more intransigent and violence-prone who are still unsatisfied.

For ghetto youth, then, there will be more ethnic studies programs and compensatory admissions and grading policies and practices and more energetic recruiting of ethnic students and faculty. But there will be less indecision or tolerance in the handling of sit-ins, seizures and other disruptions. For the radicals (ethnic as well as middle-class white), there will be greater emphasis on programs granting academic credit for extension-type activities such as tutoring of ghetto children, neighborhood seminars on consumer savvy and community organization. For the identity seekers there will be more encounter groups, more classes emphasizing "openness and honesty" in dialogue, more experiments with less structured curricula and residential communities, more "retreats," more student-initiated courses on subjects which engage their sense of "relevance" to their interests, from sex to drugs to rock. For all, there will be further loosening of the *in loco parentis* restrictions which hardly anybody in the university believes in anymore, and a little more student power (at least influence) on faculty and administrative committees. All this, combined with a more effective public-relations campaign explaining the mission of the university and its problems in coping with the consequences of prolonged adolescence, may just bring about a semblance of peace on the campus. But without peace in Vietnam, it will be an uneasy peace at best.

There will be opposition. Academic conservatives will see in these new programs the prospect of the dilution or outright abandonment of traditional standards of scholarship. The legitimation of ethnicity, the amelioration of suffering by the poor and the search for identity by the young may all be noble endeavors, they will say, but the major functions of the university are the creation and transmission of systematic bodies of abstract knowledge. Political conservatives will see in these programs harbingers of social changes which they oppose. Militant students imply more leaders and troops for restive ghettos; "the search for identity" and the self-exploratory activities the phrase suggests are redolent of the "liberalism," "permissiveness" and self-indulgence offensive to the traditional Protestant ethic which "made this country great."

Yet academic conservatives might well be reminded that the university is facing radically transformed constituencies, that academic disciplines which are well institutionalized and "traditional" today were themselves academically born in the blood of earlier periods of such transformations and that they were initially opposed by still more "traditional" fields. Political conservatives might well be reminded that student unrest was not invented by outside agitators, that its source is in social conditions conservatives affirm and that it is not repressible short of military measures. The alternatives to the adaptable university involve blood on the quad and an expendable university.

2

Lucinda Franks and Thomas Powers

Making of a Terrorist

When Diana Oughton, dead at 28, was buried in Dwight, Illinois, on Tuesday, March 24, 1970, the family and friends gathered at her grave did not really know who she was.

The minister who led the mourners in prayer explained Diana's death as part of the violent history of the times, but the full truth was not so simple.

The newspapers had provided a skeleton of facts. Diana Oughton and two young men were killed March 6 in a bomb explosion which destroyed a town house in New York's Greenwich Village. Two young women, their clothes blown off, had run unharmed from the crumbling house and disappeared after showering at the home of a neighbor. It had taken police four days to find Diana's body at the bottom of the rubble and another week to identify it.

Diana and the others were members of the violent revolutionary group known as "The Weathermen." They had turned the townhouse into what police described as a "bomb factory." Months later, they were all to be cited in a grand jury indictment as part of a conspiracy to bomb police, military and other civic buildings in their campaign to destroy American society.

The facts were clear but the townspeople of Dwight (population 3,086) could not relate them to the Diana they remembered. Her family, too had their own memories. Diana's father, James Oughton, had watched her tear away from a closely knit family and a life where beautiful and fine things were important.

Her nanny, Ruth Morehart, remembered how uneasy Diana felt about the money which set the Oughtons apart and how, when only six, she had asked: "Ruthie, why do we have to be rich?"

• • •

A few years later, a school friend who lived in a poor section of Dwight was sent away by her family to live with a grandmother. Diana came to her father in tears. "Why can't we be ordinary like them?" she asked.

• • •

When Diana walked onto the suburban, spreading campus of Bryn Mawr just outside Philadelphia in the fall of 1959 she was a tall, bony girl with short blonde hair and long aristocratic hands. A midwestern Republican, she was against Social Security, federal banking regulations and everything else which smacked of "liberalism" or "big" government. In 1960, she supported Richard M. Nixon against John F. Kennedy. She ardently defended her father's ownership of tenant farms in Lickskillet, Ala., since sold, arguing that he treated his tenants well and fairly.

During her first year, Diana was known as a light-hearted girl, always clowning around, and the kind of person you came to if you wanted to be cheered up. She was never scholarly and studied reluctantly, but still managed to get As an Bs.

• • •

Diana's senior year at Bryn Mawr in 1962–63 was a year of change for young people throughout the country. John F. Kennedy's promise in 1960 to "get the country moving again" had ended once and for all the silence of the 50s. Young people began to think about America and found it fell short of what they had always been taught to believe it was. They went on freedom rides in the South, joined voter registration projects and picketed stores which discriminated against Negroes. Students of fashionable schools like Bryn Mawr talked about social justice and racial prejudice and turned away from deb parties and champagne in the back of a fast car.

During the same period, a kind of genteel Bohemianism was becoming fashionable in the colleges. Diana was among the small advanced class of students, inspired by the beatniks of the 1950s, who grew their hair long and traded their shirtwaists and circle pins for sandals and suede jackets.

A book which made a deep impression on thousands of white students was John Howard Griffin's "Black Like Me," an account of a trip the author made through the deep South disguised as a Negro. Diana was strongly affected by it and joined a project in Philadelphia to tutor black ghetto children.

Although tutors were supposed to be limited to one child each, Diana soon had three. She took a train from Bryn Mawr into the city two days a week and spent more and more time with the children she was helping. There are few Negroes in Dwight; there was only one in her class at Bryn Mawr. Inevitably, the Philadelphia ghettos began to show Diana that the prosperous tranquility in Dwight was not the rule in America.

On one occasion, she told her sister Carol how amazed she was that 7th grade children could not read.

· · ·

By the time she had graduated from Bryn Mawr in June of 1963, Diana Oughton had traveled among the poor in the byways of Europe and worked closely with children in one of Philadelphia's decaying ghettos, but she did not really begin to learn about poverty until she went to Guatemala.

When she filled out a personal information form after being accepted by the Quaker-run, Voluntary International Service Assignments (VISA) program, she put a single word after the heading marked experience: "None."

Barbara Ann Graves, director of VISA, felt Diana's sheltered upbringing and gentle character would be a handicap and tried to dissuade her from the lonely assignments in back-country areas. Diana refused to be given special consideration, however, and was assigned to the isolated Indian market town of Chichicastenango in Guatemala.

Chichicastenango is a small, still half-primitive place where Catholic priests look the other way when the Indians burn incense to the old gods and beat ceremonial drums on the steps of the church.

When Diana first arrived she was struck by the gaudy vitality of the town, by the bright-colored shawls of the Indians, the rambling streets, whitewashed buildings, church bells and surrounding jungle, a damp rank tangle of vines and undergrowth and towering trees. She was delighted by the market where Indians from the surrounding hamlets came to sell cakes of brown sugar, earthenware, handwoven cloth, firewood, vegetables, and freshly killed goats, pigs and chickens.

Gradually, however, Diana began to see other things—the Indians' bad health, their short stature, the small, child-sized coffins sold in such numbers in the market.

She plunged into work, helping local priests to launch a nutritional program, editing a newspaper for adults who were just learning how to read and helping to care for the children who swarmed through the town.

.   .   .

The directors of VISA in Guatemala City, Bill and Donna Dreyer, began with the same doubts about Diana that Barbara Ann Graves originally felt. When they saw the speed with which Diana learned Spanish and the rapport she established with the priests and the people at Chichicastenango, their doubts disappeared.

.   .   .

After Diana had been living in Guatemala for several months she met Alan Howard, a young Fulbright scholar in Guatemala City. He was running an experimental adult reading program in the city's federal prison and long conversations with political prisoners had made him cynical about the chances of peaceful change in the country.

When Diana told him about the work she was doing in Chichicastenango, Howard said it would never end the poverty of the Indians.

"You're only delaying the revolution," he told her.

Throughout her two years in Guatemala Diana struggled with the questions of poverty, social justice and revolution. She and Ann Aleman, another VISA volunteer in Chichicastenango, had been exposed to the country's deep conservative roots as soon as they had arrived; the priests warned them bluntly that discussion of birth control or other subjects considered sensitive by the Catholic church was forbidden.

During the months that followed, both girls gradually began to see that no matter how hard they or Father Casas worked, there would always be more people than food or jobs or places to live.

.   .   .

The Diana Oughton who returned from Guatemala in the fall of 1965 was not the same young woman who had graduated from Bryn Mawr two years earlier.

Her family was bothered by her seriousness and a new air of melancholy present in everything she did. She seemed to have lost some of her sense of humor and her taste for clowning around.

After living in a single room with a dirt floor and no plumbing or electricity for two years, Diana found it hard to adjust to the luxury of the Dwight estate. Her family's way of life made her uneasy. She preferred to wash dishes herself instead of using the dishwasher. She would rummage through the attic and pull out an old sweater or a wool skirt instead of buying new ones.

.   .   .

In the spring of 1966, Diana left Philadelphia for Ann Arbor to enroll in the University of Michigan graduate school of education to get her master's degree in teaching. She was adamant about being on her own and at times tried to conceal her family's wealth. When asked what her father did, she often said, "Oh, he's a farmer," and quickly changed the subject.

In Ann Arbor, she again lived frugally, ate little, and refused to let her father give her money.

"I don't want you to give me an allowance," she said in a letter in March 1967. "It is important to me to be on my own and to feel I can support myself and have responsibility for my own life . . . I think by age 25, I have the right to live the way I want without feeling guilty that my way of life upsets you."

A variety of influences played on Diana in Ann Arbor. It was a time when opposition to the Vietnam war was growing, when many young people began to feel despondent about the failure of mass peaceful demonstrations to change American policy. At home, there was a feeling that Bob Dylan's prophecy of "a hard rain's gonna fall" was coming true; beginning in 1964 there were riots in the urban ghettos, senseless, freak violence like the murder of eight nurses in Chicago and the massacre of 14 persons by a deranged gunman from a tower at the University of Texas. A darker vision of America was emerging in the minds of many young people, but most still believed the way to combat war and violence was through non-violence and reform.

After she arrived at the University of Michigan in 1966, Diana joined the Children's Community School, a project based on the Summerhill method of education and founded by a group of students the year before. It was there that Diana met Bill Ayers, the son of the chairman of Commonwealth Edison Co. of Chicago and one of the Weathermen later indicted on bomb conspiracy charges. Ayers probably exercised the single most powerful influence over Diana until her death.

The school, a kindergarten in the basement of the American Friends Committee building, was based on the premise that something had gone wrong with America's schools. Its goals were to create an integrated student body where black and white children would be treated alike, and an unstructured classroom where the children would choose what they wanted to learn. There were no classes or grades and the kids were allowed to come and go as they pleased. They wandered from room to room free to choose from among sand tables, clay, blocks and books. A child was taught to read or write only if he expressed a desire to learn.

Diana was loved by the children and, as she had in Guatemala, plunged herself totally into the effort to make the school a success. She wrote promotional brochures and designed a button with the slogan, "Children are Only Newer People." Three years later, some of her children were to place that same button, pinned to a bouquet of flowers, on the site of the bombed-out New York townhouse where she was killed.

At the Children's Community School the students spent more time on outings than in the classroom. They visited supermarkets to learn the value of money and when one child asked what a dead person looked like, they all went off to visit a morgue. They had Sunday picnics and a huge party at Christmas 1967, where the children gave each other presents. Bill gave Diana a long Indian dress and she gave him a pair of leather pants.

Bill and Diana grew closer and eventually began to live together in an attic room near the university. Like most of the men Diana had been attracted to, Bill was charming, manipulative, and a bit cruel. Diana was always at his side and when she went home to Dwight, she talked about him frequently, quoting things he had said and talking about their plans for the school. Members of her family felt her ideas, which were becoming steadily more progressive, were a reflection of his.

• • •

Despite its early acclaim, the school began running into severe problems in the spring of 1968. The American Friends Committee complained that the kids were running wild, marking up the walls, and damaging property in their basement. Two professors withdrew their children, saying that the black students were dominating the school and terrorizing the white children and that, in fact, the school was teaching their children to become racists.

In June, the Office of Economic Opportunity (OEO) board in Ann Arbor turned down a request for funds by the school, which had previously been self-supporting. It was a double blow for Bill and Diana because members of the black community in Ann Arbor, including some with children at the school, were among those who argued most heatedly against the grant.

• • •

When the school ran into still other problems because of state zoning regulations, Bill and Diana, too disappointed to go on, looked elsewhere for involvement and became more active in the Ann Arbor chapter of Students for a Democratic Society (SDS).

Ayers had been a member of the SDS Radical Education Project for several years at a time when SDS was still a loosely organized group of students who believed in experimental schools and community projects as vehicles for change.

In June 1968, they attended an SDS convention in East Lansing where a sharp split was emerging between the Progressive Labor party (PL) and the cultural revolutionaries who naturally attracted Bill and

Diana. PL was a dour, highly disciplined but distinctly old-fashioned Marxist-Leninist party which frowned on marijuana, sexual freedom, long hair, and anything else which would offend the American working classes.

After the convention, Diana and Bill spent part of the summer in Chicago working in the SDS national office where they had intense political discussions with Mike Klonsky, an SDS national officer, and Bernardine Dohrn, a later leader of the Weathermen. Diana and Bill became convinced that direct action rather than education and peaceful reform were the way to change society.

Diana was deeply affected by the demonstrations at the Democratic National Convention that August and what she and the SDS and eventually the Walker Commission felt was a "police riot."

• • •

They returned to Ann Arbor that fall in an activist mood. At the first meeting of the Ann Arbor SDS on September 24, 1968, a sharp division in the group was apparent. Diana and Bill along with some 40 other radicals banded together against the moderates and formed a faction which they called "the Jesse James Gang."

The gang declared themselves revolutionary gangsters. They held peaceful methods of reform in contempt. They urged direct action instead of talk, individual violent confrontations instead of big peace marches. Contained in their still half-formed ideas about the role of America in the world and white radicals in America, was the germ of the Weatherman analysis which would later call for violence.

The gang disrupted SDS meetings and made vicious personal attacks on their opponents. The meetings frequently degenerated into brawls. The gang shouted and heckled and even threw eggs and tomatoes at moderate speakers. They often let it be known that their opponents were running the risk of physical beatings.

• • •

Within a period of a few weeks the Jesse James Gang triumphed within the SDS chapter at Ann Arbor. Early in October 1968, the moderates decided they had had enough and walked out to form their own group. Through psychological warfare and vague threats of violence, the gang had captured the single most important SDS chapter in Michigan, which automatically gave them a powerful voice in the national organization.

The gang carried out few actions, but when they did the entire University of Michigan campus generally knew about them. On one occasion they held a demonstration outside a campus building while the university's president, Robben Fleming, was giving a speech inside. Armed with a portable public address system, records and loaves of bread they attracted a crowd. Diana spoke during the demonstration while other gang members handed out slices of bread, shouting, "here's the bread. Get the baloney inside."

Ayers rose to a position of strength within the gang because of his ability to dominate groups through a combination of charm and the volume of his voice. Handsome and brash, he was a notorious lady's man who did not hide his promiscuity from Diana.

Diana told friends that although she was hurt by Bill's infidelity, it made her redouble her efforts to be a true revolutionary. Stung by frequent jibes that she could afford to be one because her daddy was rich, Diana struggled to make her own mark in the movement.

In November 1968, Diana became a regional organizer for the SDS in Michigan, not fully aware that the appointment was an attempt by national SDS to head off criticism by the just-born women's liberation movement that SDS was "male chauvinist." Diana's status as a token woman brought her into conflict with other women radicals, but she eventually earned acceptance as a genuine liberationist.

Early in 1969 she organized a "Cuba Month" on campus, a series of films and seminars on the Cuban revolution. Gradually she became known less as Bill Ayers' sidekick than as a radical "sister" in her own right.

Diana's upbringing made her an asset to the movement. Naturally gracious and tactful, she was used as a negotiator in disputes with other left groups, and with the university administration. As one non-SDS student put it, "she was the only one in the gang you could talk to without wanting to punch her in the nose."

● ● ●

During December 1968, Bill and Diana both began to emerge as leaders in the national SDS at a conference held in Ann Arbor. At about the same time, on December 9, 1968, she wrote in one of her last letters home:

"It gets harder and I get more reluctant to justify myself over and over again to you . . . I feel as if I've gone through a process of conscious choice and that I've thought about it a lot and people I admire agree with me, educationally important, recognized and respected people . . .

"I feel like a moral person, that my life is my values and that most people my age or even younger have already begun to sell out to materialism, status, hypocrisy, stepping on other people, etc. . . . I feel like part of a vanguard, that we speak of important change to come. . . ."

• • •

The final nine months of Diana Oughton's life were absorbed almost entirely by the disintegration of the Students for a Democratic Society (SDS) and the growth of a new, much smaller organization which turned to terrorism as the Weathermen.

In June 1969, the SDS, long troubled by deep differences on questions of ideology, suddenly burst apart at a chaotic, slogan-shouting convention in Chicago.

When the SDS was founded in 1962 it was a fluid, open group which emphasized persuasion, community organizing and broad popular participation in all important decisions. By 1969, however, the organization was locked in a power struggle between the Progressive Labor Party, a highly disciplined off-shoot of the Communist party, and a more militant faction which became the Weathermen.

By the end of the Chicago convention the Weathermen had captured control of the SDS national headquarters in Chicago's West Side ghetto. The new SDS leadership was committed to action and over the summer of 1969 gradually worked out a plan for turning student radicals into a "red army" which would fight the establishment in the streets of America.

Diana met Alan Howard in Chicago. Prior to the convention, Diana and Alan went for a long walk down Chicago's Lake Shore Drive. They talked about the impending split in SDS and the Weatherman manifesto, partly written by Diana's boyfriend, Bill Ayers. The 25,000-word manifesto—named after a line in a Bob Dylan song, "You don't need a weatherman to tell which way the wind blows"—argued that white radicals in the United States could help bring on a worldwide revolution only by fighting in the streets of the "mother country."

Howard, who had first started Diana thinking seriously about revolution in Guatemala, now found himself in the awkward position of trying to restrain her, to convince Diana that a premature attempt to bring on the revolution would be suicidal.

Diana insisted the time had come to fight.

While the SDS was beginning to plan for a four-day series of anti-war demonstrations in October, Diana's relationship with Bill Ayers and her family both came under increasing strain. Ayers had been elected one of the three national officers of the Weathermen, along with Mark Rudd and Bernardine Dohrn, and was spending most of his time in the national office. Friends of Diana and Ayers say he was increasingly fascinated by Bernardine's toughness, intelligence and hard beauty, so unlike Diana's warm, almost enveloping softness of spirit.

Ayers told Diana he would not allow himself to be tied to one woman and she began spending her time with a number of other men.

During the same period Diana's father canceled a gas company credit card she had been using on behalf of SDS and she wrote him a letter explaining why the money was being spent in a good cause.

"You speak of a revolution against capitalism," her father answered from the family home in Dwight. "This can only mean that you are developing forces against me and the rest of your family. The oldest and most reasonable form of capitalism is the ownership of agricultural land and this is what your family has been involved with for a hundred years.

"I will resist any effort to change the basic ideology governing my own life and it should be obvious I do not want to support any movement that would develop into violence against me and my family."

After Diana had returned to the United States from Guatemala, Oughton had incorporated the family-owned farmland surrounding Dwight, partly in the hope that Diana's shares in the company would give her a vested interest in the society she was turning against. The move did not strengthen her ties to Dwight or weaken her belief in revolution, however, and Oughton sometimes did not even know where to send Diana's dividend checks.

The passionate intensity with which the Weathermen took their political ideas created a state of mind in Diana which her father later called "a kind of intellectual hysteria." He found her less and less willing to really talk about politics, increasingly heated when she did. She finally refused to discuss the subject altogether.

"I've made my decision, daddy," she said. "There's no sense talking about it."

• • •

Diana's difficulty in talking about politics with her family was only a reflection of the difficulty all Weathermen found in trying to explain why violence was necessary.

The group's opponents argued that the Weathermen were repeating the errors of the "Narodniki" (Russian terrorists) who assassinated the Czar in 1881 and set back the cause of reform in Russia for decades. Like the Narodniki, the Weathermen were an elite, self-appointed body from the upper classes who wanted the revolution now and, like children, could not force themselves to be patient. The Weathermen themselves joked about their upper class origins, saying that the first requirement for a prospective member was a father who made at least $30,000 a year.

The arguments against the demonstrations planned for October were generally well thought out, but they tended to ignore the one thing which made the Weathermen determined to go ahead anyway; a profound frustration with argument and a hunger for action of almost any sort.

While sentiment against the war in Vietnam grew between 1965 and 1969, SDS had raced ahead in its thinking, rejecting the war first, then rejecting the "liberalism" which they held responsible for the war, finally rejecting "the system" they saw behind everything they opposed. By 1969 they were committed to revolution, but revolution seemed further away than ever as the radical movement broke up into squabbling factions.

It was clear the working class was not about to occupy the factories, that the hordes of rock-loving, marijuana-smoking young people were not necessarily revolutionaries, however much they fought with their parents. The country did not take the revolutionary fervor of SDS seriously, and SDS grew increasingly impatient with strategies which would take 30 years to work. They wanted to take themselves seriously.

When the Weathermen began planning for a super-militant "kick ass" street battle with police in Chicago, October 8–11, 1969, however, the remnants of SDS split again. During the summer the Black Panthers denounced the Weathermen, a serious blow from their point of view, but with each setback those who remained became more determined than ever.

The pace of events picked up after Diana and a delegation of Weathermen returned from a trip to Cuba in August marked by secret meetings with Cubans and representatives of the Viet Cong. The delegation left feeling even the Cubans were too moderate and losing their early revolutionary fervor.

• • •

That weekend Diana was attending the Cleveland SDS conference where the Weatherman strategy of total commitment to revolutionary violence finally emerged as a comprehensive position. During the following weeks Weathermen raided a Pittsburgh high school, invaded a community college outside Detroit, took a gun away from a policeman in New York, attacked Harvard University's Center for International Affairs and provoked fights at drive-in restaurants and on beaches in Chicago, Cleveland and other Midwestern cities.

The theory behind the street fights in working class districts was that tough high school students, generally referred to as "grease," felt SDS was made up of "sissy intellectuals" who would never fight. A punch in the nose would do more to radicalize the grease, Weatherman argued, than years of community organizing and patient argument.

More important than the occasional battles, however, was the attempt by Weathermen to literally recreate themselves as street fighters by a brutal process of group criticism which tended to break down their personalities. Diana's experiences in collectives in Detroit and Flint, Michigan, where she went to live after returning from Cuba, were an indication of her willingness to sacrifice herself for the movement.

People who knew her during this period say that, put simply, she and the other Weathermen went through a hell of their own making.

In the months following the June 1969 convention, Weathermen collectives ranging in size from a dozen to 30 or more people began to barricade themselves inside rented houses. They put double locks on every door and nailed chicken wire over the windows to prevent enemies, real or imagined, from throwing in bombs.

Inside they lived a 24-hour existence of intense political discussion, marked by a complete abandonment of all the bourgeois amenities of their largely middle class childhoods. Clothes were strewn everywhere, food rotted on unwashed plates, milk turned sour in half-empty containers, toilets jammed, flies and cockroaches swarmed in kitchens filled with encrusted spoons and spilled food.

Diana's dividend checks and all other money went into a common fund; every expenditure, without exception, was a matter for collective decision. When the collectives needed money for buying guns and, later, explosives, and sometimes simply as a matter of discipline, the members would go without food for days. On other occasions they would stay awake for two days or even longer to harden themselves for life in the "red army."

In a number of ways the collectives attempted to destroy the "bourgeois morality" they had been taught as children. On at least one occasion they vandalized gravestones in a cemetery as a way of destroying conventional attitudes of respect for the dead.

On another occasion, partly from a genuine hunger and partly to instill in themselves a kind of savagery, a collective killed, skinned and ate a tomcat.

The collectives also attempted to destroy all their old attitudes about sexual relationships. At the Cleveland conference the women's liberation caucus had proposed that Weathermen attempt to "smash monogamy" on the grounds that it oppressed women and at the same time created love relationships which interfered with revolutionary commitment.

• • •

For a relatively brief period the attempt to destroy traditional sexual behavior led to a situation in which any man could simply announce that he wanted to sleep with a particular woman and she would be required to submit. Women quickly came to resent the fact that this did not seem to work in the opposite direction, however, and the sexual experimentation began to moderate.

The attempts at self-transformation turned collectives into violent groups with an almost savage emotional atmosphere. The group criticism sessions inevitably led to hurt feelings and smoldering grudges. The attempt to overcome traditional niceties led to exaggeratedly crude behavior. People became stiff and unnatural, afraid they would be attacked, and perhaps even purged, if they were found lacking in commitment to the revolution. Many Weathermen became nervous, high-strung, and emotionally unstable.

The military aspects of the training—karate, target shooting, practice in street fighting and, later, the making of bombs—suffered in the chaotic atmosphere of the collectives where everyone was always overtired and underfed.

Diana's commitment to the revolution, her loyalty to her friends and her determination to repress all "bourgeois hang-ups" led her to participate fully in everything. But friends say she was deeply upset by much that was happening. A gentle woman who preferred staying with one man at a time, Diana questioned both the sexual excesses and the emphasis on violence and was brutally criticized as a result. Nevertheless, she was often the one who pressed for a rest during the long, highly-charged meetings and she tried, largely without success, to prevent the collectives from becoming excessively cold and brutal.

During street actions in Flint, where she was arrested on a minor charge (later dropped) at the end of September, Diana could not bring herself to shout obscenities at the police and she sometimes even tried to argue the issues with them.

"You're a revolutionary now, not a society bitch," a Weatherman once yelled at her when she was talking to a policeman.

•   •   •

The following day Diana joined 70 Weatherwomen who marched to Grant Park for an all-women's action. When they got there they found themselves outnumbered by the police, who threatened to arrest them if they tried to leave the park wearing their helmets and carrying Viet Cong flags at the end of long, heavy poles.

Diana was one of a dozen Weatherwomen who gritted their teeth and plunged into the police lines but were immediately overpowered. . . . [On October 11,] Weathermen began filtering into Haymarket Square for the final action of the Days of Rage.

At a signal a small group of young men and women pulled crash helmets from shopping bags and put on denim jackets with Viet Cong flags sewed to the back beneath the legend, "Motor City SDS." Then the remnants of the "red army," about 200-strong, started out through the streets of Chicago on a final rampage. When it was over 103 had been arrested and those who had managed to escape were being hunted throughout the city.

That night, still trying to find a way out of Chicago, Diana called a friend. "The pigs are picking everybody up," she said. "Can you give me a ride to the airport? I've got to get back to Detroit."

Diana was scared but elated over the phone that the Weathermen had overcome their fear and fought in the streets. Despite the arrests (290 in all), the $1 million in bail and the injuries (three Weathermen had been wounded by gunfire the first day; dozens of others had been severely beaten) she felt they had created the core of the Red army.

When Diana's friend said it would be impossible to drive her to the airport, she changed her mind and went back to Dwight where she stayed for a few days, resting and eating ravenously.

Diana's mother, distraught at the thought of her daughter fighting with police, tried to talk her into abandoning the Weathermen.

"But, honey," she said, "you're only going to make things worse. You're only going to get yourself killed."

Diana refused to argue. "It's the only way, mummy," she said, stalking back and forth in the hall. "It's the only way."

• • •

During the late fall of 1969 the Weathermen had few illusions about their ability to spark a revolution in the United States, but their fanaticism only seemed to increase as a result.

Diana Oughton, fundamentally gentle, had nevertheless been exhilarated by the violent days of rage in Chicago in October. In spite of their fear, their fewness and the hopelessness of their cause, the Weathermen had gone into the streets to fight the police and had not found their courage wanting. When Diana went to Washington for the massive November 15 demonstration against the war, it was in an almost bouyant mood.

• • •

[On the 15th,] Ayers and Diana, their faces decorated with war paint, joined in a march on the Department of Justice after the main rally. The brief collision was more a revolutionary theatrical than a serious street action, marked by shouting and scuffles with police and clouds of tear gas.

It was the last time the Weathermen found a kind of fun in politics, their last action before turning to a politics of terror which had no place for the humor that called for war paint.

That night Diana drove across Washington to visit her sister Pam and to meet Pam's husband for the only time. Diana was breathless and keyed up by the day's battle with police and said she felt the revolution was near.

"When blue collar workers are making $6 an hour, where is the support coming from?" asked Carol, another of Diana's sisters, also living in Washington.

Diana simply dismissed the question. "The revolution is here," she insisted. "It's a world-wide thing."

. . . Diana returned to Flint, Michigan, to help with final preparations for the Weatherman War Council which began on December 27, a well-publicized meeting that attracted as much attention from the Flint police and the FBI as it did within the radical movement.

The atmosphere of the convention hall was far different from the heady excitement and optimism of student meetings in the early 1960s. Guards frisked everyone entering the building, the women as thoroughly as the men. Signs proclaimed "Piece (that is, guns) now" and an eight-foot-high cardboard pistol stood by the door.

Mark Rudd, a persuasive, witty speaker, described Weathermen as a kind of political joy-ride, an explosion of creative energy made possible by total commitment to revolution and an end to the "bourgeois" fear of violence.

"It's a wonderful feeling to hit a pig," he said with the tone of a boy describing his first trip on a roller coaster. "It must really be a wonderful feeling to kill a pig or blow up a building."

• • •

Much of the argument in favor of violence centered on the killing of Black Panther leader Fred Hampton by Chicago police on December 4, 1969. Weathermen argued that the entire radical movement should have taken to the streets and avenged Hampton's death.

Others found a certain ambivalence in this, since it had been Hampton who had denounced the Weathermen as "anarchistic, adventuristic . . . masochistic and custeristic" during the days of rage. When one Weatherman argued that the white race was itself the problem—"all white babies are pigs," he said—others felt he was expressing self-hate rather than a coherent political opinion.

When Weathermen insisted blacks would be the vanguard of the revolution and that they were fighting on the side of blacks, their words rang false. Radical black groups had turned against them and the organization, despite its efforts to recruit blacks, was as lily-white as the Mississippi Highway Patrol.

Rudd urged radicals to be like Captain Ahab in "Moby Dick," who lived with "one thought—to bring down the white whale."

The rest of the movement realized that Rudd's white whale included virtually everyone with a white skin and pointed out that it was Ahab, not the whale, who was destroyed in the end. Like Ahab, they said, Rudd and the Weathermen were themselves on a "death trip."

During the four-day council in Flint, Weathermen leaders slipped away to meet secretly in a seminary across the city where they debated the fate of the organization. The enormous legal difficulties which sapped their energies and finances following the days of rage, and the hostility of much of the radical movement made it clear that "Wild in the Streets" was not a strategy that could be sustained. Before the council ended on December 30, Weathermen leaders decided they should make a final break with American society and go underground.

During the following weeks the Weatherman collectives began breaking up into smaller groups. Members severed their relationships with friends and family and one by one began to disappear. It was not an easy decision to make. Breaking windows in Chicago and making bombs were far different things, and Weathermen knew there would be no turning back.

The policy of the Weathermen was that every member would participate, so far as possible, in every illegal act, whether obtaining, making or planting explosives. They knew their chances of a normal life were being irretrievably put behind them. They knew they might have to die. Of the 400 people who attended the Flint Council, fewer than 100 went underground. For those few, committed to the revolution above all else, it was a matter of logic. Community organizing had failed. Mass demonstrations had failed. Fighting in the streets had failed. Only terror was left.

The activities of Diana and the other Weathermen between the end of the Flint Council and the bomb explosion in New York on March 6 are extremely difficult to reconstruct. People who knew what they were doing are naturally reluctant to talk and even the federal indictment handed up in Detroit in July gives only the barest outline of the alleged activities of the group's leaders.

Diana is connected with only three of the 21 overt acts cited in the indictment and those fall on two dates: December 27, when the Flint Council opened, and March 6, the date of her death.

A Weatherman who dropped out of the organization when it decided to go underground said that Diana had begun to question the policies of the group's leaders—that she was no longer sure the young, the poor and the black would ever support the kind of revolution Weathermen were committed to making. Despite her doubts, however, Diana prepared to go underground with a small group of friends.

On February 4, Diana appeared in court in Chicago and was fined

$450 for her part in the women's action the previous October 9. When her name was called the judge raised his head and asked, "Are you related to Jim Oughton, the legislator?"

With a smile of amusement, Diana admitted that she was.

•   •   •

Before going back to Detroit Diana called her parents in Dwight and told them she had paid her fine with part of the bail money put up by her father and that she intended to keep the rest.

"You know, Diana," her mother said, hurt by Diana's cold tone, "you're killing us both off."

"I'm sorry, Mummy." Diana said.

Not long afterwards Mrs. Oughton told a friend, "we have lost our daughter."

During her last weeks of life, Diana was torn by conflict, determined not to falter and yet reluctant to make a final break with her friends and family. The ambivalence ran deep. She loved people and at the same time tried to use them. On one occasion in these final weeks she tried to involve a friend in a complicated scheme to "rip off" (that is, defraud) a travelers' check company.

On Monday, March 2, just four days before she died, Diana called her sister Carol in Washington. She asked lots of little questions about the family. Carol felt that perhaps Diana was beginning to move away from the violent politics of the Weathermen. About halfway through the conversation Diana asked: "Will the family stand by me, no matter what? Will they help me if I need it?"

Carol said of course.

•   •   •

It was no accident that the Weathermen were the children of the privileged classes of America. From the very beginning of the student movement, when white students organized to support black sit-in demonstrations in 1960, the strength of their commitment was subject to ridicule and attack. Their defensive parents and teachers, their non-political friends, the public officials who always hoped they would go back to their studies, even, most painfully, the blacks they were trying to help, all suggested scornfully that white activists were summertime soldiers who would retreat into the middle class womb which had created them whenever the going became hard.

There was no way white students could defend themselves against this charge. The police might hit them over the head but the courts treated them indulgently and they would always be welcomed back by The Establishment, perhaps even valued more highly for the spunk they had shown before settling down.

It was not until they became criminals that the Weathermen proved their commitment beyond a doubt. They could not believe in themselves until they had turned against the middle class world which had made them. It was their country, their class, their families, even themselves which they considered the enemy. In Dwight, Diana had hated being rich; in Guatemala she hated being an American; in the Weathermen she finally came to hate herself. How else could she have attempted, at such a cost in suffering to destroy everything that she was?

In the end, Diana Oughton relinquished her humanity in hopes of creating a new world where she thought people could be more human. She denied her own nature and everything she loved. She grew more and more distant from her family; she gave up teaching children, the thing she loved to do best, she gave up her relationship with Bill Ayers when he argued the revolution came first. Willingly, she became an instrument of the revolution. She stopped asking questions to make bombs.

She regarded the world she saw around her as the implacable enemy of everything she believed in. Like the rest of the Weathermen, the privileged children of that world, in the end, Diana had only one ambition: to be its executioner.

The bomb which exploded a few minutes past noon on Friday, March 6, 1970, killing Diana and two other Weathermen in the town house at 18 West 11th Street in New York City, was a bomb designed to kill. It was made of dynamite surrounded by heavy metal nails which acted as shrapnel. The doctor who examined the remains of her body said she had been standing within a foot or two of the bomb when it exploded. It may, in fact, have gone off in her hands.

Four days after the explosion, bomb squad detectives found Diana's body near a workbench in the rubble-filled basement of the devastated townhouse. At the end of another week, a detective discovered the tip of the little finger from a right hand. A print taken by a police department expert was matched later that day with a set of Diana's prints in the Washington files of the FBI. The prints had been taken in Chicago following her arrest during the days of rage in October 1969.

· · ·

The accidental explosion did not end the campaign of terrorism begun by the Weathermen. Remaining members of the organization are reported to be in hiding, staying off the street almost altogether, but continuing to build bombs and plan attacks. Three of the Weathermen have reportedly gone to Cuba but the rest remain in the United States, as determined as ever.

In the months since the March 6 explosion there has been a steady stream of bombings, not all of them attributable to the Weathermen. In

New York, San Francisco, Minneapolis, Omaha and Madison, Wis., among other places, bombs planted by terrorists have caused death, injuries and destruction.

The only friend Diana contacted in New York before she died was Alan Howard. Sometime that week, probably on Wednesday, Howard and Diana met. They talked about the Weathermen. Diana told him she still believed the only course open to American radicals was the building of a "Red army" in the United States which would be part of the international army fighting for a worldwide revolution.

She admitted that the days of rage had been at least partly a failure, that the Flint War Council had weakened the Weathermen even further, that the revolution was impossible without a mass base.

Nevertheless, she insisted that her role was to physically fight in any way possible.

"We have a lot to learn," she told Howard. "We'll make mistakes." On Friday of that week one of those mistakes ended her life.

3

Gerda Lerner

Women's Rights
and American Feminism

Until very recently American historians have paid scant, almost absent-minded attention to the history of women. The field has, for many decades, been left to amateurs, feminist enthusiasts, writers and scholars from the social sciences. Psychology of a male-oriented type has weighed heavily on scholarship, so that much of the biographical and analytical work that was done reflected the conviction that the appearance of women in history needed to be "explained" by showing how deviant and maladjusted they were. The sources available to the historian in the field have long been neglected and have, in turn, served to limit the scope and range of scholarship. The two major collections of "women's materials" (those at Smith College and at Radcliffe) were the result of feminist effort and reflect primarily the interest and sources of the organized woman's rights movement. Other material on women is scattered and lies largely unidentified in collections arranged from other points of view, such as antislavery, reform, etc. As a result, the literature concerning the role of women in American history is, with a handful of exceptions, topically narrow, predominantly descriptive and generally devoid

From *The American Scholar*, Vol. 40, No. 2 (Spring 1971). Copyright ©
1971 by the United Chapters of Phi Beta Kappa. By permission of the
publishers.

of interpretation. Most of the work done by historians in recent years has been preoccupied with the woman's rights movement in its legal and political aspects. Modern historians, by and large, think that what is important to know about women is how they got the ballot. The one serious challenge to this conceptual framework was offered by Mary and Charles Beard, but it was, like so much of their work, heatedly argued, poorly proved, and thus more easily dismissed than it should have been. The impact of Mary Beard's concepts on the study of women's history was negligible, which is in my opinion regrettable. The problem of how women fit into human history, how one is to conceptualize their role, and how one is to evaluate their contributions, remains to be solved. One hopes that the present upsurge of interest in the subject will lead us to new solutions.

The scholar in this field is hampered also by semantic confusion. The terms, "woman's rights," "women's emancipation," "feminism" and, lately, "women's liberation" have frequently been used interchangeably. I would like to suggest a more precise semantic definition as a means of clarifying some of the basic assumptions with which historians approach this subject.

Just as the abolition movement is a specific phase, in time and scope, of the broader and more general antislavery movement, so the woman's rights movement is a phase, specific and limited in time and scope, of the broader American feminist movement. American feminism embraces all aspects of the emancipation of American women, that is, any struggle designed to elevate their status, socially, politically, economically, and in respect to their self-concepts. The woman's rights movement, on the other hand, has more narrowly defined the emancipation of women as the winning of legal rights. For seventy-two years it overlapped and was synonymous with the woman's suffrage movement. It was therefore a specific aspect of the broader movement, just as the civil rights movement was but an aspect of the movement for black emancipation. Of the current scene, one can say that the woman's rights movement is defined by those organizations and individuals who see the question of woman's emancipation largely as one of legal changes, whereas the feminist movement embraces the new feminism of women's liberation and a variety of other groups and causes.

What are women's rights? Essentially, they are civil rights—the right to vote, to hold office, to have access to power at every level on an equal basis with men, and to partake of the channels for upward mobility open to men. They are also property rights—the right to contract, the right to hold and dispose of property, the right to one's earnings. All of these rights are based on an acceptance of the status quo, and the groups advocating them act like "out" groups wanting "in." Their demands are essentially reformist, based on appeals to justice and equity. Needless to say, their fulfillment is long overdue.

What is women's emancipation? It is freedom from oppressive restrictions imposed by sex; self-determination and autonomy. Freedom from oppressive restrictions means freedom from natural, biological restrictions due to sex as well as from societally imposed ones. Self-determination means being free to decide one's own destiny, being free to define one's own social role. Autonomy means earning one's own status, not being born to it or marrying it. It means financial and cultural independence, freedom to choose one's own life-style regardless of sex. In order for women to have autonomy, the handicap of male orientation and male domination in social institutions must first be removed.

Obviously, society must reach a certain level of development before such emancipation can take place. The preconditions for woman's emancipation are: urbanization; industrialization with technology permitting society to remove food preparation and care of the sick from the home; the mechanization of heating and laundry; spread of health and medical care sufficient to lower infant mortality and protect maternal health; birth control; the development of transportation sufficient to permit physical mobility to all groups of the population, with its accessory freedom from parental and communal restraints; and availability of education on all levels to all children without discrimination. Clearly, women's full emancipation has nowhere on earth been accomplished. This is not so much the result of a male conspiracy as of shifting historic circumstances. The fact is that women do indeed live under disabilities of sex in societies where there is no knowledge of birth control methods, where maternal health care is poor and infant mortality high, offset only by a high birthrate. Such societies require for their survival that as many women as possible marry and rear as many children as possible. As a result, women need protection; they need providers for themselves and their offspring. In such societies, women are not "free" to engage in the same work as men do, nor are they able to conceptualize the possibility of doing so. Such primitive agrarian societies have existed everywhere on earth at various times and are marked by a division of labor between the sexes, in which biology is indeed destiny.

In the United States these conditions prevailed generally in the colonies, except for a few cities, and later in the frontier regions. It is noteworthy that during this period there was no woman's rights movement, because none was possible or conceivable, but there was feminist activity and self-conscious effort on the part of a few individuals to strive for woman's emancipation. In 1647, Margaret Brent asked for the right to cast two votes in the Maryland assembly—one as Lord Baltimore's attorney, another as a landholder and "court baron." The fact that she was granted one vote as an attorney tells us a good deal about the position of women in the colony. Similarly, one might cite Anne Hutchinson's assertion of the right of women to interpret scripture to other women, or the case of Mary Dyer, whose nonviolent resistance campaign against religious intolerance ended on the scaffold in 1660, and who with other Quaker women asserted by voluntary death the right of women to engage in such political-religious work. Mercy Otis Warren, Abigail Adams and Judith Sargent Murray are other early feminists who in various ways advanced arguments for woman's emancipation. It is significant that all of these were wealthy or well-to-do women.

Under conditions of a shortage of labor and—as in colonial New England and on the frontier—a shortage of women, a sexbased division of labor did not imply differentiation in status. All work was essential for the survival of the community, hence all work had dignity. But when the community was wealthy enough to make luxuries, such as a prolonged education, available to some, but not to others, role differentiation based on sex began to be felt as oppressive and unequal. As long as all children shared in the primitive educational opportunities, and as long as most education was carried on in the home or by private tutors, boys and girls enjoyed nearly equal educational opportunity. But when education began to be institutionalized, the exclusion of girls from higher education was an actual deprivation and implied lower status. Similarly, the access to a variety of occupations enjoyed earlier by colonial women became limited as soon as American society had advanced to a point where professionalization could take place. Professional status was restricted to those who had followed a prescribed course of education within established institutions. Since women were excluded from such institutions, they were automatically excluded from the rising professions, such as law and medicine. In the American setting, this shrinking of opportunities for women occurred in the early nineteenth century. Combined with increased opportunities for males, resulting from the spread of the franchise and from upward mobility based on entrepreneurship, this status loss, both actual and perceived by women, was very obvious. It was this deprivation that gave rise to a sense of status displacement in an educated, white, middle-class elite, and that led to the emergence of the organized woman's rights movement.

It is true all over the world that woman's rights movements are dependent on a class of educated women with leisure. But the nature of the movement depends on historic circumstances. A number of historians have wondered why the American woman's rights movement placed so much of its emphasis on the ballot, to the neglect of other reforms. The explanation has been offered that this was in some way connected with the attitude of suffragists toward morality and their total acceptance of Victorian morality. This essentially conservative attitude toward sexual reform was seen, especially by Aileen Kraditor and William O'Neill, as having a seriously crippling effect on the movement. No doubt, but one is entitled to ask why this was so.

The explanation may be that the woman's rights movement, due to its composition, was in the mainstream of American reform. Like other such movements, it tended to stress legal and constitutional reform rather than more radical changes. To cite a few examples:

The United States labor movement was decisively affected by the fact that American labor had citizenship and voting rights before it formed a mass trade union movement. This development is significantly different from the European and British patterns, in which working-class, socialist-oriented parties became a permanent feature of the political system. American women and American Negroes did not have voting rights when they organized movements for their emancipation, but they lived in a nation in which the right to vote was constitutionally guaranteed to all citizens. At the time when both of these movements were launched, voting rights had recently been extended to propertyless white males. Therefore, it was only natural that both of these movements focused on the ballot as the solution to their problems. The antislavery campaign saw its triumph in the passage of the civil rights amendments. All other needed reforms, including land distribution, were presumably to follow upon this magic enactment. The results are history. Ironically, a hundred years later, the civil rights movement was offered yet another Civil Rights Act and kindred legal reforms as a substitute for the organizational, societal, institutional changes that are needed to render such laws meaningful and effective. The woman's rights movement operated within the same tradition and suffered from the same limitations —despite the fact that alternatives existed from the start. As early as 1825 American working girls had organized in trade unions for economic demands and, briefly, used political as well as economic means to advance these demands. But their movement remained generally isolated from the woman's rights movement.

Among the advocates of other forgotten alternatives to the woman's rights movement were Frances Wright, Robert Dale Owen, Ernestine Rose, John Humphrey Noyes, Henry C. Wright, and later Charlotte Gilman, Victoria Woodhull and Margaret Sanger. These radicals had in common the convictions that the institutions of society were as oppressive to women as were its laws, that the patriarchal family was a questionable institution, and that sexual morality as hitherto defined would have to change. Their methods for attack and their specific programs varied, but they made the connection between religion, the family, sexual mores, and the social status of women. They pointed out, even if not always in specific terms, that merely constitutional changes would not basically alter the position of women.

Frances Wright, the first woman to engage in public lecturing in America, scandalized her contemporaries in a variety of ways. Not only did she advocate birth control, easy divorce and free love, but in her utopian community, Nashoba, she allowed the latter practice to flourish, and on an interracial basis. When, during her absence, the community's diary was published, revealing the shocking goings-on, she refused to disavow her fellow-utopians' actions. Moreover, she was actively involved in organizing the first labor party in the United States, the Workingman's Association—and promoted within that group, during the 1828 and 1830 state election campaigns, the principle of public education for all children, starting at age two and in boarding schools. While women's liberation was not specifically listed as one of the expected benefits, she did mention that this scheme would equalize educational opportunities for workers' children, imbuing children of all classes with the egalitarian spirit that she regarded as the essential principle of American democracy. That the public education issue split the Workingman's party in 1830, causing it serious electoral losses and probably contributing to its early demise, is not surprising. Frances Wright appeared on the scene too soon to influence the first generation of feminists directly, although some of them had certainly heard of her activities. It is noteworthy that the first volume of *History of Woman Suffrage* (edited by Elizabeth Cady Stanton, *et al.*) pays tribute to Frances Wright, though only in her role as a public speaker. Latter-day feminists ignored her advanced ideas for sexual, moral and educational reform.

Both the first and second generation of activists in the woman's rights movement had direct acquaintance with and exposure to the practices and ideas of other utopians. The Fourierists allowed women to wear a costume somewhat similar to the Bloomer costume, with ballooning pants tied at the ankles, which was certainly an improvement over the whaleboned, corsetted and bustled monstrosities, weighing upward of fifteen pounds, in which nineteenth-century women attempted to pursue their daily activities. The Fourierists collectivized housekeeping chores, but divided the work tasks in the conventional manner among men and women. But since women had full voting rights in their communes, Fourierists could certainly have served as models for possible alternatives to the Victorian family. The same holds true for other communarians, such as those at Oneida, whose moving spirit, John Humphrey Noyes, advocated free love, equality of the sexes, and male continence as a method of birth control.

Ernestine Rose, Frances Wright and Robert Dale Owen were free-thinkers or opponents of established religion, who wrote and spoke extensively and exposed the connection between the subordinate position of women and the teachings of orthodox religion. Henry C. Wright advocated greater equality in marital and sex relations, sex education and family planning. Charlotte Gilman, Victoria Woodhull and Margaret Sanger all had unorthodox life-styles—each was divorced; Charlotte Gilman voluntarily renounced custody and care of her only child in favor of her husband and his second wife, with whom she remained on the friendliest terms for years after her divorce; Victoria Woodhull not only attacked the double standard by her revelations in the Beecher-Tilden affair, but led a notoriously scandalous life herself with no effort at dissimulation.

Charlotte Gilman's major theoretical contribution was a fully developed theory of women's emancipation, based not so much on legal changes as on an economic revolution and basic changes in the institution of marriage. Margaret Sanger's singleminded pursuit of birth control as the cure-all for the "disabilities of sex" was perhaps the most significant alternative to the woman's rights approach. It is interesting that Sanger carried her lonely and at first quite unsuccessful campaign so far as deliberately to become a fugitive from the law and leave the country in order to avoid arrest for violating an obscenity law. Her justification was entirely political: she would be arrested only at a time of her choosing, when her case would advance her cause by testing the Comstock law's provision forbidding the distribution of contraceptive information and devices. While she was in Europe, she arranged for one hundred thousand copies of her magazine, carrying birth control information, to be distributed in the United States. Having thus created a clear test case, Sanger returned to New York and peacefully submitted to her arrest. This action was at least as radical and political as was the much more publicized picketing of the White House by the Woman's Party, and accomplished a good deal more for the emancipation of women. The list of early practitioners and theorists of woman's emancipation could be extended, but the point is made: they were continuously in evidence on the American scene; they provided useful radical alternatives to the Victorian family and to the strictly Constitutional approach taken by suffragists—but they were not able to influence significantly the organized woman's rights movement.

The distinction between women's rights and women's emancipation becomes crucial in dealing with women of different social classes. It is a common fallacy to blur class distinctions and to proceed on the assumption that what is true for middle-class women is true for all women. The fact is that, for members of the working class and for the poor, women's rights are essentially meaningless. In the absence of property, inheritance and other property rights are irrelevant. The right to contract means only the right to contract one's labor, and here the working-class woman must, out of need, take what the market offers, regardless of the law. In fact, equal rights and standards regulated by law often deprive the poorest women of the chance to work at all—since work is available to them only at substandard wages. To lower-class children of both sexes —and this applies to the period from the Civil War to World War I— access to education is significant only insofar as it opens doors to upward mobility, which is in their case limited by various other restraints and prejudices. For the working-class girl, spinsterhood is not synonymous with independence, since with her low wages and in the crowded housing conditions of the poor, spinsterhood means staying in her parents' house as an adult, which is hardly freedom. In fact, marriage and other sexual liaisons offer much more chance of upward mobility for the lower-class girl than does education. Working-class standards of morality take such facts into consideration and are far less restrictive and retributive than are upper-class standards, especially regarding premarital sex and illegitimate children. Historians who make generalizations about the impact of Victorian morality on American women would do well to remember that Victorian morality applied to the "better" classes only. It was taken for granted during that period and well into the twentieth century that working-class women—and especially black women—were freely available for sexual use by upper-class males.

The proverbial immorality of factory girls caused much concern to Victorian ladies, who expended prodigious energies in useless efforts at amelioration. The racist myth that most black women were immoral persisted and proved to be the greatest stumbling block to the interracial activity of women. It took decades of patient educational work by black club-women to dispel it and to prove that middle-class black women shared the moral standards of white women of their class. Class differences in marriage patterns were undeniable, although frequently ignored. Lower-class families freely separated without benefit of the law before divorce was cheaply available, and entered common-law marriages when they could not legally remarry. After divorce was legalized, they divorced at a greater rate than their middle-class counterparts. Even today the values, sexual mores, life-styles and life expectations of women of the blue-collar class are dramatically different from those of the middle class, as is shown in Mirra Komarovsky's *Blue Collar Marriage* and in *Workingman's Wife* by Lee Rainwater, R. P. Coleman and W. L. Yancey. In fact, the life-styles of working-class women are much closer to those of the majority of nineteenth-century women than to those of more privileged groups of our own society.

The case is still different for black women, who have been doubly oppressed, as Blacks and as women. Race oppression has been experienced as the primary burden, and it is a particular aspect of this burden that a far greater percentage of black women than white are poor working mothers in menial service occupations. Race, caste, class and sex discrimination fall upon them with particular severity. Historically, they have organized in separate groups as women and, for the advancement of their racial interests, have joined organizations with their men.

There is yet another difference between the status and perceived problems of middle-class women and those of lower-class women. Their position as housewives is quite different. It is obvious that historically the family has undergone important changes in structure and function, bringing about essential changes in the position of women. What Betty Friedan has described as the "feminine mystique" is essentially the symptom of a cultural lag, in which our societal and personal values are adapted to a family pattern that has long ceased to exist. The large, rural family—jointly producing most of the products for its own consumption, living self-sufficiently outside of the cash economy, training its young in the home, caring for its old, and providing both men and women with lifelong activity and work, which had the dignity of being essential to the group—needed the housewife and provided her with satisfying work.

A few decades after the Civil War this family had ceased to be the prototype of the American family. But it was not until the twentieth century that the full effect of urbanization, better medical care and longer life expectancy, combined with a lower birthrate, was fully felt. The modern urban family, which has removed all productive and most educational and welfare functions from the home and which requires the full-time services of the housewife-mother for a relatively brief span of time—five to eight years, while the children are pre-schoolers—has made the lifelong occupation of housewife archaic. As Betty Friedan pointed out, no amount of glamorizing, advertising and verbal upgrading can make homemaking anything more than a part-time job stretched out into a full-time, supposedly life-filling occupation. Since upper- and middle-class families have fewer children, employ domestic help, and can afford the various services available to lighten household chores, it is not surprising that middle-class women feel more discontented and restless in their empty, socially prescribed role.

An often neglected aspect of the problem is the money question. When the work of men became work for money, and society adopted money standards as its measure for value and worth, the unpaid labor of the housewife was again degraded, and her status, perhaps at first imperceptibly, but nevertheless decisively, lowered.

All of this is quite different for the lower-class family. Among the eleven million poor families (those with an annual income under four thousand dollars), the housewife still performs an essential function. Even the economically more privileged blue-collar worker's family could not survive, if the mother did not contribute her free labor for laundering, cleaning, home baking, haircutting and, often, home sewing. Shopping for bargains—the only kind of goods poor working people can afford to buy—is a time-consuming but, under present conditions, essential occupation. The working-class housewife's unpaid labor directly supplements the wages paid to her husband. This does not lessen her burden or exploitation, but it does make a difference in her subjective attitude toward her role. It also explains her general indifference to women's rights organizations.

If these women find little appeal in women's rights as such, their emancipation is nevertheless progressing. Labor protective legislation, welfare state measures, improvements in medical and health care, the availability of birth control information—these are all reforms that advance the status of lower-class women. Working women have traditionally perceived that the trade union movement, despite its predominant insensitivity to the problems of women, still offers their best chance for advancement. In those unions where women have been able to organize as separate entities, such as in the United Automobile Workers, considerations of their special needs could be secured, and important advances, such as job protection after maternity leaves, could be written into union contracts. This parallels the European pattern where the major legislative gains for working women were won through the pressure of strongly feminist-oriented organizations of working-class women within or without the trade union movement. This has been the exception in the United States, however, not the rule.

The preconditions for the emancipation of American women prevailed throughout most of the country for the upper and middle classes by the time of World War I. Women of all classes had by then experienced some very tangible improvements over their previous condition, which they would soon take for granted as "natural": freedom to dress so as to enjoy unhampered movement; freedom to move outside the family and escape familial or communal taboos and ostracism for deviant behavior; the right and possibility not to have one's procreative functions dominate all one's life; the right to divorce without social stigma. To middle-class women, the attainment of suffrage, and of those legal-constitutional changes they expected would inevitably follow upon suffrage, seemed adequate. This explains the waning interest in the woman's rights movement after 1920.

World War II, as had previous wars, exposed working-class women to the possibilities of well-paying jobs, free child-care centers, training opportunities for skilled employment. But, after the war, "Rosie, the Riveter" was told to go home where she belonged and produce babies, not ships. She did just that, with disastrous effects on our overcrowded schools and other institutions. One might have expected, then, that pressures for female advancement would at least come from these lower-class women.

That this did not happen is due to a familiar paradox: the women who most need reforms are helpless to enact them; the women who are most able to work for reforms are not in great need of them. The results are as one might expect: middle-class women support the more far-reaching demands of working-class women up to a point, then they relax their efforts. In this country, during the Progressive period, the interests of women of all classes briefly coincided. Suffragists needed the support of trade unionists and labor in general in order to secure their goal; working women hoped that female suffrage would serve to enact the reforms they needed—this overlapping of interests held the alliance together. After 1920, having won their "rights," middle-class women succumbed to the negative pressures of society, such as ridicule, an ideological offensive by antifeminists and red-baiting, which earlier they had been able to withstand. Working-class women, who usually bear the triple burden of work, housework and child care, without benefit of those replacement services available for money, are too weak as a group to organize and struggle in their own behalf, except for the most immediate economic gains. Still, there has been a continuous thread of organizational effort on the community level from the New Deal to the present day. Such movements as meat boycotts during World War II, consumer strikes, rent struggles, and, more recently, organization around school issues, in which lower-class women have played a significant role, deserve to be studied and interpreted by social historians.

The women's emancipation movement has experienced a sudden resurgence in the past five years. The current movement, like the woman's rights movement of the 1800s, is based on an educated elite group of white, middle-class women, who have experienced a strong sense of status displacement. Much of their effort has followed the traditional pattern of concentrating on constitutional-legal reforms that most benefit middle-class women, such as the Equal Rights Amendment. But the women's liberation movement has infused feminism with a new spirit. Despite the limitations of its composition, the more youthful and radical wing of the new feminist movement has been innovative and experimental and has striven hard to escape the historical pattern of reform and failure.

Technology and science have provided, for the first time in human history, the conditions for the potential eradication of sex-based differences among humans. Overpopulation on a world scale has raised moral questions that affect the most personal human relations. Excessive reproduction, like excessive consumption, may soon be considered against the best interests of society, if not outright immoral. With the lessening importance of their reproductive role, with altered conditions for their social functioning, women need to have oppressive institutional restraints lifted from them. There is no longer any justification for their existence.

This means, practically speaking, the kind of change in role expectations and psychological orientation women's liberationists have been talking about. It does not mean only women's rights. It means the emancipation of both men and women from a sex-dominated archaic division of labor and from the values that sustain it.

4 *Carlyle C. Douglas*

Incorporation:
A New Tactic
for Saving Black Areas

Until it had approached within a quarter of a mile, the long, white car rode anonymously in a swirl of south Alabama dust. As it drew near, however, black men in overalls began rousing themselves on the porch of the Gees Bend general store, one or two of them having recognized the driver. "Hey, how y'all," called one of them as he watched the car roll to a stop and the driver roll down his window. The straw-hatted farmer walked over to the car and leaned against the door. "Lawyer," he said, "when we go'n' git our town?"

What the farmer referred to was the incorporation as a municipality of the dusty Wilcox county hamlet, making a self-governing body of the 1,500 or so black souls who comprise the population. The prospect of incorporation and all that would go with it—self-determination, their own law enforcement officers, federal grants, telephones (until recently there were none within 20 miles) is probably the most exciting one to visit the impoverished village since neighboring white folks closed down the ferry service across the Alabama River, lengthening the traveling distance to Camden, the county seat, from seven miles to 40. While many of the whites in the county find it remarkable that it should occur to any of the

From *Ebony*, Vol. 25 (August 1970). Reprinted by permission.

blacks to incorporate their own towns, they find it even more remarkable that they should have the gumption to go ahead with that idea.

Without a doubt, it would startle these same whites to know that the phenomenon of blacks grouping to form a new town or city is not peculiar to Wilcox county. In fact, if Orzell Billingsley, a scrappy Birmingham attorney, brings his plans to fruition, more than 100 Alabama black communities, some of them rural farming villages like Gees Bend and others suburbs of major cities like Birmingham, will be incorporated over the next few years. White reaction to what some of them have judged to be a "separatist" move has been ambivalent. Billingsley is fond of repeating. "These crackers just don't know what to do!" and facts seem to bear him out. Billingsley's first successful incorporation bid was for Roosevelt City, which lies between Birmingham and Bessemer in the iron ore-rich foothills of the Appalachians. Now three years old, Roosevelt will probably become the third largest city in Jefferson county (after Birmingham and Bessemer) and the largest all-black city in the nation. Its population now stands at about 4,500, but its mayor and councilmen have launched what probably will be a successful bid to annex several neighboring unincorporated black areas which will bring its population up to about 13,000. When white Jefferson County state legislators first got wind of the plans to incorporate Roosevelt—known unofficially at that time simply as "niggertown"—a bill was rushed through in Montgomery to block incorporation of any area already within three miles of an existing town. The bill applied only to Jefferson county. Sponsored by Alabama State Sen. Richard Dominick and known as the Dominick Amendment, the bill was just days too late to prevent Roosevelt's incorporation.

Since then, things have happened pretty much as Billingsley said whites feared they would. Roosevelt has its own small but efficient police and fire departments. Recent federal grants have enabled it to begin construction of a $211,000 community center. An expected grant will provide nearly $400,000 for a sewer system. Taxes are lower than in Birmingham and Mayor Freddie Rodgers says there are no current plans to raise them. Mayor Rodgers expects that annexation and growth will eventually raise Roosevelt's population to nearly 50,000—the vast majority black. "Poor whites around here will begin to wonder about their own leadership when they see the kinds of things we will be doing," says the mayor. "We have done more in the last three years than Brownsville and Brighton (neighboring white towns which were among the five towns which had police jurisdiction over unincorporated Roosevelt) have done in 100 years. If we make the progress we're striving for, there will be more progress all around. Roosevelt City will become a seat of black power."

The mayor might have added, with much justification, that Roosevelt will also become a seat of black pride. For decades, Roosevelt and other unincorporated black areas were at the mercy of surrounding cities. Birmingham and Bessemer, each with comfortable white majorities, expanded by annexing areas near Roosevelt and skillfully gerrymandering black people. The people of Roosevelt, acting individually and through the Roosevelt Community Improvement Association headed by Jack Abernathy, older brother of Dr. Ralph D. Abernathy, sought in vain to be annexed by the larger cities. Their giant white neighbors were willing to collect taxes from Roosevelt residents (under Alabama law, businessmen in an unincorporated area must be licensed by the nearest municipality; liquor, tobacco, gasoline and utility tax refunds due the people of an unincorporated area go to the nearest municipality; traffic fines and court costs are collected by nearby municipalities) but unwilling to take them within the city limits. From a practical standpoint, there was no reason to do so. The powerless blacks of areas around Roosevelt provided an easy source of income for the white municipalities, but to annex them would have also meant further diluting a white majority with a group of people whose average family income was, and is, about $2,500 and whose unemployment rate currently stands at a depression level 14.3 per cent. Though 74 per cent of the unincorporated blacks owned their own homes and many were fine residences which would do credit to any city, most were, and are, substandard and of little tax value. So why take them in? Taxation without representation has always been a good game for the party doing the taxing. And no party in such a position has ever given it up willingly, hence the Dominick Amendment.

Upon incorporation, one of the first differences noticed by Roosevelt City officials was a "tremendous drop in the crime rate because they (white police officers from surrounding towns) had been arresting us whenever they felt like it." Though other problems have not disappeared so easily, Mayor Rodgers and the five Roosevelt City councilmen are quick to point out that the community is infinitely better off than it was Three years ago they had a budget of virtually nothing. In 1969, they operated with a balanced budget of $76,000. That figure will multiply as the population increases and federal grants begin to roll in. Though their problems are what they have always been, now there is hope of solving them. "The rough spots are all over now," the mayor says. "We plan to do 20 years of developing in the next four years. Once the sewers go in and we get our first-class recreation center built, developers will start to come in." And he's right. The planned annexations will give the city more open land and boost the tax base with the addition of light industry presently located just beyond the city limits.

Despite overwhelming evidence that the people of Roosevelt did the only thing they could do under the circumstances, some of their critics—frequently those who no doubt counted themselves among the "friends" of blacks—remained pathetically insistent that incorporation of any all-black municipality was "separatism" pure and simple. When Billingsley attempted to export his plan to Georgia where black people had recently won control of Hancock County (they outnumbered whites there by four to one), he was rebuffed by John McCown, executive director of the Georgia Council on Human Relations. "I want it made crystal clear that in Hancock County we're not interested in the least in any all-black community," said McCown at the time. He stated that the black people of Hancock County had no desire for "black separatism." Commented one Roosevelt City official: "What was he talking about? He's got a county that's almost all black and he says he don't want any separatism. What the hell is he going to do, bring in some crackers from the next county?"

John Conyers, black Democratic congressman from Detroit, took a different point of view, terming Billingsley's plan for incorporating existing black communities "a great idea." Said Conyers: "Building the political and economic power of rural communities by giving the inhabitants a larger voice in government as a group rather than as individuals will add considerably to the economic welfare of the communities and the states involved. It certainly merits the help of the federal government and all who will be directly or indirectly affected."

Though the Dominick Amendment would appear to be a major stumbling block in Billingsley's path as far as Jefferson County is concerned (the bill will have to be overturned before he can proceed with most of the eight more incorporations he plans within the county), the legislation is a bumbling, even laughable attempt to halt progress in the eyes of an attorney who leaped vigorously into early civil rights cases, represented the Muslims in some of their Southern land acquisitions and made an attempt to incorporate Resurrection City during the Poor People's Campaign. He plans to challenge the Dominick Amendment with the contention that it unconstitutionally disfranchises those residents of towns rendered unincorporable by the law. When he has had the bothersome legislation removed from the books, the new towns in Jefferson County will include Mason City, adjacent to Roosevelt, Harlem Heights, Airport City and nearly a half dozen others. He views himself not as fostering separatism, but as capitalizing on separatism which already exists and would have continued to exist in any case. Though Billingsley has carried the seed of his plan since his law school days ("People just weren't ready for it back in 1951"), he was "sidetracked" by the civil rights movement, handling sit-in, voting rights and other cases dating back to the great bus boycott in Montgomery, Ala. Even after his long involvement in the "movement" tapered off, Billingsley found that he could devote little time to his plan, the necessity of making a living providing the interference, for incorporating impoverished black towns is a losing proposition from a business standpoint. Billingsley estimates that he has spent $40,000 of his own funds to further such projects.

With the successful incorporation of Roosevelt City and Ridgeville, a northern Alabama town, however, Billingsley is finding his prospects for assistance increasing. He is hopeful that a recently enacted plan whereby students from several educational institutions offering urban planning and related disciplines will be made available to him for doing much of the legwork involved in incorporating a municipality (gathering petitions, procuring survey maps, generating enthusiasm for the idea among those affected, etc.).

Though Billingsley's plan for the incorporation of all-black towns in the South will probably be the most successful of its kind, it is certainly not the first. More than two dozen all-black hamlets were founded in Oklahoma between 1890 and 1919 as an offshoot of a post-Civil War separatist movement. In a recent article in *The Black Scholar*, Arthur L. Tolson concluded that these "black national bastions" had declined (by 1962 those which still existed had a total population of 3,335, a decrease of 1,624 over the previous decade) because "black separatism or black nationalism as such provided no permanent solution of the black question within the framework of American capitalism."

Most of the towns which have been and will be established through Billingsley's efforts, however, fall into a somewhat different category. Roosevelt City, for instance, is not dependent upon its own separate economic system. The vast majority of the community's working people hold jobs in Birmingham or Bessemer. The city may eventually expand to such a size that more people are taking money out of the town than are bringing it in, but that day will probably never come. And though most of the others are not as fortunate as Roosevelt in the availability of industrial employment, none will be facing sudden, new economic problems, for all have had to face the question of survival for many years already. They cannot help but improve their lot by incorporation. Then, too, federal aid on a level that will become available to each of the towns as they become legal municipalities was unheard of for the Oklahomans. Billingsley, who boasts with some foundation that his working knowledge of federal programs applicable to incorporated municipalities is as good as, or better than, that of any other man in the country, can cite off hand a program to suit almost any problem imaginable.

Easing his big Imperial over the dusty backroads of Gee's Bend (which will be renamed King City upon incorporation), Billingsley talked about the area, what it was and what it could be. "This has got to be one of the poorest areas in the country," he said. "You see that house there?" He gestured at a roadside hovel. "Once we get this place incorporated, we can tear that place down and regardless of what the man who lives there is making, we could put up a new house the next week that he could afford to buy. Not rent, buy." He then pointed out that most of the people of Gee's Bend own their own land, the farms averaging about 100 acres each. "These people are potentially some of the wealthiest black people in the country. This place is going to be a utopia." That potential wealth was recently increased when a dam was built across the Alabama several miles downstream from Gee's Bend, creating a lake along which much of the residents' property fronts. Property adjacent to that owned by Gee's Bend citizens has been bought by the government and declared a recreational area, giving their land values an immediate boost. Whites soon began attempting to buy some of that land, but, for the most part, the blacks have refused to sell.

Viewed by some as a circuit-riding Santa Claus carting an Imperial full of hope from town to town and by others as a devil incarnate sowing seeds of disunity, Orzell Billingsley Jr. doesn't really seem to care what those around him think of his mission. His air is one of unabrasive right-eousness coupled with a sense of practicality. He knows his plan will work and as more towns are established and made viable, there are black belt counties begging for organization. And when blacks are running a hundred towns and a score of counties, what then? Billingsley knows. But he's not saying—not just yet, anyway.

Charles E. Silberman

The Revolt
Against
Welfare Colonialism

In the last analysis, . . . Negro children will be able to climb out of their slums en masse only if they see their parents doing the same—only if the adults of the community are involved in action on their own behalf. For it is the disorganization of the community at large—the evidence on all sides that their parents are unable to control their own behavior, unable to impose sanctions on people who threaten the community's well-being —that persuades the young that the cards are stacked against them, that the omnipresent "they" will not permit them to "make it" in any legitimate form, and so leads them into apathy, withdrawal, or rebellion.

But can this be done; can the adults be mobilized? The answer, quite simply, is that it *has* been done—in Chicago, where The Wood-lawn Organization, created in late 1960, has become a major factor in that city's life and politics. Indeed, TWO is the most important and the most impressive experiment affecting Negroes anywhere in the United States. It is a living demonstration that Negroes, even those living in the worst sort of slum, can be mobilized to help themselves, and that when they are, neither the Negro community nor the city as a whole can ever be quite the same again.

From Charles E. Silberman, *Crisis in Black and White*. Reprinted by permission of Random House, Inc.

Formation of TWO represents the first instance in which a large, broadly representative organization has come into existence in any Negro district in any large American city. The Woodlawn Organization is set up as a federation of other representative groups: some eighty-five or ninety in all, including thirteen churches (virtually all the churches of any influence in the community), three businessmen's associations, and an assortment of block clubs, neighborhood associations, and social groups of one sort or another. All told, the organizations represented in TWO have a membership of about thirty thousand people; some twelve hundred of them attended the organization's second annual convention in May of 1963.

Existence of any sort of large organization in Woodlawn would seem to be almost a contradiction in terms; an oblong slum running south of the University of Chicago campus and containing between eighty and a hundred fifty thousand people, depending on how the area is defined, Woodlawn is almost a prototype of the disorganized anomic neighborhoods into which Negroes have been moving. In the 1920s, Woodlawn was part of the University community—a highly desirable residential area with broad tree-lined streets, excellent transportation facilities, and a nice admixture of private homes and apartment houses. The neighborhood began to deteriorate during the Depression, when big apartments were cut up into smaller units in an effort to rent them; and the process continued during World War Two. Even so, a report issued by the City Plan Commission in 1946 declared that "Woodlawn always has been a good community" and called for a program of neighborhood conservation to keep it that way.

The conservation program never was put into effect, however, and Woodlawn resumed its decline as the postwar rush to the suburbs got under way. Thus around about 1950, Negroes began moving in; the trickle rapidly turned into a torrent as Woodlawn became the "port-of-entry" for Negroes moving to Chicago from the South. (The Illinois Central Railroad's Sixty-third Station—the next-to-last stop on the line that runs northward from Mississippi, Louisiana, Tennessee and Kentucky—is in the Woodlawn area. There are some weeks when fully half the passengers traveling to Chicago from those states disembark in Woodlawn.) By 1960, Woodlawn had become a virtually all-Negro slum.* Al-

---

*The change in the color of Woodlawn's residents seems to have changed the area's history as well; thus, a 1962 city report on "Key Social Characteristics of the Woodlawn Community" suggests, in contradiction to the 1946 report, that as a result of "almost planless growth since the 1893 Columbia Exposition," the community had been deteriorating for more than a half-century.

though nearly 25 per cent of the area's residents receive some form of welfare, they pay an average of $84 a month in rent—more than $10 *above* the city average—for which they occupy an average housing unit of 2.2 rooms. A birth rate 25 per cent above the city's average has put pressure on the capacity of the local public schools. There is a flourishing traffic in gambling, narcotics, and prostitution, especially in one stretch under the elevated subway tracks; the commercial business district is active but declining, with large numbers of stores vacant. In short, Woodlawn is precisely the sort of obsolescent, decaying, crowded neighborhood which social workers and city planners assume can never help itself—the sort of neighborhood in which even such advocates of social action as S. M. Miller assume that "directed, concerted action toward political or any other kind of goals is extremely unlikely."

But Woodlawn *is* helping itself; it is taking concerted action toward a wide variety of goals. The impetus for TWO came from three Protestant ministers and a Catholic priest who had come together through their concern with the spiraling decline of their neighborhood and the indifference of both the city and the University of Chicago, located just to the north of Woodlawn. The clergymen had "worn out the seats of several good pairs of trousers attending an uncountable number of meetings held to 'do something about Woodlawn' "—meetings which seemed only to lead to still more meetings. "We were watching a community dying for lack of leaders, a community that had lost hope in the decency of things and people," one of the founders, Dr. Ulysses B. Blakeley, co-pastor of the First Presbyterian Church and Moderator of the Chicago Presbytery, explains. "Outsiders consider a place like this a kind of zoo or jungle; they may mean well, but they choke us. It seemed to us that any effort would be futile unless our own people could direct it, choose their own goals, and work for them, grow in the process, and have a sense again of the rightness of things."

After investigating various approaches to community organization, therefore, the clergymen "took the plunge," as Dr. Blakeley and his co-pastor, Dr. Charles T. Leber, Jr., described it in *Presbyterian Life:* they called on Saul D. Alinsky, executive director of the Industrial Areas Foundation, and invited him to help organize the Woodlawn community. A sociologist and criminologist by training, Alinsky is a specialist in creating mass organizations on a democratic basis "in order that the so-called 'little man' can gather into his hands the power he needs to make and shape his life." His organizing career began in the late 1930s, when he was one of the principal architects of Chicago's much admired Back of the Yards Neighborhood Council, which turned the stockyards area—the locale for Upton Sinclair's *The Jungle*—into one of the most desirable working-class neighborhoods in Chicago.* "When his success in organizing the Back of the Yards evoked requests to do the same in other cities, Alinsky organized the Industrial Areas Foundation, a non-profit institution which has organized some forty-four groups across the country. The most notable of these, until the formation of The Woodlawn Organization, were in California, where the IAF organized some thirty communities of Mexican-Americans and welded them together in the Community Service Organization. The Industrial Areas Foundation's President is Dr. George N. Shuster, retired president of Hunter College and now assistant to the president of Notre Dame University; the board of directors includes, among others, Mrs. Valentine E. Macy, whose husband is a power in New York Republican politics; Ralph Helstein, president of the Packinghouse Workers Union; Cecil North, former president of Metropolitan Life Insurance Company; Rev. Ralph Abernathy, second-in-command under Rev. Martin Luther King; and Meryl Ruoss, chairman of the Institute of Strategic Studies of the Board of National Missions of the Presbyterian Church.

"Took the plunge" is an apt way of describing what the Woodlawn ministers did in approaching Alinsky, however—for he is nothing if not controversial. Indeed, he delights in controversy; one of his basic premises, he likes to say, is that *all* important issues are controversial. Alinsky's opponents (few of whom have bothered to read *The Prince*) see him as Machiavelli reincarnated; Alinsky has been attacked, at various times, as a communist, a fascist, a dupe of the Catholic Church, the mastermind of a Catholic conspiracy (Alinsky is Jewish), a racist, a segregationist, and an integrationist seeking to mongrelize Chicago. His supporters are equally immoderate in their praise; as Drs. Blakeley and Leber wrote, "No one in the city is as detested or as loved, as cursed or as blessed, as feared or as respected." Certainly no one in recent memory has had as great an impact on the city of Chicago; and none in the

---

*Critics of Alinsky now point to Back of the Yards and suggest that *anyone* could have organized the area, since the residents are virtually all Catholics. But when Alinsky began his organizing work, the stockyards area quite literally was a jungle. The residents were Catholic, all right—but they belonged to an incredible number of churches, each representing a different nationality or ethnic group at war with all the others. Animosity between them was so great that Catholic priests ministering to one ethnic group literally were not on speaking terms with priests from other ethnic backgrounds. Alinsky managed to unite all the Catholics—and then to forge a working alliance between the local Churches, the Chicago Archdiocese, and the Packinghouse Workers Union—at the time (though no longer) under communist domination. Paradoxically, the Back of the Yards organization has become very conservative in recent years: *e.g.*, it has been quite effective in keeping Negroes out of the neighborhood.

United States has proposed a course of action or a philosophy better calculated to rescue Negro or white slum dwellers from their poverty or their degradation. For Alinsky is that rarity of American life: a superlative organizer, strategist, and tactician who is also a philosopher (or a superlative philosopher who is also an organizer, strategist and tactician).

The essential difference between Alinsky and his enemies is that Alinsky really believes in democracy: he really believes that the helpless, the poor, the badly-educated can solve their own problems if given the chance and the means; he really believes that the poor and uneducated, no less than the rich and educated, have the right to decide how their lives should be run and what services should be offered to them, instead of being ministered to like children. "I do not believe that democracy can survive, except as a formality," he has written, "if the ordinary citizen's part is limited to voting—if he is incapable of initiative and unable to influence the political, social and economic structures surrounding him."

The individual can influence these structures only if he has power, for power means nothing more or less than the capacity to make one's interests felt in the decisions that affect him. There are two sources of power, in Alinsky's view: money and people. Since the residents of Woodlawn and of areas like it obviously have no money, their only source of power is themselves—which is to say the creation of an effective organization. Alinsky's frankness about power is upsetting to a good many people who regard open discussion of power as somehow lacking in taste—the equivalent, almost, of discussing one's marital life in public. For power, as John Kenneth Galbraith has written, plays a curious role in American life. "The privilege of controlling the actions or of affecting the income and property of others is something that no one of us can profess to seek or admit to possessing. No American ever runs for office because of an avowed desire to govern. He seeks to serve . . . The same scrupulous avoidance of the terminology of power," Galbraith adds, "characterizes American business. The head of the company is no longer the boss—the term survives only as an amiable form of address—but the leader of the team. No union leader ever presents himself as anything but a spokesman for the boys."*

Alinsky takes delight in violating this etiquette. "The only reason people have ever banded together," he baldly states, "and the only reason they ever will, is the fact that organization gives them the power to satisfy their desires or to realize their needs. There never has been any other

---

*John Kenneth Galbraith, *American Capitalism*, Boston: Houghton Mifflin Company, 1956.

reason." In his view, people join a trade union to develop enough power to force a change in their working conditions; they join a political party in order to have a power instrument that can win an election and carry out their political objectives; they organize a church as a power instrument to convert others to their religious belief. "Even when we talk of a community lifting itself by its bootstraps," Alinsky says, "we are talking of power. It takes a great of power to lift oneself by one's own bootstraps."

To create such a power structure in an area like Woodlawn, however, requires enormous skill and effort, and a break with convention. The reason most efforts at organizing slum neighborhoods fail, Alinsky argues, is not the nature of the community but the objectives of the organizers and of the methods they use. Most approaches to community organization, as Professor Dan W. Dodson has written, involve "more of an emphasis on how to get the different vested interests together to slice up areas of 'service' than . . . a consideration of how to get people genuinely organized in fighting for the things which would bring them dignity and respect." The conventional appeal to homeowners' interests in conserving property values is useless in a community in which the majority of people rent, and in which the homeowners would have to sell if forced to comply with the building code. A call for civic pride falls flat in a community which hates its neighbors and which is convinced it is going to be bulldozed out of existence sooner or later; neighborhoods like Woodlawn are too drab and dismal to cause anyone to rally around them. Even civil rights is too much of an abstraction. "The daily lives of Woodlawn people," an early Alinsky memo on Woodlawn suggested, "leave them with little energy or enthusiasm for realizing principles from which they themselves will derive little practical benefit. They know that with their educational and economic handicaps they will be exceptions indeed if they can struggle into a middle-class neighborhood or a white-collar job." Instead of these appeals of the conventional neighborhood organizer and group worker, Alinsky uses the classical approach of trade union organization: he appeals to the self-interest of the local residents and to their resentment and distrust of the outside world, and he seeks out and develops a local, indigenous leadership.

While indigenous leadership is crucial if the organization is to mean anything in the lives of its members, the initial impetus must come from the outside, and the mean and difficult job of building the organization must be handled by fulltime organizers who know how to conquer the apathy of the slum and how to weld its disparate fragments into a unified whole. For the indigenous leaders of the slum area are not in touch with each other; without training, they lack the skills needed to keep a large organization running; and in most cases it has never oc-curred to any of them to lead a mass organization. (If any one thing is known in the Negro slum—or the white slum, for that matter—it is that you can't fight City Hall.) Just as no factory would ever be organized without stimulus and guidance from the outside, so no slum can be or-ganized without a good deal of help.

But the Industrial Areas Foundation insists that help be used to make the local community self-sufficient, not to keep it dependent. Alin-sky will not enter a community unless he is invited by something like a cross-section of the population, and he usually insists, as a condition of entering, that the community itself, no matter how poor, take over the full responsibility for financing the new organization within a period of three years.* Alinsky has a standard way of dramatizing the importance of financial independence at the convention at which a new group for-mally approves its constitution. The audience is usually full of enthu-siasm and terribly proud of the constitution, which local citizens have hammered out over a long period of time. Alinsky takes a copy of the document, looks at it briefly, and then tosses it to the floor, announcing to the startled audience: "This constitution doesn't mean a damned thing. As long as the IAF organizers are on my payroll they'll do what I damn well tell them to do and not what it says on any paper like that." After a shocked silence, someone in the audience invariably calls out, "I don't understand. I thought you were on our side!" "I am," Alinsky an-swers back. "But think of the number of people who've come down here telling you the same thing, and how many turned out to be two-timing, double-crossing S.O.B.s. Why should you trust me? The only way you can be sure that the aims in that constitution are carried out is to get the organizers off my payroll and onto your payroll. Then *you* can tell them what to do, and if they don't do it, you can fire them and get someone who will."

Once the Industrial Areas Foundation enters a community, the process of building an organization follows a fairly standard pattern:

1. Organizers from the Industrial Areas Foundation filter through the neighborhood, asking questions and, more important, listening in bars, at street corners, in stores, in peoples' homes—in short, wherever people are talking—to discover the residents' specific grievances;

2. At the same time, the organizers try to spot the individuals and the groups on which people seem to lean for advice or to which they go for

---

*Because of the poverty of Woodlawn, and even more because of the long tradi-tion of Negro dependence, Alinsky has found it necessary to stretch that period by a year or two. TWO is on its way to financial independence, however; as of January, 1964, it had $10,000 in its treasury.

help: a barber, a minister, a mailman, a restaurant owner, etc.—the "indigenous" leaders;

3. The organizers get these leaders together, discuss the irritations, frustrations, and problems animating the neighborhood, and suggest the ways in which power might be used to ameliorate or solve them;

4. A demonstration or series of demonstrations are put on to show how power can be used. These may take a variety of forms: a rent strike against slum landlords, a cleanup campaign against a notorious trouble spot, etc. What is crucial is that meetings and talk, the bedrock on which middle-class organizations founder, are avoided; the emphasis is on action, and on action that can lead to visible results.

In this way, the new organization begins to take form as a super-group comprising many existing member groups—churches, block clubs, businessmen's associations—and of new groups that are formed purely as a means of joining the larger organization. As the organization begins to move under its own steam, the IAF men gradually phase themselves out and local leaders take over. This does not mean that volunteers take over the whole work load, however. One of the cardinal principles of the IAF is that a full-time paid staff is necessary if a community organization is to continue to function; volunteers, especially in a slum neighborhood, simply do not have the time. But the local leaders take on the responsibility for making decisions and for meeting the budget; sometimes they hire one of the IAF organizers as a permanent staff head, sometimes they come up with their own organizers.

So much for general principles and procedures. The actual work of creating The Woodlawn Organization was begun in the spring and summer of 1960, eighteen months after the four ministers had called on Alinsky for help. (He had told them he would not come in to Woodlawn until a representative committee had extended the invitation.) By this time, the invitation was being extended by the Greater Woodlawn Pastors Alliance with support from most other organized groups in the community. The organizing effort was made possible by grants from the Catholic Archdiocese of Chicago, the Presbyterian Church of Chicago, and the Schwarzhaupt Foundation, a private philanthropy which has supported Industrial Areas Foundation projects elsewhere in the United States.

How do you begin to organize an area like Woodlawn? As Nicholas von Hoffman, then chief organizer for the IAF (now a reporter for a Chicago daily) put it with studied casualness, "I found myself at the corner of Sixty-third and Kimbark and I looked around." It did not take much looking or listening to discover, as might be expected in a Negro slum, that one of the things that "bugged" residents the most was cheating and exploitation by some of the businessmen of the area. In most low-income areas, credit-purchasing is a trap; naïve and semi-literate customers are high-pressured into signing installment contracts without reading the fine print or having it explained. According to Dr. Leber, there were instances of customers being charged effective interest rates as high as 200 per cent; second-hand merchandise was represented as new; and prices bordered on outright piracy: a $6 diamond chip in a gaudy ring setting would be sold for $250, with a "Certificate of Guarantee" that it was a real diamond. (It *was* a real diamond—but one worth only $6.) Credit-purchasing aside, many merchants took unfair advantage of their customers' ignorance; food stores, for example, gave short weight, overcharged, and in a few cases actually rigged their cash registers to give false totals.

Hence, when the IAF organizers started fanning through the community, complaints began to pile up. Here was an issue, moreover, on which the legitimate businessmen in the area could unite with the consumers, for the crooked merchants hurt business for everyone else. As a result, TWO—bringing together the leaders of the Businessman's Association, some of the ministers, and some of the indigenous leaders who were being turned up—worked out a Code of Business Ethics covering credit practices, pricing, and advertising. To implement the Code, TWO set up a Board of Arbitration consisting of four representatives from the Businessman's Association, four from consumer groups, with an impartial chairman from outside the community elected by the eight Board members.

If this had been all, however, TWO would have been stillborn. To publicize the Code, and to publicize the new organization, a big parade was staged in which nearly a thousand people marched through the business section carrying signs, singing, and creating enough of a stir to make the front pages of most Chicago newspapers. The next Saturday, a registered scale was set up at a nearby Catholic church, along with an adding machine; people who shopped at the markets suspected of giving false weights and improper totals brought their packages directly to the church, where they were weighed, and cash register slips checked and the false weights and false totals publicized. Most of the offending merchants quickly agreed to comply with the "Square Deal" agreement. To bring recalcitrant merchants to terms, leaflets were distributed through the community accusing them of cheating and urging residents to stay away.

The Square Deal campaign served its purpose. It eliminated a considerable amount of exploitation and chicanery on the part of Woodlawn merchants. More important, it made the residents of Woodlawn aware of the existence of the new organization and drove home the fact that through organization they *could* improve some of the circumstances of their lives. Two years later, a TWO vice-president recalled that it was the Square Deal campaign that brought him into the organization, and that really put TWO on a solid footing. "We showed people that they don't have to accept everything, that they can do something about it," he said—"but that they have to be organized to do it."

To capitalize on the enthusiasm this campaign created, the IAF staff men moved next to organize rent strikes in a number of Woodlawn buildings. Wherever a substantial majority of the tenants could be persuaded to act together, a tenants' group was formed which demanded that the landlord, within some stated period of time, clear up physical violations that made occupancy hazardous or uncomfortable—broken windows, plumbing that did not work, missing steps from staircases, inadequate heat, etc. When the landlords ignored the ultimatum, TWO organized a rent strike: rents were withheld from the landlord and deposited in escrow in a special bank account. To dramatize the strike on one block where several adjoining buildings were involved, residents spelled out "This Is A Slum" in huge letters on the outside of the building. If the landlord remained recalcitrant, groups of pickets were dispatched to march up and down in front of the landlord's own home, carrying placards that read "Your Neighbor Is A Slumlord." The picketing provided a useful outlet for the anger the tenants felt, and gave them an opportunity, for the first time in their lives, to use their color in an affirmative way. For as soon as the Negro pickets appeared in a white suburban block, the landlord was deluged with phone calls from angry neighbors demanding that he do something to call the pickets off. Within a matter of hours landlords who were picketed were on the phone with TWO, agreeing to make repairs.

Landlords were not the only ones who were picketed; over-crowded and segregated schools became a target, too. When William G. Caples, president of the Board of Education, refused to meet with TWO to discuss their complaints—he denounced the organization as "the lunatic fringe"—a delegation of eighteen Protestant and Catholic pastors staged a sit-in at the executive offices of Inland Steel, where Caples was public relations vice-president; at the same time, TWO rank-and-filers circled the building on the outside, carrying placards denouncing Caples as a segregationist. (Caples resigned the following month "because of the pressure of company business.") And when Superintendent of Schools Benjamin Willis denied that overcrowding could be relieved by transferring Negro students to all-white schools, TWO sent "truth squads" of mothers into neighboring white schools to photograph empty and half-empty classrooms. (In one elementary school, which was 81.5 per cent Negro, classes averaged 48.4 students per room; a school nine blocks away, but

99 per cent white, had an average of 28.4 pupils per room.) TWO members also staged a "death watch" at Board of Education meetings: a large
group would attend each meeting wearing long black capes, to symbolize
the "mourning" of Negro parents over the plight of their children.

It is precisely this sort of tactic that leads some of Alinsky's critics to
denounce him as an agitator who deals in hate and who incites to conflict, a troublemaker whose stated goal is to "rub raw the sores of discontent," as an early TWO memorandum put it. "The fact that a community may be stirred and organized by 'sharpening dormant hostilities'
and 'rubbing raw the sores of discontent' is not new," says Julian Levi,
executive director of the South East Chicago Commission and mastermind and director of the University of Chicago's urban renewal activities.
"The technique has been proved in practice in the assembling of lynch
mobs." (Levi and the University have been trying alternately to discredit
Alinsky and to ignore him since he began organizing Woodlawn.) As an
example of the methods to which he objects, Levi cites a TWO leaflet
naming a local food store and warning people to "watch out" for short
weights, spoiled food, and short-changing. "If this is what this merchant
is really doing," Levi says, "he should be punished by the court—but with
all the safeguards the law provides. This is not the way people should be
taught to protect themselves," he argues; they should be taught to register complaints with the Department of Health (about spoiled food), and
Department of Weights and Measures (about short weights), and the
Police Department (about short change). Levi similarly deplores the use
of rent strikes. If landlords were violating the building code, he argues,
TWO should have brought action through the Building Department, the
way the South East Chicago Commission does, instead of taking the law
into its own hands.

But slum dwellers, as Levi surely knows, have been complaining to
the Building Department and to other city agencies for years, to no
avail. The reason the South East Chicago Commission is able to get rapid
action on complaints it registers with the Building Department or any
other city agency is that it has what politicians call "clout": the Commission is the urban renewal arm of the University of Chicago, whose board
of trustees includes some of the most influential businessmen and politicians in the city.

But agitation by itself is not enough; the inhabitants of a slum like
Woodlawn must be convinced not only that a solution is possible but also
that it is probable; they must see some tangible evidence that banding
together will give them the capacity to alter the circumstances of their
lives. To use the language of war (for that is what it is), the only way to
build an army is by winning a few victories. But how do you gain a vic-

tory before you have an army? The only method ever devised is guerilla warfare: to avoid a fixed battle where the forces are arrayed and where the new army's weakness would become visible, and to concentrate instead on hit-and-run tactics designed to gain small but measurable victories. Hence the emphasis on such dramatic actions as parades and rent strikes whose main objective is to create a sense of solidarity and of community.

Once this guerilla warfare begins, the best organizing help of all frequently comes from "the enemy"—the established institutions who feel themselves threatened by the new organization. What really welded the Woodlawn community together, for example, was the University of Chicago's announcement, on July 19, 1960, that it planned to extend its "South Campus" into Woodlawn by annexing an adjacent strip a block wide and a mile long.

The controversy over the South Campus plan has been revealing in another respect. There has been a great deal of talk, in recent years, about ways of increasing "citizen participation" in city planning, especially urban renewal planning; federal legislation now requires local citizen participation in the formulation of renewal plans as a condition of federal aid. The Woodlawn experience indicates that "participation" means something very different to planners and to the academic researchers on whom they lean, than it does to the people being planned for. To the former, "citizen participation" means that the local residents are given a chance to air their views *after* the plans have been drawn, not before; planning, in this view, is a matter for experts, and "participation" is really thought of as "acquiescence."

What makes The Woodlawn Organization significant, however, is not so much what it is doing for its members as what it is doing *to* them. "The most important thing to me about the forty-six busloads of people who went to City Hall to register," Alinsky commented at the time, "was their own reaction. Many were weeping; others were saying, 'They're paying attention to us;' 'They're recognizing that we're people.'" Eighteen months later, an active member observed, "City Hall used to be a forbidden place, but we've made so many trips there and seen so many people that it's beginning to feel like a neighborhood store." Other members expressed themselves in much the same way: "We've lost our fear of standing up and expressing ourselves;" "We don't have to go hat in hand, begging, anymore. It's a wonderful feeling." What is crucial, in short, is not what the Woodlawn residents win, but that *they* are winning it; and this makes them see themselves in a new light—as men and women of substance and worth.

Besides giving its members a sense of dignity and worth, the Woodlawn Organization has given a good many people a sense of direction and purpose and an inner discipline that has enabled them to overcome the "floundering phenomenon." "This has been the most satisfying and rewarding period of my life," one TWO officer remarked in the spring of 1963. "The organization has given me a real sense of accomplishing something—the only time in my life I've had that feeling." Indeed, activity in TWO has completely reshaped this man's life; he remembers the date and even the hour of the first TWO meeting he attended; he dates events from that time, the way a happily married couple dates events from their wedding day. But TWO has done more than just give purpose and meaning to his life, important as that is. Like so many other Woodlawnites, he had been accustomed to waste enormous amounts of time and energy through sheer inefficiency, *i.e.,* personal disorganization. This made the initial organizing work more difficult than anything the organizers had ever encountered in white slums; at first, every little venture seemed to fail because of the personal disorganization. Even such an apparently simple matter as rounding up a half-dozen people to hand out leaflets at a particular time loomed as a major task: the six selected would turn up at different times, the leaflets would be lost or misplaced, the volunteers would get bored before they had finished distributing the leaflets, etc., etc., etc. Bit by bit, however, the members learned how to accept orders, how to carry out a simple task and follow through on it; then they begin to learn how to give orders, how to organize a rent strike or a rally, how to handle a meeting, how to talk on their feet and debate an issue, how to handle opposition. The result, for those who have been actively involved in the organization, has been to transform their existence, for the discipline of the organization gradually imposes itself on their own lives. And as the individual learns to organize his own life, he learns how to relate to others. "We've learned to live together and act as a community," another TWO activist says. "Now I know people all over Woodlawn, and I've been in all the churches. Two years ago I didn't know a soul."

It would be inane to pretend that Woodlawn has become a model community; it remains a poverty-stricken, crime-ridden slum, though a slum with hope—a slum that is developing the means of raising itself by its own bootstraps. Most of the problems that make Woodlawn what it is —high unemployment, lack of education, family disorganization, poor health, bad housing—cannot be solved by a community organization alone. Help is needed; enormous resources must be poured into Woodlawn in the form of compensatory education, job retraining, advice on child-rearing, preventive medicine, etc. But experience in every city in the nation demonstrates that any paternalistic program imposed from above will be resisted and resented as "welfare colonialism." *TWO's greatest contribution, therefore, is its most subtle: it gives Woodlawn residents the sense of dignity that makes it possible for them to accept help.* For help now comes (or seems to come, which amounts to the same thing) not as the result of charity but as the result of their own power; they have decided what services they need and what services they would like to have. Hence programs which the community, in the past, would have avoided with contempt as one more instance of "Mr. Charlie's brainwashing," are now eagerly sought after. Thus, negotiations between TWO and the University of Chicago have led to development of a nursery school program designed to reverse the effects of cultural deprivation. Negotiations between TWO and a team of psychiatrists enabled the latter to set up some promising experiments in group therapy; the psychiatrists and social workers work through TWO's network of block clubs to bring people into the program. When a program enters Woodlawn with TWO's endorsement and recommendation, it carries a cachet that greatly multiplies its chances of success.

The Woodlawn experience deserves—indeed, requires—the most careful study by anyone, black or white, interested in solving "the Negro problem." Unfortunately, it is not getting that attention—at least not from academic researchers and foundation executives, who seem to be repelled by the controversy in which TWO basks. Not a single social scientist from the University of Chicago, for example (as of February, 1964, at any rate) has shown the slightest interest in TWO; with the most important social laboratory in the country across the street, they have turned steadfastly the other way. The large foundations have shown much the same lack of interest.

Yet The Woodlawn Organization is invaluable not only as a demonstration that a Negro slum community can be mobilized to help itself, but because it shows that co-operation is possible between whites and Negroes of the most militant stripe. The Woodlawn experience demonstrates that white help is valuable in a number of ways. Negroes have been so conditioned to accepting their plight as inevitable that it sometimes (though less and less frequently) takes whites to convince them that the status quo can be changed. White help is invaluable, secondly, in supplying the organizational know-how, and in overcoming or compensating for "the floundering phenomenon;" white advice can be useful also in advising the indigenous Negro leaders on how to approach the whites with whom they must deal. (Many of these leaders have had no contact with whites except in an employer-employee relationship; for such a man, the first trip to City Hall or to the Board of Education can be a terrifying experience.) Because of the poverty of the Negro community and the absence of any tradition of giving, white financial support is also essential if the organization is to get off the ground.

If Woodlawn demonstrates the need for white help, it also shows that help can be given in ways that build rather than destroy the Negroes' self-reliance and dignity and pride. Unquestionably, a good many TWO members must have been suspicious of their white allies during the early months or even years. But the whites proved their credentials by yielding the reins as rapidly as possible. In the first year, white ministers supplied most of the direction and served as spokesmen. But they moved more and more into the background as indigenous leadership began to develop. By 1963, for example, some of the most active members of the Education Committee were ADC mothers.

Where will the necessary support come from? Not from the government, in all likelihood; no government, no matter how liberal, is going to stimulate creation of a power organization that is sure to make its life uncomfortable. The much-heralded "Mobilization for Youth" project on New York City's Lower East Side, for example, which has received some $14 million from the Federal, state, and local governments and from the Ford Foundation, is based upon a sociological theory very similar to Alinsky's. "The long-range target in a service program," the Mobilization prospectus argues, "should not be the individual delinquent or even the conflict gang but, rather, the community itself . . . In the long run, the young will be far more responsive to an adult community which exhibits the capacity to organize itself, to manage its own problems, to impose informal sanctions, and to mobilize indigenous resources for young people, than they will be to a community which must have these functions performed by external agents."

6

Go Fox/Stop Pollution

Most of the time he is just another mild-mannered family man living in Aurora, Ill., a small city west of Chicago. But occasionally, unpredictably, he becomes—The Fox, unremitting foe of those who would befoul America by air, land or sea, a kind of Scarlet Pimpernel of the war on pollution. During the past year and a half The Fox has crawled up an industrial sewage pipe that was spewing sudsy wastes into a stream and clogged the outlet with a plywood bulkhead; he has scaled a factory's towering smokestack and capped it with a homemade metal stopper; and he has deposited dead skunks on the front porches of executives who work for companies responsible for the pollution. Each time he has left behind a handwritten note to explain his acts—and each note has been signed: "The Fox."

The Fox's one-man battle against industrial blight, which has already made him something of a legend among ecologically minded Chicagoans, apparently sprang from a frustration familiar to millions of Americans. As he explained it by phone to *Newsweek's* Don Holt last week (without, in the process, dropping so much as a single clue to his identity), The Fox had grown appalled by the systematic destruction of his favorite fishing preserve—the Fox River, a once-lovely waterway that meanders through Aurora to the Illinois River. Today a flood of wastes from proliferating industrial plants in the area has transformed the river into a brackish, odorous and fish-less mess. "Nobody ever stuck up for that poor, mistreated stream," The Fox, told Holt. "So I decided to do something in its name."

Up until this month, The Fox had confined his guerrilla raids to nighttime and to the area immediately around Aurora. But then two weeks ago, a husky, middle-aged man wearing ordinary work clothes and sunglasses walked into the reception room of the U.S. Reduction Co. in East Chicago, Ind., and dumped a can containing 50 pounds of raw sewage on the tile floor. As horrified secretaries fled the nauseating smell, the man wordlessly handed a note to a shrieking receptionist and calmly walked out. The note denounced the water pollution caused by an aluminum company in Aurora that is owned by U.S. Reduction. It was signed: "The Fox."

Lawbreaker. Although newspaper publicity about his forays has won The Fox plaudits from many, the police remain singularly unenchanted by him. Despite the quixotic nature of his crimes, The Fox is, after all, a lawbreaker—and one whose identity remains known only to a few like-minded friends. "If we catch him we could charge him with trespassing and criminal damage to property," growled police sergeant Robert Kollwelter as he perused the thick "Fox" folder he keeps in his desk. Kollwelter and his fellow Fox hunters think that they have at least a minor clue as to their quarry's identity. The expert construction of the plywood bulkhead that The Fox used to plug up the sewage pipe leads them to conclude that he has to be a carpenter—and a pretty good one, at that. (The Fox concedes that he does indeed know something about carpentry, but he insists that he doesn't carry a union card.) But beyond this, Kollwelter admits that he has been at least temporarily outfoxed. "It's kind of hard," he explains ruefully, "to lift fingerprints from the inside of a sewer."

It is perhaps a reflection of the times that some of Kollwelter's colleagues attribute The Fox's success and their failure to run him down to the probability that the whole thing is some sort of underground do-gooder conspiracy. "It has to be some kind of anti-pollution committee," maintains one policeman. "I think we'll find that there are many Foxes." (Although The Fox admits to Holt that a few close friends occasionally lend various forms of assistance, he chuckles over the charge that he is only one of a pack. "My biggest raid consisted of two of us," he says. "That's when we climbed the smokestack. I needed help to both measure it and fit the cap over the top.")

Dignity. Even orthodox environmentalists, while far more sympathetic to The Fox's aims than the police, are dubious about the long-term effects of this kind of guerrilla action. "I understand the guy's frustrations," says Joe Karaganis, a young lawyer in the state attorney general's office. "But the whole thing has broader implications. What if somebody takes the next illogical step and throws a bomb?" Such talk clearly appalls The Fox, who considers himself to be neither a revolutionary nor a criminal. "Who's breaking the law anyway?" he demands emphatically. "Do you know where I got that raw sewage I dumped at U.S. Reduction? I just went down to the Fox River and took what came out of their pipes." And although he admits to being so nervous before a raid that he sometimes vomits, The Fox intends to keep right on playing The Fox. "There is a dignity about nature," he says, his voice somber and earnest. "Man can exploit it but he shouldn't ruin it. I'm trying to stop something that is wrong—and I'm willing to go my own route to do it."

7

Michael M. Schneider

Middle America:
Study in Frustration

There is an alarming problem in this country today, the alienation of a large segment of the population, the white working class. Forty million strong, the white workers form the bulk of this nation's labor force. Attached to them are the white civil servants, the small entrepreneurs, the shopkeepers, all the people encompassed in the term "middle America." They add up to sixty or seventy million.

The white worker earns from five or six thousand dollars to somewhere around fifteen thousand dollars a year. Typically, he has a wife, two children, a house in town or the inner suburbs. He is the buffer between the ghetto and the affluent society. He owes far too much on installment debts on his car, appliances, and home. He finds his tax burden increasingly heavy, his neighborhood services low or invisible, and his political clout diminishing.

Typically, he attended public school and graduated from high school, which was probably the high point of his life, at least socially. But school, to him, was generally an abysmal failure. It had sold him and his parents on the legitimacy of a system that abused him by putting him

Reprinted, with permission, from the November 1970 issue of *The Center Magazine*, a publication of the Center for the Study of Democratic Institutions in Santa Barbara, California.

on the vocational and general education track, meaning dead end. At seventeen he already knew he hadn't made it. All, then, that he has to look forward to is the work ethic, and he sees people making fun of it, particularly the young. He is confused, and now he is growing increasingly angry.

In the building trades, he is upset that his job status is being threatened. For at least sixty years, through the unions he was guaranteed a measure of economic security. It wasn't easy for him to get into a union. When he did he had to serve a long apprenticeship, pass stiff examinations; only then could he possibly get a job, marginal at best. But at least he was one step up the ladder. Now he sees the civil-rights organizations and the government putting pressure on the unions to bypass the apprenticeship program or inserting outside controls on them. To him this means a cheapening of his craft; in addition, he knows that in a marginal industry there is only so much work to go around. Opening up the crafts to an uncontrolled apprenticeship program without creating new jobs means unemployment for him.

A good proportion of the frustration of the white worker relates to rising prices and taxes. He gets a dollar raise and seventy cents of it goes to inflation. His wife says, "Hey, John, look, what's going on around here? We need more money." He is confused. On his TV screen, he sees angry blacks and browns getting it for themselves, and he thinks society is giving it only to them. He feels that he is supporting the poor and that the welfare and city budgets come off of his back.

The draft is another target of his anger. He believes, and it is generally true, that if you have "pull," you don't get drafted. He sees college kids who are generally exempt from the draft involved in demonstrations against the institutions that he feels he must revere and that his sons in the army are defending. Loyalty, to him, is something you don't have any choice about.

These people want to be recognized, they want to be told that they exist, and not only as a negative force in American life. They are not happy, because they don't know what to do with their lives. They are insecure in many ways. And they are fearful. The fear can produce fury in the absence of direction. Given the present conditions, you can count on them to provide a much larger vote for the George Wallace type of candidate in 1972.

I write out of a sense of desperation. I feel I have been involved with this all my life—as an electrician, a member for the last twenty years of the electricians' union. I work on building-trades jobs with white working-class America and I know whereof I speak. But I have also been interested in the politics of America. I have been involved in civil-rights and civil-liberties movements in the Bay Area, and in Democratic Party politics. I am one of the founders of the California Democratic Council.

The question is: What can be done to calm the fears, relieve the frustration, and restore a sense of self-worth to the middle-American working man and his family? This question can be answered, I think, only after we look at this man, see where he came from, how he was educated, the conditions under which he works, and the quality of his participation in trade-union and political affairs.

To analyze the white working class of 1970, we have to go back to the Depression because, even after you make allowance for their age span, most of them were born in the late nineteen-twenties or early nineteen-thirties. Today this group is the largest percentage of the voting population. Their life histories are intertwined with the Depression.

Consider that the Depression of the nineteen-thirties left thirty-four million Americans scarred by unemployment. One in five workers was unemployed or underemployed. Many Americans left the Depression impressed as never before with the built-in deficiencies of a society that could collapse on paper in one day, could close factories, and sponsor the human starvation and degradation of millions.

Slowly but surely, as time passed, the victims of the Depression came to place their reliance once more on the mechanisms of government, through the modified welfare capitalism of the New Deal. By 1940, fifteen million of them had turned to the new power represented by the A.F.L. and C.I.O. labor organizations. Yet today on the job you still hear: "Well, you don't know how it really was if you weren't through the Depression."

World War II left its mark, too. For the first time many in this group worked steadily and, with the cost-plus contracts allowing employers to pay handsomely, and with accumulated war-bond savings, millions of them had their first taste of prosperity. On top of that, they weren't doing ordinary work. They were working "to save our boys over there." There was dignity and a sense of purpose in what they did. Many of those who were serving in the armed forces shared this sense of optimism. The government had come through, hadn't it, for those working in defense; surely it would come through for them, too. Alas, this was not to be.

By and large the men who got out of the service were forgotten. The class differences for them made all the difference. Government programs for the returning veterans did not fill the gap. If the social and class motivation was there, one went to college or back into business. For millions of other veterans the period from 1945 to 1950 was one of floundering around. Government programs after the war were mostly dismal failures. Unemployment plagued both the returning veteran and the defense worker. For example, all the talk about building millions of homes turned out to be just talk. Congress did not get around to large-scale appropriations until 1953–54.

With the advent of the Korean war an economic boom started and continued with high and low peaks until 1969. Unemployment, however, remained high consistently through the nineteen-fifties and the early nineteen-sixties, rarely dipping below six per cent except for the early stages of the Vietnam war. The recovery from each recession left the country with a higher rate of unemployment than the previous one.

More California workers were jobless in July, 1970, than at any time in the last thirty years, as unemployment rose to over six hundred thousand and the seasonally adjusted rate climbed to 6.4 per cent, forty per cent higher than the 4.5 per cent just one year ago. San Diego, for example, has an unemployment rate of 14.5 per cent, and even San Francisco, which currently has a construction boom in the downtown area, still has an unemployment rate of fifteen per cent in the building trades.

Anxiety must run very heavy, especially for those millions of workers whose jobs are affected by the Vietnam war. They have not yet seen the government come up with any plans that would allow defense and its allied industries to convert rapidly to a peacetime economy. All too vividly they remember the recessions after World War II and the Korean war.

I think it useful to interject some remarks about the schools that these men went to and the schools that their children are going to, so that we may begin to see the pattern of their frustration. In the schools that they attended, and the schools their children are attending now, they are defined not by what they are but by what they are not. When we see a growing number of students from working-class families going to college we begin to assume that they are all going, and that they will all be happy and successful when they get there. Yet it is still a fact, as it always was, that the lower ranks of the economic order have the smallest chance of sending their children on, and that those who fall below the academic middle in high school tend to represent a disproportionate percentage of poor and lower-middle-class families. What kids do in school tends as always to be predetermined. The honors class is filled with the children of professionals, whose parents have gone to college. The general course and the vocational track are composed of the sons and daughters of the working class.

The tragedy of the parents and the accompanying threat to their children lies precisely in the acceptance of the low esteem in which schools and society regard them, and in the inability to learn a language to express what they feel but dare not trust themselves to say. From class to class, from school to school, from home to back, there is a kind of passing through.

After school, they get jobs in the factories, start in the building trades as apprentices, work in gas stations, at little repair shops, or in diners—and that's it. School is an extension of the home. In the suburbs it's rated on college admissions. In working-class neighborhoods of the city it tends to be judged on order and discipline. It is an incompetent school system, by and large, with teachers who purport to represent genuine intellectual achievement and are thus allowed to continue their contempt for kids behind a passion for conformity and order, and to re-affirm the idea, already favored among working-class parents, that schooling is tough, boring, vicious, and mindless. The kids of the lower middle in the order of the school system have always known that they don't have much to say about anything. They have been put down most of their lives by their parents, by contemptuous teachers, and by fellow students.

Working-class kids are still stigmatized. In school, the vocational students are called the fender benders, and occasionally especially nasty remarks are answered with sudden explosive violence. The contempt of large-city school administrators is not limited just to the complaints of the black community. The increase in the defeat of numbers of school-bond issues and tax-increase proposals is hardly a sign of growing confidence in the school people who proposed them. It might well be that white working-class parents are becoming more suspicious of the mediocrity of their schools, more aware of their crimes. I hope so.

I think something should also be said about the white workers' jobs, how they exist on them. In 1970, despite all the advances made by the labor unions and by so-called enlightened industrialists, millions of adult Americans enjoy few rewards from their work. A worker on an assembly line gets little satisfaction from placing the same screws in the same holes in one car every thirty seconds. He gets a couple of coffee breaks a day and a short lunch period, and he has to do this day after day. Even in the building trades, with more and more prefabrication, we see more and more of the same type of mindless repetition. There is little chance of his breaking out of this. A study I have read of eleven major industries estimated that well over one-half of all non-supervisory jobs lead to a dead end. In the building trades, once you have achieved journeyman status, that is where you stay. There are no programs for upgrading. Few companies have any kind of on-the-job education, and I have yet to see a community college in the Bay Area having any kind of program for upgrading purposes.

The worker's insecurity is compounded by the fact that he is among the first to feel the effects of unemployment. It is hard for building tradesmen already hard hit by the present economic policies of the government to see the virtue in programs that would not only give newcomers priority on new job openings over unemployed tradesmen (the Philadelphia Plan), but, in order to achieve racial balance, would lay off workers. In some of the mass industries civil-rights groups are demanding super-seniority for minority workers in the event of mass layoffs.

The worker feels more threatened by automation and is also more dependent on sheer physical health for his livelihood than a professional. Yet in 1970 a worker injured on the job in California receives a maximum disability payment of $87.50 a week. If he is unemployed right now he receives $62.50 a week or less, depending on his income while at work. These are the workers who presumably have made it. The truth is, the majority of people who work for a living are not part of affluent America. The median family in 1968 made $8,632, less than the so-called adequate standard defined by the government. In 1965 the average industrial worker with three dependents took home $88.06 a week. His after-taxes pay in 1969 was eighty-seven dollars. In the electrician's local, in 1969, the average income was $9,800.

When he has reached his plateau in his capacity to earn by advancement to journeyman in the crafts or to mechanic's status on the assembly line, precisely at this point his children have reached their teens and the family budget is at its peak. Expenses continue to rise. The last family members are born. He becomes a home owner. At this time, too, he may have to think about support for his aging parents. Yet inflation proceeds in its own merciless and seemingly uncontrollable way. Throughout 1968, '69, and '70, the consumer price index continued the consecutive monthly increases begun back in 1966.

The worker's paycheck power has shrunk regularly since 1954. The erosion of purchasing power becomes almost a fixed part of the American scene, so the average worker who established his standard of living when he was single or was first married finds now that he can maintain it only by having saved when he was younger, which he probably didn't do; or by moonlighting on a second part-time job; or by having his wife work, in spite of the obstacles to doing so; or by continued pressure for even larger wage increases.

The tax-reform measure of 1969 did nothing to correct the unequal tax treatment of work-connected expenses of wage earners compared to the favored treatment given high-salaried white-collar company executives. For example, a worker cannot claim a deduction for driving a car to and from work, even when no public transportation is available to him. The company executive, however, may have the free use of a company limousine and chauffeur without having to pay any taxes for these services. The wages the worker spends for his lunch to fuel up for the afternoon are fully taxable. On the other hand, the executive can take a friend to lunch in an expensive restaurant, deduct this expense, and pay no taxes on it, by merely showing that it is a business-related luncheon. Even the wear and tear on shoes and clothing the worker incurs while at work is not tax deductible.

There is no provision for tax relief as family education costs rise, either in terms of the average three hundred dollars a year that it costs to send a child to school or the larger cost of sending a child to college. In some states income is redistributed from lower-income to higher-income groups to subsidize education for the children of the latter group. The case is most apparent in the state of California, with the University of California.

Government policies on child care, designed to enable the wife to work, also give little or no relief. At present families with incomes of $5,900 or more cannot deduct child-care expenses; government child-care centers under the Head Start programs are for the poor, so do not help this group. Welfare mothers receive subsidized child care to facilitate their move from welfare to work, but working-class mothers who seek work and are outside the welfare system incur the full cost and thus frequently are really unable to add to the family income. In addition, the cost of providing transportation for the woman, wage discrimination, lack of education and retraining opportunities also discourage many working-class wives from working. Yet it is precisely working-class wives whose income could be a meaningful addition to the family finances.

"Oh, yes, they never had it so good." That litany I hear over and over so often from the media and my middle-class friends that I almost believe it myself—almost. I knew an electrician who quit a job where I work (a "steady" job) after eighteen years in order to collect his pension contributions so he could get out of debt—$13,000. That meant going back to the hiring hall with its intermittent employment. But for the first time in many years he was free of debts. Besides his mortgage and yearly taxes, he owed on two large cars, one for himself and one for his wife (no public transportation where he lives in the inner suburbs); plus payments on a powerboat for his vacations; plus a color TV console and three black-and-white sets for the children's rooms; impressive bills for dental work for himself and his wife. His younger son has to go to San Francisco from the suburbs three days a week to a private speech-impediment therapist (his school district doesn't have any program). He had to buy a car for his oldest son, who goes to a junior college thirty-five miles away (the local college would not accept him because his grades were too low and they were filled up anyway), and he has to pay tuition and buy the books because it is outside of the home district. His ten-year-old home needs extensive repairs because it was constructed on a poorly filled site. You say it sounds extreme; you would challenge some of his choices. Sure, some of the things he got into debt for were not necessities, but in 1970 isn't the model of a happy American one who has a boat and large cars and a TV set in every room? Through the mails and on radio and TV comes the message: buy—spend—put it on the charge account. And why shouldn't he have those things, he asks, and he goes out and gets them. When you consider that for most Americans television constitutes their primary source of information, the picture is clarified slightly. The America one sees on one's TV is either of upper-middle-class suburbia on the family shows or of the ghetto on the six o'clock news. Which do workers prefer? You know the answer.

The trade-union experience of the white working-class American usually turns out to be very negative. It is quite true that the unions provide a form of security which meets a legitimate need. On the other hand, workers feel that the union bureaucracies, which do not respond to them, are inhuman and overly rigid. In most unions the rank and file have no real voice in union policymaking. Workers don't feel any personal responsibility or involvement. They don't go to meetings. They grudgingly pay their dues, which by and large have increased over the years to where for example in the International Brotherhood of Electrical Workers we pay twenty-three dollars per month. So the only time most workers go to union meetings is to resist dues increases or the creation of new assessments. They go to union elections if the issues are really dramatized and there isn't too much personal inconvenience. The resultant state of affairs is rationalized cynically. On one hand they bemoan the ingrown bureaucracy of their unions, and on the other hand they lack faith in the effectiveness of any kind of a legitimate opposition.

It must be said, though, that many of the local trade-union officials benefit from the non-involvement of most of the members in the local's affairs. Although trade-union officials complain about the lack of attendance at their meetings, in reality many prefer to rule their locals with a small clique of those who are directly involved with running the affairs of the union and who can establish either monetary or social gains from being involved in the union establishment. The union ˙member who starts to play a role in the union is instantly looked at from the inside as a potential threat. Is he threatening my job as an official? Can we buy him off? The average union member responds to this kind of cynicism from the outside: "Why should I go down and participate in my union when those guys really aren't interested in me? All they want to do is make their own deals with the boss." Cynicism of this kind, I think, pervades large sections of organized labor. More and more, the average union man relates to his union in politics by not going along with the way his union wants him to vote. He resents the implication, also fostered by the newspapers, that labor controls his vote. He feels that resisting this pressure is one way of making his independence felt.

Thirty years ago during the New Deal, poor white Southerners, blacks, and trade unionists were brought together in the Democratic Party for the first time. The year 1968 saw the final collapse of this coalition. In checking the performance in San Francisco of five working-class precincts during the 1956–1968 period I found that, although the neighborhood had changed somewhat (more blacks had moved into some precincts, more Spanish-speaking people had moved into some precincts), by 1968 the Democratic loyalty in these precincts had dropped to a low of fifty-eight per cent. The vote for Wallace in the precincts averaged twenty-three per cent against his city-wide average of twelve per cent.

A generation ago most voters felt they could protect their interests best by holding steadfastly to one party. In the five Presidential elections from 1932 to 1948 just over half (fifty-one per cent) of the counties in the United States, including all of the most populous cities, cast a majority of their votes for the same party's candidates each time. But in three of the five elections that followed, from 1952 to 1968, only a fifth stuck with the same party's nominees. During these years a decisive proportion of the electorate abandoned the Democratic Party and decided to protect themselves politically by using both parties. Today working-class voters will go for whatever party is available to serve their present needs.

In looking at this phenomenon, I think we may forget that these people usually find themselves both out of mind and out of favor with the so-called "decision-makers." The mass media seem to concentrate on the violent and sensational, so those concerned seem not to focus on this inarticulate, unseen, little-understood mass of people. The working stiff, I think, is right. His vague concerns do get lost between the ballot box, where he is still supreme, and the decision-making processes, where the action is. The working-class guy feels that there is no room for him inside and no interest paid to him by the major political parties other than at election time. This attitude of indifference is dominant when he sees the local political leaders appear at election time and go into immediate hibernation afterwards, only to seek him out at the next vote-getting time.

Some other footnotes on the 1968 election: Far more young working people still punch time clocks at factories and offices than attend universities, and these young people particularly were not enchanted by the confrontation tactics of campus rebels. A measure of their alienation may be seen in the Wallace movement of 1968, which made its greatest inroads among young voters aged twenty-one to twenty-nine. Also, although now it is popular in the Democratic Party to put down the primary campaign of Eugene McCarthy, it is significant that in San Francisco McCarthy carried white working-class neighborhoods by huge margins in 1968. In the general election a lot of these same working stiffs were either unenthusiastic about Humphrey or were for Wallace. I think that one of the qualities that endeared McCarthy to many was that he stood outside of what they called politics. He did not appear to them as a politician, as they understood the term.

The elitism in the Democratic Party is currently illustrated by various comments on and off the record by Democratic candidates who keep on hoping for an economic recession so that the Democrats will have a chance of getting back into power. Most of these people have never felt the uncertainties that the working class feels during an economic recession. They have never been unemployed, or even felt the threat of unemployment. This kind of cynicism drives working-class people further and further away from politics. They see politicians caring only for their own careers. Our party structure narrows choices and tends to blur rather than sharpen differences on issues.

This is precisely what most voters don't want. To sort out their clashing emotions, they need a wider choice of candidates. They also want the candidates to speak out and tell them directly what they intend to do about the issues. They will try out candidate after candidate only to find that the men who might fit their feelings, for example on the Vietnam war, might not fit their racial emotions; or, if he has satisfied their racial emotions, he might not satisfy their economic interests. Many working-class people want to be able to influence the policies of government at all levels and all year round, not just at election time.

This group has other frustrations, less easy to describe. People in the working class are usually less mobile, less able to speak out as an organized group, and less capable of using legitimate means to protect their status or to secure changes in their favor. Consider that just about two per cent of the population engage in any organized political activities. To a considerable extent, the ninety-eight per cent feel that they are the forgotten people, and they believe not only that government has no direct concern for them, but that it has moved from being neutral to supporting big business on one side and the minorities on the other.

Among the problems that are bugging them nowadays is the fear of violent crimes. More and more in white neighborhoods you see people putting up gates on their homes, hear people talking about guns. The most damaging of the effects of violent crime is fear, which cannot be underestimated. People more and more stay behind the locked doors of their homes. The fear of crime makes them afraid to talk to each other, and that makes the circle of fear complete. Their economic immobility blocks their flight from these conditions and feeds the fear of violence in their homes and in the schools.

Since most working-class people have barely completed high school, they have very limited opportunities to change their occupation. They do not have the tools of education to use as a lever to escape from their problems. Overt hostility among ethnic and racial groups is greater among less-educated groups than among more-educated groups. Thus the white working-class guy is more likely to transfer his economic and social frustrations into racial and ethnic prejudices and now we are seeing more and more overt hostility.

Nowadays if you don't have a college education you don't have any real status. The changes in the nature of the labor force dramatize the technical and professional experts to the detriment of the working class. Working-class people have been so denigrated that their jobs have become a last resort instead of providing decent respected careers. Who wants to be called an electrician nowadays? If you are not a computer expert, you are nothing. The worker has suffered a loss of self-respect.

Schools reinforce this loss of self-esteem, since teachers know as little about the working class as the mass media do. The only publicity given to workers is when they are out on strike or during such incidents as the recent outbreak of "hard-hattism."

Also, these people are the closest neighbors of those on welfare, but often their wages are only a notch or so above the payments of welfare recipients. Yet they are excluded from social programs directed toward the so-called disadvantaged: medical aid, job training, head-start programs, and legal aid. As taxpayers they support these programs, but they see no share for themselves in the services they provide. Rather, they see government funds, manpower, and creative efforts on a large scale going in to help the poor catch up and cross the fundamental divide that separates the poverty person from the worker.

The worker more often than not feels this aid would never have gone to him in any event, but would probably have been directed to more powerful interests. Of course, there is no evidence to indicate much success yet in the effort on the part of the poor to catch up. Ghetto conditions remain an ugly reality. But the media, to which the white working class person pays heed, have portrayed it as if the promises to the ghetto were being fulfilled. So you have the blacks on TV angry because they still haven't shared the pie, and the white working-class guys who feel that they haven't got any of it either. It is not hard to see how whites hold grievances against those they feel have stolen their slice of the pie and how these grievances reduce themselves either to an indictment of the blacks and their white allies, who are supposedly taking over the country, or lead to the feeling that the government has abandoned the traditional American way of life.

The white worker needs to feel that government is concerned about him, that it is willing to take steps to meet his needs for public services. Otherwise, confidence in the government is going to decrease further. He also wants to feel that he has a way of redressing his grievances. Machinery must be set up to protect him from the petty outrages by government bureaucrats so that the government will not seem to be permanently indifferent in dealings with him.

We need to consider that his alienation and disaffection are real. We also need to start work on the problem and eliminate this alienation. Only then will it be possible for us as a nation to initiate increased commitment of the needed resources to the public sector. To improve the quality of life for the disenfranchised, we have to improve the quality of life for all of us.

I realize there are twice as many non-white Americans unemployed as white Americans. It is true, too, that this is undeniably the result of discrimination, not only in the labor market but at every crucial point in their lives, starting before they are born, with no prenatal medical care, and going through the educational system, and later to employment. However, it is precisely my point that, critical as these needs are, they cannot be met by taking jobs from other workers.

To give an example: An acquaintance of mine is a teacher. When a less formally qualified teacher was chosen for a more highly paid job because she was black, my friend was able to grin, shrug her shoulders, and return to her classroom where her old job awaited her. In contrast, the man who works next to me on the job faces weeks out of work, with income reduced to one-fourth of his wages, if he is laid off. If he yields to demands for super-seniority for black workers his family will suffer— really suffer. He will fight for his job before he will give in.

In effect, these demands, which fall so glibly from the lips of the secure upper middle class, amount to requiring the least able to subsidize social justice. I don't think they will do it. I don't think that in their place the secure upper-middle-class American would do it either.

part two

The Institutional Setting for Participation

Fragmented Responsiveness or Patterned Unresponsiveness?

The New Participation will work itself out within the framework of an old Constitution, as well as within the confines of political ideas and institutions that have evolved over the years. And therein lie some potentially profound dilemmas. Perhaps the core issue is one of achieving a subtle balance. The ideal is to preserve certain basic ideas and institutions that have proved useful in the past and still have value, but to do so while encouraging the innovation of new ideas and institutions that will be necessary in the future.

Part two provides two perspectives on this dual challenge of preserving the best of today's political ideas and institutions while also seeking guidance for tomorrow. Readings 8 through 12 focus on the constitution; readings 13 through 18 seek to illustrate the texture and quality of the broader political setting of ideas and institutions within which the New Participation will evolve.

From the perspective of the Constitution, the tension between the New Participation and existing institutions and ideas is patent. That essential tension may be expressed briefly, without undue simplification. The Constitution implies a representative or republican form of government, with multiple constituencies and numerous majorities. The underlying intent is to avoid both a tyranny of the majority as well as suppression by the few. The republican form attempted to slip between the horns of the classic dilemma of governance, then, by balancing two opposed ideas so as to avoid the extremes of each.

Many of the new participative experiments clash with this basic institutional bias, both coming and going, as it were. That is, many of today's approaches to political participation publicly adopt a democratic or a majoritarian form, reflecting a strong populist spirit that urges a kind of immediate sovereignty in a people's majority. "Power to the people" illustrates the public spirit of these approaches, although some observers dismiss that spirit as mere ideological camouflage for a clever new and tiny elite seeking to overthrow "the system."

Directly, then, the Constitution implies variously hedged political participation, and its basic structure was carefully designed with that end in mind. A variety of actions, including major decisions by the Supreme Court, have variously chipped away at this structural approach to managing participation. But the basic design remains more or less intact. The issue is whether this basic constitutional design can contain the more intense forms of participation that seem in our future, or whether new basic forms of governance will have to be innovated.

The editors do not intend to overstate this tension. It is not a black-and-white contrast; but it does exist, and more or less by specific design. That is, the Constitution does contain numerous contrasting notions, sometimes as a result of compromises that balanced opposed concepts, and sometimes as a result of an Aristotelian pursuit of the golden mean between extremes. Examples come easily. The Framers of the Constitution drew upon their shared philosophical heritage to separate powers so as to create spheres of specialization so that absolute power would not corrupt absolutely. And then they related by checks-and-balances what they had separated so as to reduce the probability that the separated powers would go their individual ways. On balance, however, the Constitution reflects a consistently republican character.

This republican or representative character is clear in the original concept of participation underlying the Constitution, as James Madison stresses in the famous "Federalist No. 10." Madison did not write for all of his colleagues at Philadelphia's Constitution Hall, but those who shared his outlook paradoxically argued the virtues of a limited pluralism to an elite audience that was homogeneous—white, male, and propertied. Federalist No. 10 seeks support for the ratification of the Constitution from that portion of the white and male property holders in New York who were literate. Madison sought their approval for the Constitution for their own good, in effect. Simply, their interests would be protected by the basic institutional arrangements the new Constitution would establish.

The Constitution was a kind of best of all possible worlds, in sum, at least for the white, male, and propertied. On one hand, the new republic would provide the propertied elite with economic protections not available under the Articles of Confederation or state constitutions. On the other hand, the strong unitary states would inhibit control by that most stubborn of factions, the potential nation-wide majoritarian coalition of those without property. This was true in two basic senses. First, the republican principle would "refine and enlarge the public views, by passing them through the medium of a chosen body of citizens, whose wisdom may best discern the true interest of their country. . . ." Second, the existence of unitary states also would help control factions, especially because the individuals states retained major powers. "The influence of factious leaders may kindle a flame within their particular States," Madison sagely noted, "but will be unable to spread a general conflagration through the other States."

The evidence suggests, in addition, that the basic institutional arrangements described by Madison also described a viable framework for other times and different problems. That basic institutional scheme, in effect, has been acted on by two basic sets of opposed forces, each of which has profound implications for political participation. These forces have sometimes tugged the basic constitutional doctrine toward majoritarianism; and the forces sometimes have edged that doctrine toward such refined forms of representation as could deny or at least delay even substantial majorities in most or all states. Through it all, the basic constitutional arrangements have provided a viable framework for the ebb and flow of these two basic forces.

The early development of the Supreme Court illustrates both tendencies. From one perspective, the Supreme Court early laid claim to a power—judicial review—that put it in a crucial position to thwart legislative and even national majorities. Ironically, Madison himself was an unwitting agent in establishing this power of the court which a century and a half later was to be of critical aid in helping one faction kindle their flame throughout the several states, even though individual states (as Madison predicted) had long been able to frustrate that effort. That faction included those devoted to equal educational opportunity, especially for blacks.

Some few facts explain the allusion above. Madison was the defendant in *Marbury v. Madison*, the details of which are not important here. Overall, Madison won the battle but lost the war. Chief Justice John Marshall at once upheld Madison in a trivial matter, while he momentously innovated a major role for the Supreme Court to balance the authority of the Congress and the president. He asserted the judiciary's authority to review the constitutionality of congressional acts and, by implication, the acts of those in the executive branch and in the states. Thereafter, the meaning of the Constitution was in the hands of the courts, when judges wanted it. Moreover, the courts were long influenced by Marshall and the Federalists, who favored a strong national government.

That power of judicial review could thwart some majorities while it helped develop others, from a second perspective. Specifically, judicial review was the tool which Marshall utilized in *McCulloch v. Maryland* to extend the boundaries of national power in relation to state and local governments. This decision no doubt ran counter to majorities in many of the states in the short run. In the long run, however, the effect was to contribute to the development of presidential power, which would encourage the growing significance of the kind of nationwide majority that Madison feared.

Some few details lend support to the broad summary above. Marshall's decision in *McCulloch v. Maryland* expanded the authority of the national government by interpreting broadly the "necessary and proper" clause of Article 1, Section 8 of the Constitution. The case states two doctrines of profound impact on the system which Madison described in Federalist No. 10: implied powers, and supremacy of national law. There were two specific issues in *McCulloch v. Maryland.* Could Congress charter a national bank, even though that power was nowhere explicitly granted by the Constitution? And if Congress could do so, could a state interfere with the bank's operations? Those citizens whose economic, occupational, ideological, and other interests could be furthered at the national level would profit from the decision in *McCulloch v. Maryland.* Economic interests it was, mostly, well into the twentieth century.

A major battleground for majoritarian versus republican tendencies in our basic political approach presently centers on the Bill of Rights. The ability of existing constitutional forms to contain contemporary participation will be determined significantly by the way in which the present controversy surrounding the Bill of Rights is resolved. The specific definition of what constitutes "free speech" and "lawful assembly," for example, will go a long way toward determining how the present participative ferment will evolve. Too strict a definition could conceivably create a suppression of some in the name of preserving participation for others, which is perverse. On the other hand, "free speech" and "lawful assembly" could be so broadly defined as to provide a license for behavior that could undercut the basic trust and agreement to tolerate differences on which meaningful participation rests in the long run.

The Bill of Rights has long been of central concern. Despite his concern about a propertyless majority, curiously, Madison did not favor a Bill of Rights to explicitly safeguard specific rights of individuals or minorities. However, ratification of the Constitution almost failed because it originally contained no bill of rights. Holdouts extracted promises of a bill of rights before they voted for ratification.

Arthur J. Goldberg reflects major concern about possible infringements on those major constitutional addenda in "Our Besieged Bill of Rights." The issues Goldberg raises imply that the crystal ball of those resisting ratification in the absence of a bill of rights was better than Madison's. Recall, Madison argued that a multitude of factions would counterbalance each other so that a majority faction could emerge to establish a tyranny over others. Madison was clearly correct in particular situations. When segregation was treated as a state rather than a national issue, for example, state segregationist majorities could have their way. Black minorities, consequently, made little impact upon governmental policies. When segregation issues were shifted to the national level of government, especially by court action in Marshall's tradition, segregationist whites became a national minority faction. The lot of blacks improved. What seems to work at times for factions may not work for individuals, or small groups, however, which somehow are at odds with prevailing majority or forceful minority opinion. Goldberg's discussion spotlights individual and group protections contained in the Bill of Rights. That discussion also suggests the forceful ways in which various majorities seek to strip some individuals and groups of the protection of the Bill of Rights.

That the New Participation poses nasty dilemmas in America also can be established via a broader perspective. For example, numerous points of access—to legislators and public administrators—often are created by the concepts and institutions that define the boundaries of acceptable political participation. Such access intentionally permits diverse interests to bear on the development or implementing of public policy. Consequently, many prepared minorities can and do participate meaningfully in shaping public decision. So far, so good. A price has to be paid for providing such opportunities, however. That is, the availability of numerous points of access can serve to delay or inhibit response to the expressed needs and wishes of even massive numbers of political participants. Clearly, there is no easy way to monitor the delicate balance. Restricting opportunities for access would limit potential abuses, of course, but the cure is worse than the disease. The dilemma must be lived with, interminably, and its harsher consequences must be avoided, if possible.

Hence the two horns of the central dilemma which American politics seek to slip between. Multiple points of access can at once heighten responsiveness to participant inputs, via fragmented ways of making and implementing decisions. Indeed, there are often so many possible points at which to influence public policy that persistence is far more necessary than ingenuity. Multiple points of access can work toward unresponsiveness as well, however, because there are so many points at which it is possible to kill or modify any proposed piece of public policy or business.

Slipping between horns of this central dilemma is probably most difficult at times like these. New participants take advantage of the available opportunities for access, and may trigger two unsatisfying consequences. The new participants may motivate efforts to restrict their access, as by restrictions on speech and assembly. Or the new participants may find themselves checkmated by persons or interests who can exercise an effective veto at some crucial point. Neither consequence is likely to satisfy new participants. Indeed, they are likely to denounce the cruelty and depravity of "the system" which provides them opportunities but not the outcomes they seek.

The last seven readings of this chapter illustrate the complex relationships which result from the basic policy of providing multiple points of access into American politics and public administration. These readings should provide further insight concerning the tension induced by the New Participation. Overall, multiple access has served to limit majoritarian tendencies, in ways that Madison did not and really could not anticipate. This is particularly the case in the burgeoning of the administrative machinery of government, whose growth Madison could not foresee. Diverse administrative agencies, many with overlapping jurisdictions, provide numerous opportunities for prepared minorities to influence the development and the implementation of public policy. To say the same thing in other words, multiple access implies a large number of filters that variously "enlarge and refine the public views" or the policy preferences of various minorities, and even of various majorities.

More specifically, the last seven readings have two foci. First, they highlight how participants seek to work their way through the maze created by the separation of powers and by checks-and-balances. The basic institutional arrangements described by Madison in "Federalist No. 10" still make their impact felt, that is to say, despite developments since the Constitutional Convention. Second, the readings stress the issues inherent in the fundamental fact that the linkages between various participants and public policy are diverse and of highly variable directness. Voters do not make public policy, for example. Some voters choose some of those who influence public policy, such as the president or congressmen. But many other critical participants are far removed from even such indirect influence. For example, public administrators help determine policy and also often interpret and apply it with wide latitude. To complicate matters, various publics develop different degrees of access to these several influencers/implementers of public policy. Conflict between the several influencers/implementers of public policy is thus not only possible, but likely.

The complexities of our institutional setting for participation are dramatically introduced by Richard E. Neustadt's "The President: Leader or Clerk?" The president may get a majoritarian mandate, but the system tends to get to him, early and decisively. Neustadt notes basically that the very forces that make the president a potential leader are the same forces that make him a clerk. The president's power inheres in the fact that everyone needs him, and that everybody nowadays "expects the man inside the White House to do something about everything." But these very demands massively undercut his ability to be a leader in fact. The presidential game, then, involves gaining some opportunities for leadership by being an effective clerk. This may seem a tedious exercise to both new participants and the old. But consider one point. A president somehow powerful enough not to play the game might be too powerful to control or even influence. Such power is the antigoal of both democratic and republican forms of government.

Sharp restrictions in presidential power and initiative are manifest in international as well as domestic affairs, even though in the former the president has a uniquely influential role. The kinds of international opportunities/ limitations that impact on the presidency are graphically reflected in Chalmers M. Roberts' careful attempt to reconstruct "The Day We Didn't Go to War," the day being Saturday, April 3, 1954. The focus in the selection is on the still-young war in Southeast Asia that later became a sink-hole for so many American lives and for so much American treasure. The proposal was to come to the aid of the beleaguered French at Dienbienphu with massive air strikes, to be followed if necessary by land strikes. Nothing more, nothing less.

President Eisenhower and his immediate aides had decided on the need for this momentous intervention in a distant war; but they also decided to marshall support for what seemed necessary. Eisenhower, through his Secretary of State Dulles, requested a joint resolution by Congress supporting the action, as Roberts recounts. And that was the beginning of a gripping drama of the constraints that limit presidential initiative in the international arena. By most opinion, that arena is the one in which the president is considered most central because of the uniqueness of his office, because of his selection by the broadest set of majorities of any elected official, and because of his constitutional responsibilities as chief of state, head of the armed forces, and so on.

The result of seeking legislative support was that the proposed action was not taken, for good or ill. The president could not function as leader, due to very serious reservations in many quarters. Hence he became a clerk, forwarding to the French his government's regrets that relief for Dienbienphu was not possible, even though its unsolicited offer somewhat earlier by an American official had left a French general flabbergasted. Eisenhower's act of clerkship only temporarily interrupted American involvement in that area of the world, however, as we know all too well.

The president also can be checkmated in domestic affairs, and perhaps even more easily. The vehicle is often a strong relationship between an agency or bureau of the huge federal bureaucracy, a committee or subcommittee of Congress, and some organized interest. This "iron triangle" has frustrated all presidents.

Depending on whose ox is being gored, opinions about the iron triangle vary. When his ox was being gored, for example, Senator Strom Thurmond (D., S.C.) had a caustic reaction. "The trouble around here," he complained about administrative actions associated with school desegregation, "is that what goes in at the top doesn't come out at the bottom." However, evidence suggests that the evaluation of even congressmen can change, as the iron triangle variously serves their interests, or those of their constituents. There inevitably will be times, in short, when all of us will fervently hope that what goes in at the top of the executive branch does not come out at the bottom.

Robert Semple argues this position forcefully in "Who Runs the Government?" He shows how the iron triangle can frustrate presidents bent on doing monumental good or perpetrating momentous evil, as well as every gradation in between. That iron triangle is a major reason that the president typically must be a very good clerk for many groups or persons before he can assert any substantial leadership.

Two points need emphasis. First, Semple's selection is pitched to the federal level, but it is representative of the dynamics at all governmental levels. Second, the situation described is not somehow new. Its essentials are as current as today's administrative dynamics, and those essentials also are a thumbnail history of the last two or three decades.

The overall picture sketched by Semple gets detailed counterpoint in J. Malcolm Moore's "To Provide for the Common Defense." Moore focuses on a delicate interface in American government, where our institutions risk stalemate as the possible price of broad support for specific policies or programs. Moore's piece well illustrates how our existing institutions and ideas about political participation seek to provide fragmented responsiveness, while they also seek to avoid attack/defend unresponsiveness. The outcome is often in delicate doubt, as Moore shows in detail.

So-called interest groups also create representational vehicles for participation, usually by minorities but conceivably even for majorities. Interest groups have a bad press, and for some very good but hardly universal reasons. For example, they are often pictured as exploitative and narrowly materialistic, but they need not be. Nor does an interest group's commitment to a cause necessarily imply defeat for those who see themselves as idealists. "Victory in the Everglades" by Marjory Stoneman Douglas provides a case in point. Douglas describes how one conservationist coalition successfully acted as an interest group. It sought to represent long-run concerns about saving some of today's environment for posterity and, consequently, served as a brake on interests with a shorter time perspective and narrower interests.

As the two selections above reflect, interest groups can influence public policy in many ways, both subtle or gross, with statesmanship or with narrow self-serving goals. And a critical way of influencing policy is to influence the choice of the people who will be deeply involved in its determination and implementation. Hence the intense concern by interest groups with personnel matters. Sometimes this means that an interest will seek to get "its man" in a legislature, in an administrative agency, or on some regulating board or commission. Just as important, the issue may be keeping the other interest's man on the outside, looking in.

Daniel K. Wanamaker sketches the approaches and emphases of several interest groups to seeing that the right people are in the proper places, as far as they are concerned, in one area of critical concern. Wanamaker focuses on the nomination of federal judges, and is especially critical not only because of what the nominees will do but also because they are very likely to be doing it as long as they can sit on the bench. Given the life tenure of judges, plus their often monumental longevity, mistakes in selecting them may have to be lived with for a very long time indeed.

More or less, Wanamaker shows that interest groups followed the basic strategy of keeping out of office some of the other guy's nominees, but not all. Where the specific line is drawn no doubt has a major effect on the quality of our politics. The names of Carswell and Haynsworth are still in public memory, if they are fading. Their experience illustrates the kind of public pressure that interest groups can bring to bear on critical personnel decisions, for good or ill.

It is easy to grow exasperated with the byzantine dynamics associated with multiple access, but there is no easy way out. For example, insulating administrative agencies from the interests would be extremely difficult to do in practice, and might induce a system in which everyone's freedom was reduced even where such insulation was accomplished. Moreover, there are administrative agencies that are but weakly responsive to the inputs from interested publics. They are not clearly superior because of that fact, however. Perhaps the best contemporary example is the system of local draft boards, especially as it existed under General Hershey. The original inspiration behind the system smelled of the grass-roots: ". . . the nation would much more willingly support compulsory military service operated by their neighbors at home . . ." History moved beyond this comfortable notion, as draft boards tended to become unrepresentative and out of touch with the communities they served. But the underlying concept and practice of the boards went on and on.

Kenneth M. Dolbeare and James W. Davis provide a picture of an administrative system as a shell of its original self, but still with a momentum borne of other days and other times. Their "Little Groups of Neighbors: American Draft Boards" suggest how quickly, and under which circumstances, an administrative agency can become self-righteously what it was not intended to be.

8

James Madison

The Federalist No. 10

To the People of the State of New York:

Among the numerous advantages promised by a well-constructed Union, none deserves to be more accurately developed than its tendency to break and control the violence of faction. The friend of popular governments never finds himself so much alarmed for their character and fate, as when he contemplates their propensity to this dangerous vice. He will not fail, therefore, to set a due value on any plan which, without violating the principles to which he is attached, provides a proper cure for it. The instability, injustice, and confusion introduced into the public councils, have, in truth, been the mortal diseases under which popular governments have everywhere perished; as they continue to be the favorite and fruitful topics from which the adversaries to liberty derive their most specious declamations. The valuable improvements made by the American constitutions on the popular models, both ancient and modern, cannot certainly be too much admired; but it would be an unwarrantable partiality, to contend that they have as effectually obviated the danger on this side, as was wished and expected. Complaints are everywhere heard from our most considerate and virtuous citizens, equally the friends of public and private faith, and of public and personal liberty, that our governments are too unstable, that the public good is disregarded in the conflicts of rival parties, and that measures are too often decided, not according to the rules of justice and the rights of the minor party, but by the superior force of an interested and overbearing majority. However anxiously we may wish that these complaints had no foundation, the evidence of known facts will not permit us to deny that they are in some degree true. It will be found, indeed, on a candid review of our situation, that some of the distresses under which we labor have been erroneously charged on the operation of our governments; but it will be found, at the same time, that other causes will not alone account for many of our heaviest misfortunes; and, particularly, for that prevailing and increasing distrust of public engagements, and alarm for private rights, which are echoed from one end of the continent to the other. These must be chiefly, if not wholly, effects of the unsteadiness and injustice with which a factious spirit has tainted our public administrations.

By a faction, I understand a number of citizens, whether amounting to a majority or minority of the whole, who are united and actuated by some common impulse of passion, or of interest, adverse to the rights of other citizens, or to the permanent and aggregate interests of the community.

There are two methods of curing the mischiefs of faction: the one, by removing its causes; the other, by controlling its effects.

There are again two methods of removing the causes of faction: the one, by destroying the liberty which is essential to its existence; the other, by giving to every citizen the same opinions, the same passions, and the same interests.

It could never be more truly said than of the first remedy, that it was worse than the disease. Liberty is to faction what air is to fire, an aliment without which it instantly expires. But it could not be less folly to abolish liberty, which is essential to political life, because it nourishes faction, than it would be to wish the annihilation of air, which is essential to animal life, because it imparts to fire its destructive agency.

The second expedient is as impracticable as the first would be unwise. As long as the reason of man continues fallible, and he is at liberty to exercise it, different opinions will be formed. As long as the connection subsists between his reason and his self-love, his opinions and his passions will have a reciprocal influence on each other; and the former will be objects to which the latter will attach themselves. The diversity in the faculties of men, from which the rights of property originate, is not less an insuperable obstacle to a uniformity of interests. The protection of these faculties is the first object of government. From the protection of different and unequal faculties of acquiring property, the possession of different degrees and kinds of property immediately results; and from the influence of these on the sentiments and views of the respective proprietors, ensues a division of the society into different interests and parties.

The latent causes of faction are thus sown in the nature of man; and we see them everywhere brought into different degrees of activity, according to the different circumstances of civil society. A zeal for different opinions concerning religion, concerning government, and many other points, as well of speculation as of practice; an attachment to different leaders ambitiously contending for pre-eminence and power; or to persons of other descriptions whose fortunes have been interesting to the human passions, have, in turn, divided mankind into parties, inflamed them with mutual animosity, and rendered them much more disposed to vex and oppress each other than to co-operate for their common good. So strong is this propensity of mankind to fall into mutual animosities, that where no substantial occasion presents itself, the most frivolous and fanciful distinctions have been sufficient to kindle their unfriendly passions and excite their most violent conflicts. But the most common and durable source of factions has been the various and unequal distribution of property. Those who hold and those who are without property have ever formed distinct interests in society. Those who are creditors, and those who are debtors, fall under a like discrimination. A landed interest, a manufacturing interest, a mercantile interest, a moneyed interest, with many lesser interests, grow up of necessity in civilized nations, and divide them into different classes, actuated by different sentiments and views. The regulation of these various and interfering interests forms the principal task of modern legislation, and involves the spirit of party and faction in the necessary and ordinary operations of the government.

No man is allowed to be a judge in his own cause, because his interest would certainly bias his judgment, and, not improbably, corrupt his integrity. With equal, nay with greater reason, a body of men are unfit to be both judges and parties at the same time; yet what are many of the most important acts of legislation, but so many judicial determinations, not indeed concerning the rights of single persons, but concerning the rights of large bodies of citizens? And what are the different classes of legislators but advocates and parties to the causes which they determine? Is a law proposed concerning private debts? It is a question to which the creditors are parties on one side and the debtors on the other. Justice ought to hold the balance between them. Yet the parties are, and must be, themselves the judges; and the most numerous party, or, in other words, the most powerful faction must be expected to prevail. Shall domestic manufactures be encouraged, and in what degree, by restrictions on foreign manufactures? are questions which would be differently decided by the landed and the manufacturing classes, and probably by neither with a sole regard to justice and the public good. The apportionment of taxes on the various descriptions of property is an act which seems to require the most exact impartiality; yet there is, perhaps, no legislative act in which greater opportunity and temptation are given to a predominant party to trample on the rules of justice. Every shilling with which they overburden the inferior number, is a shilling saved to their own pockets.

It is in vain to say that enlightened statesmen will be able to adjust these clashing interests, and render them all subservient to the public good. Enlightened statesmen will not always be at the helm. Nor, in many cases, can such an adjustment be made at all without taking into view indirect and remote considerations, which will rarely prevail over the immediate interest which one party may find in disregarding the rights of another or the good of the whole.

The inference to which we are brought is, that the *causes* of faction cannot be removed, and that relief is only to be sought in the means of controlling its *effects*.

If a faction consists of less than a majority, relief is supplied by the republican principle, which enables the majority to defeat its sinister views by regular vote. It may clog the administration, it may convulse the society; but it will be unable to execute and mask its violence under the forms of the Constitution. When a majority is included in a faction, the form of popular government, on the other hand, enables it to sacrifice to its ruling passion or interest both the public good and the rights of other citizens. To secure the public good and private rights against the danger of such a faction, and at the same time to preserve the spirit and the form of popular government, is then the great object to which our inquiries are directed. Let me add that it is the great desideratum by which this form of government can be rescued from the opprobrium under which it has so long labored, and be recommended to the esteem and adoption of mankind.

By what means is this object attainable? Evidently by one of two only. Either the existence of the same passion or interest in a majority at the same time must be prevented, or the majority, having such coexistent passion or interest, must be rendered, by their number and local situation, unable to concert and carry into effect schemes of oppression. If the impulse and the opportunity be suffered to coincide, we well know that neither moral nor religious motives can be relied on as an adequate control. They are not found to be such on the injustice and violence of individuals, and lose their efficacy in proportion to the number combined together, that is, in proportion as their efficacy becomes needful.

From this view of the subject it may be concluded that a pure democracy, by which I mean a society consisting of a small number of citizens, who assemble and administer the government in person, can admit of no cure for the mischiefs of faction. A common passion or interest will, in almost every case, be felt by a majority of the whole; a communication and concert result from the form of government itself; and there is nothing to check the inducements to sacrifice the weaker party or an obnoxious individual. Hence it is that such democracies have ever been spectacles of turbulence and contention; have ever been found incompatible with personal security or the rights of property; and have in general been as short in their lives as they have been violent in their deaths. Theoretic politicians, who have patronized this species of government, have erroneously supposed that by reducing mankind to a perfect equality in their political rights, they would, at the same time, be perfectly equalized and assimilated in their possessions, their opinions, and their passions.

A republic, by which I mean a government in which the scheme of representation takes place, opens a different prospect, and promises the cure for which we are seeking. Let us examine the points in which it varies from pure democracy, and we shall comprehend both the nature of the cure and the efficacy which it must derive from the Union.

The two great points of difference between a democracy and a republic are: first, the delegation of the government, in the latter, to a small number of citizens elected by the rest; secondly, the greater number of citizens, and greater sphere of country, over which the latter may be extended.

The effect of the first difference is, on the one hand, to refine and enlarge the public views, by passing them through the medium of a chosen body of citizens, whose wisdom may best discern the true interest of their country, and whose patriotism and love of justice will be least likely to sacrifice it to temporary or partial considerations. Under such a regulation, it may well happen that the public voice, pronounced by the representatives of the people, will be more consonant to the public good than if pronounced by the people themselves, convened for the purpose. On the other hand, the effect may be inverted. Men of factious tempers, of local prejudices, or of sinister designs, may, by intrigue, by corruption, or by other means, first obtain the suffrages, and then betray the interests, of the people. The question resulting is, whether small or extensive republics are more favorable to the election of proper guardians of the public weal; and it is clearly decided in favor of the latter by two obvious considerations:

In the first place, it is to be remarked that, however small the republic may be, the representatives must be raised to a certain number, in order to guard against the cabals of a few; and that, however large it may be, they must be limited to a certain number, in order to guard against the confusion of a multitude. Hence, the number of representatives in the two cases not being in proportion to that of the two constituents, and being proportionally greater in the small republic, it follows that, if the proportion of fit characters be not less in the large than in the small republic, the former will present a greater option, and consequently a greater probability of a fit choice.

In the next place, as each representative will be chosen by a greater number of citizens in the large than in the small republic, it will be more difficult for unworthy candidates to practise with success the vicious arts by which elections are too often carried; and the suffrages of the people being more free, will be more likely to centre in men who possess the most attractive merit and the most diffusive and established characters.

It must be confessed that in this, as in most other cases, there is a mean, on both sides of which inconveniences will be found to lie. By enlarging too much the number of electors, you render the representative too little acquainted with all their local circumstances and lesser interests; as by reducing it too much, you render him unduly attached to these, and too little fit to comprehend and pursue great and national objects. The federal Constitution forms a happy combination in this respect; the great and aggregate interests being referred to the national, the local and particular to the State legislatures.

The other point of difference is, the greater number of citizens and extent of territory which may be brought within the compass of republican than of democratic government; and it is this circumstance principally which renders factious combinations less to be dreaded in the former than in the latter. The smaller the society, the fewer probably will be the distinct parties and interests composing it; the fewer the distinct parties and interests, the more frequently will a majority be found of the same party; and the smaller the number of individuals composing a majority, and the smaller the compass within which they are placed, the more easily will they concert and execute their plans of oppression. Extend the sphere and you take in a greater variety of parties and interests; you make it less probable that a majority of the whole will have a common motive to invade the rights of other citizens; or if such a common motive exists, it will be more difficult for all who feel it to discover their own strength, and to act in unison with each other. Besides other impediments, it may be remarked that, where there is a consciousness of unjust or dishonorable purposes, communication is always checked by distrust in proportion to the number whose concurrence is necessary.

Hence, it clearly appears, that the same advantage which a republic has over a democracy, in controlling the effects of faction, is enjoyed by a large over a small republic,—is enjoyed by the Union over the States composing it. Does the advantage consist in the substitution of representatives whose enlightened views and virtuous sentiments render them superior to local prejudices and to schemes of injustice? It will not be denied that the representation of the Union will be most likely to possess these requisite endowments. Does it consist in the greater security afforded by a greater variety of parties, against the event of any one party being able to outnumber and oppress the rest? In an equal degree does the increased variety of parties comprised within the Union, increase this security. Does it, in fine, consist in the greater obstacles opposed to the concert and accomplishment of the secret wishes of an unjust and interested majority? Here, again, the extent of the Union gives it the most palpable advantage.

The influence of factious leaders may kindle a flame within their particular States, but will be unable to spread a general conflagration through the other States. A religious sect may degenerate into a political faction in a part of the Confederacy; but the variety of sects dispersed over the entire face of it must secure the national councils against any danger from that source. A rage for paper money, for an abolition of debts, for an equal division of property, or for any other improper or wicked project, will be less apt to pervade the whole body of the Union than a particular member of it; in the same proportion as such a malady is more likely to taint a particular county or district, than an entire State.

In the extent and proper structure of the Union, therefore, we behold a republican remedy for the diseases most incident to republican government. And according to the degree of pleasure and pride we feel in being republicans, ought to be our zeal in cherishing the spirit and supporting the character of Federalists.   Publius

9

Marbury v. Madison:
1 Cranch 137 (1803)

Mr. Chief Justice Marshall delivered the opinion of the Court. He noted, in part:

The question whether an act repugnant to the Constitution can become the law of the land, is a question deeply interesting to the United States; but, happily, not of an intricacy proportioned to its interest. It seems only necessary to recognize certain principles supposed to have been long and well established, to decide it.

That the people have an original right to establish, for their future government, such principles as, in their opinion, shall most conduce to their own happiness, is the basis on which the whole American fabric has been erected. The exercise of this original right is a very great exertion; nor can it nor ought it to be frequently repeated. The principles, therefore, so established, are deemed fundamental. And as the authority from which they proceed is supreme, and can seldom act, they are designed to be permanent.

This original and supreme will organizes the government, and assigns to different departments their respective powers. It may either stop here, or establish certain limits not to be transcended by those departments.

The government of the United States is of the latter description. The powers of the legislature are defined and limited; and that those limits may not be mistaken, or forgotten, the Constitution is written. To what purpose are powers limited, and to what purpose is that limitation committed to writing, if these limits may, at any time, be passed by those intended to be restrained? The distinction between a government with limited and unlimited powers is abolished, if those limits do not confine the persons on whom they are imposed, and if acts prohibited and acts allowed, are of equal obligation. It is a proposition too plain to be contested, that the Constitution controls any legislative act repugnant to it; or, that the legislature may alter the Constitution by an ordinary act.

Between these alternatives there is no middle ground. The Constitution is either a superior paramount law, unchangeable by ordinary means, or it is on a level with ordinary legislative acts, and, like other acts, is alterable when the legislature shall please to alter it.

If the former part of the alternative be true, then a legislative act contrary to the Constitution, is not law; if the latter part be true, then written constitutions are absurd attempts, on the part of the people, to limit a power in its own nature illimitable.

Certainly all those who have framed written constitutions contemplate them as forming the fundamental and paramount law of the nation, and, consequently, the theory of every such government must be, that an act of the legislature, repugnant to the constitution, is void.

This theory is essentially attached to a written constitution, and is consequently to be considered, by this court, as one of the fundamental principles of our society. It is not, therefore, to be lost sight of in the further consideration of this subject.

If an act of the legislature, repugnant to the Constitution, is void, does it, notwithstanding its invalidity, bind the courts, and oblige them to give it effect? Or, in other words, though it be not law, does it constitute a rule as operative as if it was a law? This would be to overthrow in fact what was established in theory; and would seem, at first view, an absurdity too gross to be insisted on. It shall, however, receive a more attentive consideration.

It is emphatically the province and duty of the judicial department to say what the law is. Those who apply the rule to particular cases, must of necessity expound and interpret that rule. If two laws conflict with each other, the courts must decide on the operation of each.

So if the law be in opposition to the Constitution; if both the law and the Constitution apply to a particular case, so that the court must either decide that case conformably to the law, disregarding the Constitution, or conformably to the Constitution, disregarding the law, the court must determine which of these conflicting rules governs the case. This is of the very essence of judicial duty.

If, then, the courts are to regard the Constitution, and the Constitution is superior to any ordinary act of the legislature, the Constitution, and not such ordinary act, must govern the case to which they both apply.

Those, then, who controvert the principle that the Constitution is to be considered, in court, as a paramount law, are reduced to the necessity of maintaining that courts must close their eyes on the Constitution, and see only the law.

This doctrine would subvert the very foundation of all written constitutions. It would declare that an act which, according to the principles and theory of our government, is entirely void, is yet, in practice, completely obligatory. It would declare that if the legislature shall do what is expressly forbidden, such act, notwithstanding the express prohibition, is in reality effectual. It would be giving to the legislature a practical and real omnipotence, with the same breath which professes to restrict their powers within narrow limits. It is prescribing limits, and declaring that those limits may be passed at pleasure.

That it thus reduces to nothing what we have deemed the greatest improvement on political institutions, a written constitution, would of itself be sufficient, in America, where written constitutions have been viewed with so much reverence, for rejecting the construction. But the peculiar expressions of the Constitution of the United States furnish additional arguments in favor of its rejection.

The judicial power of the United States is extended to all cases arising under the Constitution.

Could it be the intention of those who gave this power, to say that in using it the Constitution should not be looked into? That a case arising under the Constitution should be decided without examining the instrument under which it arises?

This is too extravagant to be maintained.

In some cases, then, the Constitution must be looked into by the judges. And if they can open it at all, what part of it are they forbidden to read or to obey?

There are many other parts of the Constitution which serve to illustrate this subject.

It is declared that "no tax or duty shall be laid on articles exported from any State." Suppose a duty on the export of cotton, of tobacco, or of flour; and a suit instituted to recover it. Ought judgment to be rendered in such a case? Ought the judges to close their eyes on the Constitution, and only see the law?

The Constitution declares "that no bill of attainder or *ex post facto* law shall be passed."

If, however, such a bill should be passed, and a person should be prosecuted under it, must the court condemn to death those victims whom the Constitution endeavors to preserve?

"No person," says the Constitution, "shall be convicted of treason unless on the testimony of two witnesses to the same overt act, or on confession in open court."

Here the language of the Constitution is addressed especially to the courts. It prescribes, directly for them, a rule of evidence not to be departed from. If the legislature should change that rule, and declare one witness, or a confession out of court, sufficient for conviction, must the constitutional principle yield to the legislative act?

From these, and many other selections which might be made, it is apparent that the framers of the Constitution contemplated that instrument as a rule for the government of courts, as well as of the legislature.

Why otherwise does it direct the judges to take an oath to support it? This oath certainly applies in an especial manner to their conduct in their official character. How immoral to impose it on them, if they were to be used as the instruments, and the knowing instruments, for violating what they swear to support!

The oath of office, too, imposed by the legislature, is completely demonstrative of the legislative opinion on this subject. It is in these words: "I do solemnly swear that I will administer justice without respect to persons, and do equal right to the poor and to the rich; and that I will faithfully and impartially discharge all the duties incumbent on me as ————, according to the best of my abilities and understanding, agreeably to the Constitution and laws of the United States."

Why does a judge swear to discharge his duties agreeably to the Constitution of the United States, if that Constitution forms no rule for his government—if it is closed upon him, and cannot be inspected by him?

If such be the real state of things, this is worse than solemn mockery. To prescribe, or to take this oath, becomes equally a crime.

It is also not entirely unworthy of observation, that in declaring what shall be the supreme law of the land, the Constitution itself is first mentioned; and not the laws of the United States generally, but those only which shall be made in pursuance of the Constitution, have that rank.

Thus, the particular phraseology of the Constitution of the United

States confirms and strengthens the principle, supposed to be essential to all written constitutions, that a law repugnant to the Constitution is void; and that courts, as well as other departments, are bound by that instrument.

10

McCulloch v. Maryland: 4 Wheaton 316 (1819)

Mr. Chief Justice Marshall delivered the opinion of the Court. He noted, in part:

In the case now to be determined, the defendant, a sovereign State, denies the obligation of a law enacted by the legislature of the Union; and the plaintiff, on his part, contests the validity of an Act which has been passed by the legislature of that State. The Constitution of our country, in its most interesting and vital parts, is to be considered; the conflicting powers of the government of the Union and of its members, as marked in that Constitution, are to be discussed; and an opinion given, which may essentially influence the great operations of the government. . . .

If any one proposition could command the universal assent of mankind, we might expect it would be this: that the government of the Union, though limited in its powers, is supreme within its sphere of action. This would seem to result necessarily from its nature. It is the government of all; its powers are delegated by all; it represents all, and acts for all. Though any one State may be willing to control its operations, no State is willing to allow others to control them. The nation, on those subjects on which it can act, must necessarily bind its component parts. But this question is not left to mere reason: the people have, in express terms, decided it, by saying, "this Constitution, and the laws of the United States, which shall be made in pursuance thereof," "shall be the supreme law of the land," and by requiring that the members of the State legislatures, and the officers of the executive and judicial departments of the States, shall take the oath of fidelity to it. . . .

A constitution, to contain an accurate detail of all the subdivisions of which its great powers will admit, and of all the means by which they may be carried into execution, would partake of the prolixity of a legal code, and could scarcely be embraced by the human mind. It would probably never be understood by the public. Its nature, therefore, requires that only its great outlines should be marked, its important objects designated, and the minor ingredients which compose those objects be deduced from the nature of the objects themselves. That this idea was entertained by the framers of the American Constitution, is not only to be inferred from the nature of the instrument, but from the language. . . .

Although, among the enumerated powers of government, we do not find the word "bank,' or "incorporation," we find the great powers to lay and collect taxes; to borrow money; to regulate commerce; to declare and conduct a war; and to raise and support armies and navies. The sword and the purse, all the external relations, and no inconsiderable portion of the industry of the nation, are entrusted to its government. It can never be pretended that these vast powers draw after them others of inferior importance, merely because they are inferior. Such an idea can never be advanced. But it may, with great reason, be contended, that a government, entrusted with such ample powers, on the due execution of which the happiness and prosperity of the nation so vitally depends, must also be entrusted with ample means for their execution. The power being given, it is the interest of the nation to facilitate its execution. It can never be their interest, and cannot be presumed to have been their intention, to clog and embarrass its execution by withholding the most appropriate means. Throughout this vast republic, from the St. Croix to the Gulf of Mexico, from the Atlantic to the Pacific, revenue is to be collected and expended, armies are to be marched and supported. The exigencies of the nation may require, that the treasure raised in the North should be transported to the South, that raised in the East conveyed to the West, or that this order should be reversed. Is that construction of the Constitution to be preferred which would render these operations difficult, hazardous, and expensive? Can we adopt that construction (unless the words imperiously require it) which would impute to the framers of that instrument, when granting these powers for the public good, the intention of impeding their exercise by withholding a choice of means? If, indeed, such be the mandate of the Constitution, we have only to obey; but that instrument does not profess to enumerate the means by which the powers it confers may be executed; nor does it prohibit the creation of a corporation, if the existence of such a being be essential to the beneficial exercise of those powers. It is, then, the subject of fair inquiry, how far such means may be employed. . . .

We admit, as all must admit, that the powers of the government are limited, and that its limits are not to be transcended. But we think the sound construction of the Constitution must allow to the national legislature that discretion, with respect to the means by which the powers it confers are to be carried into execution, which will enable that body to perform the high duties assigned to it, in the manner most beneficial to the people. Let the end be legitimate, let it be within the scope of the Constitution, and all means which are appropriate, which are plainly adapted to that end, which are not prohibited, but consist with the letter and spirit of the Constitution, are constitutional. . . .

It being the opinion of the court that the act incorporating the bank is constitutional; and that the power of establishing a branch in the State of Maryland might be properly exercised by the bank itself, we proceed to inquire:

Whether the State of Maryland may, without violating the Constitution, tax that branch? . . .

That the power of taxation is one of vital importance; that it is retained by the States; that it is not abridged by the grant of a similar power to the government of the Union; that it is to be concurrently exercised by the two governments: are truths which have never been denied. But, such is the paramount character of the Constitution, that its capacity to withdraw any subject from the action of even this power, is admitted. The States are expressly forbidden to lay any duties on imports or exports, except what may be absolutely necessary for executing their inspection laws. If the obligation of this prohibition must be conceded— if it may restrain a State from the exercise of its taxing power on imports and exports; the same paramount character would seem to restrain, as it certainly may restrain, a State from such other exercise of this power, as is in its nature incompatible with, and repugnant to, the constitutional laws of the Union. A law, absolutely repugnant to another, as entirely repeals that other as if express terms of repeal were used.

On this ground the counsel for the bank place its claim to be exempted from the power of a State to tax its operations. There is no express provision for the case, but the claim has been sustained on a principle which so entirely pervades the Constitution, is so intermixed with the materials which compose it, so interwoven with its web, so blended with its texture, as to be incapable of being separated from it, without rending it into shreds.

This great principle is that the Constitution and the laws made in pursuance thereof are supreme; that they control the Constitution and laws of the respective States, and cannot be controlled by them. From this, which may be almost termed an axiom, other propositions are deduced as corollaries, on the truth or error of which, and on their application to this case, the cause has been supposed to depend. These are, 1. That a power to create implies a power to preserve. 2. That a power to destroy, if wielded by a different hand, is hostile to, and incompatible with, these powers to create and preserve. 3. That where this repugnancy exists, that authority which is supreme must control, not yield to that over which it is supreme. . . .

If we apply the principle for which the State of Maryland contends, to the Constitution generally, we shall find it capable of changing totally the character of that instrument. We shall find it capable of arresting all the measures of the government, and of prostrating it at the foot of the States. The American people have declared their Constitution, and the laws made in pursuance thereof, to be supreme; but this principle would transfer the supremacy, in fact, to the States. . . .

The court has bestowed on this subject its most deliberate consideration. The result is a conviction that the States have no power, by taxation or otherwise, to retard, impede, burden, or in any manner control, the operations of the constitutional laws enacted by Congress to carry into execution the powers vested in the general government. That is, we think, the unavoidable consequence of that supremacy which the Constitution has declared. . . .

The Bill of Rights

Article 1.

What this means is "freedom" to subvert!

Congress shall make no law respecting an establishment of religion, or prohibiting the free exercise thereof; or abridging the freedom of speech or of the press; or the right of the people peaceably to assemble and to petition the Government for a redress of grievances.

Article 2.

A well-regulated militia being necessary to the security of a free State, the right of the people to keep and bear arms shall not be infringed.

Article 3.

No soldier shall, in time of peace, be quartered in any house without the consent of the owner, nor in time of war but in a manner to be prescribed by law.

Article 4.

Must be changed! We're shackling the police!

The right of the people to be secure in their persons, houses, papers, and effects, against unreasonable searches and seizures, shall not be violated, and no warrants shall issue but upon probable cause, supported by oath or affirmation, and particularly describing the place to be searched, and the persons or things to be seized.

Article 5.

Sure! and let all the crooks and Commies off the hook!

No person shall be held to answer for a capital or other infamous crime unless on a presentment or indictment of a Grand Jury, except in cases arising in the land or naval forces, or in the militia, when in actual service, in time of war or public danger; nor shall any person be subject for the same offense to be twice put in jeopardy of life or limb; nor shall be compelled in any criminal case to be a witness against himself, nor be deprived of life, liberty, or property, without due process of law; nor shall private property be taken for public use without just compensation.

Article 6.

Keep this & we'll have murderers roaming the streets!

In all criminal prosecutions, the accused shall enjoy the right to a speedy and public trial, by an impartial jury of the State and district wherein the crime shall have been committed, which districts shall have been previously ascertained by law, and to be informed of the nature and cause of the accusation; to be confronted with the witnesses against him; to have compulsory process for obtaining witnesses in his favor, and to have the assistance of counsel for his defense.

Article 7.

In suits at common law, where the value in controversy shall exceed $20, the right of trial by jury shall be preserved, and no fact tried by a jury shall be otherwise re-examined in any court of the United States than according to the rules of the common law.

Article 8.

Excessive bail shall not be required, nor excessive fines imposed, nor cruel and unusual punishments inflicted.

Article 9.

The enumeration in the Constitution of certain rights shall not be construed to deny or disparage others retained by the people.

Article 10.

The powers not delegated to the United States by the Constitution, nor prohibited by it to the States, are reserved to the States respectively, or to the people.

11

Arthur J. Goldberg

Our Besieged
Bill of Rights

There is a controversy in American law that reflects the uncertainty and division of contemporary American society. A universal and understandable concern with the rising rate of crime has led to a frustrating search for solutions. The frustration has bred drastic and desperate demands, among them, various proposals to alter the Constitution—or recent Supreme Court interpretations of it—in the hope that, thereby, law and order may be "restored." Some of the proposals have been made into slogans; for example, "Take the handcuffs off the police." Even more sophisticated suggestions are based on the idea of "liberating" officials from constitutional restraints. These critics do not put forth merely new and much-needed devices for the prevention of crime, such as better training and higher pay for the police, sufficient manpower for effective patrol or improved techniques and equipment. They propose to alter the fundamental balance established in the Bill of Rights between the power of government and the autonomy of the individual. The Bill of Rights is to be adjusted to meet our concern over crime. In particular, the Fifth Amendment has been attacked as a luxury we cannot afford in the current crisis. Even such an eminent jurist as Henry Friendly of the Federal

Court of Appeals, Second Circuit, has gone so far as to propose a constitutional amendment to reverse recent interpretations of the self-incrimination provisions of the Fifth Amendment. Judge Friendly has been joined in this demand by others in the judicial and law-enforcement professions. One of the most outspoken is former governor of New York Thomas E. Dewey, who has said, "We could get along just as well if we repealed the Fifth Amendment." In a time of such panic-inspired rhetoric, it is necessary to examine the reasons for our constitutional protections.

A Bill of Rights reflects wisdom. Its limits are based on the knowledge that a society may take hasty action that it will later come to regret. Thus, a wise society provides itself with parchment counsel intended to prevent those actions that history teaches us are most often lamented. A Bill of Rights also expresses the essential optimism of a people, for it is based upon a belief that there will be a future worth aiming the nation toward.

It is a glory of the United States that it has maintained a Bill of Rights for almost two centuries. This is not an easy thing, for it is an implicit assumption of constitutional limitations that they will frequently be unpopular in specific application. If the Government and the people could be counted on always to act according to the *principles* of the Bill of Rights, there would be no need for the document. But it was recognized by the people of this new nation, who would not accept a Constitution without a Bill of Rights, that there would be temporary passions, passing emergencies, apparently changed circumstances—all of which might appear to justify abridgment of liberty. It seems intrinsic to human nature that the closer we are to an event, the less reliable is our judgment. The Bill of Rights provides the detached wisdom that we require when basic freedoms seem to block the path of necessity.

The general value of constitutional freedoms is illustrated by the First Amendment's provision for freedom of speech. This freedom has been constantly under attack from the days of the discredited Alien and Sedition Laws. Comstockian censors rallied against the amendment when it protected some of the world's great literature from the imposition of their narrow vision. The First Amendment always has rough going when it protects war dissenters, at least until the war is over. And it has done extraordinary service in protecting the rights of peaceful civil-rights demonstrations. In fact, whenever there are two sides to an issue, the minority depends on the First Amendment for the right to present its side. We all have at least one opinion that someone, somewhere, thinks we should not express. Knowing this, we value the amendment that protects those with whom we disagree.

We easily see that the freedom of the First Amendment protects us; but the rights of criminal suspects seem less personal. They are often presented as limitations that the law-abiding society adopts only out of an exaggerated sense of fair play. And when a confession or illegally seized evidence is excluded from a criminal trial, we hear that we cannot afford to give such an advantage to the adversary. But it is not someone else whom the Fourth, Fifth and Sixth amendments protect. Especially, it is not only someone else who will lose if the proposals against the Fifth Amendment succeed. For to trim the privilege against self-incrimination will also trim the autonomy of every individual, which is the essence of the Bill of Rights.

The autonomy of the individual comprises freedom of thought, speech and association. Necessary at times to all of these is privacy. Privacy exists not as an absolute concept but as a relationship with other entities. One may maintain physical privacy against the world with a wall, even though a mailman, milkman and salesman regularly come through one's gate. Passers-by may peer through the chinks and children may scale one's wall in search of errant balls. Yet there is privacy in the enclosure, in the sense that one can act with reasonable assurance that he is not, in fact, being observed.

Privacy vis-à-vis the Government is similarly incomplete and erratic. But it must have the quality that allows the feeling that one is unnoticed, at least some of the time. The Government naturally requires information of various types, and there will be occasions when almost a total account of one's life may be required. But to preserve the feeling of autonomy, those occasions must be rare, like the breaches of a solid wall. The individual must know that, in the usual case, his life is his own, not his Government's.

Privacy has already suffered a major invasion in those sections of the 1968 Crime Act that authorize wire tapping and electronic surveillance. Under these provisions, the Attorney General or any local chief prosecutor may seek an order allowing the interception of any conversation of a person suspected of any of a long list of crimes, some of them quite minor. Under the law, the police can tap one's phone or eavesdrop electronically even if they only suspect that one "is about to" commit a crime without informing the person spied upon until long after the event. Thus, we may be overheard in the supposed privacy of our homes, without a realistic chance to protest.

The Attorney General has said he will use the wire-tapping authority to protect us from threats to national security and from organized crime only. But there are not even these restrictions on local police. They may listen for any crime carrying a penalty of over one year. This means that, for example, whenever one were suspected of allowing his teenage children to sip beer or wine on a festive or sacramental occasion, the police could spy on his bedroom. (The act allows interception of oral, as well as telephonic, communications.) Of course, no district attorney is likely to sanction the use of so awesome a weapon for so minor a transgression. But small crimes may be used as a pretext to eavesdrop for suspected evidence of larger ones, as those who have traced judicial efforts to limit exploratory searches know too well.

The problem here is that one never knows for what reason electronic gadgetry—such as the device widely advertised as The Snooper— will be used. Even if you act in accord with community mores today, you cannot predict when a new district attorney will attempt to build his reputation on your supposed transgressions. Can we afford to maintain the privacy of the home against such a variety of intrusions by the inquisitive state? This question—as well as "Will it help catch criminals?" —must be answered. And my answer is that we *must* afford privacy. It is the principal distinction between a free society and the sullen tyranny of Big Brother.

The most vocal of today's attacks on the Bill of Rights are directed against the Fifth Amendment. A rising crime rate is associated with Supreme Court rulings dealing with the privilege against self-incrimination. Critics seem to believe that if that privilege were eliminated or weakened, there would be more confessions, and that if there were more confessions, there would be less crime and we would all be better off. But they offer no evidence that limiting the Fifth Amendment would substantially limit crime. They really propose that we experiment with the liberty we enjoy, in order to receive a benefit that may not exist.

The privilege not to "be compelled in any criminal case to be a witness against" oneself derives from an earlier, crueler age than ours. Then, people did not wonder at the necessity of the privilege to remain silent in the face of criminal accusation. They were too familiar with torture and long imprisonment as means of acquiring information.

But the Middle Ages are gone. Why do we still have the Fifth Amendment? One reason is fear that without it, the brutality of the extorted confession will continue to plague us. Forty years ago was not the Middle Ages, yet the Wickersham Commission, appointed by President Herbert Hoover in 1929 to investigate law-enforcement procedures, discovered that police still used torture to gain admissions of guilt. Today is not the Middle Ages, yet the crew of the Pueblo discovered that the need for the Fifth Amendment has not disappeared. One might say we are 40 years and 7000 miles from such incidents and, generally, we are. But that statement is testimony to the effectiveness of the privilege, not to its superfluity.

That we still need protection against coercion is demonstrated by the amount of violent interrogation that has been discovered in the past decade. The Civil Rights Commission found violence directed at Negroes for many reasons, among them the obtaining of confessions. A study in New Jersey found coercion to be a common questioning technique, used with impartiality against both white and black suspects. Lest anyone think that this represents the irreducible level of violence, the same study showed that in nearby Philadelphia, coercion was a rare phenomenon. The difference was attributed to the determination of Philadelphia authorities to respect the privilege.

Even when the zeal of law enforcers does not extend to physical brutality, threats and promises can be equally effective in breaking the will of a suspect. For the law-enforcement resources of an entire state to close around a lone suspect and intimidate him into confessing is unseemly. And it is dangerous. If a little fear makes a guilty man confess, a lot might move the innocent to admit guilt. More likely, it could make a minor criminal exaggerate his deeds, clearing the police files of unsolved crimes. These are too common realities, and judicial enforcement of the Fifth Amendment is the primary limit on their occurrence.

The Fifth Amendment privilege protects against more than physical and psychological brutality; it is intrinsic to the individual's right of privacy. The dwindling of privacy has been as frequently noted as the rise of crime. In the modern world, we have only belatedly realized that privacy is an increasingly scarce social resource and one that must be vigilantly protected against the claims of efficient social ordering. We have, luckily, so far prevented the establishment of a national computer bank, for example. The projected uses of the computer seem perfectly legitimate: Some well-meaning men want an efficient means of arranging all the information the Government already has, in order that it may be better used for the good of all. What is wrong with that? Simply this—that everyone has something to hide; not something that he is necessarily ashamed of but that he wants for his own. That he once registered as a Democrat, for example, or made an improvident investment, or engaged in a youthful escapade not even criminal, or bought an Edsel. These are the sorts of facts that the state knows but that we do not want it to know too well.

Perhaps the best way to appreciate what the privilege against self-incrimination really means is to imagine a system without it. There are, of course, countries that have neither a Fifth Amendment nor tyranny. But they have developed other restraints in dealings between state and citizen. From the record of coercion in the United States, even with the privilege, it is apparent that we have developed no substitute for the amendment. And repeal in the present context would hardly provoke a search for substitutes. If we "liberate" our officialdom from the Fifth, it will not be because the officials have so internalized its values as to render it superfluous. Rather, it will be because we have decided we can no longer afford the restraints it imposes. Politically, repeal would represent positive encouragement to do what formerly the amendment prohibited. Post-repeal America would not be a non-Fifth society; it would be an anti-Fifth society.

What could happen without the amendment would seem to many a whole new order of police behavior. One can imagine the investigator calling the citizen in for a chat about the events of the past few days, weeks or years: "Come down to the station and bring your diary with you," he might say. "What crimes have been committed in your vicinity in the past month? Do you take a morning walk? Why that route?" At this point, the citizen may keep silent, which will no doubt interest a jury, or he will have to defend his innocent private habits.

How many details of one's life are perfectly legal and honorable, yet personal? What is more totalitarian than having to report on these things at the insistence of some bureaucrat who naturally views his task as more important than your privacy? Yet it is only an explicit prohibition such as the Fifth Amendment that prevents the state from seeking such total knowledge. The ends are legitimate (investigating crime) and the means seem mild enough in the individual case (just a few polite questions). But if the interrogation is limited only by the number of crimes to solve, there is no limit at all.

But the Fifth Amendment does not merely protect us against embarrassment. It keeps us out of jail. Four hundred years ago, Montaigne wrote, "No man is so exquisitely honest or upright but he brings his actions and thoughts within compass and danger of the laws, and that ten times in his life might not lawfully be hanged." In the intervening centuries, the number of crimes for which we may "lawfully be hanged" has been reduced. But the number for which we may be imprisoned has multiplied a hundredfold. How many tax underpayments are the result of unwitting errors by the taxpayer? How much simpler prosecution would be if the taxpayer could be interrogated alone, without either his lawyer or his records.

There is a more insidious possibility for law enforcement in a post-Fifth Amendment era. Instead of investigating specific crimes in which a suspect might have been implicated, the state can call in people for general investigations. Who has not wittingly or unwittingly exceeded the speed limit or littered the sidewalk or crossed a street against the red light? When asked, "Have you committed any crimes?" what does one say? To say no is to lie. If done in court, this is perjury; out of court, it may be called obstructing justice. To confess is to pay penalties just because some official has singled one out for reasons that will never be known. In effect, the state can make either a criminal or a perjurer out of most anyone it chooses. Pity the unfortunate man who falls out of favor with his local district attorney!

In fact, today's large number of crimes necessitates some sort of selection by law enforcers, but the criteria of selection are never specified by the legislature. Some law-enforcement agencies concentrate on street crimes; others perceive a threat in subversion and question suspects about their politics; yet others spend their time enforcing civil rights laws. But the decision may as easily be made not according to what crime seems most important but according to what group one hates or fears most. Crime can be investigated while keeping an alert eye on ethnic or political minorities. Membership in one of these groups can become an invitation to inquisition. Political leaders, in fact, are inclined to define law-enforcement priorities in terms of the anxieties of their electoral constituencies.

Even those who fall on the right side of prosecutor discretion today ought not to be so sure that they can get along better without the Fifth Amendment. It was only 15 years ago that the clamor of McCarthyism threatened the privilege against self-incrimination. That campaign was not directed against street crime but against the right to hold one's own political beliefs, the right to believe differently from Senator McCarthy without being publicly harassed. McCarthy is gone, and the Fifth Amendment and we are still here, but that is no assurance that another witch-hunt will not occur. The Fifth Amendment is part of our essential insurance against that day.

Not only the Fifth Amendment but our whole heritage of individual liberty rejects inquisitorial law enforcement. Those who would tamper with this heritage argue that it will be more difficult to catch criminals if we cannot make them confess. Of course, there are times when no other evidence is available, although not so often as is frequently asserted. I must emphasize, however, that liberty is worth this small price. We should not rush to abandon our autonomy as individuals just because it creates inefficiencies in the apprehension of criminals. Democracy may be an inefficient means for determining policy, but we do not rush to abandon democracy. We are justifiably concerned with crime, but the criminal's power is nothing compared with the power of the state.

Proponents of new measures argue that "adjusting" the Fifth Amendment will not unleash the entire force of the state. They claim that the Fifth Amendment that protects us against arbitrary intrusions by the state is something different from recent judicial interpretations. It is said that the courts have enacted a new code of criminal procedure under the guise of interpreting the Constitution. It is true that the Supreme Court has prescribed precise rules that, understandably, are not present in the Constitution. But such rules are the only way to make the Constitution a reality. When *Wolf vs. Colorado* left enforcement of the Fourth Amendment to the states, it was too widely taken as a green light to search and seize at will. The Court has not expanded the privilege against self-incrimination: It has created effective remedies and extended their protection to the poor and ignorant.

The test of the constitutionality of a confession has long been whether it was voluntary or not. A confession could not constitutionally be beaten out of a suspect. It *could* be extracted through more subtle psychological pressures playing upon the fears of the suspect. What the Court did in the *Miranda* decision was to apply the same standards to the reality that confronts the poor and the ignorant defendant. Organized criminals have their lawyers and know enough to call them when they confront the law. When they volunteer a confession, it is a bargain, exchanging help to the police for lesser charges and lighter sentences.

But a lawyerless defendant facing the law for the first time has no knowledge of such bargains. Ignorant of his rights, the suspect sees no limits to what his captors can do. Indeed, interrogation manuals suggest creating the impression of police omnipotence. And even if there are limits, who enforces them against the police? The suspect in this position frequently has no real choice in his behavior. This produces results for the inquisitor. It also provides an incentive for the police to violate other rights. Although the Fourth Amendment requires probable cause for arrest, the availability of information from the uninformed prisoner encourages the arrest of large numbers of people on "suspicion," in the hope that some of them will reveal incriminating information under the stress of custody.

Miranda is closely tailored to the coercive atmosphere in which interrogation occurs. The police are not forbidden to ask questions; they are not required to warn informants who are not suspects; and volunteered statements are perfectly acceptable evidence. What *Miranda* does require is the warning of a suspect that what he says can be used against him and that he has a right to remain silent and to have a lawyer—free, if he cannot afford one. These are not new rights. They are all means of effectuating the long-recognized privilege against self-incrimination, based on the appreciation that rights are useless if the holder is ignorant of them. *Miranda* upholds the proposition that the poor first offender is as entitled as any of us to the right that anything he says should be voluntary.

If *Miranda* were overturned, it seems clear that the poor, disproportionate numbers of whom are black, would be most affected. Organized
criminals, as we have said, do not talk, even in the face of illegal threats.
The police are usually careful not to harass well-to-do suspects (who
have lawyers, anyway). So, in effect, a separate system of interrogation is
established for the poor. The counterargument—in favor of abridging
the Fifth—is that all that is sought is an efficient system of criminal investigation that accidentally affects the poor somewhat differently than
others. It is a fact of life that the poor suffer in many ways. A fact of life
it may be, but not one we can overlook when the practical effect of a
proposed rule change clearly would be even greater discrimination
against the poor, who could be pressured to talk more easily than others.

The poor know that whatever happens to the Fifth Amendment,
business-crime suspects are unlikely to be grilled at the station house.
And this may explain why proposals to weaken the amendment come
mainly from the better off. To establish this mode of law enforcement is
to abandon something fundamental to America, equal justice.

We cannot afford to abandon equality. We have already seen some
of the costs of a racially divided society. These costs include joblessness
and riots and the very crime wave we want to diminish. It is true that
equality is slowly achieved and will only slowly affect the crime rate, but
it is essential to peace in our cities. Whatever short-term gains may flow
from repression will not be worth deepening the alienation of the repressed. A state of seige cannot be the goal of law and order.

So far, we have assumed that the protection of the Fifth Amendment exacts its price through crime. But there has been no sufficient
showing that abrogation of the amendment will significantly affect crime.
Interrogation is a technique for solving crimes, not preventing them.
Even in solving crimes, confessions are not usually essential. The district
attorney of Los Angeles County has stated that *Miranda*-type warnings
have not significantly affected his conviction rate.

The Supreme Court is *not* one of the significant causes of urban
crime, but the way our society handles the availability of addictive drugs
and guns is. In virtually all of our cities, an appalling proportion of
property crime is committed by addicts. We *can* do something constructive about this crime. Addicts commit crimes for money to support their
habits. Simply prescribing maintenance doses of addictive drugs, either
free or at a cost of less than a dollar a day, would eliminate a substantial
cause of crime.

Uncontrolled ownership of guns also contributes to violence. The
mere availability of a gun has turned more than one family quarrel into
a murder. Easy access to guns paves the way for armed robbers. This is,
again, a problem about which we have the power to do something yet

refuse to act adequately. It is ironic that some of the most vociferous opponents of the Supreme Court also oppose gun-control legislation. If they really wished to control crime and preserve liberty, their positions should be reversed on both issues.

Experimentation with such steps as dispensing drugs and restricting the sale of firearms is a practical approach to the crime problem as is a determined effort to eliminate poverty and other underlying causes of crime. If such proposals do not work out in practice, they can be modified or abandoned. But constitutional experimentation is far more difficult. Constitutional restrictions serve a more complex function than to provide statute law and guide judicial decisions. The constitutional rule, by instructing officialdom as to its primary duties to citizens, inculcates a basic respect for individual dignity. To alter the rules every so often devalues the social policy underlying them. The entire relationship between citizen and state is altered, with results neither foreseeable nor easily correctable. Perhaps with this in mind, we have never fundamentally altered the Constitution. And we have never even tampered with the Bill of Rights.

Establishing the basic relationship between the citizen and the state is the greatest task of the constitution maker. It is a task difficult to do well, because the arrangement must last far beyond what the wisest man can foresee. Whenever adjustments are required, the immediate demands of the state always seem so pressing and legitimate. In any single case, it is difficult to resist the demands of necessity, as the Japanese-Americans who spent World War Two in concentration camps learned. What if the Bill of Rights had been written during that crisis? We are in the midst of another crisis now and it is an equally bad time to rewrite the Constitution. Especially, we should not rewrite it in response to proposals that trade away liberty for the illusion of security. In the end, we would be protected from neither the state nor the criminal. If we sacrifice only the least aware of our fellow citizens, we exacerbate the causes of violent conflict, without eliminating any of the symptoms. There are many ways of fighting crime, but neither for rich nor for poor are there many ways to protect the privacy and integrity of the individual—rights and values that are the very essence of constitutional liberty and security.

One of the tenets of the legal profession is that bad cases make bad law. Times of stress make even worse law. It would be bad law and bad policy to weaken the Fifth Amendment, for it is even truer today than it was 178 years ago that we can afford liberty. And we must preserve those laws that guarantee it.

12 Richard E. Neustadt

The President:
Leader or Clerk?

In the United States we like to "rate" a President. We measure him as "weak" or "strong" and call what we are measuring his "leadership." We do not wait until a man is dead; we rate him from the moment he takes office. We are quite right to do so. His office has become the focal point of politics and policy in our political system. Our commentators and our politicians make a specialty of taking the man's measurements. The rest of us join in when we feel "government" impinging on our private lives. In the third quarter of the twentieth century millions of us have that feeling often.

This book is an endeavor to illuminate what we are measuring. Although we all make judgments about presidential leadership, we often base our judgments upon images of office that are far removed from the reality. We also use those images when we tell one another whom to choose as President. But it is risky to appraise a man in office or to choose a man for office on false premises about the nature of his job. When the job is the Presidency of the United States the risk becomes excessive. Hopefully, this book can help reduce the risk.

We deal here with the President himself and with his influence on

From Richard E. Neustadt, *Presidential Power: The Politics of Leadership.* Copyright © 1960 by John Wiley & Sons, Inc. Reprinted by permission.

governmental action. In institutional terms the Presidency now includes 2000 men and women. The President is only one of them. But *his* performance scarcely can be measured without focusing on *him*. In terms of party, or of country, or the West, so-called, his leadership involves far more than governmental action. But the sharpening of spirit and of values and of purposes is not done in a vacuum. Although governmental action may not be the whole of leadership, all else is nurtured by it and gains meaning from it. Yet if we treat the Presidency as the President, we cannot measure him as though he were the government. Not action as an outcome but his impact on the outcome is the measure of the man. His strength or weakness, then, turns on his personal capacity to influence the conduct of the men who make up government. His influence becomes the mark of leadership. To rate a President according to these rules, one looks into the man's own capabilities as seeker and as wielder of effective influence upon the other men involved in governing the country. That is what [I] will do.

"Presidential" on the title page [of the book from which this article is reprinted] means nothing but the President. "Power" means *his* influence. It helps to have these meanings settled at the start.

There are two ways to study "presidential power." One way is to focus on the tactics, so to speak, of influencing certain men in given situations: how to get a bill through Congress, how to settle strikes, how to quiet Cabinet feuds, or how to stop a Suez. The other way is to step back from tactics on those "givens" and to deal with influence in more strategic terms: what is its nature and what are its sources? What can *this* man accomplish to improve the prospect that he will have influence when he wants it? Strategically, the question is not how he masters Congress in a peculiar instance, but what he does to boost his chance for mastery in any instance, looking toward tomorrow from today. The second of these two ways has been chosen for this book.

To look into the strategy of presidential influence one must decide at whom to look. Power problems vary with the scope and scale of government, the state of politics, the progress of technology, the pace of world relationships. Power in the Nineteen-sixties cannot be acquired or employed on the same terms as those befitting Calvin Coolidge, or Theodore Roosevelt, or Grover Cleveland, or James K. Polk. But there is a real likelihood that in the next decade a President will have to reach for influence and use it under much the same conditions we have known since the Second World War. If so, the men whose problems shed most light on White House prospects are Dwight David Eisenhower and Harry S. Truman. It is at them, primarily, that we shall look. To do so is to see the shadow of another, Franklin D. Roosevelt. They worked amidst the remnants of his voter coalition, and they filled an office that his practice had enlarged.

Our two most recent Presidents have had in common something that is likely to endure into our future: the setting for a great deal of their work. They worked in an environment of policy and politics marked by a high degree of continuity. To sense the continuity from Truman's time through Eisenhower's one need only place the newspapers of 1959 alongside those of 1949. Save for the issue of domestic communists, the subject matter of our policy and politics remains almost unchanged. We deal as we have done in terms of cold war, of an arms race, of a competition overseas, of danger from inflation, and of damage from recession. We skirmish on the frontiers of the Welfare State and in the borderlands of race relations. Aspects change, but labels stay the same. So do dilemmas. Everything remains unfinished business. Not in this century has there been comparable continuity from a decade's beginning to its end; count back from 1949 and this grows plain. There even has been continuity in the behavior of our national electorate; what Samuel Lubell nine years ago called "stalemate" in our partisan alignments has not broken yet.

The similarities in Truman's setting and in Eisenhower's give their years a unity distinct from the War Years, or the Depression Era, or the Twenties, or before. In governmental terms, at least, the fifteen years since V-J Day deserve a designation all their own. "Mid-century" will serve for present purposes. And what distinguishes mid-century can be put very briefly: emergencies in policy with politics as usual.

"Emergency" describes mid-century conditions only by the standards of the past. By present standards what would once have been emergency is commonplace. Policy dilemmas through the postwar period resemble past emergencies in one respect, their difficulty and complexity for government. Technological innovation, social and political change abroad, population growth at home impose enormous strains not only on the managerial equipment of our policy-makers but also on their intellectual resources. The gropings of mature men at mid-century remind one of the intellectual confusions stemming from depression, thirty years ago, when men were also pushed past comprehension by the novelty of their condition. In our time innovation keeps us *constantly* confused; no sooner do we start to comprehend than something new is added, and we grope again. But unlike the Great Difficulties of the past, our policy dilemmas rarely produce what the country feels as "crisis." Not even the Korean War brought anything approaching sustained national "consensus." Since 1945 innumerable situations have been felt as crises inside government; there rarely has been comparable feeling outside government. In the era of the Cold War we have practiced "peacetime" politics. What else could we have done? Cold War is not a "crisis"; it becomes a way of life.

Our politics has been "as usual," but only by the standard of past *crises*. In comparison with what was once normality, our politics has been *un*usual. The weakening of party ties, the emphasis on personality, the close approach of world events, the changeability of public moods, and above all the ticket-splitting, none of this was "usual" before the Second World War. The symbol of mid-century political conditions is the White House in one party's hands with Congress in the other's—a symbol plainly visible in eight of the past fifteen years and all but visible in four of the remaining seven. Nothing really comparable has been seen in this country since the Eighteen-eighties. And the Eighties were not troubled by emergencies in policy.

As for politics and policy combined, we have seen some precursors of our setting at mid-century. Franklin Roosevelt had a reasonably comparable setting in his middle years as President, though not in his first years and not after Pearl Harbor. Indeed, if one excepts the war, mid-century could properly be said to start with Roosevelt's second term. Our recent situation is to be compared, as well, with aspects of the Civil War. Abraham Lincoln is much closer to us in condition than in time, the Lincoln plagued by Radicals and shunned by Democrats amidst the managerial and intellectual confusions of twentieth-century warfare in the nineteenth century. And in 1919 Woodrow Wilson faced and was defeated by conditions something like our own. But save for these men one can say of Truman and of Eisenhower that they were the first who had to fashion presidential influence out of mid-century materials. Presumably they will not be the last.

We tend to measure Truman's predecessors as though "leadership" consisted of initiatives in economics, or diplomacy, or legislation, or in mass communication. If we measured him and his successors so, they would be leaders automatically. A striking feature of our recent past has been the transformation into routine practice of the actions we once treated as exceptional. A President may retain liberty, in Woodrow Wilson's phrase, "to be as big a man as he can." But nowadays he cannot be as small as he might like.

Our two most recent Presidents have gone through all the motions we traditionally associate with strength in office. So will the man who takes the oath on January 20, 1961. In instance after instance the exceptional behavior of our earlier "strong" Presidents has now been set by statute as a regular requirement. Theodore Roosevelt once assumed the "steward's" role in the emergency created by the great coal strike of

1902; the Railway Labor Act and the Taft-Hartley Act now make such interventions mandatory upon Presidents. The other Roosevelt once asserted personal responsibility for gauging and for guiding the American economy; the Employment Act binds his successors to that task. Wilson and F.D.R. became chief spokesmen, leading actors, on a world stage at the height of war; now UN membership, far-flung alliances, prescribe that role continuously in times termed "peace." Through both world wars our Presidents grappled experimentally with an emergency-created need to "integrate" foreign and military policies; the National Security Act now takes that need for granted as a constant of our times. F.D.R. and Truman made themselves responsible for the development and first use of atomic weapons; the Atomic Energy Act now puts a comparable burden on the back of every President. And what has escaped statutory recognition has mostly been accreted into presidential common law, confirmed by custom, no less binding: the "fireside chat" and the press conference, for example, or the personally presented legislative program, or personal campaigning in congressional elections.

In form all Presidents are leaders, nowadays. In fact this guarantees no more than that they will be clerks. Everybody now expects the man inside the White House to do something about everything. Laws and customs now reflect acceptance of him as the Great Initiator, an acceptance quite as widespread at the Capitol as at his end of Pennsylvania Avenue. But such acceptance does not signify that all the rest of government is at his feet. It merely signifies that other men have found it practically impossible to do *their* jobs without assurance of initiatives from him. Service for themselves, not power for the President, has brought them to accept his leadership in form. They find his actions useful in their business. The transformation of his routine obligations testifies to their dependence on an active White House. A President, these days, is an invaluable clerk. His services are in demand all over Washington. His influence, however, is a very different matter. Laws and customs tell us little about leadership in fact.

Why have our Presidents been honored with this clerkship? The answer is that no one else's services suffice. Our Constitution, our traditions, and our politics provide no better source for the initiatives a President can take. Executive officials need decisions, and political protection, and a referee for fights. Where are these to come from but the White House? Congressmen need an agenda from outside, something with high status to respond to or react against. What provides it better than the program of the President? Party politicians need a record to defend in the next national campaign. How can it be made except by "their" Administration? Private persons with a public axe to grind may need a helping hand or they may need a grinding stone. In either case who gives more satisfaction than a President? And outside the United States, in every country where our policies and postures influence home politics, there will be people needing just the "right" thing said and done or just the "wrong" thing stopped *in Washington*. What symbolizes Washington more nearly than the White House?

A modern President is bound to face demands for aid and service from five more or less distinguishable sources: from Executive official-dom, from Congress, from his partisans, from citizens at large, and from abroad. The Presidency's clerkship is expressive of these pressures. In effect they are constituency pressures and each President has five sets of constituents. The five are not distinguished by their membership; membership is obviously an overlapping matter. And taken one by one they do not match the man's electorate; one of them, indeed, is outside his electorate. They are distinguished, rather, by their different claims upon him. Initiatives are what they want, for five distinctive reasons. Since government and politics have offered no alternative, our laws and customs turn those wants into his obligations.

Why, then, is the President not guaranteed an influence commensurate with services performed? Constituent relations are relations of dependence. Everyone with any share in governing this country will belong to one (or two, or three) of his "constituencies." Since everyone depends on him why is he not assured of everyone's support? The answer is that no one else sits where he sits, or sees quite as he sees; no one else feels the full weight of his obligations. Those obligations are a tribute to his unique place in our political system. But just because it is unique they fall on him alone. *The same conditions that promote his leadership in form preclude a guarantee of leadership in fact.* No man or group at either end of Pennsylvania Avenue shares his peculiar status in our government and politics. That is why his services are in demand. By the same token, though, the obligations of all other men are different from his own. His Cabinet officers have departmental duties and constituents. His legislative leaders head *congressional* parties, one in either House. His national party organization stands apart from his official family. His political allies in the States need not face Washington, or one another. The private groups that seek him out are not compelled to govern. And friends abroad are not compelled to run in our elections. Lacking his position and prerogatives, these men cannot regard his obligations as their own. They have their jobs to do; none is the same as his. As they perceive their duty they may find it right to follow him, in fact, or they may not. Whether they will feel obliged *on their responsibility* to do what he wants done remains an open question. . . .

13 *Chalmers M. Roberts*

The Day
We Didn't Go to War

Saturday, April 3, 1954, was a raw, windy day in Washington, but the weather didn't prevent a hundred Americans from milling around the Jefferson Memorial to see the cherry blossoms—twenty thousand of them from watching the crowning of the 1954 Cherry Blossom Queen.

President Eisenhower drove off to his Maryland mountain retreat called Camp David. There he worked on his coming Monday speech, designed, so the White House said, to quiet America's fears of Russia, the H-bomb, domestic Communists, a depression. But that Saturday morning eight members of Congress, five Senators and three Representatives, got the scare of their lives. They had been called to a secret conference with John Foster Dulles. They entered one of the State Department's fifth-floor conference rooms to find not only Dulles but Admiral Arthur W. Radford, chairman of the Joint Chiefs of Staff, Under Secretary of Defense Roger Kyes, Navy Secretary Robert B. Anderson, and Thruston B. Morton, Dulles's assistant for Congressional Relations. A large map of

From *The Reporter* (September 1954). Copyright 1954 by Fortnightly Publishing Company, Inc. Reprinted by permission.

the world hung behind Dulles's seat, and Radford stood by with several others. "The President has asked me to call this meeting," Dulles began.

URGENCY AND A PLAN

The atmosphere became serious at once. What was wanted, Dulles said, was a joint resolution by Congress to permit the President to use air and naval power in Indo-China. Dulles hinted that perhaps the mere passage of such a resolution would in itself make its use unnecessary. But the President had asked for its consideration, and, Dulles added, Mr. Eisenhower felt that it was indispensable at this juncture that the leaders of Congress feel as the Administration did on the Indo-China crisis.

Then Radford took over. He said the Administration was deeply concerned over the rapidly deteriorating situation. He used a map of the Pacific to point out the importance of Indo-China. He spoke about the French Union forces then already under siege for three weeks in the fortress of Dienbienphu.

The admiral explained the urgency of American action by declaring that he was not even sure, because of poor communications, whether, in fact, Dienbienphu was still holding out. (The fortress held out for five weeks more.)

Dulles backed up Radford. If Indo-China fell and if its fall led to the loss of all of Southeast Asia, he declared, then the United States might eventually be forced back to Hawaii, as it was before the Second World War. And Dulles was not complimentary about the French. He said he feared they might use some disguised means of getting out of Indo-China if they did not receive help soon.

The eight legislators were silent: Senator Majority Leader Knowland and his G.O.P. colleague Eugene Millikin, Senator Minority Leader Lyndon B. Johnson and his Democratic colleagues Richard B. Russell and Earle C. Clements, House G.O.P. Speaker Joseph Martin and two Democratic House leaders, John W. McCormack and J. Percy Priest.

What to do? Radford offered the plan he had in mind once Congress passed the joint resolution.

Some two hundred planes from the thirty-one-thousand-ton U.S. Navy carriers *Essex* and *Boxer*, then in the South China Sea ostensibly for "training," plus land-based U.S. Air Force planes from bases a thousand miles away in the Philippines, would be used for a single strike to save Dienbienphu.

The legislators stirred, and the questions began.

Radford was asked whether such action would be war. He replied that we would be in the war.

If the strike did not succeed in relieving the fortress, would we follow up? "Yes," said the chairman of the Joint Chiefs of Staff.

Would land forces then also have to be used? Radford did not give a definite answer.

In the early part of the questioning, Knowland showed enthusiasm for the venture, consistent with his public statements that something must be done or Southeast Asia would be lost.

But as the questions kept flowing, largely from Democrats, Knowland lapsed into silence.

Clements asked Radford the first of the two key questions: "Does this plan have the approval of the other members of the Joint Chiefs of Staff?"

"No," replied Radford.

"How many of the three agree with you?"

"None."

"How do you account for that?"

"I have spent more time in the Far East than any of them and I understand the situation better."

Lyndon Johnson put the other key question in the form of a little speech. He said that Knowland had been saying publicly that in Korea up to ninety per cent of the men and the money came from the United States. The United States had become sold on the idea that that was bad. Hence in any operation in Indo-China we ought to know first who would put up the men. And so he asked Dulles whether he had consulted nations who might be our allies in intervention.

Dulles said he had not.

The Secretary was asked why he didn't go to the United Nations as in the Korean case. He replied that it would take too long, that this was an immediate problem.

There were other questions. Would Red China and the Soviet Union come into the war if the United States took military action? The China question appears to have been sidestepped, though Dulles said he felt the Soviets could handle the Chinese and the United States did not think that Moscow wanted a general war now. Further, he added, if the Communists feel that we mean business, they won't go "any further down there," pointing to the map of Southeast Asia.

John W. McCormack, the House Minority Leader, couldn't resist temptation. He was surprised, he said, that Dulles would look to the "party of treason," as the Democrats had been called by Joe McCarthy in his Lincoln's Birthday speech under G.O.P. auspices, to take the lead in a situation that might end up in a general shooting war. Dulles did not reply.

In the end, all eight members of Congress, Republicans and Democrats alike, were agreed that Dulles had better first go shopping for allies. Some people who should know say that Dulles was carrying, but did not produce, a draft of the joint resolution the President wanted Congress to consider.

The whole meeting had lasted two hours and ten minutes. As they left, the Hill delegation told waiting reporters they had been briefed on Indo-China. Nothing more.

This approach to Congress by Dulles and Radford on behalf of the President was the beginning of three weeks of intensive effort by the Administration to head off disaster in Indo-China. Some of those at the meeting came away with the feeling that if they had agreed that Saturday to the resolution, planes would have been winging toward Dienbienphu without waiting for a vote of Congress—or without a word in advance to the American people.

For some months now, I have tried to put together the bits and pieces of the American part in the Indo-China debacle. But before relating the sequel, it is necessary here to go back to two events that underlay the meeting just described—though neither of them was mentioned at that meeting.

On March 20, just two weeks earlier, General Paul Ely, then French Chief of Staff and later commander in Indo-China, had arrived in Washington from the Far East to tell the President, Dulles, Radford, and others that unless the United States intervened, Indo-China would be lost. This was a shock of earthquake proportions to leaders who had been taken in by their own talk of the Navarre Plan to win the war.

In his meetings at the Pentagon, Ely was flabbergasted to find that Radford proposed American intervention without being asked. Ely said he would have to consult his government. He carried back to Paris the word that when France gave the signal, the United States would respond.

The second event of importance is the most difficult to determine accurately. But it is clear that Ely's remarks started a mighty struggle within the National Security Council, that inner core of government where our most vital decisions are worked out for the President's final O.K. The argument advanced by Radford and supported by Vice-President Nixon and by Dulles was that Indochina must not be allowed to fall into Communist hands lest such a fate set in motion a falling row of dominoes.

Eisenhower himself used the "row-of-dominoes" phrase at a press conference on April 7. On April 15, Radford said in a speech that Indo-

China's loss "would be the prelude to the loss of all Southeast Asia and a threat to a far wider area." On April 16 Nixon, in his well-publicized "off-the-record" talk to the newspaper editors' convention, said that if the United States could not otherwise prevent the loss of Indo-China, then the Administration must face the situation and dispatch troops. And the President in his press conference of March 24 had declared that Southeast Asia was of the "most transcendent importance." All these remarks reflected a basic policy decision.

It is my understanding, although I cannot produce the top secret NSC [National Security Council] paper to prove it, that some time between Ely's arrival on March 20 and the Dulles-Radford approach to the Congressional leaders on April 3, the NSC had taken a firm position that the United States could not afford the loss of Indo-China to the Communists, and that if it were necessary to prevent that loss, the United States would intervene in the war—*provided* the intervention was an allied venture and *provided* the French would give Indo-China a real grant of independence so as to eliminate the colonialism issue. The decision may have been taken at the March 25 meeting. It is also my understanding that this NSC paper has on it the approving initials "D.D.E."

On March 29, Dulles, in a New York speech, had called for "united action" even though it might involve "serious risks," and declared that Red China was backing aggression in Indo-China with the goal of controlling all of Southeast Asia. He had added that the United States felt that "that possibility should not be passively accepted but should be met by united action."

The newspapers were still full of reactions to this speech when the Congressional leaders, at the April 3 secret meeting with Dulles and Radford, insisted that Dulles should line up allies for "united action" before trying to get a joint resolution of Congress that would commit the nation to war.

The Secretary lost no time. Within a week Dulles talked with diplomatic representatives in Washington of Britain, France, Australia, New Zealand, the Philippines, Thailand, and the three Associated States of Indo-China—Vietnam, Laos, and Cambodia.

There was no doubt in the minds of many of these diplomats that Dulles was discussing military action involving carriers and planes. Dulles was seeking a statement or declaration of intent designed to be issued by all the nations at the time of the U.S. military action, to explain to the world what we were doing and why, and to warn the Chinese Communists against entering the war as they had done in Korea.

In these talks Dulles ran into one rock of opposition—Britain. Messages flashing back and forth between Washington and London failed to crack the rock. Finally Dulles offered to come and talk the plan over personally with Prime Minister Churchill and Foreign Secretary Anthony Eden. On April 10, just a week after the Congressional meeting, Dulles flew off to London and later went on to Paris.

Whether Dulles told the British about either the NSC decision or about his talks with the Congressional leaders I do not know. But he didn't need to. The British had learned of the Congressional meeting within a couple of days after it happened. When Dulles reached London they were fully aware of the seriousness of his mission.

The London talks had two effects. Dulles had to shelve the idea of immediate intervention. He came up instead with a proposal for creating a Southeast Asia Treaty Organization (SEATO). Dulles felt this was the "united front" he wanted and that it would lead to "united action." He thought that some sort of *ad hoc* organization should be set up at once without waiting for formal treaty organization, and to this, he seems to have felt, Churchill and Eden agreed.

Just what the British did agree to is not clear, apparently not even to them. Dulles, it appears, had no formal SEATO proposal down on paper, while the British did have some ideas in writing. Eden feels that he made it plain that nothing could be done until after the Geneva Conference, which was due to begin in two weeks. But he apparently made some remark about "going on thinking about it" in the meantime.

At any rate, on his return to Washington Dulles immediately called a SEATO drafting meeting for April 20. The British Ambassador (who at this point had just read the Nixon off-the-record speech in the newspaper) cabled London for instructions and was told not to attend any such meeting. To cover up, the meeting was turned into one on Korea, the other topic for the Geneva Conference. Out of this confusion grew a thinly veiled hostility between Dulles and Eden that exists to this day. Dulles felt that Eden had switched his position and suspects that Eden did so after strong words reached London from Prime Minister Nehru in New Delhi.

EDEN AT THE BRIDGE

A few days later, Dulles flew back to Paris, ostensibly for the NATO meeting with Eden, France's Georges Bidault, and others during the week-end just before the Geneva Conference opened.

On Friday, April 23, Bidault showed Dulles a telegram from General Henri-Eugene Navarre, then the Indo-China commander, saying that only a massive air attack could save Dienbienphu, by now under siege for six weeks. Dulles said the United States could not intervene.

But on Saturday Admiral Radford arrived and met with Dulles. Then Dulles and Radford saw Eden. Dulles told Eden that the French were asking for military help at once. An allied air strike at the Vietminh positions around Dienbienphu was discussed. The discussion centered on using the same two U.S. Navy carriers and Philippine-based Air Force planes Radford had talked about to the Congressional leaders.

Radford, it appears, did most of the talking. But Dulles said that if the allies agreed, the President was prepared to go to Congress on the following Monday, April 26 (the day the Geneva Conference was to open) and ask for a joint resolution authorizing such action. Assuming quick passage by Congress, the strike could take place on April 28. Under Secretary of State Walter Bedell Smith, an advocate of intervention, gave the same proposal to French Ambassador Henri Bonnet in Washington the same day.

The State Department had prepared a declaration of intentions, an outgrowth of the earlier proposals in Washington, to be signed on Monday or Tuesday by the Washington ambassadors of the allied nations willing to back the venture in words. As it happened, there were no available British or Australian carriers and the French already were fully occupied. Hence the strike would be by American planes alone, presented to the world as a "united action" by means of the declaration of intentions.

Eden, on hearing all these details from Dulles and Radford, said that this was a most serious proposition, amounting to war, and that he wanted to hear it direct from the French. Eden and Dulles thereupon conferred with Bidault, who confirmed the fact that France was indeed calling desperately for help—though no formal French request was ever put forward in writing.

Eden began to feel like Horatius at the bridge. Here, on the eve of a conference that might lead to a negotiated end of the seven-year-old Indo-China war, the United States, at the highly informal request of a weak and panicky French Government, was proposing military action that might very well lead to a general war in Asia if not to a third world war.

DULLES' RETREAT

Eden said forcefully that he could not agree to any such scheme of intervention, that he personally opposed it. He added his conviction that within forty-eight hours after an air strike, ground troops would be called for, as had been the case at the beginning of the Korean War.

But, added Eden, he alone could not make any such formal decision on behalf of Her Majesty's Government. He would fly to London at once and put the matter before a Cabinet meeting. So far as I can determine, neither Dulles or Bidault tried to prevent this step.

Shortly after Eden flew off that Saturday afternoon, Dulles sat down in the American Embassy in Paris with his chief advisers, Messrs. MacArthur, Merchant, Bowie, and McCardle, and Ambassador Dillon. They composed a letter to Bidault.

In this letter, Dulles told Bidault the United States could not intervene without action by Congress because to do so was beyond the President's Constitutional powers and because we had made it plain that any action we might take could only be part of a "united action." Further, Dulles added, the American military leaders felt it was too late to save Dienbienphu.

American intervention collapsed on that Saturday, April 24. On Sunday Eden arrived in Geneva with word of the "No" from the specially convened British Cabinet meeting. And on Monday, the day the Geneva Conference began, Eisenhower said in a speech that what was being sought at Geneva was a *"modus vivendi"* with the Communists.

All these events were unknown to the general public at the time. However, on Sunday the New York *Times* printed a story (written in Paris under a Geneva dateline) that the U.S. had turned down a French request for intervention on the grounds Dulles had cited to Bidault. And on Tuesday Churchill announced to a cheering House of Commons that the British government was "not prepared to give any undertakings about United Kingdom military action in Indo-China in advance of the results of Geneva" and that "we have not entered into any new political or military commitments."

Thus the Geneva Conference opened in a mood of deepest American gloom. Eden felt that he had warded off disaster and that now there was a chance to negotiate a peace. The Communists, whatever they may have learned of the behind-the-scenes details here recounted, knew that Britain had turned down some sort of American plan of intervention. And with the military tide in Indo-China flowing so rapidly in their favor, they proceeded to stall.

In the end, of course, a kind of peace was made. On June 23, nearly four weeks before the peace, Eden said in the House of Commons that the British Government had "been reproached in some unofficial quarters for their failure to support armed intervention to try to save Dienbienphu. It is quite true that we were at no time willing to support such action . . ."

This mixture of improvisation and panic is the story of how close the United States came to entering the Indo-China war. Would Congress have approved intervention if the President had dared to ask it? This point is worth a final word.

On returning from Geneva in mid-May, I asked that question of numerous Senators and Representatives. Their replies made clear that Congress would, in the end, have done what Eisenhower asked, provided he had asked for it forcefully and explained the facts and their relation to the national interest of the United States.

Whether action or inaction better served the American interest at that late stage of Indo-China war is for the historian, not for the reporter, to say. But the fact emerges that President Eisenhower never did lay the intervention question on the line. In spite of the NSC decision, April 3, 1954, was the day we *didn't* go to war.

14 *Robert Semple*

Who Runs
the Government?

Americans are taught in their high school civics courses that the people rule this nation through an elective process—every two, four or six years —that sufficiently changes the composition of the Federal Government to guarantee that the will of the people will prevail. As usual, however, high school civics and the conventional wisdom are deficient—not totally, but enough to make anyone who knows how Washington actually functions feel very uneasy, indeed.

For the fact of the matter is that we are ruled only partly by our elected officials. We are more pervasively ruled by what is, for all practical purposes, a hidden Government—hidden in the CIA, the Federal Reserve Board and the lowliest echelons of the Department of Housing and Urban Development and all the other vast agencies—a largely invisible but hugely powerful apparatus composed of men, some former business cronies of politicians, who are appointed to their positions (or who win them through competitive Civil Service examinations, thereby ensuring permanent tenure), whose performance is never reviewed by the public at large and whose influence often increases as their careers span different Administrations. These are the members of the permanent

144

bureaucracy—and to many observers they, more than any others, are the real voice and muscle of the Government.

If this sounds alarmist, I would present as evidence a rather cagey politician who does not routinely act on impulse: Richard M. Nixon. Among the more tedious aspects of Mr. Nixon's first four weeks in office, back in 1969, was his systematic effort to win friends and influence people in the sprawling bureaucracies of the capital. His strategy included courtesy calls on each agency and, as White House correspondent for *The New York Times*, I followed him around. My friends thought I had lost my mind, for the visits were seemingly routine and produced little hard news. After the fourth or fifth such visit, I had begun to share their doubts; then I saw something scrawled on a blackboard in a nondescript room on the fourth floor of the Treasury building, which Nixon was scheduled to visit that afternoon. It read in its poetic entirety:

> Roses are red
> Violets are blue
> The President is coming
> To see you.

Quite infantile—and, besides, it didn't scan. But it justified my otherwise barren pilgrimage, because in its simple sarcasm it explained rather well why the President had decided to court the bureaucrats: A lot of them didn't need him, a lot of them didn't like him and he, in turn, was concerned whether, as a minority President propelled into office by the slimmest of margins, he could bend them to his purposes and views.

A few minutes after my discovery, in another room, Mr. Nixon (who did not, as far as I could tell, notice the joyless welcome chalked on the blackboard down the hall) addressed a group of senior civil servants. He commended them for their devotion to nonpartisan duty and pleaded for their continuing loyalty and energy in the years ahead. His ingratiating and at times sanctimonious performance was not without irony. For here was Dick Nixon, a conspicuously loyal member of an earlier Administration that, in 1952, was at best indifferent to and at worst contemptuous of the bureaucrats, especially if they happened to be Democrats. Here, too, was the man who had promised, during the 1968 campaign, to clean house at the State Department. But instead of cleaning house at State or anywhere else, he invited the entrenched army of the Potomac to go right on keeping house.

And all for a very good reason: The bureaucracy is not what it was in 1952. It is larger, and probably more sluggish, and certainly more confident and self-assured. Each agency has built large and loyal constituencies among the public. And each is filled with men who owe their appointments to some earlier President and are protected either by Civil Service regulations or by exemptions written into the law by Eisenhower in 1954 and Johnson in 1966. Like the press—and members of the bureaucracy often regard themselves as a fourth branch of Government—they know that while Presidents and Cabinet members come and go, they remain, guardians of the past and custodians of much of the future.

The presence and the power of the permanent bureaucracy stirs annual debate in the capital and leads to periodic efforts by elected officials, especially the President, to reform the apparatus, to make it a more efficient and responsive instrument of the popular will. It would be a mistake, of course, to think that the continuing struggle between elected officials and the Civil Service involves a perennial fight pitting *all* elected officials against *all* appointed officials. The hostility between the two groups is not endemic. An elected official like the President is responsible, after all, for a good many of the most important Federal appointments (although not so many as is commonly supposed, as we shall see) and—especially if he is clever and chooses shrewdly—he can use those appointments to carry out the policies and pledges set forth in his campaign. He can also use his appointees to obstruct or soften or otherwise obfuscate his announced policies; for example, by naming a conservative administrator to implement proposals that appeared liberal during the campaign. Mr. Nixon's appointment of Maurice Stans as Secretary of Commerce is a case in point; under Stans's guidance, Nixon's repeated campaign pledge to give Negroes a "piece of the action" through black capitalism has come to virtually nothing.

The real issue in Government is not between the elected President and the top men he appoints; Cabinet Secretaries and Undersecretaries can be made to serve his purposes. The real issue is broader: the continuing tension between those who are in some sense vulnerable to the wishes of the electorate (Presidents, Congressmen, even Cabinet members who usually leave office when the President who appointed them is defeated or retires) and those who remain insulated from the electorate through seniority, skill, tenacity, influence or simple anonymity. They make up the permanent bureaucracy. Government cannot work unless the men who carry the popular will to Washington every few years can make an impact on them; and so far, our elected officials haven't been very successful.

This issue—and the tension it produces—is very real and equally frustrates a wide range of men who would not ordinarily be caught in the same room. The late Robert F. Kennedy, for example, was baffled, beaten and ultimately reduced to helpless anger by the refusal of bureaucrats in the Department of Agriculture to cut red tape and deliver free food to the starving children of Mississippi. But it was Senator Strom Thurmond, not widely known for his sensitivity to hungry blacks, who framed the matter most succinctly when he discovered that despite the soothing assurances of a succession of Secretaries of Health, Education and Welfare, the Office of Civil Rights was still sending enforcement agents to South Carolina hell-bent on desegregating Thurmond's school districts. "The trouble around here," he complained, "is that what goes in at the top doesn't come out at the bottom."

That, slightly restated, is the reason Mr. Nixon spent all that time visiting the agencies in the first month of his Presidency. He simply wanted to make certain (or, more precisely, give himself a fighting chance) that the policies he put into the agencies at the top through his appointed Cabinet Secretaries and Undersecretaries would emerge at the bottom, in time, as operational programs. As economist and management expert Peter Drucker has astutely observed, the "strong" President nowadays is not a man of shining vision but one who knows how to make the lions of the bureaucracy do his bidding. Some would argue—as Tom Wicker did in *Playboy's* October 1970 issue—that more is required of a President than administrative skill, especially in these times; but it is equally true that a President who fails to tame the bureaucrats is doomed to an unhappy tenure.

It is to the White House, of course, that the sensible man takes himself when he wants to find governmental frustration of the purest sort. For it is at the White House—even the Nixon White House—that the visions are the largest and the eagerness to influence the rest of the body politic most evident. It is there that the bureaucrat who resists official policy, or fails to understand it, or simply bungles it, causes the most pain. Consider the following example.

Last year, my wife and I invited one of the President's senior domestic advisors and his wife to dinner at the Five Crowns restaurant in California's Newport Beach, a favorite hangout for key Nixon staffers when their boss is resting at his elegant compound in San Clemente, some 25 miles down the coast. At one point in the evening, my wife innocently asked our guest how she could effectively join the fight against pollution. The aide first suggested that she join some citizens' campaign to clean up the Potomac. Then he paused, as if dissatisfied with his answer, and, at a decibel level he rarely reaches (judging by the startled expression on his wife's face), he said with passion: "The other thing you can do is go sit on Carl Klein's doorstep, and sit there and sit there, until he gets off his tail and does something!"

Carl Klein was then the Assistant Secretary of Interior for Water Resources, and it was the White House's considered judgment that he had done little or nothing to assist the Administration's efforts to enforce water-pollution standards and chase down errant industrialists and dirty municipalities. As it turned out, my wife was not required to track down Klein at the Department of the Interior, since he was gone a few weeks later. He had been appointed by the President—more precisely, rammed down the President's throat by the late Everett McKinley Dirksen, whose protégés are still scattered all over the Government—and when the time came for his dismissal, he was forced to accept the awful uncertainty that burdens most Presidential appointees. As Wally Hickel discovered, the Lord giveth and the Lord taketh away.

But there are not many men like Klein whom the President can easily get at if he decides they aren't measuring up. The reason is that his true powers of appointment are less than they are commonly supposed to be. A study by *Congressional Quarterly* early in the Administration, for instance, pointed out that the potential political patronage open to the new regime amounted to about 6500 Federal jobs with a total minimum annual salary of $106,400,000. But this was a misleading figure, because no President can expect to fill all those jobs with new people (there's never enough time); many of the officials he does manage to appoint become captives of the bureaucracies they're supposed to run; and a sizable percentage (nearly one third) of the 6500 posts are already occupied by holdovers with status acquired through good service and seniority, who cannot be removed except for cause—moral or professional turpitude—that is usually impossible to prove.

It should also be noted that the 6500 posts over which the President theoretically has some influence constitute only a tiny fraction, a mere platoon, of the Federal army, which now numbers some 3,000,000 civilian employees. And these are not all mail carriers. Among them are men with the capacity, judgment and acumen to make or break policy by expediting or obstructing programs at the middle and lower levels.

Finally, there seem to be entire agencies (never mind the individual bureaucrats) that remain impervious to Presidential suggestion, because they have either powerful allies in Congress or influential constituencies among the citizenry. The Soil Conservation Service, the Forestry Service and some of the regulatory agencies—most notably, the Federal Trade Commission—have acquired independent lives of their own, as Ralph Nader never tires of pointing out. Neither John Gardner nor Bob Finch could make a dent in the welfare bureaucracy at HEW; thus, the only hope for a radical change in the welfare system would seem to be an overhaul of the laws governing that agency, as implied in Nixon's proposed Family Assistance Program. The Office of Economic Opportunity was dominated (until Nixon effectively reduced the scope of its power last year) not so much by the Republicans he named to run it as by holdover Democrats wedded to the more aggressive pace of Lyndon Johnson's Great Society. Meanwhile, the Bureau of Public Roads has remained a powerful obstacle to the efforts of successive Secretaries of Transportation to make highways the servant, rather than the master, of constructive land use and population growth. And every time the President or some conservation-minded Congressman sets out to save this or that ecological treasure, he finds that the Army Corps of Engineers has already planned some project in the area and is stubbornly resisting efforts to cancel it.

The outstanding case of bureaucratic isolation from the popular will is, of course, the Federal Reserve Board, whose independence stems from the deep-seated and honestly motivated conviction that politicians should not be allowed to monkey around with the money supply. Johnson ranted and raved at William McChesney Martin when L. B. J. wanted easier credit, but his shouting came to little, because Martin—then nearing the end of the 14-year term of which FRB chairmen are assured—was legally accountable to no one but himself and his system. Mr. Nixon seems to be getting along quite well with Arthur Burns, his choice to succeed Martin, but there are signs of strain below the surface.

The usual Presidential response to the problem of ineffective and sluggish bureaucracies is to strengthen the White House staff, in the apparent belief that enough manpower and expertise concentrated at the top can overcome timidity and/or inertia down below. This phenomenon has been noted by Robert C. Wood, a former political scientist at the Massachusetts Institute of Technology and now president of the University of Massachusetts. Wood served as Under-secretary of the Department of Housing and Urban Development in the Johnson Administration, an experience that taught him as much as he had ever imparted to his students about the practical problems of translating the wishes of elected officials into administrative reality. During Wood's tenure, for instance, longtime employees of the Urban Renewal program (which had been a separate entity before the creation of HUD) showed little enthusiasm for —and in one case, to my personal knowledge, lobbied against—the Model Cities program proposed by L. B. J. and authorized by Congress, on grounds that the new program would diminish the funds available for urban renewal. During this same period—just to add to the Under-secretary's frustrations—the Federal Housing Administration (another separate entity in the pre-HUD days) actively resisted administrative orders and legislative proposals requiring Model Cities to provide insurance for homes built in low-income areas. FHA had always spent most of its mortgage money in the suburbs, where the risks were low, and its officials did not relish the thought of (a) overturning three decades of tradition, a powerful influence in most bureaucracies, and (b) risking their good records with the General Accounting Office by placing the full faith and credit of the Federal Government behind rehabilitated housing in the slums.

However, as Wood has observed, the predictable response to these and similar problems—strengthening the supervisory capability of the President and increasing the size and visibility of the White House staff—has not solved them. On the contrary, the predictable response has produced a predictable result: the creation of even more bureaucracies that, without meaning to, further erode the President's capacity to turn the general guidelines of Government policy into actionable programs that fulfill the promise of that policy. The classic illustration is the old Budget Bureau, which has evolved over the years from a modest accounting organization charged with drawing up the annual budget—a rather generalized form of bureaucratic overview—into an immensely powerful, immensely professional agency that has added to its original functions an enormous degree of *operational* authority. The average Cabinet member cannot make a move, practically speaking, without getting prior clearance from the Budget Bureau. In Wood's time, for example, the Budget Bureau not only determined how much the housing agency could ask for to finance its Open Space program for the central cities but also—after Congress had appropriated the funds—involved itself intimately in the political and administrative process of allocating the money among competing cities and suburbs.

A case can be made—and probably ought to be—that the increasing powers of the Budget Bureau are the inevitable result of the failures of the lower bureaucracy, that the vast agencies of Government would never accomplish anything unless the Budget Bureau, acting as the loyal, competent, unbiased servant of the President, constantly prodded those agencies into some form of action. This would be a compelling argument, except for one small but ineluctable fact: This is still a Government in which the Cabinet occupies a large role, however symbolic that role may be. We have not figured out a way to get rid of the Cabinet. Cabinet officers still run the departments, at least in theory. Federal employees still look to their Secretaries and Undersecretaries for leadership and guidance. They regard the Budget Bureau—and this is important—as just another level of the bureaucracy, to be obeyed but not to be inspired by. In their view, the Budget Bureau intimidates and, in the end, emasculates their own bosses, who must grapple with it at budget time, surrender to its business-office mentality and, if so ordered, abandon programs on which those very bureaucrats, not to mention the Secretary himself, may have spent a great deal of time, energy and imagination. Thus, the Budget Bureau historically has tended to dampen agency morale and has inhibited the very efficiency in execution that, through its intervention in operational matters, it is trying to achieve.

Much the same criticism has been aimed at Mr. Nixon's recent reorganization of his own staff, which in itself demonstrates that the impulse to reshuffle at the top in order to achieve results at the bottom remains unabated among those who occupy, with mounting frustration, the theoretical pinnacle of power. In brief, what Mr. Nixon did last year was to name White House staffer John Ehrlichman chief executive officer of a new Domestic Council to oversee the creation of domestic policy; simultaneously, he named George Shultz—then Secretary of Labor—to head the new Office of Management and Budget, whose mandate includes not only the budget-making functions of the old Budget Bureau but also a vastly expanded management operation. In effect, Shultz is supposed to ride herd on the agencies and thus make sure that Ehrlichman's policies are translated into workable programs.

It sounds beautiful—and may turn out to be, in actual practice—but there are those who wonder whether the old problems (of morale and efficiency) won't soon begin to resurface. Despite the disclaimers of the new scheme's architects—a commission headed by Roy Ash of Litton Industries, who recommended the reorganization to the President—it may be that OMB interposes yet another layer (a supermanagement agency, if you will) between the President and the Cabinet departments, demoting the latter yet another notch. Given the obstructionism of lower-level bureaucrats in the old days, when things were pretty well decentralized, it may be a very good idea, indeed, to concentrate more responsibility in the Executive office of the President. But one wonders how many men of stature and competence will henceforth take on demanding Cabinet and sub-Cabinet jobs when they know they will be dealing not with the President but with a couple of guys named Shultz and Ehrlichman and their successors.

Beyond that: Can *any* reorganization at the top of the Executive branch solve the problems below? As I have suggested, the problems are formidable and are complicated by tenure, by timidity, by politics, by some inherent malaise that seems to turn bright men into paper-shuffling ciphers. What, for example, can Ehrlichman-Shultz do about Mississippi Congressman Jamie Whitten? Nick Kotz, an enterprising reporter for

The Washington Post, once called Jamie Whitten the Permanent Secretary of Agriculture. He is not a bureaucrat but an elected official who knows how to manipulate bureaucrats and exploit their fears. As chairman of the House Appropriations Subcommittee on Agriculture, Whitten has used the power of the purse for 20 years to persuade middle-echelon officials in the Department of Agriculture to promote those programs that help the commercial farmer (cotton growers, in particular), while blocking or minimizing the impact of nearly every constructive effort to alleviate hunger among the black poor. During the Johnson Administration, for example, when the White House and the Budget Bureau were chock-full of well-intentioned liberals, Whitten managed to persuade officials in both Agriculture and HEW to drop Mississippi from a list of states targeted for a malnutrition survey. Kotz accurately points out that in the quiet process of hidden power, a bureaucrat in the Agriculture Department reacts more quickly to a raised eyebrow from Jamie Whitten than to a direct order from the Secretary himself.

There is very little that any President can do—especially if he wants Whitten's votes on other issues—to curb this sort of power. He might as well attempt to dislodge the chairman of the Federal Reserve Board, for Whitten's constituents seem disposed to grant him permanent tenure— and, besides that, there are probably any number of officials in the Department of Agriculture who would suffer some kind of professional collapse if Whitten were suddenly no longer around to give them guidance.

The long and short of it is that any President—confronted with a bureaucracy that succumbs to the Whittens of this world—has very little leeway. After Eisenhower was elected in 1952, Harry Truman was overheard to remark: "He'll sit right here and he'll say, 'Do this, do that,' and nothing will happen. Poor Ike! It won't be a bit like the Army. He'll find it very frustrating." Or, as McGeorge Bundy, who tussled with the problems of national security in the Kennedy Administration, has observed, "The ablest of Presidents, with the most brilliant and dedicated of Executive office staffs, simply cannot do it alone."

Ironically, however, there is one area of public policy in which the President has great leverage to work his will: foreign affairs. While the Whittens and the obstructionists at HUD cannot easily be removed, the strangle hold that various bureaucrats and appointed dignitaries have had on the conduct of foreign policy for 20 years can easily be broken simply by not appointing them again. It is worth mentioning the existence of an entrenched foreign-policy bureaucracy, if only because when people start complaining of inertia in Government, they tend to think exclusively of the domestic agencies. But the international arena also abounds with people who are similarly immune from public review. One need only peruse the columns written by James Reston of *The New York Times* to discover who some of them are: the Achesons, Lovetts, McCloys, Nitzes, Harrimans, Cliffords, Gilpatrics and McNamaras. Many arose in the Truman years and went to ground in the Eisenhower era, but the first thing John Kennedy did after pledging to get the country moving again was to reach back and resurrect them. Richard Nixon has his own equivalents, all cut to the same establishmentarian, Cold Warrior pattern. He kept Henry Cabot Lodge at the Paris peace talks (David Bruce, another old hand, replaced him) and he has stuck with Ellsworth Bunker as ambassador in Saigon. And there has been no real house cleaning at State.

To the anti-Cold Warrior who resents the refusal of Presidents to infuse the foreign-policy process with new blood and who regards the foreign-policy establishment as so many interchangeable parts, the solution is instantly clear: Fire or sensibly retire the architects of the old order or elect a President with a new foreign policy. In short, find a new boy, someone who has not so fully absorbed the diplomacy of the Cold War that he feels compelled, quadrennially, to seek counsel from those who have provided the rhetoric and the policies that sustain the Cold War. But this simple remedy, unfortunately, is not applicable to the domestic agencies, to the middle-level officials in HEW nor HUD nor the Bureau of Roads nor the Corps of Engineers nor the OMB nor the Agency for International Development nor the Departments of Interior and Agriculture and Justice. Canonized by some earlier ruler, their positions secured by acceptable performance and consolidated by tenure, they remain fugitives from the men who are supposed to exercise some authority over them—but easy prey for the Jamie Whittens. Is it therefore true that nothing can be done to give elected officials greater control over the bureaucracy they inherit? No. The prospects for reform are not hopeless. One partial remedy would be to strengthen the roles of individual Cabinet members. The people on the Ash Commission who devised the reorganization plan under which Ehrlichman became head of the Domestic Council and Shultz boss of the OMB genuinely hoped that the scheme would strengthen the ties between the President and his principal appointive officers instead of inserting another layer between them. To his credit, Ehrlichman has attempted, through a complex system of *ad hoc* subcommittees that meet regularly at the White House, to bring Cabinet members into an intimate, day-to-day relationship with himself and other key members of Nixon's palace guard. If successful, this system ought to give members of the Cabinet a larger stake in policy making and, in time, infuse the vast structures around them with a greater sense of purpose.

Moreover, once it's clearly established that policy is to be made at the top, the men in the middle and at the bottom may acquire a sharper definition of their own roles, which are (or ought to be) essentially operational, nonpolitical and professional. Robert Wood recalls that when he was Undersecretary of the Department of Housing and Urban Development, both Congress and the White House tried hard to arrange for greater coordination between ordinary citizens and local governments in the administration of antipoverty programs. Federal administrators at the local level, however, he complains, "never changed the signals." The will of the President and Congress was thus thwarted, and Wood suggests that new disciplinary measures be devised by the bureaucracy itself to ensure that people on the operational level behave like trained professionals rather than amateurs "intoxicated by visions" of making policy on their own.

When Wood complains about operational types in the permanent bureaucracy who imagine themselves to be policy makers, he and others who share his objections are expressing (sometimes tacitly, often openly) the wistful hope that someday the American Civil Service might be refashioned to resemble more nearly its British counterpart. It is generally conceded that the British version works infinitely better and the reasons are not hard to find. One—as Wood has already suggested in his plea for more professionalism in American Government—is that to be a public servant in Britain is to occupy a post of considerable public prestige. The British civil service is free from patronage and its members are not routinely regarded as drudges or even, for that matter, as bureaucrats, which in America is not a kind word. Henry Kissinger, for instance, is constantly referring to men in the State Department as bureaucrats and the contempt in his voice is not calculated to elevate morale in Foggy Bottom. More important, perhaps, is the fact that a clear distinction is and always has been made in Britain between the functions of elected officials and those of the civil service. In Britain, the Prime Minister and his Cabinet (whose officers must all be elected members of Parliament) are solely responsible for *policy* in the broadest sense. The civil service is responsible for the *operation* of that policy. There is none of the confusion of roles that so bedeviled a man like Wood, who found his underlings continuously meddling with what he thought was his and the President's policy.

But unless we can transform our own Civil Service overnight (and I seriously doubt that we can), my feeling is that Government will not work until Congress makes it work. The President and his principal officers in Government can do very little to master the agencies as long as the bureaucrats can play Congress off against the Executive—as long as they can run to Congressman Whitten or to somebody like him whenever they get into trouble or whenever they disagree with orders passed down by their superiors. The public may want a national malnutrition survey; the President may want it; the Cabinet and sub-Cabinet officers (appointed by the President and, therefore, responsive to him) may want it. But the middle-echelon shuffler, responsive to Whitten, may not want it, and if he can get enough like-minded people together, he can either dissuade his boss from undertaking the project or simply sabotage it. But the Whitten example is an extreme one. The fundamental problem goes beyond the Whittens to embrace not only those isolated Congressmen who, hand in glove with their bureaucratic allies, work actively to sabotage policy but also all those in Congress who, because of apathy or overwork, just don't care what happens to their programs after the legislative process has ended and the bureaucracy has taken control. What we're talking about, in short, is Congressional accountability for the performance of the Executive branch.

Astoundingly enough, given the amount of energy expended by Congress to invent programs, not to mention the enormous sums authorized for them, the men on the Hill make very little effort to monitor the subsequent performance of their own creations. Bad programs—flawed at conception—not only survive but flourish. Good programs are allowed to founder. Programs with a terminal date of, say, five years are often renewed with little opposition. By then, they have acquired momentum and allies—a bureaucracy in Washington to manage them and a constituency in the country to keep them alive. Ask a typical Congressman how he keeps track of the bureaucracy and he will reply, "Through the GAO"—the General Accounting Office, an extension of Congress that not only publishes the least-read reports in Washington but concerns itself almost exclusively with accounting procedures. The GAO is interested mainly in discovering waste in Government programs and establishing efficiency; but the GAO never really asks the relevant questions, namely: Is the program doing the job expected of it by Congress and are the men in charge of it any good?

Some brand-new mechanism will have to be devised to make crucial value judgments like these. There has never been any shortage of suggestions. I recall with nostalgia Daniel Patrick Moynihan's appearance five years ago before the subcommittee on government reorganization chaired by Senator Abraham Ribicoff. The hearings still stand as the largest compendium anywhere of good (and unused) suggestions on how the Government might better organize itself to attack the problems of the cities. Among the simplest and best of the ideas was Moynihan's proposal for a permanent, well-staffed office to monitor the effectiveness of Government programs. The office would be directly responsible not to the bureaucracy but to Congress and would make stiff recommendations for improving flawed programs or for canceling them altogether, along with the various bureaucratic appendages that have lost their usefulness. On a more modest level, Charles L. Schultze, L. B. J.'s Budget Director, has suggested that Congress can do as much if not more than the Executive branch to control the dollar-happy bureaucrats in the Pentagon; he suggests, for this purpose, that Congress set up a joint committee on the military budget to help establish priorities in the national-security area. Both committees would be staffed with skilled professionals capable of making tough judgments and remaining immune from bureaucratic or political pressures.

It may be argued that, by superimposing Congressional review on the workings of the bureaucracy, we might risk years of patient effort to protect the administrative structure from the political process. This of course, is a basic rationale for having a Civil Service in the first place. However, as Drucker has noted, the safeguards we have devised to protect the existing machinery from the distortions and pressures of politics "also protect the incumbents in the agencies from the demands of performance." And the monitoring functions that Moynihan and Schultze suggested would not require intense surveillance and day-to-day snooping. They would simply produce well-researched judgments as to whether agency A or bureau B or program C was effectively producing the results originally intended. The committees would then recommend revision or automatic abandonment or at least extensive public hearings to put the agency or the program back on course. Given this prospect, even the most deeply entrenched official would soon become more responsive —to his superiors, to the President and (through them) to the public, which nowadays has little notion of what the bureaucrat is up to and an even slimmer chance of finding out.

15 J. Malcolm Moore

To Provide
for the
Common Defense

A constitutional mini-crisis manufactured in the House Armed Services Committee in 1961 threatened so many other military policy makers into reaction that a rare opportunity emerged—an opportunity to dissect United States military policy making and to examine *who* does *what* and *how* they do it. *How* decisions are made and *who* makes them regularly determine *what* they are. The RS-70 aircraft was the center of this unusual dispute which spotlighted military policy-making routines.

In terms of money spent and personnel employed, to say nothing of national survival, decisions concerning the military have greater impact than decisions in any other realm of U.S. national governmental policy. Critical as such decisions are, the U.S. Constitution is scant help in an effort to determine *how* military policy is made. Specific situations frequently place two or more provisions of the Constitution into conflict. This is true even when each provision is clear on its face, which is not always the case. The sections of the Constitution which create the framework for establishing U.S. military posture are examples of just such am-

This selection was written expressly for this volume.

biguity: Congress shall "provide for the common Defense and general Welfare," "raise and support Armies," and "provide and maintain a Navy," but the president is Commander-in-Chief of the Armed Services. Does this mean that the president is in supreme and complete command of forces which are selected and armed by Congress? Of course not, but the relationship often remains ambiguous and obscure.

Military policy is not unique. Those who must make the Constitution work find that the generalities of the Framers frequently left open the specific rules for policy making. What the rules are and how they changed between 1945 and the second anniversary of the Nixon presidency are the topics which anchor this essay. Four specific themes recur. First, members of Congress possess certain techniques and labor under definite limitations as they encounter policies formed in the executive branch. Second, both congressional and executive policy makers treat *structural* (domestic) aspects of military policy differently from the way they treat *strategic* (international) components. Third, congressional-executive patterns of interaction underscore the importance of strategic decision-making procedures in the executive branch. Finally, changes in forms, formats, and forums of decision making impose trade-offs; advantages gained through change usually mean that other advantages, previously enjoyed, are lost.

THE RS-70 CONTROVERSY

The RS-70 controversy overflowed with illustrations of decision-making trade-offs. The B-70 bomber was redesignated RS-70 in 1962 and given a reconnaissance-strike mission after two presidents and four secretaries of defense refused to fund fully the prototype development program. The B-70 first became an Air Force budget request item for fiscal year 1954 (FY54). It was conceived as a manned bomber designed to fly at about 2,200 miles per hour at altitudes of about 70,000 feet. The aircraft originally was scheduled to be operational in 1964. The program was terminated some ten years after it began, although cutbacks began in 1958. Spokesmen for the Air Force continued to hope, during most of the ten years, that by the early 1970s North American Aviation, Inc. would produce and that the Air Force would have the RS-70, nee B-70.[1]

Air Force representatives were active rather than passive in at-

---

[1] U.S. Congress, House, Subcommittee of the Committee on Appropriations, *Hearings on Department of Defense Appropriations for 1961*, 86th Congress, 2nd Session, 1960, Part 2, pp. 249–59; Part 6, pp. 33–38; and the *New York Times* (March 8, 1952), p. 14.

tempting to realize their hopes for the RS-70. They convinced the chairman and members of the House Armed Services Committee that funding for the RS-70 program for FY63 should be $491 million instead of the $171 million asked by President John F. Kennedy and his secretary of Defense, Robert S. McNamara.

Constitutional Threats and Tests

Chairman Carl Vinson exploited an unusual, possibly unique, tactic as he sought to boost the president's RS-70 budget request to the total sought by Air Force spokesmen. He and the other members of the House Armed Services Committee threatened a constitutional test between Congress and the Executive. Specifically, they threatened to recommend, to the full House, *authorizing* legislation which *directed* the secretary of the Air Force to enter into contracts that had been forbidden by the secretary of defense. If passed, the legislation would have directed the secretary of the Air Force to utilize an authorization of $320 million more than President Kennedy requested in FY63 for an RS-70 weapons system.[2]

A move to "direct" expenditures deviated dramatically from the usual approach in committees which authorize the Executive to act and to spend. Members of such committees typically recommend to their parent houses that an executive official be *authorized* to spend specific amounts for stated purposes. Each authorization bill, if and when it passes both houses of Congress, contains two implied conditions. The first condition is that the Appropriations Committees and the Congress will appropriate enough money to fulfill the authorization, which often does not happen. The second condition is that the president or his subordinates will spend any or all of the appropriated money, which sometimes does not occur either.

Threats by members of Congress to direct specific action by an executive official exposed the sensitive, gray area where congressional and executive authority overlap. Implemented to its fullest, this concept would leave the Commander in Chief with command of his forces and also with his forces armed with weapons selected and supplied against the presidential will by another authority—Congress.

The threatened directive also set Congress against itself in complicated ways. Members of the House Armed Services Committee raised

2U.S. Congress, House, Committee on Armed Services, *Hearings on Military Posture and H. R. 9751, Authorizations for Aircraft, Missiles, and Naval Vessels,* 87th Congress, 2nd Session, 1962, pp. 3171–77, 3897–3920, and 3988. Cited hereafter as *Hearings on H.R. 9571,* 1962.

a potential challenge to several other committees, especially the Senate Armed Services Committee and the Appropriations Committee in each house. Even if the threatened directive were accepted in the House, members of the Senate Armed Services Committee might be unwilling to recommend such a proposal to their parent body. Should they be both willing and able to engineer the directive through the Senate, the House and Senate Appropriations Committees would be severely challenged. In the Appropriations Committees, particularly the House Committee, members traditionally exercise their own independent judgment about how much money should be *appropriated* regardless of how much more has been *authorized*. This is as true for the two Military Appropriations Subcommittees as it is for the parent committees.

Some of the questions raised by the threatened directive suggest why the participants were delighted when the dispute was resolved without the conflict and disruption which answers would have required. (1) If the directive to the Air Force Secretary passed in the House, would members of the House Military Appropriations' Subcommittee be denied their independent judgment on how much money should be appropriated? (2) What would the relevant Senate committees do? (3) If the secretary of defense or the president refused to permit their subordinate to execute the RS-70 contracts, would any of the three of them be subjected to impeachment proceedings? (4) Would the legal duty imposed upon the secretary of the Air Force result in the release of funds by the president? (5) What would occur if the secretary of the Air Force executed contracts against the orders of his superiors in the executive branch?

Whether or not such questions were ever formally posed, they were never answered. President Kennedy and Chairman Vinson reached a compromise the day before the proposal went to the floor of the House. The offending word "directed" was struck and "authorized" was substituted. In exchange for the revised wording, the president and Secretary McNamara agreed to have the RS-70 reevaluated, a commitment McNamara had made more than a month earlier. Vinson made certain, however, that the "proper" interests were represented in the RS-70 re-evaluation group.[3]

Relationships Under Stress

Neither the president nor Vinson nor anyone else forced answers to questions such as those posed above. Answers will not be forced in

---

[3] U.S. Congressional Record, 87th Congress, 2nd Session, 1962, CVIII, pp. 4309–10. Cited hereafter as *C.R., CVIII, 1962.*

this essay either. Instead, this examination is of the relationships among those who shared in governing as they attempted to avoid the tests of strength and will which answers would have required.

The RS-70 disputants did not sink the ship of state; they did rock the boat a bit. When Vinson proposed to *direct* the secretary of the Air Force, he exposed many links which bind together those who share in governing—bind them in ways which make them appear on the verge of flying apart. The particular links which ultimately withstood Vinson's tests were not only within Congress but also within the executive branch and between the two.

Consider the ways in which congressmen are alert to chinks in executive solidarity. Fragmentation in the executive branch often is generated by its three parts: the career bureaucracy (military and civilian), politically appointed members of the administration, and members of the president's staff, institutionalized in the Executive Office of the President.

Bureaucracy. In the RS-70 controversy, the *bureaucracy* was a major spokesman. Bureaucrats constitute the permanent government. They are on the job when any particular president is inaugurated, and they will be there when he leaves. Members of the bureaucracy are often understood to be civilians only, but the military is also a career bureaucracy. Bureaucrats obtain their positions, are retained, and are promoted upon the basis of merit rather than patronage. They are charged with implementing policies made by themselves or by others in the executive branch of Congress, but the ways of implementation may subtly affect these policies or even change them radically.

Administration. Of the 8,000-odd presidential appointees who constitute a president's administration, the ones considered here are department heads and their deputy, under, and assistant secretaries, plus a few others. Appointed by the president, these officials can find their loyalties whip-sawed from above and below. A department head must rely upon the bureaucrats of his department in many essential ways. However, they may, and often do, have policy preferences contrary to the president's and/or the department head's. The buffeting which a member of the administration takes is compounded when his personal preferences differ from those of both his subordinates and his superiors.

Executive Office of the President. Members of the president's staff are often lumped under the term "administration" with department heads and other appointed members of the line organization, but here the "presidency" or the "president's staff" refers to those 1,500 men and women in the Executive Office of the President. With their offices in the

White House or next door in the Executive Office Building, they are physically closer to the president than are bureaucrats and administrators. The members of the president's staff often are psychologically closer to the president, also. If a president is to realize his preferences over those of his administration and the bureaucracy, he usually must rely heavily upon those in the Executive Office of the President. They include, among others, the White House Staff, the Bureau of the Budget (BOB) (and its beefed-up successor the Office of Management and Budget), the Council of Economic Advisors, and the National Security Council.

Participants from Congress, the bureaucracy, the administration, and the Executive Office were involved in the RS-70 controversy and had vested interests in its resolution.

CONGRESSIONAL-EXECUTIVE RELATIONS

The floors of the two congressional houses are major stages where representatives and senators go to posture and to be on display. Committee rooms are where they work, and this is the reason for the emphasis upon committees throughout this essay.

Members of Congress in their committees do not deal with the president; they deal with personnel from the Executive Office of the President. They deal sometimes with department heads, their deputies and assistants; but most often, they deal with the bureau chiefs and those who work in the bureaus. During their annual pilgrimage to Capitol Hill, some bureau spokesmen confront members of committees who seek to *control* them, others who seek to *supervise* them, and others who are content merely to *oversee* them.[4] Some congressmen ask questions that direct attention and tend toward *control:* "Which problems shall we examine?" Another type of question goes toward *supervision,* solving problems and setting priorities: "Which course of action is better?" Other questions simply seek to find out the score so that congress-

---

[4]Malcolm E. Jewell and Samuel C. Patterson, *The Legislative Process in the United States* (New York: Random House, 1966), pp. 484–509; Cornelius P. Cotter, Legislative Oversight, *Congress: The First Branch of Government,* coordinator, Alfred de Grazia (Washington, D.C.: America Enterprise Institute for Public Policy Research, 1966); William E. Rhode, *Committee Clearance of Administrative Decisions* (East Lansing: Michigan State University Bureau of Social and Political Research, 1959); and Joseph P. Harris, *Congressional Control of Administration* (Garden City, N.Y.: Anchor Books, Doubleday, 1964), pp. 9, 195–97, 233–36, and 246–48.

men can watch over what takes place in the bureau: "How well are we doing?"[5]

Control

The most vigorous efforts at *control* occurred in the pre-Constitution period (1775–1781) when members of Congress attempted to administer government through their committees. In the last half of the twentieth century, however, legislators can be said to *control* when they gain their preferences by employing either or both of two techniques: (1) when they specify the exact organizational structure for the bureaus with which they deal, or (2) when they compel bureau personnel to clear administrative decisions with committee members or with committee staff personnel before they can be implemented. *Control* may be exercised by members of Congress individually or collectively, through their committee or through their committee's staff.

Members of the House Armed Services Committee have established their *control* over a limited range of issues, especially real estate transactions. A relatively common device was engineered in 1951; it required personnel in the Defense Department to "come into agreement" with the Armed Services Committees on any military real estate purchase or sale which (1) exceeded $25,000, or (2) equaled $25,000 for a lease of one year or more. After several actual and threatened vetoes, the tactic was changed. Members of the House Armed Services Committee in 1960 substituted the requirement that all military real estate transactions for $50,000 or more be submitted in advance to them and their counterparts in the Senate. A simple resolution passed in either house could negate any transaction.

When administrative decisions, before they are implemented, must first be cleared through committee members or committee staff members, there is the possibility that attention directing, problem solving, and score card questions will be asked both in the Congress and in the executive branch. *Control* does not necessarily mean that every issue will be scrutinized in a congressional committee to determine which problems to solve, how to solve them, or how previous decisions are working. The potential for questioning every issue is there, however. Risks for bureaucrats and their superiors are higher when they ignore that potential with committees which *control* than when they ignore it with committees which *supervise* or *oversee*.

[5]See James G. March and Herbert A. Simon, *Organizations* (New York: Wiley, 1963), pp. 161–62.

When committee members *control* the bureaucracy, policy initiation and innovation (new ideas, new decisions, new policies) flow or grind from complex interactions among committee and bureau personnel. It is usually impossible to determine who proposed (1) problems for solution, (2) alternative solutions, or (3) methods of evaluating the solutions chosen; in any case, congressmen are more likely to initiate and innovate for those issues they *control* than they are for those they *supervise* or *oversee*.

Supervision

Supervision is a less restrictive form of intervention into administrative activities by members of congressional committees. *Supervision* occurs when congressmen basically take for granted that personnel in the Executive are looking at the proper problems. The questions posed by members of such committees are basically limited to *problem solving*. Instead of considering all possible courses of action, congressmen tend to question the specific emphases or priorities established in the executive branch. This means that the persons who decide *what* is to be done and who partially decide *how* it is to be done are administrators not legislators. Congressmen who *supervise* through the activities of their committees substitute their own values, perceptions, preferences, judgment for those of executive officials. The substitution is limited, however, to the order of and emphasis in methods of attacking problems identified by those same executive officials. Innovation and initiation of policy are left to personnel in the executive branch; legislators intervene to change the priorities of those who have already identified not only problems but also solutions.

Members of the House and Senate Appropriations Committees, particularly the House Committee, regularly *supervise*. By rearranging the amounts of money available for specific purposes, members of these committees force priorities to conform to their own preferences.

Oversight

When members of a committee *oversee*, they neither *control* nor *supervise*; they neither innovate nor rearrange priorities established by executive personnel. Through familiarity with a bureau's organization and implementation of policy, legislators use their committee as a "watchdog." They use the telephone and personal meetings to stay abreast of what is taking place. They observe through the press, through complaints from constituents, through information developed as they investigate executive personnel, decisions, and policies.

When members of such committees agree that executive personnel are looking at the wrong problems, coming forward with the wrong solutions, or attacking problems in the wrong order, the congressmen tend to avoid taking over the tasks themselves. In essence they say, to executive officials, "You have things fouled up. Go back and rethink the entire situation: find out what the real problems are; generate genuine solutions; and establish realistic priorities which have a fair chance of solving the actual problems. Put your solutions into operation. Then we will evaluate what you have done."

Oversight by members of congressional committees occurs after innovation and initiation have been launched by executive personnel. Committee members focus upon what personnel of the executive branch are doing, how they are doing it, and with what results. At the outset, decisions about what to do and how to do it are left for those in the executive branch.

Members of the House and Senate Armed Services Committees tend to *oversee* strategic decisions and policy; they prefer to *control* real estate matters.[6]

MILITARY POLICY DECISIONS AND CONGRESSIONAL-EXECUTIVE RELATIONS

Members of every congressional committee face many quandaries: whether to *control*, or to *supervise*, or to *oversee*; to do so *continuously* or *sporadically*; to strive for mastery over issues in the *long run* or in the *short run*. How have these puzzles been resolved by members of the four committees most immediately involved with military policy? In attempting to answer this question for the House and Senate Armed Services Committees and the Military Appropriations Subcommittees of each house, it is essential to differentiate two types of military policy: *structure* and *strategy*. These distinctions then force consideration of a statutory change in 1959 which had a direct bearing upon the RS-70 controversy.

Structure and Strategy

Professor Samuel P. Huntington found that between 1945 and 1960, members of both Armed Services Committees and both Military

---

[6]Harris, *Congressional Control*, pp. 9, 243–50; Lewis Anthony Dexter, "Congressman and the Making of Military Policy," *Components of Defense Policy*, ed. Davis B. Bobrow (Chicago: Rand McNally, 1965), p. 99; and Jewell and Patterson, *The Legislative Process*, p. 491.

Appropriations Subcommittees "participated" with members of the executive branch on matters of *structure* for the armed forces. Structure consists of (1) budget decisions on the size and distribution of the budget; (2) personnel decisions on number, procurement, retention, pay, and working conditions of servicemen and other employees; (3) material decisions on the amount, procurement, and distribution of supplies; and (4) organizational decisions on methods and forms utilized in organizing and administering the armed forces. Structural decisions are made in the "currency of domestic politics": economic prosperity, individual freedom and welfare, inexpensive government, low taxation, economic stability, social welfare. "Participation" in the real estate aspects of structural decisions tended to be in the form of committee *control* by the Armed Services Committees.[7]

During the same 1945 to 1960 period, Professor Huntington found that Congress *did not* play a decisive part in decisions on *strategy*. Strategy includes (1) program decisions dealing with (a) the strength, composition and readiness of military forces, and (b) the readiness, number, type, and development rate of their weapons (for example, *the RS-70*), and (2) use decisions dealing with deployment, commitment, and employment of military forces. Strategic decisions are made in the "currency of international politics": conquest, influence, power, territory, trade, wealth, empire, security.

Members of Congress, between 1945 and 1960, appeared unwilling to interject themselves more decisively into strategic policy making for two reasons. First, members of Congress and executive personnel were generally in agreement concerning foreign policy goals. Such agreement relegated controversy to disputes over alternative solutions rather than disputes over goals. Disputes over programs to reach strategic goals were between and among officials from several executive agencies: the separate branches of the armed services, the Defense Department, the State Department, the Treasury Department, the Budget Bureau, and a few others. Second, no congressional committee possesses either the legal power or the political capability to: (1) bring together and balance all the conflicting interests existing among the executive agencies involved, or (2) effect a compromise among them on strategic programs.

The *site* of strategic decision making between 1945 and 1960 was in the executive branch, but its *character* was legislative. The traditional patterns of legislative conflict and compromise occurred among execu-

[7]Samuel P. Huntington, *The Common Defense: Strategic Programs in National Politics* (New York: Columbia University Press, 1961), pp. 3–4, 131–32, 146–74, 304. Unless otherwise noted, discussions concerning military policy making between 1945 and 1960 are from this source.

tive personnel. A detailed study of the defense budget for fiscal 1950 essentially confirms these conclusions about the *site* and *character* of strategic decision making.[8]

Between 1945 and 1960, members of the two Armed Services Committees and the two Military Appropriations Subcommittees manipulated both control and oversight techniques. Issues which were defined by decision participants as structural (domestic) drew committee *control* or at least *supervision*. On the other hand, when committee members defined an issue as strategic (international), they resorted to *oversight*.[9]

Dispersion of authority in Congress makes it difficult for members of any committee to generate more than *oversight* on strategic issues. Secretaries of state and defense must cultivate close ties with ten committees or subcommittees, and they often must confront some fifteen more committees in justifying important programs or parts of programs.[10] Chairman of the Senate Foreign Relations Committee, J. William Fulbright (D., Arkansas) has observed that Congress occasionally initiates marginal policies (Fulbright exchange scholars, for example) and serves as "legitimator" of Executive policies.[11] This means that when members of Congress approve programs originated within the executive branch, such programs are viewed as legitimate and worthy of citizen compliance.

Insofar as the Indo-Chinese War and Fulbright's committee are adequate indicators of current trends, two tentative conclusions appear reasonable. First, when members of *just one* committee withhold or withdraw their stamp of legitimacy, this rare event has important, restrictive implications for future strategic decisions made by executive personnel. Second, members of a committee do not necessarily *control,* even when they can develop restrictions upon executive flexibility such as the 1971 Cooper-Church resolution, which formally prevents U.S. ground troops from entering Cambodia and Laos. They can put certain decisions off-limits, but they do not then come forward with their own coherent plan for ending or withdrawing from the Indo-Chinese War. They say, in essence, "You have not decided well. With this new guid-

[8]Warner R. Schilling, Paul Y. Hammond, and Glenn H. Snyder, *Strategy, Politics, and Defense Budgets* (New York: Columbia University Press, 1962), pp. 1–272.
[9]Elias Hunzar in his *The Purse and the Sword: Control of the Army by Congress, 1933–1950* (Ithaca, N.Y.: Cornell University Press, 1950) suggests that this relationship predated 1945.
[10]Holbert N. Carroll, "The Congress and National Security Policy," *The Congress and America's Future,* ed. David B. Truman (Englewood Cliffs, N.J.: Prentice-Hall, 1965), p. 152.
[11]James A. Robinson, *Congress and Foreign Policy,* rev. ed. (Homewood, Ill.: Dorsey, 1967), pp. 171–213.

ance and with specific alternatives denied (ground troops in Laos or Cambodia), rethink your strategic problems and alternative solutions.[12]

This approach is somewhat stronger but similar to the mode of the Armed Services Committees and Military Appropriations Subcommittees between 1945 and 1960. When members of these four committees contested strategic decisions, during this fifteen-year period, they operated, for all practical purposes, as lobbyists. They challenged, petitioned, and harrassed decision makers within the executive branch to examine again and defend again their original decison.

If not greater, complexities in military strategy and other foreign policy are less familiar to congressmen than complexities in domestic affairs. Relatedly, only a small portion of the citizenry is attentive to, or conversant about issues of foreign policy. Constitutional, institutional, and behavioral obstacles largely bar congressional initiative and innovation in international relations.[13] Nonetheless, members of the Armed Services Committees, in 1959, engineered through Congress a statutory change with the potential to rearrange their docility in strategic decisions.

The Military Construction Act of 1959: Section 412(b)

From the Senate Armed Services Committee emerged the impetus for section 412(b) of the Military Construction Act of 1959, Public Law 86–149.[14] This section requires *authorizations* prior to appropriations for procurement of aircraft, missiles, or naval vessels (strategic weapons). The authorization measure for fiscal 1963 expanded §412(b) to include all authorizations prior to appropriations for research, development, test, and evaluation for strategic weapons.[15] Subsequent expansions of §412(b) have been for tactical weapons.

Prior to §412(b) members of the two Armed Services Committees

---

[12]Eugene P. Dvorin, ed., *The Senate's War Powers: Debate on Cambodia from the Congressional Record* (Chicago: Markham, 1971), particularly pp. 38ff.

[13]Gabriel A. Almond, *The American People and Foreign Policy* (New York: Praeger, 1961); James N. Rosenau, *Public Opinion and Foreign Policy* (New York: Random House, 1961); and Robert A. Dahl, *Congress and Foreign Policy* (New York: Norton, 1964).

[14]Edward A. Kolodziej, *The Uncommon Defense and Congress, 1945–1963* (Columbus: Ohio State University Press, 1966), pp. 372ff.; and Bernard K. Gordon, "The Military Budget: Congressional Phase," *Journal of Politics*, 23, No. 1 (November 1961), pp. 689–710.

[15]*U.S. Congressional Record*, 87th Congress, 2nd Session, 1962, CVIII, pp. 5833, 5932–33.

had contented themselves with granting general authorities such as one to the Secretary of the Army in 1956. He was to procure "guided missiles," with no item particularized.[16] To obtain particular authority over strategic weapons, members of the Armed Services Committees made their move through structural legislation, a construction bill.

Strategic weapons such as the RS-70 are the concrete manifestations of abstract goals, concepts, and plans. With specific weapons certain strategic goals probably can be realized and particular concepts can be operationalized; others cannot. In other words, a strategic goal such as the defense of Western Europe requires strategic concepts about how that goal can be attained. Strategic weapons become the tools through which the concepts are put into operation. When committee members have an opportunity to ask questions about strategic weapons they possess the potential to question the concepts and the goals those weapons are designed to fulfill. Should questions about strategic concepts and goals flow from questioning about weapons, the trend could be toward *control* and attention direction: Which strategic problems shall we look at? Alternatively, questions about strategic weapons might move toward *supervision,* problem solving and priority setting: Which course of action is better?" Instead, it appears that members of the Armed Services Committees continued to *oversee*; they continued to ask scorecard questions: "How well are we doing?" Under §412(b), they had greater access to and they could focus upon strategic weapons decisions, but they exercised *oversight* techniques; they neither *controlled* nor *supervised* those decisions.[17] House Armed Services Committee Chairman, Carl Vinson, said as much in 1961:

> Up to this time the Departments merely had to request and obtain appropriations for the procurement of these items under these very broad authorities. I am afraid that the end result of this procedure was that members of the Appropriations Committee were the only ones in Congress who actually had very much knowledge of the tremendous programs and expenditures which the Congress was called upon to pass each year. It is my hope that Section 412 has called to a halt this situation. If it did nothing else, it brought 37 more members of the House into the heretofore exclusive area of knowledge of these very large problems.[18]

16Peter Woll, *American Bureaucracy* (New York: Norton, 1963), p. 119.
17Raymond H. Dawson, "Congressional Innovation and Intervention in Defense Policy: Legislative Authorization of Weapons Systems," *American Political Science Review,* 56, No. 1 (March 1962), pp. 42–57; and John Malcolm Moore, "Military Strategy and Legislative Oversight" (Unpublished Ph.D. dissertation, Department of Political Science, University of Georgia, 1969), pp. 60–62, 213–15, 243–55. See, also, Kolodziej, *The Uncommon Defense* pp. 374–401.
18*U.S. Congressional Record,* Daily Edition, May 24, 1961, p. 8218.

Lessons from the RS-70

If new congressional access to and focus upon strategic decisions lie unexploited for control or supervision, what purpose is served by §412(b)? In the RS-70 case, Chairman Vinson and his colleagues employed their broadened warrant to threaten several of those who must deal with them regularly. Without §412(b), the threats would have been unlikely; with §412(b), they were possible. If Vinson settled for no more than a re-examination of the RS-70 that he had already been promised, the threats which §412(b) permitted did not accomplish much—or did they?

Vinson told his fellow members of the House that his accomplishments were fourfold. First, he had dramatized the unwillingness of thoughtful men to rely upon a strategy of massive retaliation only. Second, he had impressed upon the Executive the dangers to the nation of junking manned bombers. Third, he emphasized the depth with which members of the Committee felt about these two issues. Fourth, he wrung from the secretary of defense a reversal of his previous unwillingness to spend more than the requested $171 million for the RS-70.

Vinson explained to the House how this had been accomplished:

> The president is interested now.
> He has injected himself right into the middle of the whole matter.
> And another thing, the committee will get a full assurance that the group making this study will have not only scientists and representatives of the secretary of defense in it, but will have people from the Air Force, not only the technical ones but the policy ones; not only civilians, but military people whose background and experience in the development and operation of bombers gives them special understanding of the problem we are talking about.[19]

At least Vinson and the other members of his committee had put the president and his secretary of defense on notice that some members of Congress have definite expectations concerning the proper composition of decision-making groups within the executive branch. The RS-70 restudy was left to the executive branch, but those participants were selected, at least in part, by Chairman Vinson with the backing of his committee.

Authority in Congress is scattered among many committees, however. The effects of this dispersion appear in a subsequent agreement between Secretary McNamara and members of the House Appropriations Committee. Their authority to reach independent judgments

[19]*C.R.*, CVIII, 1962, p. 4310.

about appropriations also was threatened by Vinson's proposed "direction" to the Secretary of the Air Force and, more generally, by §412(b). Their agreement with McNamara assured members of the House Appropriations Committee that he would not spend the entire appropriation which was itself a reduction to $362 million from the $491 million authorized.[20]

Chairman Vinson overtly grasped for *control* in the RS-70 conflict. Without influential allies in the House Appropriations Committee, it is unclear whether McNamara could have withstood Vinson's use of §412(b) to exercise greater *control* over strategic decisions. The argument here is that the short-run implications of the RS-70 conflict are different from the long-run implications. In the short run, that is, in the RS-70 incident itself, Vinson had particular types of decision makers added. This would fit the earlier definition of *control*, if the change in decision makers had produced a different outcome. It did not, which leads to consideration of long-run outcomes.

"Congress does not want to run the Department of Defense— Congress just wants to sit at the table and get across an idea once in a while."[21] In this quotation, Vinson indicates that his goals might not have been as grand as *control*. In future decisions, what might members of Congress demand? What might they object to? The RS-70 case gave Secretary McNamara a firm clue. When he cut particular types of personnel from specific decision-making forums, some members of Congress would consider that decision questionable. And they would question it, even if this required constitutional confrontations. Thus constrained, executive decision makers might be encouraged to let Congress "sit at the table and get across an idea once in a while."

STRATEGIC DECISIONS WITHIN THE EXECUTIVE BRANCH

Whether Secretary McNamara was inhibited by what he anticipated that members of Congress might do is a moot point. When Chairman Vinson and members of the House Armed Services Committee disputed the RS-70 decision, McNamara was already in the throes of major changes which rearranged the participants in and their impact upon strategic decision making.

McNamara's program of change centered upon four types of proc-

[20]Richard F. Fenno, Jr., *The Power of the Purse: Appropriations Politics in Congress* (Boston: Little, Brown, 1966), p. 72; and Woll, *American Bureaucracy* p. 128.
[21]*C.R.*, CVIII, 1962, p. 4312.

esses for making decisions, introduced here but explained and illustrated subsequently. At the time of the RS-70 confrontation, McNamara already had taken dynamic strides toward introducing *extreme rationality* into the executive decision-making processes which he inherited, barely a year earlier. His special targets were processes characterized as *pluralistic, logrolling,* or *procedurally inclusive.*[22] It is doubtful that Congress could sit at McNamara's table; there was hardly room for many who had sat there previously.

McNamara's format for strategic decision-making eventually overwhelmed many who had participated in such decisions between 1945 and 1960. McNamara and the personnel of his office gained the ability to *direct* or *command* strategic decisions by imposing the extreme rationality of systems (ends-means) analysis. Ends-means analysis requires that the links between needs, objectives, and capabilities be confronted head-on: all were to be exposed, articulated, scrutinized, and examined critically. A program and performance budget system (PPBS) and cost-effectiveness analysis were utilized by McNamara and his staff to accomplish this change which centralized strategic decision making in them. They were able to direct or command particular decisions as a look at an organization chart might mislead one to believe secretaries of defense had done all along. Of course, directions from the secretary's office might be resisted from within a branch of service, as the RS-70 illustrates.

McNamara's techniques struck at the decision-making format utilized at each of three levels: (1) where the size of the military slice from the national budgetary pie was set; (2) where the size of the slice was determined for each branch of service; and (3) where its share was divided within each branch of the armed forces. As the national budgetary pie sliced and the military portion was determined, McNamara's extreme rationality replaced the pluralistic conflict and compromise format which had existed among personnel from several executive agencies: the separate branches of service; the Defense, State, and Treasury Departments; the Budget Bureau; and a few others. As the size of the slice to be devoured by each service branch was determined, McNamara's extreme rationality replaced the pluralistic conflict and compromise format which had existed among the Joint Chiefs of Staff (JCS) as they sought to gain all that they could for their individual service branches. As strategic plans were budgeted within each branch of the armed forces, McNamara's extreme rationality replaced both logrolling and proce-

---

[22]Cf. Paul Y. Hammond, "A Functional Analysis of Defense Department Decision Making in the McNamara Administration," *American Political Science Review,* 62, No. 1 (March 1968), pp. 58–64. Subsequent discussion relies heavily upon this article.

durally inclusive processes. Personnel from one branch of service did not meddle with the internal plans of another branch (logrolling). These internal plans were produced through procedures which had been designed so that personnel were included in decisions which affected their areas of responsibility.

Pluralism

Conventional notions of the free marketplace assume that the "best" product or idea prevails over its competitors, because consumers somehow possess the skills and tools to determine the "best." This is the heart of the pluralist argument.

There are real problems with the pluralist approach. In practice, pluralistic decision making produces a definition of "best" that does not mean "maximum." "Best" more nearly means "satisfactory," that is, that most, if not all, of those affected by a decision can live with it. A way to insure that decisions are tolerable to those directly affected is to have their spokesmen included in the decision-making group. They can put their positions before spokesmen for different economic, ideological, organizational, or other interests. Spokesmen can learn the assumptions and restraints operating among those representing other interests. This does not mean necessarily that anyone will persuade anyone else. It does place participants in a forum where they can bargain, trade, and possibly reach tolerable accommodations.[23]

Bargains, trades, and tolerable solutions were the characteristics of pluralistic decisions which, between 1945 and 1960, allocated dollars for defense and dollars for each branch of service. Pluralism reigned as decisions were made concerning the ratio of military expenditures to domestic expenditures as well as the division of funds among the various branches of the armed forces.

Dollars for defense. Strategic posture for the U.S. was set by the same officials who set specific money amounts which would be asked of Congress for implementation. In the pluralistic format identified by Professor Huntington in the 1945–60 period, participants answered three questions: What are the problems? What are we going to do about them? How much are we going to spend doing it? This latter question throws strategic policy into conflict with domestic programs since money spent for one is not available for the other.

[23]See Almond, *The American People.* Robert A. Dahl, *Who Governs?* (New Haven, Conn.: Yale University Press, 1961), and *Pluralist Democracy in the United States* (Chicago: Rand McNally, 1967). Cf. March and Simon, *Organizations,* ch. 6.

The participants in strategic planning and funding decisions between 1945 and 1960 brought to their task several different perspectives and priorities. These differences were reconciled through pluralistic or command compromise rather than by direction or command from the President or anyone else. The Chief-of-Staff and members of his staff for each branch of service spoke for the various Army, Navy, Air Force, and Marine Corps interests which they represented in the Defense Department. The secretary of defense and other civilian appointees of the president in the Defense Department spoke from their perspectives, wedged as they were between the priorities of the president and the priorities of the diverse interests of each service branch which they purportedly directed. The secretary of state and his staff members brought to strategic decisions the demands that their particular foreign policies might impose. For example, the North Atlantic Alliance, constructed by Secretary of State John Foster Dulles, demanded particular numbers and placement of military personnel and equipment as well as certain amounts of money. The Treasury Department houses not only the revenue collectors and the revenue but also economists who project future revenue collections and needs. Personnel from Treasury, therefore, possess data concerning levels of funding available for strategic programs as well as domestic programs. Secretary of the Treasury George Humphrey also was reportedly President Eisenhower's closest advisor on matters of the economy as was Dulles for foreign affairs.[24] Presidential budgeting expertise during the 1945 to 1960 period was in the Bureau of the Budget (BOB). BOB personnel traditionally have enforced presidential priorities upon the bureaucracy and funneled disputes about funding upward to the president. Personnel from the White House Staff as well as those from BOB (both in the Executive Office of the President) supported presidential priorities, domestic and foreign, when they differed from those of departmental participants. Conflict followed by compromise among these officials specified strategic problems, general solutions to those problems, and how much of the national treasure the president would ask Congress to devote to solutions.

Dollars for each branch of service. Answers to a pair of questions were left to those charged with putting strategic plans into operation: (1) Who is to spend what monies, and (2) for what are the monies to be spent? The first of these questions was also answered in a pluralistic format by the Joint Chiefs of Staff (JCS) during the 1945 to 1960 period.

---

[24]Patrick Anderson, *The President's Men* (Garden City, N.Y.: Anchor Books, Doubleday, 1969), p. 176.

The second of these questions was answered differently, and it will be discussed in the context of logrolling and procedural inclusiveness.

Members of the JCS wear two hats. Individually, they are the ranking members of their branch of the armed forces: Chief of Staff of the Army, Chief of Naval Operations, Chief of Staff of the Air Force, and Commandant of the Marine Corps. With their chairman added, they serve collectively as the top military committee advising the president and the secretary of defense. Much of their behavior in the executive branch and in front of congressional committees suggests that they are more comfortable in their individual than in their collective roles.

Decisions about who was to spend what monies illustrate the pluralistic conflict generated by the bias toward individual rather than collective responsibility. After the Joint Chiefs of Staff (JCS) knew how much money the president would request, they were left to divide it among their respective service branches. A bitter battle ended with an obscure but real compromise among the Chiefs of Staff which gave the Air Force 46 percent, the Navy (and Marine Corps) 28 percent, and the Army 23 percent of all military appropriations.[25]

Logrolling and Procedural Inclusiveness

Once each Chief of Staff captured the largest possible share of the budget for his service branch in pluralistic settings, logrolling triumphed among branches. Personnel within a branch of service adopted a posture of noninterference in respect to each other branch. Within each branch, procedural inclusiveness characterized much of the interaction among decision makers during the 1945 to 1960 period. The combination of logrolling noninterference between services and procedural inclusiveness within each service contained tremendous potential for uncoordinated strategic decisions. This potential will be illustrated following the description of logrolling and procedural rationality.

Logrolling is typically associated with legislatures, but legislators are not alone in swapping support and restraint, particularly restraint. An exchange such as "you support my measure; I'll support yours" contains an important understanding of noninterference. A close approximation of the mutual restraint exercised among the individual services between 1945 and 1960 is contained in the implied provision of a logrolling trade: "Don't criticize my proposals, and I won't criticize yours."

25Theodore H. White, "An Inside Report on Robert McNamara's Revolution in the Pentagon," *Look*, April 23, 1963, p. 34; and Huntington, *The Common Defense*, p. 424.

Logrolling noninterference by personnel of one service made for another service meant that formats for decision making did not need to be coordinated. Although they were not coordinated, formats were similar in that they were procedurally inclusive.

Procedures are inclusive when they insure that everyone who is affected is consulted for a statement of his needs, preferences, and recommendations before a decision is made. Carbon copies marked "For your information" and "For your action" abound. What is often labeled "red tape" slowed final decisions between 1945 and 1960. In the sense of slower decisions, procedural inclusiveness produced inefficiency. In the sense of providing decision makers with the available information, procedural inclusiveness was probably more efficient than pre-World War II techniques. Before World War II, for example, supply personnel selected the equipment which they would procure without consulting those who had to utilize the supplies. Procedural inclusiveness between 1945 and 1960 permitted operating personnel to put in their bid for what they needed, as they saw it, not as it was seen for them by procurement personnel.[26]

Procedural inclusiveness does not preclude decisions made by direction or command, pluralistic, or logrolling techniques. Every affected person might be consulted and then one in a superior organizational position might direct or command his subordinates to follow a particular course of action. On the other hand, he might let or encourage his subordinates to fight out their differences and reach pluralistic compromises. Still another alternative, would be for a superior to permit his subordinates to practice logrolling noninterference in the area of expertise of another. We lack data which would indicate the mix of command, pluralism, and logrolling within the various branches of the armed forces during the period of procedural inclusiveness between 1945 and 1960. Trends would seem to be toward command and away from logrolling. Whether decisions were directed, pluralistically compromised, or logrolled, the ultimate decision maker(s) seldom had to articulate his criteria and analysis in formal and explicit terms.

Uncoordinated decisions. No matter how rational the procedures used within each branch of the armed forces, the procedures seldom incorporated those from other branches who might have been affected by within-branch decisions. Logrolling restraint among branch personnel was dominant, and this lack of coordination produced duplication and inflated costs.

26Hammond, "Analysis of Defense Department," pp. 58–64; and Peter Blau, *Bureaucracy in Modern Society* (New York: Random House, 1962), pp. 13–14.

During the 1945 to 1960 period, requirements for the armed forces were calculated branch-by-branch within the budgetary lines established previously by the JCS. Army strategists would plan not only the role of the Army but also the role for each other branch of service. If their best plan cost more than was allotted, they would produce another total plan until they were within budgetary limits. Budget requests for the Army then would be based upon the Army role in the Army plan. So it was with each other branch of service. Duplication was rampant. If strategic plans of one service fit with others, the fit was by accident rather than by design.[27]

Requirements were established to fulfill missions which were assumed by the Joint Chiefs of Staff or assigned by higher authority. An example of such a mission would be the defense of Western Europe from invasion by the Soviet Union. In setting its requirements, the Army might place heavy emphasis upon quickly airlifting many U.S. and allied troops from these homeland or other stations to Western Europe. There would be no assurance that the Air Force personnel would build transport aircraft into their requirements. In comparison to the Army, the Air Force would not need to move many people and mountains of equipment quickly. Besides, glory and morale for aviators are not in hauling cargo; headlines are garnered by demolishing the enemy. Moreover, both the Air Force and the Navy might purchase aircraft to provide close air support for troops the Army could not get into position because of a lack of transportation.

Between and among the branches of service, strategists neither scrutinized nor criticized the planning of other strategists. If strategists could not fit their concepts into their money amounts, they sought additional funds from Congress. They pleaded the merits of their case, asking for more in total rather than asking for part of someone else's share. This was the case for years as Air Force personnel sought more B-70 funding.

Extreme Rationality

Robert S. McNamara's form of *extreme rationality* took under seige each of the *pluralistic, logrolling,* and *procedurally inclusive* decision-making practices which he inherited in January of 1961 when he became secretary of defense. His brand of rationality was extreme in that it forced decision makers to spell out what they knew, perceived, understood, or believed, and it forced them to distinguish among know-

---

27White, "McNamara's Revolution," p. 34; and William W. Kaufmann, "The McNamara Strategy," *The Politics of the Federal Bureaucracy*, ed. Allan A. Atlshuler (New York: Dodd, Mead, 1968), pp. 179–96, particularly p. 181.

ing, perceiving, understanding, and believing. Criteria for making judgments about what was needed were made explicit, and then, these criteria were utilized to compare proposals against similar proposals.

Secretary McNamara and the personnel of his office imposed the *extreme* rationality of systems (ends-means) analysis. Ends-means analysis requires that the links between objectives, capabilities, and needs be confronted head-on: All were to be exposed, articulated, scrutinized, and examined critically. A program and performance budget system (PPBS) and cost-effectiveness analysis were utilized by McNamara and his staff to accomplish this change. The cost of each alternative was weighed against its projected effectiveness. If a weapons system could provide 80 percent protection for half the cost of a similar weapons system which could provide 95 percent protection, McNamara wanted to know. During the 1945 to 1960 era of *procedural inclusiveness*, decision makers within each branch of service tended to choose the greater protection so long as they had money enough to buy it.[28] McNamara's changes had additional impact upon decision making both within and outside of the Department of Defense (DOD).

Extreme rationality in DOD. No longer was it enough for a service Chief or JCS, collectively, to say, "In my (our) professional judgment, . . ." Program budget categories were established in the Office of the Secretary of Defense and cost versus effectiveness calculations were made to compare the capabilities of different weapons systems which accomplish the same function or purpose. For example, sea-based missiles (intermediate range and intercontinental) were compared to similar land-based missiles and to strategc bombers (such as the B-70) under the Strategc Relatiatory Forces category. Thus, sea-based missiles no longer competed for funds with naval air, conventional submarines, fleet escorts, mine sweepers, etc. Sea-based missiles began to compete for funds with the land-based missiles and strategic bombers of the Air Force. The Marine Corps, a part of the naval service, began to compete with similar forces of the Army under the General Purpose Forces budget category.[29]

Different decision makers perceive, understand, and know the same facts differently. They attach different weights to criteria of cost, risk, and advantage. Under McNamara, the disputes among the service

[28]Cf. Robert J. Art, *The TFX Decision: McNamara and the Military* (Boston: Little, Brown, 1968), pp. 32–33 (note), 58.

[29]The six additional program budget categories which were established are Continental Air and Missile Defense Forces, Airlift and Sealift Forces, Reserve and Guard Forces, Research and Development, General Support, and Civil Defense. See *Study Report on Programming for the Secretary of Defense*, prepared by the Office of the Assistant Secretary of Defense (Comptroller), Programming Directorate for Systems Planning, June 25, 1962.

branches were settled by decisions from him and others in his office. This centralization replaced the pluralistic conflict, bargaining, and compromise among the Joint Chiefs of Staff which preceded his administration. Decisions in the Office of the Secretary of Defense went more deeply into the service branches themselves where the Chief of Staff, members of his staff, line officers, and decision-making committees previously had prevailed.[30] When the Joint Chiefs of Staff were united, early in McNamara's term, he was forced to compromise on missile procurement rather than pay (and have the president pay) the political price of public disputes before Congress.[31] As his tenure endured, this type of trade-off became less and less characteristic of McNamara's style.

Members of the Joint Chiefs of Staff made their strategic and budgetary recommendations and were essentially through with their portion of budget construction in the spring of each year. McNamara's systems analysts would render their decisions on the basis of cost-effectiveness analysis. Then in September and October, McNamara would preside over efforts to reconcile differences between personnel from components of DOD and Bureau of the Budget (BOB) officials.[32]

Extreme rationality outside DOD. McNamara also had a major impact on BOB officials, whom presidents regularly use to enforce their priorities upon their administrations as well as the bureaucracy.[33] Indeed, McNamara was able to marshal such a mass of data and analysis that few chose to contest with him before the president. Neither experienced strategists nor experienced budgeteers harbored many hopes of winning a dispute with the Secretary of Defense.

One former director of BOB argues that the person in that position is valuable and viable to a president only insofar as the director makes the same decision that the president would make were he there. If the director's decisions are appealed to the president and regularly overruled by him, more and more decisions will be appealed, eliminating the usefulness of BOB.[34] It seems as likely from their experience with Mc-

30Art, *The TFX Decision*, particularly pp. 157–66. Cf. Adam Yarmolinski, "Ideas into Programs," *The Presidential Advisory System*, eds. Thomas E. Cronin and Sanford D. Greenberg (New York: Harper & Row, 1969), pp. 284–94.
31David Halberstam, "The Programming of Robert McNamara," *Harper's Magazine*, February, 1971, p. 54.
32*New York Times*, September 29, 1969, pp. 1 and 27.
33Richard E. Neustadt, "Presidency and Legislation: The Growth of Central Clearance," *American Political Science Review*, 48, No. 3 (September 1954), pp. 642–50; Kermit Gordon, "The Budget Director" in Cronin and Greenberg, pp. 284–94; and James W. Davis and Randall B. Ripley, "The Bureau of the Budget and Executive Branch Agencies: Notes of their Interaction," *Politics, Programs, and Budgets*, ed. James W. Davis, Jr. (Englewood Cliffs, N.J.: Prentice-Hall, 1968), pp. 63–77.
34Gordon, "The Budget Director," pp. 284–94.

Namara that BOB personnel might quit contesting with members of the administration who regularly won appeals to the president.

What appears to have happened until near the end of the Johnson presidency is that those involved in constructing budgets and strategists at top levels found that Secretary McNamara was making the decisions the president would make if called upon to do so. McNamara took precedence over persons of equal and closer organizational position to the president.

TRADE-OFFS

Secretary McNamara's *extreme rationality* provided highly coherent, coordinated programs, but it traded away the advantages of fragmented and decentralized decision making which included among its advantages the involvement of a greater number and range of participants. Whether or not it was a worthwhile trade is a judgmental question. In the ongoing business of government, probably the most important judgments to examine are those of a different president and his secretary of defense. Richard M. Nixon and Melvin Laird, during their first two years in office, have made changes which undoubtedly reflect their evaluation of McNamara's techniques.

The changes they have wrought within DOD are the products of the Defense Programs Review Board. This Board is chaired by the president's foreign policy advisor, Henry Kissinger, and its other members are the deputy secretary of defense, the under secretary of state, the director of the Office of Management and Budget (BOB expanded and strengthened), the chairman of the Council of Economics Advisors (CEA), and the chairman of the Joint Chiefs of Staff. They review and evaluate programs devised in the armed services in response to strategic decisions made in the National Security Council. The institutional homes of these officials, with one exception, are the same as the pre-McNamara, top-level military strategy/budget setters. The chairman of CEA has been substituted for a Treasury representative. Otherwise, the Board is structured much the same as the key group which determined the size of the military slice from the national budget between 1945 and 1960.

President Nixon appears willing to trade the highly coherent, centralized strategic and budgetary planning of McNamara for a return to a *pluralistic* format similar to the one McNamara abandoned in a shower of cost-effectiveness data.

Trade-offs within DOD

Similar, recent changes have been made in DOD, and they constitute a postscript on the RS-70 dispute. During Laird's first year as secretary, cost-effectiveness analysts were downgraded in the Office of the Secretary of Defense. At the same time, members of JCS—wearing, also, their other hats as ranking member of their particular branch of service —were upgraded, and cost-effectiveness analysis was made a tool for use by them rather than by the secretary of defense. Secretary McNamara turned the strategic and budgetary recommendations of the Joint Chiefs over to his cost-effectiveness analysts in the spring. On the other hand, Secretary Laird plans to continue the participation of the Chiefs of Staff throughout the annual budget-preparation cycle.[35] This seems to place the service Chiefs in a better position to resist decisions which go against their preferences. Before the McNamara changes, the Chiefs of Staff and those around them (so long as they stayed within preestablished budgetary ceilings) essentially could seek the interests of their separate services without outside interference. There is a considerable difference between a Chief of Staff being able to resist the preferences of others.

It is not yet clear how much influence and authority the Chiefs of Staff have gained from Laird's changes. Whatever their current influence and authority, it exceeds that which they had during the McNamara period; they participate longer, in more decisions, with more data and better analyses. The potential implications of these recent changes are analyzed in the context of the 1961 dispute over the RS-70.

The RS-70

The RS-70 incident was among the first where McNamara rearranged 1945–1960 patterns; he intervened in allocations of research and development funds for the Air Force. The controversy foreshadowed changes to come and illustrates two important trade-offs. First, McNamara's categories for analysis, no matter how rational they were, traded away certain types of comparison. Second, extremely rational decisions require articulated, explicit, formal reasoning but deny the intuitive hunch, the nagging doubt of the experienced professional.

It is not certain that McNamara's embryo, functional categories forced Air Force strategists to redesignate the B-70 as the RS-70. Nonetheless, the redesignation and the subsequent conflict spotlight the capa-

[35]*New York Times*, September 29, 1969, pp. 1 and 27.

bilities of different analytic schemes. Air Force strategists quit attempting to add the B-70 as a first-strike weapon. They argued instead that the RS-70 could follow a missile strike. After missiles had eliminated surface-to-air defenses, the RS-70 could reconnoiter the damage and strike priority targets which survived the missile attack.[36] McNamara continued to compare its capabilities to those of first-strike missiles.

Chairman Vinson of the House Armed Services Committee, on the other hand, utilized a different method of analysis. He ascertained that no other existing or projected weapons system would be available for the reconnaissance-strike task, and he judged that task to be important. Vinson needed no more cost-analyses before attempting to strengthen the RS-70 program.

The first trade-off is that functional categories which permit (not necessarily insure) results to be judged in terms of costs may shut out weapons systems or even strategic concepts which do not fit the categories of analysis. Vinson perceived that use of McNamara's categories was producing a single strategy—massive retaliation.[37]

Throughout the RS-70 conflict, a more general and troubling trade-off seemed to motivate Vinson. He preferred to satisfy the parochial interests and the stated needs of Air Force spokesmen. He feared that centralized decision makers would overlook a national vulnerability that might be covered, at least partially, by fragmented, logrolling strategists in the separate service branches. Centralized decision making might promise short-run savings at tremendous long-run costs.

Centralized decision making does not necessarily insure lower costs any more than fragmented decision making insures that all reasonable strategic contingencies will be covered. Vinson opted for the latter probability, however. He supported the intuitive, nagging concern of professional strategists and rejected the *extreme rationality* of McNamara's professional budgeteers, whom he considered unreliable as strategists. Vinson had no guarantee that the McNamara-type *extreme rationality* could differentiate valid professional concerns from efforts simply to enhance the position of a service branch.

These trade-offs cannot be evaluated here. It is impossible to judge the strength of arguments in favor of fragmented professionalism until more is known about how many and which decisions were directed, pluralistic, or logrolled within each branch of service before Mc-

---

[36]U.S. Congress, House, Committee on Armed Services, *Authorization for Aircraft, Missiles, and Naval Vessels*, 87th Congress, 2nd Session, 1962, *H. Rept. 1406* to accompany *H.R. 9751*, p. 9.

[37]*C.R.*, CVIII, 1962, p. 4310; and Roland Evans, Jr., "The Sixth Sense of Carl Vinson," *Reporter*, April 12, 1962, p. 26.

Namara's changes. Whatever the earlier combination, McNamara's lasting change may be in the use of systems analysis and program and performance budgeting within the branches of the armed forces. Insofar as these techniques continue, it is safe to predict that more and more decisions will be decentralized in the Chief of Staff for each branch.

16 *Marjory Stoneman Douglas*

Victory in the Everglades

After a violent controversy between conservationists and the promoters of a huge jet airport in the Everglades, peace descended in Florida at last in November 1969. On Thanksgiving Day, President Nixon announced that he had made his personal decision that the jetport could not be built at that site. It was peace of a sort, because a landing strip for jet planes, already built, was allowed to function only so long as it was proved, after 90 days, that it did not destroy wildlife, pollute or contaminate its environment and threaten the water supply of the Everglades National Park and the lower West Coast of Florida. The first few jets began to land at the training airport in January 1970, after a contract, carefully stating the restrictions, was signed between the Federal government, the State of Florida and the Dade County Port Authority. It was agreed also that after another jetport site had been approved, the training strip would be moved.

It was the greatest victory yet won in the United States by national and local conservation organizations and concerned individuals every-

From *Interplay* (March 1970). Copyright © 1970 by Interplay. Reprinted by permission.

where, with the support of the major national magazines, newspapers, TV and radio, against the exploitation by large private interests of our valuable and dwindling natural resources.

To the great aviation interests the Florida Everglades, with the Everglades National Park at its southern tip, looks, from a flying airplane, like an old wet carpet. To many Florida businessmen and newcomers it seems only a vast stretch of empty land waiting to be used to bring more people and more money into the state of Florida. But to conservationists and scientists, that great central region from Okeechobee to Cape Sable is the source of wildlife and sea life and the whole water supply of the region so that it can truly be called the heart and life of all South Florida.

The conflict over the Everglades jetport developed long after the Dade County Port Authority first decided that it needed a much larger airport, far away from urban areas and the rising complaints of residents against plane noise. By 1967, the Federal Aviation Administration had approved the Port Authority's search for a site with a planning grant of $500,000. The Authority floated a bond issue of $52 million, of which $44 million was to go to build a jetport at some undesignated site, preferably in Dade County. Nine different places, some as far away as the Bahamas, were studied and declared impractical. Comments from the Port Authority indicated that they were considering Collier County as a location. The Everglades were not mentioned.

In 1967 Joseph Browder, a Miami radio man and member of the Tropical Audubon Society, the local chapter of the National Audubon Society, was startled to hear, at a meeting of the Port Authority, that the jetport was likely to be built in eastern Collier County in the general area of the Big Cypress. The Big Cypress is a swamp north of the Tamiami Trail on the edge of the Everglades and the location of a Mikasuki Indian hunting ground with several villages. He called this to the attention of the National Audubon Society, which was the group which first stopped the killing of Everglades birds by plume hunters for the New York millinery trade, with a Federal act. It was instrumental in establishing the Everglades National Park in 1947. They were assured by the Port Authority that every precaution would be taken by jetport planners to protect the wildlife and the water supply of the Park, which lies immediately to the south. Conservationists ruefully admit now that their fears had been soothed by the reassurance of the Authority so that they did not begin their active protest until 1968.

Demands from the Superintendent of the Everglades National Park to know exactly how the Port Authority meant to protect the Park from the jetport, and its inevitable surrounding development of hit-or-miss urban sprawl, were met by the reply that they meant to build only one training strip to be run by a crew of not more than ten men.

Then Robert Padrick, chairman of the Central and Southern Florida Flood Control District, discovered that the Port Authority planned to cut a four-lane highway from Miami to the jetport straight through the Everglades, a highway hardly necessary if the Port Authority meant what it said about the single training strip. It was soon made clear that the Port Authority all this time had been quietly buying up land for a 39-square-mile jetport right there.

Representatives of many state and national conservation societies— Gerri Souci of New York, for the Eastern branch of the Sierra Club, Joseph Browder, now representing the National Audubon Society, Superintendent Raferty of the Everglades National Park, the representative of the Florida Fish and Wildlife Service—got together at once to try to force a public confrontation with the Port Authority. It would be required to reply publicly and in writing to 119 questions about the jetport, compiled and edited by the Florida National Resources Board. The answers sent back by the Port Authority were so vague, evasive and unsatisfactory, generally consisting of the phrase "under study," that the idea of a public confrontation was given up as useless. The general attitude of the Port Authority to the whole question was that these protests against a multi-million-dollar project by people who were only "alligator lovers and bird watchers" were not important enough to be bothered with.

CONSERVATIONIST FEARS CONFIRMED

In April 1969, the Department of Federal Transportation announced an appropriation of $200,000 for a multi-million-dollar high-speed transportation system to the jetport. In May, after a meeting in Naples, a Collier County businessman revealed that the Port Authority expected to build around the jetport an urban complex for heavy industries, the devastating effect of which would be exactly what the conservationists had most feared.

They learned then, if they had not learned it before, that the Port Authority had no intention of trying to keep even the vague promises they had made to safeguard the Everglades National Park and the water supply of the lower West Coast.

At this point, exhausted conservationists would have given in to despair except that new men, like Dan Paul, an attorney, joined them with bolder plans for fighting the increasing threat. Twenty-two national conservation organizations throughout the United States joined forces to bring the fight to Washington.

In June, they appealed to Senator Jackson of the Senate Committee on Interior Affairs who, with Senator Nelson, held a series of hearings on the threat to the Park by the proposed jetport. As a result, Secretary Hickel of the Department of the Interior ordered a study of the jetport's effect on the environment by Dr. L. B. Leopold of the Department of the Interior, aided by Arthur Marshall, Field Coordinator of the U.S. Fish and Wildlife Service. At the same time, the National Academy of Science began making its own study of the situation.

By late August the word began to leak out that both reports were completely adverse to the jetport. And for the first time, the Port Authority began to realize that they might be forced to abandon their plan. Ex-Secretary of the Interior Stewart Udall was hired by them to make a third environmental study. It was also reported that the Metro Commission of Dade County was so impressed by the evidence against that jetport site that they had begun negotiations with the State Cabinet of Florida to trade it for land elsewhere. Governor Kirk suggested that the port be moved to Palm Beach.

The Dade County Port Authority compounded the confusion by issuing a series of statements to the local press, in varying but less lofty tones of voice. They said they had acted in good faith with the approval of the Federal government, by which they meant the support of the Federal Aviation Administration; that they had already spent $13 million and hated to see that money go to waste; that they were sure something could be done so that the Everglades National Park would not be damaged, although they never said what; and they insisted that conservationists had delayed so long before making their first protests that the land for the jetport had already been acquired before the Port Authority learned there would be objections. This in the face of the fact that the Port Authority had bought up the land with what would seem to be deliberate secrecy.

By September 3, 1969, the fight was taken by the coalition of national conservation societies to the highest governmental levels in Washington. Secretary of the Interior Hickel held a series of meetings with Secretary of Transportation John Volpe to try to come to some agreement that would save the Park. He was increasingly irritated by the Port Authority's arrogant assumption that what they said was above question: this in the face of the adverse scientific reports, including that by Stewart Udall, which advocated moving the jetport.

THE MEDIA ENTER THE FRAY

Suddenly the pages of many of the most important national newspapers and magazines burst forth with articles and photographs on the dangers to the Everglades National Park: *Life, Time, Newsweek,* the *New York Times,* the *Christian Science Monitor,* the *Audubon Magazine,* with much pro-Park talk on national radio and TV hookups. The general public was increasingly aroused.

Secretary Hickel found that he and Secretary Volpe could not reach an agreement on the removal of the jetport site. He therefore took the issue directly to President Nixon for his personal decision, who announced on Thanksgiving Day that the jetport was not going to be built on the Everglades site. That was that.

Work on the training strip that had brought the roar of bulldozers to the Mikusaki Indian villages and the planes to the very edge of the ancient Square Ground, scene of the immemorial Green Corn festival with its religious rites, was at once stopped. A compromise was reached by the signing of the contract stating the terms by which another jet site must be searched for by the Port Authority, the Everglades land already acquired disposed of, and what part of the expenses the Federal government was prepared to pay. If, after 90 days, the training strip was found to pollute or contaminate the environment and affect the water supply, it was to be discontinued at once. It would be moved permanently when another jetport site was found.

There is an apprehension among the embattled conservationists, elated as they are by the President's epoch-making decision, that the Port Authority may still hope to retain the jetport site by insisting that no other possible site can be found. It is quite evident that the coalition of national conservation societies, created for this emergency, as well as thousands of private citizens and many Florida organizations, especially the newly formed "Friends of the Everglades," are prepared to bring an unrelenting vigilance to the protection of the great region.

A WATERY EDEN LOST FOREVER

There is, of course, no question that the unique and remarkable Everglades can ever be restored to what it was in the 5,000 years of its development since the last of the risen sea water ran off at the beginning of the last Polar Ice Age.

Then the fresh water from Florida's great average rainfall flowed south through lakes and creeks into Okeechobee, from which, in rainy seasons, the excess water spilled out eastward through the Loxahatchee Slough to the Atlantic, westward slowly through the meandering Caloosahatchee, but chiefly flowed, as fast as four miles an hour, down the long curving course of the Everglades to the delta of the Ten Thousand Islands. The whole region, with the bristling sawgrass which sprang up to make it a true river of grass, was then an example of one of the most perfectly balanced natural engineering systems in the world. In dry times the fresh water glades were protected from the constant pressure of salt sea water by the rock rims of both coasts. In rainy seasons the excess fresh water flowed over natural dams, the rapids and rocks in the short rivers. Where the fresh water flowed into the salt, at the tip of Florida, astronomical quantities of tiny sea creatures were spawned, to move out to enrich the teeming Florida seas. Early man and early animals lived well throughout the Everglades then, never disturbing that wonderful, life-giving balance.

It was only the American, who, as late as 1906, first brought the threat of destruction to this system of the Glades. That was the year when Governor Napoleon Bonaparte Broward, having campaigned on a promise to drain the Everglades and create an "Empire of the Sun," sent the first dredge to digging a canal up the north New River at Fort Lauderdale, to Lake Okeechobee.

The history of the Everglades since then has been one of change and encroachment by the pressure of population, since boom days, into south Florida. The jungles south of the Lake were cut down so that vast vegetable and sugar cane fields spread and burn up the 30-foot-deep rich peaty-muck accumulated in the first 5,000 years. By the year 2000 the soil will be gone, mined out by vegetable growers. The fresh water dams in rivers, blown up for transportation, no longer prevented the encroachment of salt water, which has crept in everywhere, requiring that the well fields of growing East Coast cities be moved farther toward the Glades.

More canals were built: the St. Lucie canal from the Lake eastward, the lovely Caloosahatchee ruined by another. To keep the water table at the right level for vegetable growers around the Lake, billions of gallons of fresh water were discharged from the Lake and eastward into the Atlantic. At Stuart, the excess fresh water killed off the salt water fish in the protected inland waterways. There were complaints that there was not enough water for East Coast cities. In 1947 the Everglades National Park was established in the lower Glades.

The Army Engineers' development of a system of canals and pumps and dikes, making three great water conservancy areas for the East Coast counties, managed to cut off the vital flow of water to the Everglades National Park, thus creating a situation of great and immediate danger. Water in abundance was allowed to flow into the Park only after the conservationists' protests had an effect in Washington. Water standing in the conservancy basins, like a series of lakes, still evaporates under the Florida sun almost as fast as it can be run in. This problem has not yet been solved, along with that strange one—the surplus of fresh water in Lake Okeechobee allowed to run in billions of wasted gallons east and west into the Atlantic and the Gulf of Mexico.

A "THIRTEEN MILLION DOLLAR EDUCATION"?

It has been argued that the Everglades has been so changed that nothing that happens to it matters. That is an impossible belief. The Everglades are still there, if battered. The porous rock is there that holds water like a reservoir, as well as the Lake. The Florida rains and hurricanes bring their great supply of fresh water, in cycles of wet and dry. Despite the statement of some officials that the cities are threatened with water shortages, it is not unreasonable to demand wise replanning without waste, to insure water enough for all the people and cities that can be supported by South Florida, along with farms, industries, wildlife, sea life, wilderness and recreation areas and the Everglades National Park. This can be done only if the Everglades region is considered to be a related whole, one and indivisible.

Perhaps, after all, the great jetport controversy may be considered a $13 million education, if it has brought wisdom about the Everglades to millions of people, including the President of the United States.

17 *Daniel K. Wanamaker*

Your Son
May Never Become
a
Supreme Court Justice

Although most nominations to the Supreme Court have been rapidly confirmed by the Senate, interest groups have begun to play important roles in battling for and against recent confirmations. The power of pressure groups opposing the nominations made Johnson and Nixon the first presidents in modern times to have their Supreme Court nominees rejected by the Senate; and President Johnson became the only recent president to have his nomination for Chief Justice not confirmed by the Senate.

The focus here is on interest group interventions in several recent nominations to the Supreme Court. The emphasis is on which interests have been concerned, and on the thrust of their basic strategies for raising their concern.

"Your Son May Never Become a Supreme Court Justice if He is Not Liked by Certain Interest Groups: Patterns of Interest Group Activity in Nominations of the Court" was written expressly for this volume.

THE FORTAS NOMINATION

On June 13, 1968, Chief Justice Earl Warren informed President Johnson that he wanted to retire. However, the Chief Justice indicated that he would stay until a successor was confirmed by the Senate. The rationale for this focus is direct. The concern by interest groups may reflect the major political role of the Supreme Court. And the strategies of the interest groups may have broad implications not only for who gets on the Court, but on who is willing to run the gauntlet of objective interest groups. Some thought that Chief Justice Warren was resigning because of the animosity between Warren and the leading Republican presidential contender, Richard M. Nixon. The argument is straightforward. During the 1952 Republican convention, Warren was the favorite son candidate for president of the California delegation. Junior Senator Nixon, also of California, was credited with breaking the favorite son pledge of the delegation. Nixon was able to lead a portion of the delegation for candidate Dwight D. Eisenhower, which may have cinched Nixon's nomination as Eisenhower's runningmate. By resigning in June 1968, Warren may have tried to insure that Nixon would not be able to appoint the next Chief Justice even if Nixon were nominated and elected.

On June 26, President Johnson nominated his close friend, Associate Justice Abe Fortas, for Chief Justice. Johnson also named Judge Homer Thornberry of the Fifth Circuit Court of Appeals to replace Fortas as Associate Justice. Some Republican Senators reacted negatively to both nominations. For example, Senator Robert P. Griffin (R., Michigan) argued that the nominations were based on "cronyism," since both nominees were close friends of the president. Fortas had been an advisor to the president before serving on the court. Thornberry's relationship to President Johnson was perhaps a closer one. He had been elected congressman from Johnson's district when Johnson was first elected senator from Texas. Along with eighteen other Republican senators, Senator Griffin signed a statement opposing the nominations. The resolution said that since the November presidential election was less than five months away, the Supreme Court vacancies should be filled by the newly-elected president. This fact may have motivated Griffin's resolution, of course.

Support for the Fortas Nomination

The hearings on the nominations were conducted between July 11 and July 23, 1968, before the Senate Committee on the Judiciary chaired by James O. Eastland (D., Mississippi). The first entry in the record was the usual letter from the Standing Committee on the Federal Judiciary of the American Bar Association (ABA). "Our Committee is of the view that Associate Justice Fortas is 'highly acceptable from the viewpoint of professional qualifications'."[1] The president-elect of the ABA wrote, "If I were a member of the Judiciary Committee of the Senate, I would vote without reservation to recommend the confirmation of Mr. Justice Fortas as Chief Justice" (p. 3).

Most of the testimony at the hearings centered around the Fortas nomination because of the importance and influence of the Chief Justice. In addition, there would not be a vacancy for Thornberry as Associate Justice if Fortas were rejected for Chief Justice.

Besides the nominees, a number of witnesses appeared before the Committee including Attorney General Ramsey Clark, Senators Robert P. Griffin (R., Michigan), Ralph Yarborough (D., Texas), Albert Gore (D., Tennessee), and Deputy Attorney General Warren Christopher. All these witnesses favored the nominations except Senator Griffin. The remainder of the testimonies were from interest group representatives, most of whom opposed the nominations.

Opposition to the Fortas Nomination

"Soft" on Communists. Several lobbyists from the right side of the political spectrum appeared first to oppose the Fortas nomination. For example, the National Chairman of the Conservative Society of America and publisher of the *Conservative Journal* testified against the Fortas nomination. His arguments against Fortas were based on his beliefs that Fortas was siding with the members of a Communist conspiracy (p. 77). The Chairman of the Council Against Communist Aggression opposed Fortas for the same reason (p. 79).

Too Permissive Decisions. On July 22, 1968, two other conservative pressure groups testified before the Committee. The Executive Secretary of the Liberty Lobby argued that the confirmation of Justice Fortas as Chief Justice would accelerate the ascension of a philosophy of permissiveness in society (pp. 283–84). The second lobbyist was an attorney for the executive board of the National Organization, Citizens for Decent

---

[1]Letter from Albert E. Jenner, Hearings Before the Committee on the Judiciary, United States Senate, Ninetieth Congress, Second Session, *The Nomination of Abe Fortas, of Tennessee, to be Chief Justice of the United States and the Nomination of Homer Thornberry, of Texas, to be Associate Justice of the Supreme Court of the United States,* p. 1. (Unless otherwise footnoted, all other citations in the section about Fortas are from these hearings. The page number is given at the end of the citation.)

Literature, Inc. This group's opposition was based on Fortas' judicial philosophy, which could be gleaned from the fact that Fortas voted to reverse the jury and State court obscenity determinations in each of the cases he acted upon during the 1966 and 1967 terms (p. 294).

Extra-Judicial Activities. The remaining hearings before the Judiciary Committee were postponed until after the Republican and Democratic National Conventions. Opponents of Fortas made good use of the time. For example, on September 16, Senator Griffin cited a magazine article which stated that Fortas, while Associate Justice, had helped President Johnson with his 1966 State of the Union message. Senator Allott (R., Colorado) argued that Fortas wrote certain legislation for President Johnson. For example, the Senator charged that ". . . Fortas wrote an amendment to an appropriations bill dealing with Secret Service protection of presidential candidates" (p. 1359). Legislators, usually interested in the separation of powers, might well take heed.

On September 13, the Dean of the Law School of American University said that Justice Fortas had been paid $15,000 to conduct law seminars during the summer of 1968. This was a princely sum, and apparently raised further concerns about Fortas' expenditures of energies.

In any case, the Senate Judiciary Committee voted on September 17 to send the nomination to the full Senate. On the floor of the Senate, however, a coalition of Republicans and Southern Democrats began to filibuster to block the confirmation. This filibuster started on September 25 and continued through September 30. Senate Majority Leader Mansfield (D., Montana) got the Senate to agree to bring to a vote a motion on cloture (a motion to stop the filibuster) on the next day, October 1. Before the cloture voting, Minority Leader Everett McKinley Dirksen (R., Illinois) announced his opposition to the Fortas nomination. Dirksen, the Ranking Minority Member on the Senate Judiciary Committee, previously had favored confirmation in the Committee report. Dirksen attributed his switch in position to the case of *Witherspoon v. Illinois* (1968) in which Fortas was in the majority. In this case, the Supreme Court held that prospective jurors could not be eliminated in capital cases because they opposed capital punishment. Although the *Witherspoon* case may have been the reason for the Dirksen switch, one source observed, perhaps uncharitably, ". . . it was clear that as Griffin's following of Republican Senators [opposing the nomination] grew, Dirksen's control as . . . [Minority] leader diminished."[2] The vote on the cloture motion was 45 to 43. Although a majority, the vote was short of the two-thirds majority needed to stop the debate.

[2]"Attempt to Stop Fortas Debate Fails by 14-Vote Margin," *1968 Congressional Quarterly Almanac, 24,* 531.

Fortas apparently got the message. Several days later, he asked President Johnson to remove his name from further consideration as Chief Justice.

The Threat of a Fortas Impeachment:
More Extra Judicial Activities

Although Abe Fortas continued to serve as Associate Justice, his political troubles were not over. The *Congressional Quarterly* reported that

> according to an article in *Life* magazine, Fortas in January 1966, accepted a $20,000 check from a foundation established by multimillionaire industrialist, Louis E. Wolfson. In September, 1966, Wolfson was indicted for selling unregistered securities. In December, 1966, according to the article, Fortas returned the $20,000.[3]

Under threats of impeachment, Fortas resigned as Associate Justice in a letter to Chief Justice Warren on May 14, 1969. He explained:

> Since becoming a member of the Court, I have not, at any time, directly or indirectly, received any compensation from Mr. Wolfson or members of his family or any of his associates for advice, assistance or any reason whatever, except the Foundation fee which was returned. There has been no wrongdoing on my part. There has been no default in the performance of my judicial duties in accordance with the high standards of the office I hold. So far as I am concerned, the welfare and maximum effectiveness of the Court to perform its critical role in our system of government are factors that are paramount to all others. It is this consideration that prompts my resignation which, I hope, by terminating the public controversy, will permit the Court to proceed with its work, without the harassment of debate concerning one of its members.[4]

Thus, the new president, Richard Nixon, now had two appointments to make to the Supreme Court—a Chief Justice and an Associate Justice.

THE BURGER NOMINATION

On May 21, 1969, President Nixon nominated Warren Earl Burger to be Chief Justice. The Burger nomination had strong support and was

3"Justice's Resignation First Under Impeachment Threat," *1969 Congressional Quarterly Almanac,* 25, 136.
4"Text of Fortas Letter Explaining Resignation," *1969 Congressional Quarterly Almanac,* 25, 137.

rapidly confirmed by the Senate by a vote of 74–3. In the Committee hearings, there were a number of letters and telegrams from various members of the ABA. For example, the Acting Chairman of the ABA's Standing Committee stated that the ABA was unanimously of the opinion that Judge Burger "is highly acceptable from the viewpoint of professional qualifications for this appointment."[5] Except for the telegrams, no lobbyists testified before the Committee. In fact, only two Senators and the nominee appeared to make statements at the hearing.

THE HAYNSWORTH NOMINATION

On August 18, 1969, President Nixon nominated Judge Clement F. Haynsworth, Jr., of the Fourth Judicial Circuit Court of Appeals as Associate Justice to fill the Fortas vacancy on the Supreme Court. When Chairman Eastland (D., Mississippi) opened hearings on the nomination, the first witnesses besides the nominee were Senators Strom Thurmond (R) and Ernest F. Hollings (D), both of South Carolina, who favored the nomination. As excerpts of the testimony from the hearings demonstrate, interest group activity was greater in this nomination than in the Fortas or Burger nominations.

Support for the Haynsworth Nomination

Although most of the witnesses opposed the nomination, there were a few who testified on behalf of Judge Haynsworth. On September 18, the Chairman of the ABA Standing Committee on the Federal Judiciary testified that he and the Committee had found no impropriety in Judge Haynsworth's conduct. The Committee had found Judge Haynsworth to be professionally qualified to fill the vacancy. They saw no reason for opposing him.[6] John Bolt Culbertson, the president of the Greenville County (South Carolina) Bar Association, also testified on behalf of Judge Haynsworth. Culbertson stated that he was a practicing attorney

5Letter from Cloyd LaPorte, Hearing Before the Committee on the Judiciary, United States Senate, Ninety-First Congress, First Session, *The Nomination of Warren E. Burger, of Virginia, to be Chief Justice of the United States*, p. 1. (Unless otherwise footnoted, all other citations in the section about Burger are from these hearings. The page number is given at the end of the citation.)
6Testimony by Lawrence E. Walsh, Hearings Before the Committee on the Judiciary, United States Senate, Ninety-First Congress, First Session, *The Nomination of Clement F. Haynsworth, Jr., of South Carolina, to be Associate Justice of the Supreme Court of the United States*, p. 139. (Unless otherwise footnoted, all other citations in the section about Haynsworth are from these hearings. The page number is given at the end of the citation.)

confining his practice to representing poor people, the laboring class of people, and the indigents. He said that as far as he was concerned, the Republicans had a right to nominate someone with their philosophy as long as they were honest. Culbertson felt that Haynsworth was absolutely honest. In addition, he stated that Haynsworth had one of the best and most decisive legal minds he had ever known (p. 215). Another witness, a former president of the Virginia Bar Lawyers' Association, argued ". . . that Judge Haynsworth will make a great judge, and he will be another great Justice Black from the South" (p. 231).

Opposition to the Haynsworth Nomination

Conflict of Interest. Others were to express concern about Haynsworth's action, especially about conflicts in the *Darlington* and *Brunswick* cases which the Judge had helped adjudicate as a member of a three-judge panel. Haynsworth owned one-seventh of Vend-A-Matic, a company which did business with several plants owned by Deering Milliken. The *Darlington* case involved one Deering Milliken plant, and Haynsworth did not make his interest a matter of record. Irving Abramson, attorney for the International Union of Electrical Radio and Machine Workers (IUE), spoke for the IUE in opposing Haynsworth because of this "conflict of interest."

> Mr. Abramson: Yes, my opinion is that he should disqualify himself or, failing that, he should inform both parties about his former connections, and make that as a matter of record. . . . refer to opinion No. 594 contained on page 206 of the American Bar Association's "Opinions on Professional Ethics." A judge is not prohibited from sitting in a case because his former firm is counsel in such case. However, to avoid any inference of impropriety, the judge shall decline to sit where the case was in the firm at the time he was a member, where a regular client of the firm at the time he was a member is a party to the case. . . .
> So while the bar association is saying that as a matter of law he is not prohibited from sitting, that the standards of ethics . . . suggest to him that he should not sit (pp. 401–2).

Union attorney Abramson also revealed that one of the strongest supporters of the Haynsworth nomination, Senator Sam J. Ervin, Jr. (D., North Carolina), had also been involved in the *Darlington* case. He suggested that Ervin should disqualify himself from the Haynsworth hearings. The *Hearings* reveal Ervin's response:

> Senator Ervin: I will be glad to hear that, because I think that is the funniest thing I have heard since Bud Fisher started drawing Jeff and Mutt (p. 406).

Overall, union representatives noted that Haynsworth seemed more culpable than Fortas (p. 358), who was forced to resign from the Court. Elliott Bredhoff, General Counsel of Industrial Union Department, AFL-CIO, noted that:

> As a major stockholder in Vend-A-Matic, Judge Haynsworth had the same substantial interest in preserving and expanding the Vend-A-Matic business with Deering Milliken and keeping the goodwill of other textile companies . . . (p. 336).

In addition, Bredhoff listed fourteen specific points to show Judge Haynsworth's interest in Vend-A-Matic. He also mentioned that under the Landrum-Griffin Act, which protects against corrupt labor union practices, union officers are required to report any stock or income derived from a company in which the union does substantial business, e.g., represents the workers in collective bargaining. The lawyer argued that if a requirement was made of labor union officials to eliminate possible conflict of interest, a similar requirement should be made of judges (pp. 344–45).

In addition to Judge Haynsworth's holdings in the Vend-A-Matic Company, the judge apparently had holdings in another company involved in litigation before him. To clear up any doubts, Arthur J. McCall, the judge's stockbroker, was asked to testify. McCall confirmed that Judge Haynsworth had purchased 1,000 shares of Brunswick Corporation on December 26, 1967. This information was particularly damaging to the nominee's confirmation, since Judge Haynsworth served as Chief Judge of a three-member panel which was hearing a case involving the Brunswick Corporation when he bought the stock. The 1,000 shares of Brunswick Corporation amount only to .0005 percent ownership of the company by Haynsworth. However, Senator Bayh (R., Indiana) pointed out that $16,000 or $17,000 is a sizable sum to most people. This type of judicial impropriety or conflict of interest should be avoided, Bayh added (p. 249).

> . . . the nomination of Judge Haynsworth should not be rejected by the Committee on the Judiciary. . . . It should be withdrawn by Judge Haynsworth himself. The true test of the ethical sensitivity of any man . . . is the degree of embarrassment to which he will subject his friends and supporters in the pursuit of his personal ambition. . .

> For certainly Judge Haynsworth must know by now that he has embarrassed his high sponsors from President Nixon down by his admissions of cupidity and stupidity. Cupidity in the Carolina Vend-A-Matic transactions and stupidity in the Brunswick stock purchase (p. 542).

Randolph Phillips outlined three reasons why the Committee for a Fair, Honest and Impartial Judiciary opposed the nomination. First,

> Strom Thurmond was promised . . . that in return for his 394 votes at the August 1969 Republican Convention he could name as Associate Justice . . . a sitting Federal judge (p. 547).

Second,

> . . . as a judge of the U.S. Court of Appeals for the Fourth Circuit, Judge Haynsworth failed to disclose the facts already set forth in the record about Carolina Vend-A-Matic, prior to hearing argument in and joining in the 3-to-2 decision that decided in favor of the company in the Deering Milliken *(Darlington)* case (p. 544).

Third,

> . . . it is apparent that the nomination of Judge Haynsworth is motivated by considerations about winning the 1970 congressional and the 1972 presidential elections (p. 544).

Civil Rights Position. The second major objection to Judge Haynsworth was his opposition to school desegregation. The witnesses who opposed him for his position on civil rights were extremely pointed. This intense opposition may have played a large role in Haynsworth's defeat.

Joseph Rauh, Counsel for the Leadership Conference on Civil Rights, argued that in a number of cases, Judge Haynsworth was trying to find a way around the 1954 desegregation case of *Brown v. School Board of Topeka.* This line of argument was also taken by other witnesses. A group of eight Congressmen, seven of whom were black, argued that Judge Haynsworth had played a very prominent role in the 15 years of frustration and delay which have followed the Brown decision (p. 473).

Rauh's statement that Haynsworth was avoiding the *Brown* decision was supported by the National Chairman of the Black American Law Students Association, J. Otis Cochran. He mentioned some of Haynsworth's "obstructionist" tactics in dealing with civil rights cases.

> The typical Haynsworth opinion pays lip service to the principles of desegregation while further delaying relief to black civil rights complainants by remanding cases to the district courts for further investigation, refusing to grant relief pending State court action, or simply granting inadequate relief (p. 582).

> Judge Haynsworth has, throughout his career, stood for obstructionist technique and philosophy, squarely contrary to the whole thrust of mod-

ern Supreme Court decisions. His appointment to that post would make a mockery of the path the court has forged over the last 15 years (p. 583).

Although unable to testify before the Committee, Floyd B. McKissick filed a statement on behalf of the National Conference of Black Lawyers. This statement contained familiar arguments. It stated that although Judge Haynsworth had ruled in favor of *some* black litigants,

> . . . he almost invariably took a segregationist position where the Court was sharply divided on civil rights issues. As a dissenter from progress he has shown himself hostile to the fundamental Constitutional rights of black Americans (p. 612).

Many supported McKissick. Illustratively, Nils R. Douglas, a black man, testified for the Americans for Democratic Action (ADA). He firmly believed that Judge Haynsworth was helping deny the Negroes of their constitutional rights.

> I am here because I think the rate, the shape, the color, the tone and quality of life, everyday life for Negroes in America is being . . . determined now and in the foreseeable future, shall be determined by the legal philosophy of the members of the U.S. Supreme Court (p. 532).

> I . . . know what the needs and wants of the black people are in America, and for this Committee to act favorably upon the nomination of Clement F. Haynsworth . . . is to confirm in the minds of any thinking Negro the notion that the 13th amendment and the 14th amendment to the Constitution do not mean what they claim to mean (p. 532).

Antilabor Philosophy. The third and last major objection to Judge Haynsworth was his antilabor philosophy. However, those attacking Haynsworth's antilabor position usually emphasized issues relating to conflict of interest and civil rights.

George Meany, president of the American Federation of Labor and Congress of Industrial Organizations (AFL-CIO), emphasized that this was only the second time in forty years that the American trade union movement had actively opposed the nomination of a judge to the Supreme Court. The opposition was based on three points: (1) Haynsworth's decisions proved him to be antilabor; (2) he had demonstrated indifference to the legitimate aspirations of Negroes; and (3) he had demonstrated a lack of ethical standards, while on the bench, that disqualify him from consideration for promotion (p. 163).

The flavor of other labor contributions is easy to characterize. A letter from I. W. Abel, president of the Industrial Union Department and the United Steelworkers of America also opposed the nomination, and it is typical. Abel explained:

> The United Steelworkers of America and the Industrial Union Department of the AFL-CIO regard the decision by the President to nominate Judge Haynsworth to the Supreme Court as extremely unfortunate for workers and minority groups, and we . . . urge the Senate to reject the nomination (p. 333).

And so it went, as far as organized labor was concerned.

Haynsworth Committee Report

On October 9, the Senate Judiciary Committee voted 10–7 to send the nomination to the full Senate. The majority report concluded that Judge Haynsworth was "extraordinarily well qualified" to become a Supreme Court Justice. This report refuted all the charges made against the nominee. It stated:

> . . . the contention that Haynsworth should have disqualified himself from the case of *Darlington Manufacturing Co. v. NLRB* (1963)—because he owned one-seventh interest in a company which did business with the company which owned Darlington—was contrary to all precedents for judicial disqualification.

> . . . neither federal law nor the canons of ethics were violated by Haynsworth's actions in regard to the case of *Brunswick Corporation v. Long* (1967), after he purchased 1,000 shares of Brunswick stock . . . the case had been decided, if not announced, before the stock purchase (and) . . . Haynsworth's interest in the case was far short of "substantial" and . . . he did not profit through the purchase or the decision.

> . . . Haynsworth could not fairly be described as unsympathetic to minorities, segregationist, or antilabor. He had . . . frequently voted in favor of persons claiming deprivation of their civil rights. In labor cases he exemplified the "evenheaded treatment of litigants according to law" ruling sometimes for labor and sometimes for management.[7]

Many Senators in the minority filed individual reports on the nomination. Senators Bayh, Burdick, Hart, Kennedy, and Tydings felt that President Nixon should withdraw the nomination. Senator Bayh was the most ardent critic of the nomination.

[7]"Senate Rejects Haynsworth Nomination to Court," *1969 Congressional Quarterly Almanac, 25*, 346.

The Haynsworth Defeat

During the hearings, President Nixon continued to pressure for confirmation of Haynsworth. After allegations of conflict of interest in the hearing, the ABA's Standing Committee on the Federal Judiciary met again and reaffirmed their support of Haynsworth. Other ABA pressures were exerted. For example, Senator Eastland (D., Mississippi) received a telegram from sixteen past presidents of the ABA, not including the then-president or immediate-past president, urging confirmation of Haynsworth. On the other side, on October 27, the American Trial Lawyers Association asked that the nomination be withdrawn or disapproved by the Senate.[8]

Finally, on November 21, a roll call vote of 45–65 defeated the Haynsworth nomination. Ironically, some key Republican leaders voted against the nomination. These included: Senators Hugh Scott (Pa.), the Minority Leader; Robert P. Griffin (Mich.), the party whip; Margaret Chase Smith (Maine), chairman of the Senate Republican Leadership Conference; and John J. Williams (Del.), chairman of the GOP Committee on Committees.

THE CARSWELL NOMINATION

President Nixon nominated another southern jurist, George Harold Carswell, for the Supreme Court on January 19, 1970. As usual, the nomination was referred to the Senate Judiciary Committee, chaired by Senator Eastland.

Supporters took a consistent approach.[9] For example, the president of the Florida Bar Association representing the Boards of Governors of the association testified for the Carswell nomination. The former governor of Florida, Leroy Collins, also testified for the nominee. Others who testified for Carswell included Senator Spessard L. Holland (D., Florida), Senator Edward J. Gurney (R., Florida), and Representative Don Fuqua (D., Florida). Chairman Eastland submitted letters from five judges in the Fifth Circuit Court of Appeals endorsing the Carswell

---

[8]Ibid., p. 348.
[9]Letter from Lawrence E. Walsh, Hearings Before the Committee on the Judiciary, United States Senate, Ninety-First Congress, Second Session, *The Nomination of George Harold Carswell, of Florida, to be Associate Justice of the Supreme Court of the United States,* pp. 1–2. (Unless otherwise footnoted, all other citations in the section about Carswell are from these hearings. The page number is given at the. end of the citation.)

nomination. One of the letters was from Judge Homer Thornberry, a recent Supreme Court nominee. Judge Thornberry described Carswell as

> . . . a man of impeccable character. He is dedicated in his work and vigorous in its application. As a member of our Court, his volume and quality of opinions is extremely high (p. 5).

In addition,

> Judge Carswell has the compassion which is so important in a judge. I believe Judge Carswell possesses the professional and judicial qualifications to be a distinguished Associate Justice of the Supreme Court of the United States (pp. 5–6).

Opposition to the Carswell Nomination

Women's Rights. Opposition for Carswell took two basic forms. First, one of his earlier decisions affected working women, and their spokesmen rose to the defense. Most prominent among these was the president of the National Organization for Women (NOW) and author of *The Feminine Mystique,* Betty Friedan. She stressed that Judge Carswell's voting to deny a rehearing in the *Martin Marietta* case

> . . . would permit employers . . . to fire 4 million working mothers who have children under 6. These mothers comprise 38 percent of the nearly 11 million mothers in the labor force today (p. 89).

> At the very least, Judge Carswell's vote in the *Martin Marietta* case reflects a total blindness to the very real problems women face today, in attempting at long last to use the rights guaranteed in the Constitution to assume full participation in American society . . . (p. 91).

Civil Rights—White Supremacy Speech. Second, civil rights also played a major role in the Senate Hearings. Congressman John Conyers, Jr. (D., Michigan) testified with the support of eight other black Congressmen. His position was clear and direct:

> I am here again to prevail upon you to establish the basic principle that any person of a racist or segregationist persuasion is per se unqualified to serve on the U.S. Supreme Court (p. 206).

Congressman Conyers read part of the famous 1948 white supremacy campaign speech of Carswell. Carswell was quoted as stating:

> I am a southerner by ancestry, birth, training, and inclination, belief and practice. I believe that segregation of the races is proper, and the only

practical and correct way of life in our States. I have always so believed and I shall always so act. I shall be the last to submit to any attempt on the part of anyone to break down and to weaken this firmly established policy of our people. If my own brother were to advocate such a program, I would be compelled to take issue with him and to oppose him to the limits of my ability. I yield to no man, as a fellow candidate or as a fellow citizen, in the firm, vigorous belief in the principles of white supremacy, and I shall always be so governed (p. 207).

Civil Rights—The All White Country Club. Carswell's position was apparently the same in 1956. Julian Proctor, an incorporator of the Capital City Country Club, in Tallahassee, Florida, testified that Carswell had been one of the original twenty stockholders of the club. A newspaper clipping from the *Tallahassee Democrat* on February 15, 1956, carried the story that the city council had leased the municipal golf course to the Tallahassee Country Club.

> The vote was 4 to 1, with Mayor J. T. Williams registering the objection. On a motion by Commissioner Fred Winterle, the commission also agreed to make the same deal on a Negro golf course now under construction to "any responsible group" that wants to take it over.

> Asked if the course would be open to the public, Robert Parker, who represented the country club group, said "any acceptable person will be allowed to play" (p. 261).

Later that year, on May 4, 1956, the Tallahassee Country Club assigned its lease to the Capital City Country Club. The inference was that Carswell had been an incorporator of a private country club which was set up to exclude blacks.

Antagonistic to Civil Rights Attorneys. Leroy D. Clark represented the National Conference of Black Lawyers, and sought to establish that Carswell's approach to civil rights had remained consistent through the very recent past. Attorney Clark had formerly been in charge of all civil rights litigation in Florida for the NAACP. He noted:

> CLARK: . . . I would suggest that there is not a lawyer in the country today who has appeared before Judge Carswell on more cases with specific references to civil rights matters . . . (p. 221).

> Judge Carswell was the most hostile Federal District Court judge I have ever appeared before with respect to civil rights matters . . . (p. 227).

> CLARK: Judge Carswell was insulting and hostile. I have been in Judge Carswell's court on at least one occasion in which he turned his chair away from me when I was arguing. . . . it was not an infrequent experience for Judge Carswell to deliberately disrupt your argument and cut across you, while according, by the way, to opposing counsel every courtesy possible.

It was not unusual for Judge Carswell to shout at a black lawyer who appeared before him while using a civil tone to opposing counsel (p. 227).

Attorneys John Lowenthal, Ernest H. Rosenberger, and Norman Knopf worked in the summer of 1964 as volunteers for Lawyers' Constitutional Defense Committee of the American Civil Liberties Union defending civil rights and voter registration workers in northern Florida. They also indicated that then District Judge Carswell expressed displeasure with out-of-staters, particularly northern lawyers representing civil rights workers (p. 195).

Summary of Civil Rights Arguments. Two other civil rights leaders also testified in opposition to the nomination. The first was Clarence Mitchell, Legislative Chairman, Leadership Conference on Civil Rights, and Director of Washington Bureau of the NAACP. The second witness was Joseph L. Rauh, Jr., General Counsel of Leadership Conference on Civil Rights and Vice Chairman of the Americans for Democratic Action. Rauh summarized his objections to Carswell as follows:

> There is a presumption that a man who says he is a white supremacist, is a white supremacist until he proves the contrary. I say that the record before you, instead of proving the contrary, buttresses the 1948 white supremacy speech.
> There is the golf course incident, in which Judge Carswell has not only been implicated deeply, but lacking in candor before this committee. There is the civil rights hostility running down to the present. I think Leroy Clark said he was there until as late as 1966, being insulted, "never letting me finish a sentence, turning his back on me." Do you really believe that Rosenberger, Knopf, Lowenthal, and Clark were not telling the truth? You could not believe that if you saw them. They have nothing to gain out of this.
> So you have a record buttressing the white supremacy statement. And then you have the cases. You have 15 cases of unanimous reversal, nothing in his favor (p. 306).

Lack of Professional Qualifications. Organized labor introduced a final body-blow. Carswell's nomination was political in the narrowest sense, without the redeeming virtue of sufficient professional qualifications. Thomas E. Harris, Associate General Counsel of the AFL-CIO appeared in behalf of President George Meany to oppose the Carswell nomination. He explained:

> We do not do so because we view Judge Carswell as antagonistic to the interests of organized labor, . . . rather the premise of our opposition is that this nomination is based exclusively on calculations of partisan political advantage, and was made without regard to professional or judicial merit (p. 234).

. . . the administration's sole guide in making its selections was its southern political strategy.

That strategy requires a relatively youthful nominee from the South, preferably a State in which the Republicans have made headway and have a good chance to make more, with a poor civil rights record and a good chance of confirmation. Judge Carswell meets the requirements of this standard perfectly (pp. 235–36).

Meany's charges of the lack of professional competence were supported by Louis H. Pollak, Dean of Yale Law School:

On the basis of the nominee's public record, together with what I have read of his work product, I am forced to conclude that the nominee has not demonstrated the professional skills and the larger constitutional wisdom which fits a lawyer for elevation to our highest court.

. . . I am impelled to conclude that the nominee presents more slender credentials than any nominee for the Supreme Court put forth in this century . . . (p. 242).

Senate Rejects Carswell

At first, administration forces thought they might have won confirmation for Carswell when they defeated an effort to send the nomination back to the Senate Judiciary Committee by a vote of 52–44.[10] This recommittal effort, if it had been successful, would have defeated the nomination without an official vote. Recommittal was an attempt by anti-Carswell forces to kill the nomination by burying it. This apparent victory for the pro-Carswell leaders was short-lived, when confirmation was defeated two days later on April 8 by a vote of 45–51.[11]

Once again, key Republican Senators who the president needed for confirmation voted against the nominee. Senators Marlow W. Cook (R., Kentucky), a leader in the pro-Haynsworth forces, Margaret Chase Smith (R., Maine), and Winston L. Prouty (R., Vermont) who voted for Haynsworth, all voted against Carswell. Carswell soon resigned his judicial post to run for the Republican nomination for Senator from Florida. He was defeated in the primary election.

THE BLACKMUN NOMINATION

On April 14, 1970, President Nixon nominated Harry Andrew Blackmun, a judge of the Eight Circuit Court of Appeals, for the Su-

---

[10]"Senate Rejects Carswell Nomination to Supreme Court," *Congressional Quarterly Weekly Report, 28,* No. 15 (April 10, 1970), 943.
[11]Ibid.

preme Court.[12] A native Minnesotan and friend of Chief Justice Burger, Blackmun fit President Nixon's requirement as a "strict constitutional constructionist." It was apparent from the outset that the Blackmun nomination would have an easier time with the Senate than the last two Nixon nominations. Former Vice-President Humphrey felt the nominee was " . . . the kind of man I'd like to see on the Court . . . completely devoid of any racial bias . . . [a man] of moderate political persuasion."[13]

On April 29, the Senate Judiciary Committee began hearings on the Blackmun nomination. The ABA's Standing Committee on the Federal Judiciary endorsed the nomination as they had the other three nominees. Except for the ABA endorsement, interest groups did not testify in the one day hearings. On May 5 the Committee voted unanimously to report his nomination favorably to the full Senate.[14] On that same day the AFL-CIO released a letter from its President George Meany endorsing the nomination.[15] The Senate confirmed the nomination unanimously by a vote of 94–0. This confirmation made a complete court of nine justices.

CONCLUSION

It is clear that interest groups played an important role in lobbying against the nomination of certain recent Supreme Court nominees. In fact, rarely has interest group activity been as extended and as intense over court nominations. A number of pressure groups with a wide variety of interests participated in the lobbying efforts. Most pressure group activities were negative—a blocking effort—and were influential in defeating the nominations of Fortas, Haynsworth, and Carswell. The activities and subsequent rejections of these three nominees by the U.S. Senate suggest that future appointments to the Supreme Court must not only be carefully selected, but must also be acceptable to a variety of interest groups and their allies in the Senate.

12"Minnesota Judge is Third Nominee to Supreme Court," *Congressional Quarterly Weekly Report, 28*, No. 16 (April 17, 1970), 1044.
13Ibid.
14"Blackmun Nomination," *Congressional Quarterly Weekly Report, 28*, No. 19 (May 8, 1970), 1218.
15"Blackmun Unanimously Confirmed for Supreme Court," *Congressional Quarterly Weekly Report, 28*, No. 20 (May 15, 1970), 1271.

18 *Kenneth M. Dolbeare and James W. Davis, Jr.*

Little Groups of Neighbors: American Draft Boards

With a new Administration, a new Congress, and the prospect of a reduced need of soldiery, the reform of the Selective Service System may
once again become a public issue. In 1967 the system received only a
perfunctory review in Congress, despite (or, perhaps, because of) loud
complaints from all sides and some provocative findings from a Presidential commission. In the last two years not much has changed. The
problems are if anything worse:

There is an even greater surplus of manpower over needs, making
even more important the manner of selecting the minority (about 45
percent of the eligible age group) who *are* required to serve.

Guaranteed deferments for those young men in college, frequently
followed by occupational, Reserve, or National Guard deferments, in-
troduce a strong economic bias into conscription. (The lowest-income people do gain some compensation from the fact that so many of them fail
the physical and mental examinations.) Therefore, the threat of induction hovers most compellingly over the sons of the working and lower-

From *Trans-Action* (March 1969). Copyright © March 1969 by Trans-
action, Inc., New Brunswick, New Jersey. Reprinted by permission.

middle classes. In Wisconsin, the military-service experience of qualified men in some low-income, rural counties is 50 percent higher than qualified men in wealthy urban areas.

Finally, each of the nation's nearly 4,100 local boards has different standards and practices—so that the man who would be deferred in one area may be quickly drafted in another.

These facts were all well established in 1967, of course, when Congress brushed aside proposals for reforming the system. And it may be that the Vietnam War, the preferences of House Armed Services Committee Chairman L. Mendel Rivers, or the political artistry of Selective Service Director Lewis B. Hershey will serve again to prevent serious consideration of the anachronisms of the draft.

The major argument for retention of the system in its present form —and the argument that General Hershey has made since he acquired responsibility for conscription in the 1930s—is that the crucial act of selecting men for induction should be made through the discretionary judgments of local boards of part-time volunteers in each local community across the nation. These "little groups of neighbors," in General Hershey's oft-used phrase, must remain the foundation of the Selective Service System—because these men are representative of their communities, they know who can best be spared from the community (and therefore the need for broad discretion in decision-making), and they are known and trusted by their fellow citizens to the extent that public acceptance of conscription itself rests on the existence of local boards.

This is the way General Hershey put the matter in a prepared budget presentation to the House Appropriations Committee in 1966: "The . . . functions [of Selective Service] are carried on in the local boards which are composed of little groups of neighbors on whom is placed the responsibility to determine who is to serve the nation in the Armed Forces and who is to serve in industry, agriculture, and other deferred classifications." And later in 1966, in response to the House Armed Services Committee's friendly queries about the need for change in the system: "It would be essential to avoid in any way interfering with the present decentralized approach of the system. . . . The decentralized, or local board, or grass-roots operation of Selective Service began with the First World War and demonstrated that the nation would much more willingly support compulsory military service operated by their neighbors at home. . . ."

But research conducted since 1967 shows conclusively that *every major assumption made by General Hershey and the Selective Service System concerning local boards is wrong.* The "little groups of neighbors" that Selective Service and (apparently) Congress are so attached to are by and large *not* "neighbors" in any representative sense, they are *not* in contact with registrants, they are *not* known or widely trusted by local citizens (their discretionary powers are particularly resented), and they are perhaps a principal reason for public *disapproval* of conscription. Conducting conscription through the local-board system is costing Selective Service popular confidence and support; it is exaggerating the economic biases inherent in deferment policies; and it is creating the arbitrariness and lack of uniformity which are the hallmarks of the system. In short, only memories of turn-of-the-century rural America—and General Hershey's fear that change can mean only a return to the type of draft conducted during the Civil War—sustain the local-board principle.

Let us examine the findings in each major part of the "little groups of neighbors" argument.

The representativeness of local-board members. Early in 1967, the National Advisory Commission on Selective Service (the President's Commission, chaired by Burke Marshall) released data on the social characteristics of local-board members throughout the country. Even for such a devotedly backward-looking organization as Selective Service, it came as something of a surprise to find that 22 percent of all board members were over 70 years of age and nearly half were over 60. Two-thirds of all board members were veterans, and far more had their service experience in World War I—which ended 50 years ago—than saw service in the Korean War. The typical five-member draft board included three veterans, at least one of them from World War I; at least one member who was over 70; and no more than one member under 50. (In 1967 Congress responded to the system's superannuation by soberly enacting amendments limiting terms of service on local boards to 25 years, and requiring retirement at age 75. These amendments were not without effect, of course: Maine's Appeal Board, for example, lost four of its five members, ages 93, 81, 78, and 77. Yet the amendments did not give much impetus to a substantial turnover in membership.)

Board members were unrepresentative in other ways, too. In 1966 only 1.3 percent were Negroes, although Negroes constitute 11 percent of the male population and an even larger share of the armed forces. In four Southern states with heavy concentrations of Negroes, there were no board members who were black; other Southern and border states had only a few, and most Northern cities had only token black membership. (These figures have been improved in the past two years, according to Selective Service, but the basic pattern still survives.) Occupationally, board members were drawn chiefly from such upper middle-class strata as professionals, managers, and proprietors. Although half of the male labor is employed in blue-collar jobs, only 9 percent of all board members reported that they were blue-collar workers.

States varied widely in the occupational makeup of their boards—apparently in response to the policies of state draft headquarters and to local political realities. New York City emphasizes lawyers—nearly one-third of all its board members are lawyers, even though registrants are legally prevented from bringing lawyers with them when they appear. (General Hershey says procedures are so simple that registrants don't have to be represented by counsel.) North Dakota avoids having lawyers on boards: In 1966, not one of its 213 board members was a lawyer. In some states (Florida and Pennsylvania among them) boards are heavily dominated by proprietors and managers; the highest percentage of blue-collar men (15 percent) is in Massachusetts, and the lowest (3 percent) in Washington.

Our own research in Wisconsin and elsewhere allows us to elaborate on the nature of board members' unrepresentativeness and the reasons for it. Age is a serious problem in Wisconsin, as it is nationally. Among the 81 percent of Wisconsin's 387 board members who answered our questionnaire, almost three times as many were over 60 as were under 45, and 26 percent were over 70. On the average, then, a Wisconsin local board would have two men who are retired from business (over 65) for each member whose job experience dates from World War II or after. Many men stay on their local boards long after they retire, and some actually join after retirement, in both cases apparently because they want to have something to do with their time. The job is not taxing, and they perceive it as important. Selective Service officials actually encourage long service, because it is not easy to find replacements and because long service makes life easier for the state headquarters: Experienced board members are more predictable, and require less guidance in times of stress than new men with new ideas.

Occupationally, board members are drawn from a special grouping within the middle class. Missing are the more mobile and higher-status occupations, like salesmen and physicians. Instead, board members are men with geographically fixed livelihoods—government employment, retail stores, farms, or family enterprises—suggesting that they have both long residence and a concern for the social and political management of the community. Vacancies in Wisconsin as in many other states are filled by having the remaining members nominate one of their acquaintances to the state headquarters, which passes the recommendation on to the Governor and thence to the President for appointment. Thus, the recruitment of new members is for the most part self-perpetuating. Occasionally, the state headquarters has to find a new man. In Wisconsin, this has created a remarkable overrepresentation of post-office employees, because the field man from state headquarters frequently begins his search by consulting the local postmaster. Whatever the route by which men reach their boards, the process only rarely reflects efforts toward representation of any kind on the boards.

If boards are therefore unrepresentative of their communities—or, perhaps more accurately, representative of only the social-control and political-control structures of their communities when the system was re-established 20 years ago—consider how they look to their clientele, the registrants. To today's generation 18 to 25 years old—mobile, lacking their parents' experience with World War II, Korea, or Depression "hard times"; pressured by the Vietnam War; and only too aware of the pace of technological change—these "little groups of neighbors" are little more than a cruel joke. Selective Service requires that a registrant be subject to the board at which he registered at 18, despite any subsequent moves on his part to other locations and jobs around the country, so that often boards are not even "neighbors" in the geographical sense of the word.

Board members know their communities and who can best be spared for military service. In some rural counties, where there are few registrants and there has been little change in the last 20 years, board members may in fact know their registrants and the needs of their communities. One could enter some reservations even here, though: We found some board members enthusiastic about their opportunity to support community norms by inducting men who fail to get a job in timely fashion, men who leave their wives, etc. But for the majority of registrants, who live in the nation's more urban areas, such intimacy of knowledge on the part of board members is wholly impossible.

Board members of such advanced ages, drawn so arbitrarily from such a narrow segment of the middle class, are unlikely either to have much of an idea of the needs of their communities or to know their registrants at all, let alone to know who can best be spared. In many cities, the jurisdiction of a board follows ancient ward or precinct lines, or some other boundary equally irrelevant for purposes of defining social or economic units that might be "communities." Two or three square miles of apartment houses containing perhaps 20,000 registrants don't constitute a "community" with specific needs and priorities, nor is it likely that board members would know more than a tiny fraction of such a number of registrants. (Urban boards have 20,000 registrants on the average, though some have more than 50,000.)

Evidence from both local-board members and registrants indicates that board members are generally unfamiliar with their clients. Thus, we asked Wisconsin local-board members how often they had contact of *any* kind with *any* of their registrants. The results are:

Board Members Contact With Registrants

	Frequent Contact	Occasional Contact	Rare or No Contact
Urban Board Member	3%	25%	72%
Small-city Members	15	48	37
Small-town Members	19	55	26

The majority of urban-board members rarely or never have contact with registrants, the majority of small-city members had occasional, rare, or no contact; and the majority of small-town members had only occasional contact. Next, we asked a sample of University of Wisconsin students to name members of their local boards: Only a handful, even of rural residents, could name even one. And perhaps understandably, registrants showed a lack of trust in their boards. If you were to seek information from your local board, we asked the students, would you be willing to give your name? One-third of registrants in rural areas and one-half of urban registrants said No. Many registrants also seem to think that board members are chockful of bias and prejudice: When presented with hypothetical questions about their boards' criteria in selecting among equally qualified men for induction, nearly half of our respondents were convinced that race, class, or occupational factors would control their boards' decision-making.

These findings suggest that local-board members, for the most part, neither know their "communities" nor their registrants—because their communities don't exist as such; because in any event they are too far detached from them; because there are too many registrants (many of whom have moved from the area); and because the contact between board members and registrants is usually slight, and often marked by fear and distrust on the part of registrants. Board members sometimes do receive and act upon bits of knowledge about their registrants, of course, but not always in the direction of a more rational decision process: The President's Commission reported that men who had moved out of their board's jurisdiction since age 18 were placed in 1-A classifications considerably more often than equally qualified men remaining in the jurisdiction!

Local boards are known and trusted by local citizens, and they are the key to public acceptance of conscription. If possible, Selective Service's assumptions are even more mythical here than elsewhere. In September 1966, using the services of the University of Wisconsin's Survey Research Laboratory, we obtained responses from a sample of Wisconsin's adult population to a series of questions about the draft and the Selective Service System.

We discovered first that barely half the population was aware that the draft was conducted through local boards—despite almost daily publicity about the draft in the news media. A full 39 percent said flatly that they did not know *who* administered the draft; some associated it with units of local government; and only 52 percent gave responses that—with the most generous interpretation—we could define as indicating some knowledge about local boards. Of those who *were* aware of the existence of local boards, only one in ten could give the name of a member. And because half of the names given were female, while *all* board members were then male, these names may have been those of clerks. (No effort was made to verify the accuracy of the handful of names given.)

Next, we found that among those people who *were* aware of the existence of local boards, a narrow plurality thought that the local-board principle was *not* a good idea. As for those who had no prior knowledge about local-board administration, when acquainted with the practice, *they* said it was *not* a good idea by a ratio of about five to three. The combined sample delivered a clear plurality against local management of the draft.

Interestingly, there were sharp differences by class in people's attitudes toward the local-board principle. Professionals, managers, proprietors, officials, and farmers—in short, those *like* board members themselves—supported the local-board idea by sometimes more than two-to-one ratios. Blue-collar workers and housewives *opposed* local management by the same ratios.

Finally, we found that there was almost no relationship between people's attitudes toward local boards and their attitudes toward conscription. For one thing, many more people were aware of the existence of the draft, a majority of them considering it to be fairly administered. Those who considered the draft unfair tended to be people with the most in the way of financial outlay or education invested in a civilian career, for whom military service was an unwanted interruption. Blue-collar people, perhaps because service was not such a comparatively bad alternative to their other prospects, tended to think the draft was fair. But the very people most convinced of the unfairness of the draft itself (professionals, for example) were most likely to be those who expressed the greatest confidence in local boards, while the people who opposed the local-board idea (i.e., blue-collar workers) were *not* adverse to conscription.

There was only one important correlation between people's attitudes toward local boards and their attitudes toward the fairness of the draft: Of those who knew about local boards, those who believed that boards "just followed orders from Washington" were much *more* likely to think the draft was fair than those who believed that local boards could "decide for themselves" who should be drafted. Because this finding flies so squarely in the face of the system's conviction that discretion is necessary for local-board efficacy, these data are worth presenting in full:

	Local boards "Decide for themselves"	Local boards "Just follow orders from Washington"
The draft is fair	39%	62%
The draft is unfair	61	38
	100%	100%
	(Number: 67)	(Number: 148)

The implications of all these findings are clear: Local boards cannot be the source of public acceptance of conscription, for local boards are neither known nor approved—and not even the knowledgeable people approve of their discretionary powers. But local boards *may* be the price of acquiescence from that politically powerful segment of the middle class that itself mans and controls the local boards. In this case, of course, the local-board system boils down to a cynical grant of power to the middle class to draft the sons of the working class in the least visible manner possible.

WHAT DO LOCAL BOARDS CONTRIBUTE TO SELECTIVE SERVICE?

From the evidence examined here, local boards seem to create antipathy in the majority of people and fear and distrust on the part of registrants. On the other hand, local boards seem to quiet any anxieties of those people who may be politically weighty—because such people are reassured that others like themselves run the boards. From the President's Commission Report and from our research—and from the daily observation of most citizens—eloquent testimony is available as to the lack of uniformity injected into conscription by the existence of so many legally autonomous local boards. Selective Service, perhaps because of its conviction about the necessity of local boards, makes a virtue out of this fact, arguing in effect that no two men in the nation are so similarly situated that they might reasonably expect to be similarly treated.

Not so readily obvious is the fact that local boards, by the mere fact of multiplying the number of jurisdictions on which induction calls must be made, both exacerbate nonuniformity and exaggerate the economic biases of national deferment policy. If there were only one (national) manpower pool from which all calls were made, local differences in percentages of men attending college or failing to meet induction standards would average out and conscription would be nationally uniform, calling similarly situated men from all over the nation at once.

The local-board principle, therefore, does definite harm—and very little in the way of benefit. What holds it up? How long can it endure as the central commitment of the American system of conscription? Our view is that, as a substitute for facts, there is nothing better than ideology—particularly when ideology may serve, as here, as a cloak for advantage.

Only the foolhardy are likely to venture forth against the assembled weight of the status quo of conscription and its mechanisms. Selective Service's local-board system is the beneficiary of a combination of an internally generated and thoroughly self-deluding conviction ("little groups of neighbors"), an all-encompassing decentralization ethic in and out of government, and a perhaps even more significant central core of sophisticated political achievement. In a 1967 Task Force Report, Selective Service triumphantly "rebutted" all the President's Commission's findings and proposals, chiefly because it did not question the basic premise that local boards were useful and essential. It defended their "achievements" without ever examining them.

Decentralization of government responsibilities commands support from many without regard for the specific consequences. National uniformity in the sharing of national burdens or benefits, though well established in such similar areas as Internal Revenue or Social Security or the Veterans' Administration, in regard to the draft still faces the accretions of decades of ideology and superstition. And because our public policies reflect the power distributions and proclivities of Congress more accurately than the merits of problems *or* the preferences of majorities of the people, and because those with the greatest political power are content with Selective Service, the local-board system—unfortunately—is likely to endure into the foreseeable future.

part three

Participation at the Higher Levels

Interacting Effects of Elites and Institutions

This chapter deals with participants at the higher political levels and with the political institutions and ideas they respond to or create. These elite participants include presidents, heads of federal departments, and governors. The political institutions or ideas with which they interact include both time-honored ones and innovative ones like "maximum feasible participation," which was intended to permit a new role for individuals served by various public programs.

The spectrum of attention here is broad, but the point is a simple one. The quality of the political drama is the product of an incredibly diverse and subtle adjustment of institutions to participants, and participants to institutions. Sometimes the interaction is direct and immediate, at other times it is circuitous and long-range. But the signs are always there, for the prepared eye. And the basic dilemma is always there, whether in democracies or in representative systems. Participants at "higher political levels" must be variously enabled to help guide what needs doing, while they also must somehow be tethered short of that degree of power that poses a threat to the liberty of "rank and file" participants. The balance, ideally, is a shifting one. For example, during a war the balance will shift toward providing higher political levels with more power.

This chapter emphasizes a critical reality, then. In the complex mutual adjustment of political institutions and specific political figures, as in much of life, some actors will always be more equal than others. This will be due to both personal skills and ambitions, as well as to specialization by some in governance. In both cases, the challenge is to permit broad influence upon the political elite without shackling them.

Political reality achieves this balance only imperfectly. Consider Linda Carstarphen's narrative, "New England Challenges the Oil Import Policy." She traces the impact upon long-standing institutional arrangements that can be exerted by presidents who, if they pick their spots, can be far more equal than other political actors. Carstarphen's narrative also suggests that established oil interests have major interests in influencing public policy, and that they have advantages in seeking to express those interests. In this case, as in many others, the key question is whether other interests adequately participated or were represented. These "other interests" include such diffuse aggregates as "the northeastern consumers of oil."

The inequalities common in political life are clearly illustrated by Carstarphen. Two U.S. presidents were variously not persuaded about the case for lowering fuel oil prices in Maine and the upper northeast by the development of a refinery complex at a proposed foreign trade zone in Machiasport, Maine. And these two presidents were able to convert their lack of persuasion into nondecisions. Only the tactics varied. Initially, nondecision was the product of simple delay. Later, nondecision was fostered by the tried and true method of appointing study group after study group, and then studiously neglecting their studied recommendations.

The point here is not to demean either process or participants. Indeed, if more or less pleasantly arrived at, some nondecisions may be the very height of political statesmanship. Politics is the art of the possible; but it also has much to do with responding to aspirations in ways that give them their day in political court, even if those aspirations must be denied. In this sense, Presidents Johnson and Nixon were able to respond to both the established oil interests and their potential competitors. The two presidents were able to rise to the occasion by variously adapting procedures and policies to the exigencies of the moment.

Presidents also can be more equal in making things happen as well as in keeping them from happening, be it noted. That point is patent in "Sit Tight, Wally," by Clyde E. Teasley III. Wally—or Walter J. Hickel—had been chosen by Nixon as his Secretary of the Interior. Wally was later to be given a direct presidential directive to resign, despite his preference to "sit tight" in the face of less direct invitations to resign. The president won this one, at least in the sense that Wally Hickel did leave.

In short, Hickel was not able to overcome the institutional framework in which he found himself. From a revealing perspective, Hickel's strategy could not win for losing. As every department head must, Hickel had to develop a base of support for his leadership and his programs. For various reasons, Hickel was most successful with conservationists and the Now Generation. However, his unexpected romance with the conservationists did not endear him to a major client group of Interior, the oil interests. And his growing role as self-appointed administration spokesman for the young won him no great credit in the White House, either.

Just as he succeeded, then, so also did Wally Hickel fail. Despite more or less subtle hints to leave the administration which he increasingly sought to instruct in the error of its ways, Wally initially sat tight. But matters did not improve. Eventually, exit Wally.

The institution simply overwhelmed the man in this case. The institutional realities are plain. Hickel was Nixon's appointee, and traditionally presidents are given wide latitude in selecting and changing their team. From another point of view, Hickel's strategy may have been a good one in an election campaign. But he was a presidential appointee, and keeping in the private good graces of the boss is more critical in this case than the public hosannas one receives. This is true unless an appointee is very powerful, which Hickel not yet was but might have become. Indeed, Teasley may be describing a case in which a department head was seen as getting too big for the britches that President Nixon wished him to wear.

In addition to the political elites taking one another's measure—as in the Hickel case—campaigns, elections, and votes are usually seen as the major vehicles for somehow influencing or controlling those who have been vested with more than equal political power. Delmer D. Dunn sorts the sense from the nonsense of the common presumption about the crucial role of elections and the vote. "The Meaning and the Meaninglessness of American Elections" looks closely at the "mandate theory" of elections, and finds it seriously oversimple.

Dunn does not argue that elections are meaningless—far from it, in fact—but he finds that their meaning often conflicts with conventional wisdom. For example, the "mandate theory" maintains that elected officials will guide their behavior by the policies on which they won the *last* election. In less direct ways, Dunn argued in counterpoint, it is the *next* election which provides at least as significant direction for office holders. The election is still important, as Dunn sees it. But he argues that the conventional wisdom pays too much attention to the wrong election.

Whatever the value of the mandate theory, there is an increasing question of who controls whom at election time. The technology for inducing the electorate to make the "correct decision" has grown in both sophistication and cost, in about equal proportion. Heightened sophistication and increased cost generate grave doubts about both elections and the vote as prime vehicles for participation, whether in a true democracy or a republic. This is the essense of the *National Observer's* story on "The Almost Perfect Political Campaign," which reports on the 1966 New York gubernatorial campaign of Nelson D. Rockefeller. The story concludes on this concerned note:

> Is there a lesson in New York that anyone can be elected, given money, television, experts, and time? Perhaps not. Mr. Rockefeller, after all, is a great campaigner, and has been, many people think, a strong and effective governor.

There was, in all the confusion and the bitterness, a product to be sold, albeit in a battered and dusty package.

Yet, a note of doubt remains. These new techniques are so overwhelming, so terribly effective. Some day, maybe they will elect a truly dangerous and sinister man to high public office.

The preventive, perhaps, is a general understanding of what it's all about.

There are also other possible major preventives, like the development of vehicles for participation in addition to the vote. This is no easy piece, with two significant qualifications. First, there have been some major formal changes in power sharing via enhanced participation in this country, of course. These include the universal extension of voting rights to women in 1919–20, and just recently to 18-year-olds in national elections. And these extensions may have major effects on public policy outcomes. But the focus here is on new representative devices, as opposed to extensions of existing vehicles for participation. Second, various extralegal approaches to participation seem to be developing. For example, "ecotage" is such a new participative form. "Ecotage" is a manufactured word, combined from ecology and sabotage. Ecotage techniques might include kidnapping executives of firms that pollute, or somehow planting a tree in the middle of a highway. These extralegal participative techniques alike imply that: "Harassment is one of the few catalysts left to make people respond to problems."[1] The focus here is not on such approaches to enhanced participation.

The recent past suggests that major new vehicles for participation will be hard to develop and even harder to sustain, however. This is the dual message of Daniel A. Dye's "Maximum Feasible Participation: An Irony of the 'War on Poverty.'" Dye was the executive director of a local agency for community action, one of whose challenges was to develop "maximum feasible participation," or MFP. MFP was an attempt to develop a new participative vehicle for those served by poverty programs.

The obstacles to implementing the MFP concept were great, Dye reports, and there seems a broader message in his experience. "Maximum feasible participation," he concludes, often was interpreted as "minimum acceptable interference with the status quo." Existing institutions will not simply roll over and play dead, that is to say. And that is probably as it should be, unless those institutions are corrupt and without redeeming virtue.

[1]*Newsweek*, August 23, 1971, p. 50.

19 Linda Carstarphen

New England Challenges
the
Oil Import Policy

INTRODUCTION

One of the first lessons that students of politics learn is that politics, as David Easton and others have pointed out, involves the allocation of society's scarce resources. These resources include both intangibles—such as civil rights, opportunities, and values—and tangibles—such as wealth, property, and natural resources. Some of the most hotly contested political issues in United States history concern the control and distribution of natural resources. Very prominent among these conflicts are those pertaining to oil resources. Our history is full of such issues. For example, there was the "Hot Oil Case" in 1935, which pitted federal authority against state authority and the courts against the legislative and executive branches, *Panama Refining Company v. Ryan*, 293 U.S. 388, 55 S. Ct. 241, 79 L. Ed. 446. There is also the long running issue of

"New England Challenges the Oil Import Policy: A Case of Delayed Decision Making" was written expressly for this volume. The author wishes to acknowledge the contribution to this article made by the students in her Public Administration class at the University of Maine in the fall of 1969. Also, she wishes to thank Mr. Peter Bradford, Federal-State Coordinator for the State of Maine, for his invaluable assistance in checking the original draft for inaccuracies and omissions.

the oil depletion allowance which gives a tax advantage to the oil interests. The conflict between the oil companies and the conservationists receives constant attention in the daily press. These are only a few of the examples of the conflicts which the distribution and control of our oil resources have generated.

This particular case involves a conflict between the oil interests and the New England states; it is just another in the long series of issues that surrounds this valuable natural resource. Those who benefitted from established policies sought to prevent others from undermining their advantages in this sphere. Established interests appeared to be successful in their endeavors, and this case illustrates how they utilized the power structure to maintain their benefits. The nature of the decision making structure and the procedures involved made their task easier. Of particular interest here is the manner in which decisions were prevented. When decisions are prevented, the status quo prevails and when this happens, the interests which benefitted in the past continue to do so. This case demonstrates how difficult it can be to bring about change in a system where power is dispersed to the extent that no individual or agency can act without the support or compliance of others. The thrust of this study is to show how participants can manipulate values, myths, political institutions, and procedures to prevent a decision or to obtain a negative decision. In 1963, the Port Authority of the State of Maine was authorized by the Maine Legislature to apply to the Foreign Trade Zones in Washington, D.C., for authority to establish a foreign trade zone in Maine. A foreign trade zone is the equivalent of a foreign country for import-export purposes and was provided for in the Foreign Trade Zones Act of 1934. The federal act "authorizes the establishment of processing activities in domestic areas which are treated for purposes of the customs laws as foreign territories. Raw materials are allowed to enter free of quota or duty, and the finished products may be either exported or imported into the United States subject to the same restrictions as would apply to products manufactured abroad."[1]

Preliminary Events

Around 1965, Maine officials began serious efforts to persuade oil companies to build an oil refinery in the proposed trade zone to be located at Machiasport, a natural deep water harbor capable of accom-

---

[1]U.S. Cabinet Task Force on Oil Import Control, *The Oil Import Question: A Report on the Relationship of Oil Imports to the National Security.* (Washington, D.C.: U.S. Government Printing Office, 1970), p. 83 (hereinafter referred to as *The Oil Import Question*).

modating super tankers. The efforts to establish a foreign trade zone and oil refinery stemmed from the fact that New England has no indigenous sources of crude oil, that New Englanders consume a large quantity of heating oil every year, and that prices for oil purchases are considered to be higher in New England than elsewhere. The Governor of Maine, Kenneth M. Curtis, pointed out in October 1968 that "more than 70 percent of the homes in New England are heated by oil, and that householders there have had to pay more. There are 291 refineries in 44 states in the country, but none in New England . . . We just want a fair shake. I believe New England is being exploited."[2]

Maine officials believe that the construction of an oil refinery in the proposed foreign trade zone would lower the cost of oil and oil products for New England, especially home heating oil. Low cost foreign crude oil could be imported and refined and then shipped into the New England area under an import quota. This would eliminate the import taxes that boost the cost of oil and oil products.

These activities by Maine officials culminated in June 1968. The Maine Port Authority applied to the Foreign Trade Zones Board for a zone at Machiasport; Occidental Petroleum Corporation applied to the Oil Import Administration in the U.S. Department of the Interior for a license to import oil products from the trade zone under an import quota. These two separate but related actions have produced a situation which now involves several departments and agencies of the federal government, various cabinet secretaries, the president, numerous U.S. senators and representatives, officials of the state of Maine and other northeastern states, and a host of interest groups not only in Maine and throughout the New England area, but the rest of the United States as well. (Since this case involves numerous events spanning a three year period a chronology of events is presented in the Appendix at the end of the chapter to assist the reader in keeping track of each occurrence.)

The Two Decisions

There are two distinct but related decisions involved. The first concerns the establishment of a foreign trade zone. Maine's application for a zone in Machiasport was filed with the Foreign Trade Zones Board, an interdepartmental board composed of the secretary of the army, the secretary of the treasury, and the secretary of commerce, the official head of the board. Approval for foreign trade zones has always been a routine matter. In fact, the Foreign Trade Zones Board, in its 35-year history,

[2]*New York Times*, October 6, 1968, p. 17.

has never rejected an application.[3] Approval is automatic if it can be shown that: (1) foreign commerce will be enhanced, and (2) that no adverse effects on the United States balance of payments will result. In September 1968, at the suggestion of foreign trade zone administrators, the Maine Port Authority revised its application to make Portland a foreign trade zone for nonoil products and Machiasport a subzone for oil and oil products.

The actual decisions of the Foreign Trade Zones Board have always been made by a board of alternates consisting of the undersecretaries of the army, treasury, and commerce. The alternates evaluate the requests and then recommend acceptance or rejection. Members of the Board have a history of automatically accepting the alternates' recommendations.

The second decision concerns a request for an import quota for products manufactured in the oil refinery. The responsibility for this decision rests with the Oil Import Administration in the Department of Interior. This agency administers the nation's oil import program, established in 1959 by President Eisenhower. Under the program, oil imports are limited for the purposes of developing and conserving the nation's petroleum resources. The justification usually given for the program is that it is essential for national security. The oil import quota has been promoted as a national security measure. It is designed to protect essential military and civilian demands against possible interruptions of foreign supplies. The essence of this argument is simply that it is safer to rely on foreign supplies than to risk a threat to national security if such supplies are cut off. Eisenhower's proclamation established the types and quantities of oil which may be imported, and allocates these among oil importers according to eligibility requirements.[4]

Occidental Petroleum Corporation requested permission to import 300,000 barrels per day of crude oil into the trade zone and to ship 100,000 barrels per day of finished products into the country. This would involve an amendment to or a change in the established quota system.

Theoretically, the decision on the foreign trade zone could be made independent of the oil import quota decision.[5] However, events have

---

[3]Fact sheet distributed by Occidental Petroleum Corporation of Los Angeles, California, on September 13, 1969. The document is entitled "The Machiasport Refinery Project."

[4]For a full description of the existing oil quota system see *The Oil Import Question*, pp. 8–15.

[5]*The Oil Import Question*, p. 84.

conspired to make the issues almost inseparable. Basically, the established oil interests[6] and spokesmen for the oil-rich states of the West and Southwest sought to prevent a decision on either issue which might be detrimental to them politically and economically. In order to accomplish this, the spokesmen and representatives for the oil industry manipulated "dominant community values, myths, and political institutions and procedures."[7]

This analysis below will focus on the activities of numerous individuals in institutional positions, both public and private, who participated in the political process in order to influence the outcome of a decision. The group of participants on one side was trying to force a favorable decision on what normally would have been a routine matter obscured from public attention. The opposing group of participants was trying mainly to prevent any decision at all because the status quo was biased in their favor.

THE JOHNSON ADMINISTRATION: DELAYED DECISIONS

Trade Zone Hearings. The free trade zone and quota change applications were submitted in June 1968. No substantial action was forthcoming until October 10 of that year when a three man panel of examiners for the Foreign Trade Zone Board held hearings in Portland, Maine. Governor Kenneth Curtis, who presented the case for the State of Maine, was supported by the governor of New Hampshire, John W. King. The primary spokesman for the oil interests was Representative Hale Boggs from Louisiana who claimed that "the refinery proposition could mean the end of the domestic oil industry and could wreck the economy."[8] Boggs' concern stems from the belief that an increase in oil imports would cause a decrease in production in the U.S. petroleum industry. This in turn could affect the national economy by creating unemployment, decreasing government revenues, and affecting investments. Also supporting the position of the oil states was Ben Barnes, speaker of the

---

[6]The established oil interests would include such companies as Gulf, Standard Oil, Shell, and Sinclair. The Occidental Oil Corporation is not among the established oil companies and is often considered to be a maverick among the oil companies.

[7]Peter Bachrach and Morton S. Baratz, "Decision and Non-decisions," *American Political Science Review*, 57 (September 1963), 632.

[8]*New York Times*, October 11, 1968, p. 67.

Texas House of Representatives. Barnes' role in the hearings suggests how serious that state was about the matter.

On the day following the hearings the chairman of the Examiners Committee, N. Norman Engleberg, announced that a decision on Machiasport would probably come before the Nixon Administration took office in January 1969.[9]

Oil Industry Response. Concern among the oil interests was mounting. On October 30, 1968, Sinclair Oil Company took the first of many delaying tactics by filing a suit in the U.S. District Court for the Southern District of New York for an injunction to stop the proceedings on both the foreign trade zone and the oil import quotas. The suit asked for two injunctions: one against Stanley R. Resor, secretary of the army, C. R. Smith, secretary of commerce, and Henry M. Fowler, secretary of treasury, to halt action on the free trade zone application; and another injunction against Stewart Udall, secretary of interior, to stop proceedings on oil import quotas.[10]

The pressure apparently had begun to build. In mid-November, Udall made an I-might-if-I-could announcement. He might make a decision on the oil import quota before he left office, he noted, although he could not act until the Federal Trade Zones Board made its decision. Shortly thereafter, a suit similar to that of Sinclair Oil was filed in federal court in behalf of the State of Oklahoma charging that the Foreign Trade Zones Board lacked the authority to establish the free trade zone.[11]

Udall Proposes Alternatives. On December 8, Udall made a final and perhaps somewhat symbolic gesture. He submitted two proposals regarding the import quotas. One proposal allowed the secretary of the interior fairly broad discretion in permitting oil processed in foreign trade zones into the United States. The other proposal would have based imports of refined oil from the zones on the amount of domestic oil processed there.[12] Udall allowed interested parties thirty days to comment on his two proposals. Only the first of these proposals would have suited the purposes of Occidental. The latter was based on domestic oil refined in the trade zone, and Occidental planned to use foreign oil.

Smith Defers Decision. Following the submission of Udall's two proposals, another delaying action occurred. Secretary of Commerce Smith announced that the decision of Maine's application for a trade

[9]A release from the Atlantic World Port, Inc., of Machiasport entitled "A Chronology of Machiasport Events," dated June 25, 1969.
[10]*New York Times*, October 31, 1968, p. 68.
[11]Ibid., November 23, 1968, p. 68.
[12]Ibid., December 8, 1968, p. 65.

zone would be deferred until the Nixon Administration took office in January of the next year. In making his December 13 announcement, Smith explained that he was postponing the decision in order to give the Nixon Administration "an opportunity to examine the far-reaching policy implications of this application."[13] Outgoing administrations are not always so generous to the incoming administration of another party unless they have more to lose than gain by making a decision.

Response to Smith's Action: State Level. Smith's action precipitated a series of countermeasures. Governor Curtis announced on December 18 that Maine would file a suit in U.S. District Court to force Smith and the other members of the Foreign Trade Zone Board to make a decision. The action would have been the equivalent of a *writ of mandamus*. Almost simultaneously Senator Edward Kennedy of Massachusetts proposed that his state join Maine in challenging the constitutional basis of the oil import quota system. Kennedy also announced that he was calling for an investigation of possible violations on antitrust laws in actions of those seeking to prevent the establishment of the free trade zone. The Massachusetts senator requested both the Justice Department and the Senate Antitrust and Monopoly Subcommittee to investigate the matter, thereby involving Congress and yet another agency of the Executive Branch.

Governor Curtis also tried to contact President Johnson about the delays. Curtis was told by a presidential aide that "Johnson was adhering to his long-standing policy of referring all oil matters to the secretary of interior to avoid being charged with prejudice because of his Texas background."[14] Whatever his reasons, Johnson patently neither wanted to become involved in the matter, nor to have members of his administration make a decision on it.

Response to Smith's Action: Federal Level. Almost immediately after Smith's announcement, Senator Thomas McIntyre, a New Hampshire Democrat and Chairman of the Senate Small Business Subcommittee, announced that his committee would begin hearings on December 19. Secretary Smith, scheduled to testify before the committee, refused to do so claiming that "he and other departmental officials could not testify because of law suits pending in the case."[15] At that time both Oklahoma and Alaska had suits pending in federal courts. The Sinclair suit had been dismissed after Commerce Secretary Smith, against whom an injunction was sought, had announced that the decision would be deferred

13Ibid., December 14, 1968, p. 7.
14Ibid., December 18, 1968, p. 18.
15Ibid., December, 1968, p. 7.

for the Nixon Administration. McIntyre threatened to subpoena Smith to appear before the subcommittee, but never carried out this threat.

Smith Disqualifies Himself. On January 11, 1969, in the waning days of the Johnson Administration, Smith disqualified himself from making the foreign trade zone decision because he wanted to avoid conflict of interest charges. Smith, a native of Texas and former president of American Air Lines, had held securities in oil companies, but these had been placed in a trust over which he had no control.[16] It was later learned that Smith would join the New York investment firm of Lazard Frères which was thought to be the principal investment banker for Shell Oil Company, a role which Lazard Frères denied.[17]

Smith's self-disqualification meant in effect that the Foreign Trade Zones Board would not make a decision before the Johnson Administration left office. Since no decision would be made on the trade zone, supposedly no decision could now be made on the oil import quota. This meant that the Nixon Administration would fall heir to a thorny political question.

THE NIXON ADMINISTRATION: FURTHER DELAYS

Board of Alternates Approves Application. Once the new administration was barely in office, things began to happen. Maine's application for a foreign trade zone was unanimously approved by the Board of Alternates on February 11, 1969. The recommendation by the alternates followed a unanimous recommendation for approval by the members of the Examiners Committee of the Foreign Trade Zones Board which had held the Portland hearings several months before.

Recommendations of the Board of Alternates traditionally were accepted by the Foreign Trade Zones Board members, but as soon as the alternates announced their recommendation it became apparent that the Machiasport matter would not be treated in routine fashion. The Board members, consisting of the secretaries of commerce, treasury and army, announced that they would meet in formal session to discuss the matter. "The meeting . . . would be the first formal session of the panel since the establishment of foreign trade zones was authorized by Congress in 1934."[18] The Board was scheduled to meet on February 26 to consider Maine's proposal.

Nixon Announces Review of Oil Import Policy. Five days before

[16]Ibid., January 11, 1969, p. 39.
[17]Ibid., March 5, 1969, p. 50.
[18]Ibid., February 11, 1969, p. 41.

the Board was to meet, Nixon·introduced another delaying tactic. He announced that there would be a full review of oil import policy in general, and he personally assumed full responsibility for this policy. The message was heard loud and clear, apparently, and some curious reversals occurred. Following this action, the cabinet members responsible decided to put off making a decision on the foreign trade zone. Secretary of Commerce Maurice Stans, chairman of the Foreign Trade Zones Board, cancelled the February 26 meeting and explained that the review of oil import policy was likely to affect the issue of oil allocation in foreign trade zone refineries.[19] This development is ironical. The decision on oil import quotas initially was delayed on the grounds that a decision on the trade zone had to come first. Then the trade zones board claimed it could not act until a decision was made on oil imports. This had a touch of *Catch 22* about it.

Stans' action meant indefinite delay, and understandably roused the ire of New Englanders. Particularly irked was Senator George Aiken of Vermont, a member of the president's own party. Aiken claimed that he had received very strong assurances, supposedly from Stans, that a decision would be made before the end of February. Aiken said, "It's the first rift in the honeymoon. The Republicans, like the Democrats, are working with the oil companies."[20] The six New England governors were in Washington for the National Governors Conference at the time Stans made his announcement, and they sent him a telegram demanding that he call the Foreign Trade Zones Board back into session to make a decision.

Congressional Hearings. The next move was by a Congressional subcommittee. Senator Philip Hart, a Michigan Democrat, convened the Senate Antitrust and Monopoly Subcommittee to hear testimony on the oil import quota system. The hearings, which began in March, brought testimony from such pro-oil politicians as Senators Roman Hruska of Nebraska and Russell Long of Louisiana. Hruska make a strong defense of the present policy, describing it as "essential to national security."[21] His argument rests on the assumption that national security depends upon a reliable supply of oil and oil products which only domestic production can assure. The present oil import policy was established to assure domestic production.

Some shots also were heard from opponents of the oil import policy. Professor Morris Adelman of Massachusetts Institute of Technology said that "most Government research on oil economics had been directed

19Ibid., February 28, 1969, p. 51.
20Ibid.
21Ibid., March 12, 1969, p. 61.

toward 'the preservation of special interests.' "[22] At a later hearing by the same subcommittee, another critic of the program, Joel B. Dirlam of the University of Rhode Island estimated that the oil import policy of the Federal government was costing New England residents approximately $325 million per year.[23]

Nixon Appoints Task Force. The antitrust hearings continued until July, but the subcommittee delayed issuing an official report at that time. Apparently, this was due in part to an action by President Nixon. On March 25, he appointed a task force to study the oil import system and to make recommendations concerning needed changes in present policies. The task force consisted of six cabinet secretaries and representatives of six other departments and agencies. The president, apparently seeing no urgency in the situation, did not set a deadline for a report by the task force. Ronald Zeigler, the president's press secretary, acknowledged that Maine's application for a foreign trade zone would be reviewed by the task force,[24] thereby formally bringing the two issues together.

There is no evidence that a crash program was contemplated. Within two weeks of its appointment, the Cabinet Task Force on Oil Import Control announced an agenda that would take approximately six months to complete. A Harvard Law School antitrust specialist, Professor Philip J. Areeda, was named the executive director. The agenda of the task force extended beyond the six months originally announced. In the course of reviewing the oil import restrictions, the task force examined relevant documents, testimony from Congressional hearings, and testimony from staff experts in various departments and agencies. They also urged interested parties to submit written comments, and over 10,000 pages of written testimony and comments were submitted in response.[25]

Differences of opinion were expressed by representatives of federal agencies. One noteworthy difference occurred between the Antitrust Division of the Department of Justice and the Department of Interior. According to the Antitrust spokesmen, "the present system imposes serious costs to the economy, higher prices to consumers, and is unnecessary 'to the attainment of any national security goal.' "[26] The Antitrust

---

[22]Ibid., p. 73.
[23]Ibid., April 2, 1969, p. 71. When the President's Task Force on Oil Import Controls submitted its report it estimated that the costs for the New England states was somewhere around $393 million per year. See Table A-2 of that report on pp. 26–27.
[24]*New York Times*, March 27, 1969, p. 65.
[25]*The Oil Import Question*, p. 2.
[26]*New York Times*, August 14, 1969, p. 1.

Division representative recommended that the quota system be ended. The Interior Department spokesmen, however, said that it was necessary to retain the quota system "because a free market would not assure an adequate oil supply. The national interests require the United States to have secure sources, namely its own domestic supply."[27] The two agencies whose views, it was reported, did not necessarily reflect the views of their department heads, disagreed over the validity of the oil import program. They did, however, agree that any change should be made gradually so as to prevent economic and administrative disruption.

In mid-December 1969, reports began appearing which indicated that the task force had concluded its study and was prepared to recommend replacing the oil import quota system with a tariff system that would permit more low-cost for foreign oil into the United States.[28] While a tariff system did not represent any radical departure from past policy, it did imply some change which would affect the beneficiaries of the present system and which would offer some relief for those who sought an alteration in the established policy. In the final analysis, however, a tariff system represented more of a symbolic change than anything else. In all probability, it was the result of a compromise between the two sets of interests represented on the task force. Reports of the recommended change mentioned a split in task force membership, with five favoring a switch to tariffs and two opposed.

According to a *New York Times* article, the task force study was sent to Nixon on December 30, 1969.[29] However, on January 20, 1970, the *Times* reported that the oil quota report was being delayed until late January or early February. No reason for the delay was given.[30] Finally on February 9, the president acknowledged receipt of the report and promised to release it to the public along with his comments at a later date.

Nixon Appoints Oil Policy Committee. Eleven days later, Nixon released the report of the task force along with his comments. Essentially, he proposed to postpone indefinitely any major change in the oil quota system. As expected, the task force did recommend abolishing the quota system and establishing a tariff system of control. The following passage is taken from the task force report:

> A majority of the Task Force prefer tariffs over quotas as the basic method of restriction because tariffs (1) encourage greater efficiency in

---

27Ibid.
28Ibid., December 20, 1969, p. 50.
29Ibid., December 31, 1969, p. 43.
30Ibid., January 20, 1970, p. 55.

domestic markets, (2) permit full federal control over this national security program, (3) lessen the dependence of domestic buyers on particular suppliers, (4) substitute the market place for government allocation of import licenses, (5) eliminate vested interests in quota allocation which often impede necessary changes in the control system, and (6) assure that the benefit of much low-cost imports as are permitted is fully realized by the public rather than by recipients of quota allocations. The resulting revenues could, if desired, serve as the basis for legislation for security reserves or other steps that might contribute to petroleum security.[31]

Though Secretaries Rogers and Laird both voted with the majority, each expressed some reservations. Both felt that it was necessary to consult with other countries about the recommended changes.[32] The task force reported Laird's position as follows:

Therefore to insure a continuous surveillance and adjustment of the program in relation to national security needs, his concurrence is conditioned on the adoption, as is recommended in the report, of an interdepartmental management and control organization, which is not restricted by pre-established levels. This organization should be chaired by the Director of the Office of Emergency Preparedness and must include Defense membership.[33]

The Laird position provided Nixon with the necessary justification for his next move to delay a decision. His tactic was to appoint another group to study the question further. The new group, the Oil Policy Committee included all of the former members of the task force except one. Two members were added to the group, Attorney General John Mitchell and Paul W. McCracken, Chairman of the Council of Economic Advisors. In appointing the group, Nixon spelled out their task in the following manner.

I expect the Oil Policy Committee to consider both interim and long-term adjustments that will increase the effectiveness and enhance the equity of the oil import program. While major long-term adjustments must necessarily await the outcome of discussion with Canada, Mexico and Venezuela, and other allies and affected nations, as well as the information developed in the proposed Congressional hearings, I will direct the new committee to begin its work immediately.[34]

Response to Nixon's action was not unexpected. It was praised by politicians from the West and Southwest, as well as spokesmen for the oil industry. And it was highly criticized by New Englanders as another

[31]*The Oil Import Question*, p. 134.
[32]The positions of Secretaries Rogers and Laird are given in *The Oil Import Question*, pp. 131–32.
[33]*The Oil Import Question*, p. 132.
[34]*New York Times*, February 21, 1970, p. 47.

unnecessary delay. The Machiasport issue, which was at that time nearly two years old, was still unresolved. The task force had looked into the question of foreign trade zones and had made the following recommendation:

> Opinions may vary about the utility of foreign trade zones, but so long as they remain an authorized instrument of United States trade policy their administration can and should by kept distinct from that of any oil import program that may remain in effect. This would mean that zone applications satisfactory to the Foreign Trade Zones Board could be approved in the ordinary course.[35]

In effect, the task force seemed to be saying that applications for foreign trade zones such as the one for Maine should be approved regardless of what further decisions regarding oil imports may have to be made. Despite the task force's recommendations on this point Nixon aides indicated that the Oil Policy Committee, "would continue to deal with the 'principles' of the whole import control system and that a decision on Machiasport would have to await a decision on the principles."[36]

Nixon Decides Against Change. The most recent action on the oil import issue was taken August 17, 1970, when Nixon dropped completely the idea of shifting controls on oil imports from quotas to tariffs. In announcing this decision, Nixon released a letter received from George A. Lincoln, Director of the Office of Emergency Planning, who had been a member of the Cabinet Task Force on Oil Import Control and who was now serving as the head of the Oil Policy Committee. In the letter, Lincoln said that the rest of the committee "concurs in my judgment that we discontinue consideration of moving to a tariff system of control, but rather continue our efforts to improve the current program."[37] Lincoln had been one of the five-man majority on the cabinet task force who had supported the recommendation to switch to a tariff system of controls. Explaining his change in position, Lincoln said: "Recent developments have increased misgivings about moving to a tariff system as a feasible method of controlling oil imports."[38]

Since August 1970 there have been no major actions regarding Machiasport.[39] The issue seems to be in a state of limbo. The Foreign

---

[35]*The Oil Import Question*, p. 84.
[36]*New York Times*, February 21, 1970, p. 47.
[37]Ibid., August 18, 1970, p. 1.
[38]Ibid.
[39]Senator Edmund S. Muskie of Maine, Chairman of the Senate Subcommittee on Air and Water Pollution, who was seeking reelection at the time, held two days of hearing at Machiasport on September 8 and 9, 1970 to determine the "possible environmental effects of oil development in the area." A summary of the hearings can be found in the *Portland Press Herald*, September 8, 1970, p. 6; September 9, 1970, p. 1; and September 10, 1970, p. 1.

Trade Zones Board has taken no further action on the Maine application, and the Oil Import Administration has not acted on the Occidental request for a change in the oil quotas. Unless Occidental is granted a quota to allow it to bring oil which it refines in the trade zone into the United States, its goal of lowering the cost of oil and oil products for the New England consumers would be lost. It has been almost three years since Maine's application and Occidental's request were submitted. The only thing which seems to have been accomplished is a negative decision.

SUMMATION

The ultimate outcome in the Machiasport issue exhibits characteristics of both a negative decision, i.e., a deliberate decision not to decide on an issue which has been made public, and a nondecision, where the dominant values and institutions prohibit any changes in the status quo.

The negative decision in this case is Nixon's decision not to change the oil import quota system. The issue had been made a public one involving many individuals and groups; the strategy had been one of delaying a decision; and the ultimate outcome was a decision not to decide. The members of Nixon's administration seem to have taken their cue from the chief executive. The Maine Port Authority and Occidental still await an answer to their requests.

The outcome resembles a nondecision in that the dominant values and political institutions and procedures played an important role in preventing a decision thus far. The dominant values salient to this issue were those concerning national security. The institutional features which made delaying decisions an easy matter consisted of an administrative structure where responsibilities of two agencies overlapped with one another. While national security and overlapping responsibilities may not be all of the reasons for the negative decision, they would appear to be two of the more important reasons.

National Security. Ever since World War II, the United States has been highly preoccupied with the defense of the nation's security. Witness the proportion of the U.S. budget which is allocated for defense purposes and the escalation of the arms race. Because of this kind of preoccupation with defense matters, politicians and interest groups have often found that if a program can somehow be related to national defense it enhances the change of passage. The oil import program is a typical example of justifying programs on the basis of national security, even though the evidence is debatable.

Oil import policies may well have an effect on our national security, but there seem to be real differences of opinion on the question. The task force which studied the matter in great depth concluded that the quota system of controls "is not adequately responsive to present and future security considerations."[40] However, the members of the task force did agree that probably some type of control over oil imports was essential for national security purposes, and they seemed to think that "national security will be adequately protected by adopting as a first step a revised control system [i.e., tariffs] and a modest immediate reduction in import restraints."[41] So, while oil import controls of some type may be essential to our national security, there is substantial evidence to indicate that the present method of oil import quotas is not the most effective measure to accomplish that end. Yet the present policy remains in effect and continues to be justified on the basis of "national security."

The present case also reflects two concepts of the "national security." The view held by members of the oil industry conflicts with the view held by the promoters of the Machiasport refinery. The perception of the national interest as articulated by oil spokesmen appears to have prevailed in this case. It is a variation of the philosophy behind the now famous statement made by Charles Wilson, former head of General Motors, that what is good for General Motors is good for the country. Only in this case what is good for the oil industry is deemed good for the country.

The oil industry has much to lose if the present oil import quota system is altered. The Cabinet task force noted that, "Without import controls the domestic wellhead price would fall from $3.40 per barrel to about $2.00 which would correspond to the world price. . . . American consumers would save about $5 billion annually now and over $8 billion annually by 1980."[42] These figures illustrate why most of the oil companies are opposed to abandoning the oil import system. Their strategy, not unlike the strategies of other economic interests, has been to cloak their private interests in patriotic language about the national interest and national security. The effect of this strategy is to make those who challenge programs justified on security grounds appear to be unpatriotic or un-American.

Overlapping Administrative Responsibilities. All political structures have some kind of bias which favors one group of interests over another. These institutional biases may be built in intentionally, such as the seniority system in Congress. Or they may be unintended biases which

40*The Oil Import Question*, p. 128.
41Ibid.
42Ibid., p. 124.

have developed over time, such as the bias of the electoral college which favors the two party system and discourages third parties.

In the Machiasport issue, the bias was of the second type. Two agencies, the Oil Import Administration and the Foreign Trade Zones Board, were responsible for making decisions which touched upon one another. Each agency found it convenient to delay a decision by waiting for the other to make the decision first. The bias in this instance, which is an unintended consequence, favors the status quo. Since the status quo favors the oil industry, the bias of the administrative structure rewards the oil interests at the expense of consumers, especially those in New England. Even if the organizational structure in this instance was not deliberately biased in favor of the oil interests, it still had the effect. The oil interests exploited this organizational bias to their own advantage.

APPENDIX

An Analysis of the Major Events in the Machiasport Case and the Interests Favored by Each Event*

		Interests Favored	
Date	Event	Oil Interests	Machiasport Promoters
June 1968	Maine Port Authority applies to the Foreign Trade Zones Board for a trade zone at Machiasport.		+
June 1968	Occidental Petroleum Corporation applies to Oil Import Administration for an oil import quota.		+
October 30, 1968	Sinclair Oil files suit for an injunction to stop both proceedings.	+	
November 22, 1968	Secretary Udall announces he cannot act until Foreign Trade Zones Board makes its decision.	+	
December 13, 1968	Commerce Secretary Smith postpones decision for Nixon Administration to handle.	+	
December 18, 1968	Curtis announces possible court action by State of Maine against Smith.		+
	Senator Kennedy requests investigation by the Justice Department and Congressional committee.		+
December 19, 1968	Senator McIntyre initiates hearings by Senate Subcommittee for Small Business.		+
	Secretary Smith refuses to testify at hearings.	+	
January 11, 1969	Smith disqualifies himself from making the Machiasport decision.	+	
February 11, 1969	Board of Alternates recommends approval of Maine's application for trade zone.		+

| Date | Event | Interests Favored | |
		Oil Interests	Machiasport Promoters
February 21, 1969	Nixon announces review of all oil import policy and personally assumes responsibility for such policy.	+	
	Commerce Secretary Stans cancels scheduled meeting of the Foreign Trade Zones Board.	+	
March 11, 1969	Senator Hart initiates hearings by the Senate Antitrust and Monopoly Subcommittee.		+
March 25, 1969	Nixon appoints a cabinet level task force to study oil import policy.	+	
February 9, 1970	Task Force report received by Nixon recommends switch from quotas to tariffs and the approval of trade zone applications separate from oil import decisions.		+
February 20, 1970	Nixon releases task force report and appoints an Oil Policy Committee to study the issue further.	+	
August 17, 1970	Nixon, upon recommendation by members of the Oil Policy Committee, drops all consideration of changing from quotas to tariffs for controls.	+	

*Any measure which delayed making a decision is considered here to have favored the oil interests since they continued to gain as long as the status quo prevailed.

20 Clyde E. Teasley, III

Sit Tight, Wally

The firing by President Richard Nixon of Interior Secretary Walter J. Hickel was not just a question of mutual confidence as the president claimed. The firing of Wally Hickel was a product of President Nixon's strategy and was, in that way, symbolic of his administration's policies. This case study centers on the following two questions. First, what is the role of department heads in policy making? More specifically, how active a role should a cabinet member expect to play in policy making? Second, and perhaps more important, what is the link between policy making and public opinion? Who links policy to the desires and needs of the public in a democratic society?

Richard Fenno has argued that president-cabinet relations cannot be completely understood by assuming that the cabinet member is the "devoted keeper of the President's confidences whose career in public life is one single-minded endeavor to act as the agent and servant of his superior."[1] Fenno then proposes a more complex model:

[1]Richard F. Fenno, "President-Cabinet Relations," in Ronald Moe and William Schultze (eds.), *American Government and Politics* (Columbus, Ohio: Charles E. Merrill, 1971), p. 173.

This selection was written expressly for this volume.

240

A Cabinet member is typically the chief executive of an administrative organization, constantly interacting with its members, with [a] variety of private groups. . , with the legislators . . , and with partisan factions. . . . He is a man with a particular departmental viewpoint, responsive to particular clientele interests and pursuing a particular program. His political behavior is shaped to a large degree by the kinds of extra-presidential relationships he establishes as he seeks solutions to his particular problems —the support of his policies, the survival of his organization, the control of his environment. . . .

. . . The conditions which [this] system of fragmented power sets for the success and the survival of a Cabinet officer encourage him to consolidate his own nexus of power and compel him to operate with a degree of independence from the President.[2]

Thus, both the president and the cabinet head lead political organizations—coalitions of political power centered around their respective offices. And the degree of allegiance and subordination of a cabinet member to the president is determined largely by two factors: either their similarity of policy positions, and/or the amount of political influence the cabinet member can muster.

No easy predictions can be made beyond this point. If the president perceives a cabinet official to be very powerful, he is likely to grant the official more freedom and autonomy. On the other hand, the president may decide to clip the wings of a secretary who seems to be gaining uncomfortable and unexpected support and power.

The Nixon-Hickel confrontation implies some such dynamics. A contest for power seems to have characterized the relationship between President Nixon and Walter Hickel. Perhaps underlying that contest, and in his own peculiar way, Wally Hickel was the conscience of the Nixon administration. Thus, Walter Hickel, the man, the cabinet officer, was in a power struggle with the president. While Wally, the symbol and the conscience, was engaged in another and perhaps related struggle.

THE STRANGE CASE OF WALTER HICKEL

In the late 1960s, the ecology issue captured public attention, even to the extent of competing with other domestic issues such as the urban crisis and race relations. After all, many ecologists were forecasting the world's doom because of toxic chemicals in air, water and food, and because of overpopulation. President Nixon even pushed ecology as a major theme of his first State of the Union address in January 1970.

2Ibid., p. 183.

Nixon had selected the governor of Alaska, Walter Hickel, as his Secretary of Interior in 1969. Hickel was a multimillionaire land developer before he became governor, and his record indicated no intense involvement in the ecology issue. Indeed, he was linked to the gas industry and as governor he had tried to open the oil rich Kenai Moose Range to the oil industry in 1968.[3]

Conservationists were incensed by his nomination and they made their opposition felt during a rigorous Senate committee hearing on the confirmation of the secretary. In order to mollify this hostility, Nixon had leaked the appointment of Russell Train as Hickel's undersecretary. Train was a noted conservationist. In 1961 he had founded the African Wildlife Leadership Foundation and for the four years prior to his nomination he had headed the Conservation Foundation.[4]

The Senate Hearings, which delayed Hickel's being sworn in until two days after his cabinet colleagues, showed that he was unwilling or unable to account for his record in Alaska but that he was eager to accept the new challenge.[5] And on January 24, 1969, Hickel did indeed become the new interior secretary. On that day also, President Nixon, speaking of Hickel, said that the "last shall be first as far as this administration is concerned."[6]

Despite his relatively poor credentials, Hickel performed rather admirably at his new position—at least from a conservationist's point of view. Michael McClosky, acting executive director of the conservationist Sierra Club observed that "Conservationists remain to be convinced by Hickel, but I think their minds are not closed to welcome evidence."[7] And Senator Gaylord Nelson (D., Wis.), who had voted against the Hickel nomination, noted at the secretary's removal: "Conservationists have lost a great fighter and a great friend."[8]

Hickel had begun developing support from one of the Interior Department's publics—the conservationists. And he may have intended that the ecology issue would broaden his support base because several subsequent actions changed the minds of many conservationists and enlisted their favor. For example, Hickel took Chevron Oil to court. That cost the oil company one million dollars in fines for spilling oil in the Gulf of Mexico. He helped stop the building of a jetport in Florida's Everglades.

[3]"Hickel's Headaches," *Time*, January 17, 1969, p. 17.
[4]"Man With the Right Causes," *Time*, February 7, 1969, pp. 16–17.
[5]"Conservationist," *The New Republic*, January 25, 1969, p. 9.
[6]Don Oberdorfer, "Hickel Shift Suggested by Mitchell," the *Washington Post*, November 24, 1970, p. A-1.
[7]"Apprentice Noah," *Time*, March 21, 1969, p. 18.
[8]Carroll Kilpatrick, "Nixon Fires Hickel From Cabinet," the *Washington Post*, November 26, 1970, p. A-1.

He supported legislation to make it a federal offense to ship animals threatened with extinction, their skins, pelts or plumage, across state lines. And he acted to protect the rights of Paiute Indians against a powerful California-Nevada water pact that threatened to reduce the Pyramid Lake, the reservation's water source, to a saline desert sink.

But Walter Hickel did much more. On May 6, 1970, a letter from Hickel to President Nixon was leaked to the public. In the letter, Hickel suggested that the president had lost touch with the youth of the country and that there was a communications gap between the cabinet members and their superior.[9] One reason was Nixon's decision to expand the Southeast Asian War into Cambodia. This was in the face of growing public discontent over the war, especially among college students. This decision touched off a string of campus demonstrations and strikes. The consequences were tragic. They included the killing of four Kent State University students and two Jackson State University students, as well as the closing of scores of colleges and universities either for a few days or for the remainder of the school year.

Hickel went further still. On national TV, Hickel revealed that word was passed through the administration to the effect that the public furor over the killing of the four Kent State students by the Ohio National Guard would blow over in a day or so. It did not. By going on television, Hickel had broadened his following on issues which were not specifically within the Interior Department's realm, and thus he increasingly became a political threat to President Nixon.

Shortly thereafter, a decision was made to remove Walter Hickel. It was decided, however, to delay the actual announcement until after the 1970 November elections. Apparently, Hickel had become enough of a force to create fear that such a move would hurt the chances of Republican candidates that fall. However, White House staff aides did leak news of Hickel's impending departure several times, perhaps as an invitation for him to resign, but he did not.[10] Then Attorney General John Mitchell went to Hickel and another attempt to get a resignation was equally unsuccessful. On the television show *Sixty Minutes* Hickel told of the Mitchell meeting and that the Attorney General had told him to "sit tight." Hickel added further that "If I go away, I'm going with an arrow in my heart and not a bullet in my back."[11]

The arrow was shafted on November 25, 1970, at about 4:00 P.M. George P. Schultz, director of the Office of Management and Budget,

---

9"Listen to Youths, Hickel Writes Nixon," *U.S. News and World Report*, May 18, 1970, p. 68.
10Oberdorfer, "Hickel Shift," p. A-1.
11Ibid.

called Hickel and requested that he come to the White House. There Hickel was ushered in for one of his few private visits with the president. And just before 6:00 P.M., White House Press Secretary Ronald Zeigler announced that Nixon had asked for and received Hickel's resignation, effective immediately.[12]

WHY WAS HICKEL CHOSEN? THE NIXON STRATEGY

The Nixon presidency divided itself roughly into two parts. For the first two years of his term, the president took a definite go-slow stance—one which was geared towards making few mistakes and being able to recover rather easily from those that were made.[13] Furthermore, Republican party officials are generally more conservative and business oriented than the general public.[14] And during the first half of his term, Nixon seemed not only to buy time, but to attempt at least to pay off his party debts and then to gear his political coalition toward the 1972 presidential election. Within this framework, ecology was never a primary concern. And indeed, the whole spectrum of domestic policy seemed to play second fiddle to foreign affairs—especially the Vietnam War, which by this time had become a political time bomb.

In this context, and because of Hickel's past, the administration may have expected him to be more of an ally of business, especially of oil. But Hickel claimed to be his own man and he added, "that's probably the problem." Speaking openly about the Chevron Oil decision, Hickel rationalized, "I maintained the decision I thought was right for everyone concerned, never forgetting the administration nor my responsibility to 200 million Americans. I had to do it my way. . . ."[15]

THE JOB OF SECRETARY–THE NIXON STYLE

President Nixon's emphasis on image and public relations has been well portrayed in Joe McGinniss' *The Selling of the President 1968.*[16]

[12]Kilpatrick, "Nixon Fires Hickel," p. A-1.
[13]Max Frankel, "These Are the Words for Richard Nixon After His First Year," *New York Times Magazine*, January 18, 1970, p. 46.
[14]Herbert McClosky, Paul Hoffman, and Rosemary O'Hara, "Issue Conflict and Consensus Among Party Leaders and Followers," *American Political Science Review*, 54 (June 1960), 406–27.
[15]Oberdorfer "Hickel Shift," p. A-8.
[16]Joe McGinniss, *The Selling of the President 1968* (New York: Trident Press, 1969).

The image seemed inconsistent with reality in the Hickel case. Speaking on the presidency, Nixon observed, "The days of the passive presidency belong to a simpler past. . . . We should bring dissenters into policy discussions, not freeze them out. We should invite constructive criticism, not only because they have a right to be heard, but also because they have something worth hearing. . . . Officials of a new administration will not have to check their conscience at the door or leave their powers of independent judgment at home."[17] Walter Hickel claimed to have acted on conscience; even his famous letter, he observed, was a gesture of the heart, not disloyalty.[18]

Nixon and Hickel seemed to have different views of the world and of life. Compared with the cool, uninvolved President Nixon, Hickel was loud and rustic as well as candid and blunt—traits which did not characterize the Nixon team. The *Washington Post* editorialized on Hickel's departure: "He demonstrated a great sensitivity to the issues of the times and did not seem particularly moved by pressures brought to bear on him by economic interests. . . ."[19] Hugh Sidey also pointed out that "Hickel stood apart from the other Nixon men. He was welcome on campus, he was a bird-watcher's delight. He received hosannas from liberals, even from Democrats. In the mirthless and myopic ranks of White House aides, however, Hickel smelled of disloyalty." Sidey also painted a vivid election night scene. In it several cabinet members were watching the 1970 election results with Vice President Spiro Agnew who was walking in front of the screen exclaiming over the news of the defeat of one of his targets, "We killed that son of a bitch. . . . We killed that son of a bitch." Several of the cabinet members were appalled, but it was only Walter Hickel who left early.[20]

EXECUTIVE POLICY MAKING

The move to dismiss Walter Hickel as interior secretary accomplished at least two goals. First, it removed Hickel who had been a constant thorn in the Republican's side—thus destroying some of the foundations of what may have become an opposing faction within the Republican party. And second, since Rogers Morton inherited Hickel's job, it opened the party's national chairmanship to a person more dy-

---

17"Nixon on the Presidency," *Time*, September 27, 1968, p. 18.
18Hugh Sidey, "The Casting-Out of Wally Hickel," *Life*, December 4, 1970, p. 6.
19"Firing A Secretary, Frontier Style," the *Washington Post*, November 28, 1970, p. A-18.
20Sidey, "The Casting-Out of Wally Hickel," p. 6.

namic and possibly more politically successful than Morton had been. There was undoubtedly much consternation among high-ranking Republicans over their setbacks in the 1970 elections in spite of the administration's victory claims.[21]

Richard Nixon will probably be entered in history books as one of America's most politically oriented presidents. His chief aim, it seems, was to become president and, upon achieving that goal, to be elected for a second term. Other motives and pressures appeared secondary to those objectives. As such, Nixon kept only his closest and most reliable advisors in his inner circle. These included his friend and campaign manager Attorney General Mitchell, Robert Finch, George Schultz, John P. Erlichmann, and Henry Kissinger. And it was these men who tended to dominate policy decisions, not the various department heads.

The Times They're a Changin' went an old Bob Dylan song, and indeed it does seem that politics is taking a different twist. Young people are becoming more involved politically; colleges are excusing them from classes to campaign and now eighteen-year-olds in all states can vote. But Richard Nixon seems to have been outside of this political change. He appears as much as any of his political contemporaries to embody the ideas and philosophy of a past generation. And it was toward this weak linkage of the Nixon administration to public opinion that Hickel directed attention.

The answers of the two opening questions above are these—if the Hickel case is indicative. First, the role of the Cabinet official in policy making varies with a number of factors. Among these one would include: (1) the fit of a department's area of policy with presidential priorities, (2) the similarity of policy positions of the president and the cabinet member, (3) the prior relationship of the cabinet member with the president and his inner circle, and (4) the political support the cabinet member possesses.

As was shown above, ecology was not a primary concern for Nixon during his first two years, but it was crucial for Hickel if he were going to develop any political support among new Interior clientele. As such, Nixon and Hickel differed in their policy orientations. Furthermore, Hickel was not a member of the inner circle. In fact, he was quite different from its members in background, style and policy. Consequently, in order for Hickel to develop political support, he had to sever many of his ties to Nixon. Thus, his independence coupled with a growing level of clientele support made Hickel a political liability.

Second, who links public opinion with policy? During a period of

[21]Kilpatrick, "Nixon Fires Hickel," p. A-13.

time when the people, especially the youth, of the country became less satisfied with politics and the environment was an obvious national concern, the Nixon administration seemed uninvolved in these policy areas. And Walter Hickel was quick to articulate this gap between the president's policies and public opinion—even to the point of using television to do so. This was both embarrassing and threatening to Nixon, thus forcing Hickel's elimination.

Because of Hickel's popularity, Nixon waited for the most opportune moment between elections to dismiss his secretary of the interior. But Wally was the symbol of the problem, not the problem itself. The problem centered on the Nixon administration's inability to perceive public opinion and to incorporate it into effective policy. Certainly, in a democratic society this is a crucial linkage. And Hickel's dismissal testifies that the Nixon administration, at that time, was unwilling to have that linkage developed.

21 *Delmer D. Dunn*

The Meaning and Meaninglessness of American Elections

The goal of American elections is often interpreted as providing a "mandate" which controls or guides public policy until the next election. Neophyte voters and seasoned political commentators alike tend to analyze election outcomes in the context of an implicit belief in the mandate theory of elections. Thus, it is not surprising that when an election is close, as it was in the 1960 and 1968 presidential elections, common opinion concluded that the winner had no "mandate." Since the collective decision of that election did not ring down strongly on the size of the winner, goes the underlying argument, the citizenry expressed no clear policy preferences. According to this view, Presidents John Kennedy and Richard Nixon had no mandate.

The connotation of "not having a mandate" is negative, and leaves the impression that the lack of a mandate is either unusual or avoidable. Actually, neither is the case. If mandate means the expression of policy preference by the American people through the collective vote decision, few elections produce such a mandate.

Indeed, several features of elections actually render the voting act

This selection was written expressly for this volume.

meaningless as an instrument through which citizens can articulate policy preferences to elected public officials. This is the case even if Americans base their voting decisions on policy preferences, an issue about which researchers differ widely.[1]

Numerous features of most elections make it difficult for many voters to translate their policy preferences into voting decisions. First, many voters do not have policy preferences and, if they vote, base their decisions on other factors.[2] These "other factors" include assessment of the candidate's personality and reactions to it.[3] Many react positively to a candidate's "style." Others interest themselves in a candidate's family life, his religion, or even his leisure activities. As voters base their decisions upon such factors, they provide few if any clues regarding their policy preferences.

Even if citizens possess policy preferences, they may face difficulty in translating them into policy-relevant behavior. All candidates contesting a given office, for example, may provide no alternatives on the issue deemed important by the voter.[4] The candidates may voice the same views on the issue. For example, many would argue that candidates Nixon, Humphrey, and Wallace agreed on law and order and the Vietnam War in 1968. The voter who disagrees has little choice, except perhaps to stay home. Or none of the candidates may take a stand on issues which the voters view as important. A person desiring to express his preference for less restrictive national abortion laws, for example, would have been unable to do so in the 1968 presidential election. For those who would assert that agreement by all candidates on a given issue signifies a substantial pool of agreement among the electorate let it be said that such conditions do not *test* this pool of agreement in the only way it can be really tested through an election—by offering an alternative position.

If candidates deliberately hedge on issues, or obscure them, voters encounter another major barrier to articulating policy preferences through

1See, for example, Bernard R. Berelson, Paul F. Lazarsfeld, and William N. McPhee, *Voting* (Chicago: The University of Chicago Press, 1954); Angus Campbell, *et al.*, *The American Voter* (New York: Wiley, 1964); and V. O. Key, *The Responsible Electorate* (New York: Random House, 1966).

2Campbell, *et al.*, *The American Voter*, pp. 99–105.

3Ibid., pp. 15–30.

4For a discussion of the 1968 presidential campaign issues, see Theodore H. White, *The Making of the President 1968* (New York: Atheneum, 1969), esp. pp. 3–34, 219–60, and 438–45. Campbell *et al.*, *The American Voter*, write "Only 40 to 60 per cent *of the informed segment* of the population (that is, the part that holds an opinion on an issue) perceive party differences and hence can locate one or the other party as close to their 'own' position" (p. 104, their emphasis).

the voting act. Candidates have been known to take such approaches. They can appear to take stands on "important" issues while speaking in generalities so that the issue position may be interpreted as favorable by persons with widely divergent views on the issues.[5] A common device is to dramatize a problem which needs action, but fail to mention the solution needed to solve the problem.[6] This strategy is a pragmatic one which permits the office seeker to include divergent elements in his coalition. But no matter how pragmatic or plausible this strategy, it does impede the voter's ability to express policy preferences through his voting decision.

Even if competing candidates take divergent stands which they express clearly, and even if voters have preferences on such issues, the translation of these preferences into a voting decision may be rendered imperfect by yet another obstacle. Voters may experience difficulty in associating even a clear preference with the correct candidate.[7] Voting studies have shown that citizens misperceive the stands of office seekers, even when candidates take straight-forward positions on issues. Voters have a tendency to perceive that candidates they prefer agree with them, regardless of the candidate's expressed view on the issue.[8] Such misperceptions increase the difficulties of translating policy preferences into voting decision.

There are thus a number of barriers which make it difficult to connect the policy preference to a voting choice. A victorious candidate's winning coalition is derived from citizens who choose him for numerous, and often conflicting, reasons. Some choose him because they dislike the other candidate's personality, issues, or party. Some vote for the winner because they are attracted to personality-related factors. And those who vote their policy preferences may vote for the same candidate to express different and often contradictory policy views. President Richard Nixon, for example, received votes in the 1968 election from persons who desired to see an end to the Vietnam War. Some believed he would end it by stepping up the fighting, while others felt he would end it by scaling

---

[5]Candidate Richard Nixon provided an excellent illustration of this common campaign technique during the 1968 presidential campaign. He announced that he had a "plan" to end the Southeat Asia hostilities, but refused to disclose it.

[6]See Joe McGinniss, *The Selling of the President 1968* (New York: Trident Press, 1969), esp. pp. 90, 92–95, and 223–53.

[7]Voters do not always perceive that parties differ on the issue they have an opinion about and sometimes have difficulty identifying which party stands nearest their own party policy preference. See Campbell *et al., The American Voter,* pp. 104–8.

[8]See Berelson, Lazarsfeld, and McPhee, *Voting,* pp. 215–33. This phenomenon illustrates the impact of cognitive dissonance which is discussed in Robert E. Lane and David O. Sears, *Public Opinion* (Englewood Cliffs, N.J.: Prentice-Hall, 1964), pp. 44–53.

down the hostilities. Still others voted for the Republican candidate b\
cause they believed he would bring law and order to the land. Some
probably thought his "black capitalism" approach promised to alleviate
urban strife. Still others felt that farmers would "do better" under
Republicans.

These considerations imply a clear conclusion. Because a winner's
coalition is comprised of voters with many different policy views (none
of which all agree upon), the voting act—even when based on issues—
generates no clear expression of policy preferences which the victor can
then translate into policy action. For these reasons, the election is actually meaningless in a futuristic sense, that is, in the classic textbook
sense of providing clear policy mandates for future official behavior. The
only clear result of any election is that more voters express a preference
for one *candidate* than for others, and that this preference is derived
from a number of factors. *The "mandate" is for the candidate.* The
victor can choose to interpret the policy direction of his mandate in almost any way he wishes.

If the voting act is meaningless for expressing preferences about
future policy decision, do American elections affect government decision
making? Elections do have an impact on policy making in this country,
but this impact is not derived from providing the electorate an opportunity to translate their policy preferences into candidate selection. Rather,
because elections generally decisively determine who will hold office in
the United States, they affect the perspectives of the winning candidate.[9]
Elections can alter these perspectives in several ways. Candidates frequently learn from the responses they receive to speeches and general
campaign thrusts as they travel through their constituencies, for example.[10] Most candidates are supersensitive to that response. They are in
direct contact with the electorate in numerous activities during a campaign. Coffee klatches, fund-raising dinners and cocktail parties, and
plant-gate visits provide direct contact with voters. During this interaction, expressions of sentiment and reactions to the candidate's positions
often occur. A citizen may say "I sure like what you're saying about Vietnam!" or "Give 'em hell on the farm program!" Although these comments are usually positive, they nevertheless assist the candidate in
forming some impression of the salient issues and the constituency
temper at a given time.

Candidates often use speeches to gauge constituency opinion. Positions receiving applause from a listening crowd are likely to be repeated.
Those receiving no applause will tend to be deleted. Some candidates use

---

[9]For a discussion of the impact of elections upon candidates, see John W. Kingdom, *Candidates for Office* (New York: Random House, 1968), esp. pp. 20–106.
[10]See also ibid., pp. 97–100.

speeches to test hunches about the mood of the electorate. Congressman Frank Thompson, who represents the Trenton-Princeton area of New Jersey, campaigned in the 1970 election with the help of many student volunteers. He believed that the "antikid" line often espoused by Vice President Spiro Agnew was a political mistake. He vigorously articulated his faith in the young and the future they envisioned. To middle-class and academic adults he spoke of the need to listen to the youth, and vented his despair at those who attempted to split the generations. To working-class audiences his theme consisted of the simple American tenet "We have become a better country because each generation has worked —and worked hard—to make it better for the next generation." He would then point out some personal examples from among his audience, many of whom he had known since childhood. "At times we have wondered if the next generation was to fulfill our hope." He would then point out some examples in his audience, those who had made good despite the dire predictions of peers, priests, parents, teachers, and, sometimes policemen. Laughter usually would greet Thompson's examples. But it was kind laughter, for the individuals in his examples somehow always made it, despite the doubts. Thompson would then move to the inevitable conclusion: "Now we have those in the country who would separate us from our kids, our hope of the future, for momentary political gain. I don't like it! I know the kids and students of today. And 99 percent of them are the most decent, the smartest, and the most honorable people on the face of the earth!"

Although the exact wording of the message differed for different audiences the meaning was the same. And the response, usually a standing ovation, was also the same, regardless of the audience. The hunch was confirmed while the Congressman spoke about a conviction which meant a great deal to him.

Visual clues also confront candidates during their campaigns which say something about a constituency. The West Virginia poverty conditions were revealed to Senator John F. Kennedy as he saw and visited homes, observed closed mines, and observed the appearances of people who attended his rallies. The empty or busy storefront, the idle or booming factory, the existence and condition of natural resources etch an impression of the problems and hopes of a constituency.

The scientific opinion poll can also provide candidates a fairly precise reading of the state of opinion in their constituency at a given moment—providing they can afford to employ this costly device.[11] In-

[11]See ibid., pp. 90–93; David A. Leuthold, *Electioneering in a Democracy* (New York: 1968), pp. 51–60; and Dan Nimmo, *The Political Persuaders* (Englewood Cliffs, N.J.: Prentice-Hall, 1970), pp. 84–100.

creasingly, candidates use polls to target voter groups, to plan their issue appeals, and to locate weaknesses in opponents. This, of course, provides candidates (and officeholders) some intelligence about their constituency. Much of the incentive for gathering such information stems from the necessity of successfully campaigning for office.

Candidates also gather information about their districts or constituencies through the contacts they make with interest group representatives during campaigns.[12] This contact takes numerous forms. Sometimes a group may be crucial in raising funds for the campaign. At other times, a candidate's organization may rely heavily upon interest groups to assist in precinct voter registration drives and election day services designed to get out the vote. Candidates also use loaned equipment (ranging up to the use of airplanes for traveling) to facilitate the campaign effort. Groups providing these services find numerous opportunities to communicate information to the candidate and his entourage. The candidate typically is predisposed to listen, even more important. Candidates or their staffs, in addition, may seek out group representatives for information about how a group stands on a given issue. This may range from trying to ascertain how an economic condition affects an industry (e.g., how an increase in interest rates affects the lumber industry) to ascertaining the position of the group on an issue. Interest group representatives also approach candidates with their views on issues. The campaign consequently presents ample opportunity for a candidate to apprise himself of interest group positions. And if the group represents a sizeable interest in his constituency, it may prove especially helpful to the candidate as he attempts to inform himself about the concerns of his constituency.

Finally, candidates frequently interact with local party leaders during their campaign.[13] In national campaigns, candidate advance men touch base with local leaders to become informed of the problems of local areas. Frequently these leaders travel with the candidate throughout his stay in a state, county, or congressional district. The bourbon bashes aboard the "Cornpone Special" as it trekked through the South during the 1960 campaign are credited with helping to hold several states in the region for the Kennedy-Johnson ticket, for example. These encounters are thus another means for candidates to learn which issues to avoid, which to emphasize, and what the constituency believes to be the most salient problems during the campaign.

12For a discussion which discusses some of these contacts see Leuthold, *Electioneering*, pp. 61–73. See also David B. Truman, *The Governmental Process* (New York: Knopf, 1951), pp. 288–320.
13See Kingdon, *Candidates for Office*, pp. 93–95; and Leuthold, *Electioneering*, pp. 38–47.

We have seen thus far that the voting act itself provides only an imperfect means of translating policy preferences into candidate choices. The vagueness of this process provides election victors great flexibility in interpreting the "mandate" provided by the election. The campaign itself provides many interaction sites where citizens may communicate policy preferences to candidates that assist the ultimate victor in determining the outlines of his "mandate." This information exchange does affect the ultimate victor. The 1968 presidential primary elections, in which voters chose state delegates to represent them at the Democratic National Convention, provides a recent and dramatic example of this impact. Delegates from these states—regardless of which slate won, or the dominant issues involved—were noticeably more vociferous in their support of a "stronger" Vietnam peace plan in the party platform than were delegates from other states selected by other means. Their differing electoral experience no doubt accounted for a large part of this.

For these reasons, much of the impact of the election on officeholders' policy positions occurs as a result of the information exchange which transpires during the course of the campaign. But this is not the only way that elections affect decision makers' policy positions. Once policy makers take office the factor which looms largest is the *next* election. It is almost axiomatic in American politics that elected officials judge their success by their ability to achieve reelection. The prime task of most officeholders is therefore to conduct their office and behavior in such a way as to maximize the chances of being reelected. Because the next election will determine who will be reelected (and thus who will continue to hold office), that future election conditions an officeholder's behavior. It constantly poses a threat to their continued tenure, more so, of course, as the election approaches closely. Decision makers thus conduct their affairs with at least one eye focused on this future day of accounting—for it is there that voters will either ratify or veto present performance of office (which is hardly a positive, determinative act articulating clear expressions about future policy). Officeholders must anticipate what the electorate will want at that time, and how they will judge possible alternative performances.

Future elections may thus have more impact on an official's conduct in office than did the election in which he was elected. The election in which a decision maker was elected achieves its impact as it conditions his calculations about the future election. That is, his anticipation of what voters will want at future elections will be affected by the information he receives from the electorate during the campaign. The combination of these two devices—information transmission during the present campaign, coupled with the anticipation of voter judgment during future campaigns—provide the mechanisms by which elections have an impact on public officials' performance in office.[14]

14Elections, if they were truly democratic, might make the voting act more powerful for expressing policy preferences. For example, if financial burdens did not exclude some potential candidates, voters might have more meaningful choices. The mechanisms which are discussed in this paper are those which enable elections as they now exist to have an impact on policy. If the electoral process were reformed, it might strengthen this impact by activating additional mechanisms that would permit more direct translations of policy preference into voting decisions.

22 *James M. Perry*

The Almost Perfect Political Campaign: Nelson Rockefeller's Last Hurrah

Nelson A. Rockefeller, the happiest multimillionaire, repeated those magic words last week: "I do solemnly swear that I will . . . faithfully discharge the duties of the office of governor according to the best of my ability."

Sweet words for a man no one ever thought could be elected to a third term. Costly words. To win re-election, some $260,000 was spent for each lovely little word. Nelson Rockefeller's winning campaign was far and away the most expensive state-wide effort ever put together in this country. Not only the most expensive, but the most professional, the most astute, the most imaginative, and perhaps the most ruthless. It was, in fact, the closest thing to a perfect political campaign this democracy has ever seen.

Some supporting evidence:

1. No state-wide candidate has ever used television so much, so well. A National Observer survey indicates that 3,027 commercials were shown on New York State's 22 commercial television stations in behalf of Mr. Rockefeller. The actual figures, given the inconsistency of reporting methods, might run as high as 4,000.

From *National Observer* (January 9, 1967). Reprinted by permission.

256

2. No state-wide candidate has ever distributed so much literature and campaign paraphernalia. The Rockefeller forces distributed 27,000,000 buttons, brochures, and broadsides. That's about 4½ items for every person who turned out to vote.

3. The candidate himself, traveling by bus, by jet, by helicopter, even by seaplane—and constantly in radio touch .with his 84-room headquarters at the New York Hilton—visited all 62 counties in the state. In August alone, he shook hands at 17 county fairs in upstate New York. Mr. Rockefeller spent his energy with just as much abandon as he and loyal members of his family spent their cash.

THE LAST CAMPAIGN?

"Never again," says one of his chief advisers, "will we see another campaign like it." He may be right, for Mr. Rockefeller insists his recovery from Presidential fever is complete, and his advisers take him at his word. Presumably, this campaign was Nelson Rockefeller's last hurrah.

It is, of course, ironic. Here, the picture of rugged good health at the age of 58, is a man who has mastered the mysterious arts of the new politics; or, at least, these arts have finally been mastered by the men around him. But, just as he and his experts have reached the top of their political form—in a technical sense—the game is up.

Mr. Rockefeller may leave many legacies; he has been, after all, an activist as governor of New York. He leaves, too, a political legacy, and it's his winning campaign for a third term as governor. From this day hence, this campaign will be the apotheosis. Already, wise men are traveling to New York to talk and listen; professionals from the British Labor Party have been here and so have Scandinavians. The men who seek to win the Republican nomination for George Romney are wooing the men who worked for Nelson Rockefeller (so far without much luck).

And for the ordinary voter, living anywhere, the Rockefeller campaign is significant. After all, this campaign, like any other, was ultimately directed at that lone voter, buffeted by personal problems and petty concerns and hardly willing or able to devote more than peripheral attention to politicians or to political issues. In this campaign, new techniques were used to win that lone voter's attention and his support. Some of these techniques—if improperly used by sincere men or properly used by insincere men—may be dangerous. They at least should be understood.

Here then is the story—told in detail for the first time—of how the almost-perfect campaign was planned and waged.

To start at the beginning, there was Nelson Rockefeller. A very unpopular Nelson Rockefeller. At his side was a heavy-set man named William J. Ronan, one-time dean of the New York University Graduate School of Public Administration and Social Services. Mr. Ronan—Dr. Ronan, really—is an issues man, and the politicians held him in contempt. A thinker, they said; you don't win elections with intellectuals. As usual these days, the politicians were wrong. Dr. Ronan planned the Rockefeller campaign; he was its architect.

"We had a problem," Dr. Ronan recalls. "In January of 1966 the position of the governor in the polls was not very good. Indications were that almost anyone could beat him. There were so many negatives. He had been in office for almost eight years and he had made a lot of decisions that irritated some people; other people just thought they were aggrieved. He'd raised taxes twice in a major way. One was a sales tax. And he got full credit for all these new taxes.

"Then he had this very long session with the Legislature and a struggle over Medicaid [New York's program for medical care for the elderly]. The compromise was higher than the original bill, and the governor got credit for it. It was only after the bill was passed that newspapers pointed out its cost to state and local government. The result was a furor in the Buffalo and Syracuse areas.

"Also, there was the so-called personal problem. Some people alleged it was still there." Dr. Ronan meant, of course, Mr. Rockefeller's celebrated divorce and his remarriage to a younger woman who was a divorcee herself.

"On the other side, Rockefeller had accomplished more in eight years than any other governor. But these positives weren't apparent. He'd done so much it was all kind of a blur—the state university, highways, aid to local governments, health, parks, right across the board.

"Adding it all up, the governor just wasn't popular. People didn't like him any more."

"FORTUNE FAVORS THE BRAVE"

That's almost an understatement. The Rockefeller problem was so serious that some Republican leaders actually were calling for him to step aside in favor of U.S. Senator Jacob Javits. Even some of the people closest to Rockefeller were privately saying that defeat was inevitable. But things weren't quite as bad as they looked. As Dr. Ronan says, "Fortune favors the brave."

One of the secrets of the Rockefeller campaign's success was its early start. First, there was Dr. Ronan, ready to go on issues. Then there was "the other Bill"—William L. Pfeiffer, an old professional who had worked for Mr. Rockefeller before. This time, he actually went to work for Rockefeller on December 1, 1964. His assignment was to organize the 1966 campaign—to pick the personnel, to open a headquarters, to lay out a schedule. Bill Ronan was the ideas man; Bill Pfeiffer was the organization man. Ultimately, Mr. Pfeiffer put together a *paid* staff of 307 people, 190 of them working out of headquarters at the New York Hilton. In a more traditional way, his operation was just as brilliant as Dr. Ronan's. And almost as costly.

Yet, with all credit to Mr. Pfeiffer and the professionals working for him, the major assignment was Dr. Ronan's. He had to sell Nelson Rockefeller just as Miles Laboratories sells Alka-Seltzer. He had to make an unpopular governor an acceptable product.

THE SUBSTANTIVE ISSUES GROUP

And so he formed a small committee, himself at its head, grandiloquently called the Substantive Issues Group. Like Dr. Ronan himself, this elite group—never numbering more than five—was exclusively intellectual.

"We undertook a pre-campaign approach," says Dr. Ronan. "We wanted to improve the governor's position before the state convention [the ticket in New York is chosen by party convention, not by direct primary]. Since people were down on the governor, we decided to sell his accomplishments without using him at all."

The key decision was the choice of an advertising agency. "We wanted to depart from the usual political approach," Dr. Ronan notes. "We moseyed around the field and we found Jack Tinker & Partners, part of the Interpublic complex. We liked their different approach. It was off-beat and it had been successful in restoring some products." One of those restored products was Alka-Seltzer; another, Braniff Airways, Inc.

The scene switches, in wonderful contrast, from the stark, businesslike office of Dr. Ronan to the swinging offices of Jack Tinker & Partners. The door opens upon a large living room, a well-stocked bar ready to go at one end. The couches are deep and modern. Miniskirted girls dash breathlessly from room to room, carrying mugs of coffee. This is the place where the celebrated Mary Wells used to work, until she quit to open her own agency. Not so surprisingly, her first account turned out to be Braniff airways.

A DIFFERENT KIND OF AGENCY

But, with or without Mary Wells, Tinker has an air and a style about it that is almost singular. It's a different kind of agency. The favorite word of the people who work there is *creative*. The trademark of a Tinker commercial is its rapport with the person who is expected to look at it. Says Jack Conroy, who supervised the Rockefeller account: "Each of our commercials tries to talk with the viewer. You talk to the people in front of their sets in their own terms. This is almost automatic with the Tinker people."

The Tinker people had never handled a political client. But, when they heard the account was up for grabs, they went after it. The Tinker presentation was made by Mary Wells, shortly before she quit. It won the day.

Tinker learned it had won the account about the first of April, fully five months before the Republican State Convention was due to convene. The Tinker people still remember their first meeting with Governor Rockefeller and his people. "It was held in his private offices on 55th Street," one of them recalls. "He was there and so was Ronan, and his private pollsters too. We were impressed by the governor's own evaluation of his problems. One of the pollsters got up and said to him, 'You couldn't be elected dog-catcher.' "

THE TIME TO WORK

The creation of good television takes time. Mr. Rockefeller, because he was an incumbent and because of his own farsightedness, had the time. His ultimate Democratic opponent, Frank D. O'Connor, never did have the time and the quality of his television showed it.

"Advance planning is so damn important," says Tinker's Mr. Conroy. "I don't see why a lot of incumbents don't start planning a lot sooner. And, in fact, I don't see why the out-party couldn't start early too. The state committee could easily put together a program attacking the incumbent and his record, even without having a candidate of their own."

And so the work began, Dr. Ronan and his team deciding on the issues to be stressed, and the agency people developing these issues into brilliant television commercials. As Bill Pfeiffer puts it: "We had to sell the record, associate it with the governor. And it had to be done so subtly it crept up on you before you knew what the hell had happened to you."

Tinker commercials are prepared by teams. Each team is composed of a copy-writer and an art director. Unlike most agencies, the two members of the team follow the commercial all the way through the production process, from writing the script to directing the filming to editing the sound. Two of these teams were assigned to the Rockefeller account. Working on the No. 1 team were Eugene Case, writer, and Bob Reitzfeld, art director. Mr. Reitzfeld has since defected to Mary Wells' agency.

QUALITY COMMERCIALS

The first commercials produced by these teams all were 60 seconds in length. Each was done in a process called sound-on-film; it's slower to produce but the quality is better. Moreover, a creative team can do more with film than with tape. It is not surprising that most of the Rockefeller commercials were sound-on-film; that all of the Democratic commercials were videotape.

The first Tinker commercial set the whole tone of the early phase of the campaign. The title of the commercial is "Fish Interview." Stage directions read: "Open on hand wearing a press hat and microphone to resemble a reporter talking to a fish puppet."

The script reads, in part:

REPORTER: You, sir.
FISH: Uh huh.
REPORTER: How do you feel about Governor Rockefeller's Pure Waters Program?
FISH: His pure what?
REPORTER: Pure waters.
FISH: Oh, oh yeah.
REPORTER: This program, sir, is wiping out water pollution in New York within six years.
FISH: Well, it was pretty smelly down here.
REPORTER: By the end of summer, the governor will have called in every major polluter for a hearing.

And so on, for an exchange or two more.

Bill Pfeiffer remembers looking at the first Tinker commercials with a number of political leaders. "The politicos," says Mr. Pfeiffer, "said it was no damn good. They're so used to the staged stuff, to the candidate standing there talking. You had to wait out these Tinker commercials to find out what they were all about. But the politicos thought they were just a waste of time. That's when I knew we had done the right thing."

A GERM OF TRUTH

Each commercial dealt with a single subject, directly and imaginatively. The commercials were amusing and they were interesting. And each of them contained a germ or two of truth.

The second Tinker commercial was classic in its utter simplicity. A camera was mounted on a hood of a car, and the commercial showed what the camera photographed as the road slipped by. The script reads: "If you took all the roads Governor Rockefeller has built, and all the roads he's widened and straightened and smoothed out . . . if you took all these roads, and laid them end to end, they'd stretch all the way to . . . Hawaii."

At that point—the Hawaii bit—the sound swells; it's all crashing breakers and hula music. Then the car obviously backs up and turns around. The road starts to slip by again. The voice returns: "All the way to Hawaii . . . and all the way back."

Then came "Butterfingers" (about state scholarships) and all the rest. Nelson Rockefeller didn't appear in any of these commercials. His voice wasn't even used. The Tinker agency picked a professional—actor Ed Binns—to read the scripts. It is this same Ed Binns that millions of Americans hear on television every day—talking about Alka-Seltzer and Gillette razors.

The first of the soft-sell Tinker commercials began popping up on screens in July. Just as Bill Pfeiffer says, they "crept up" on the viewer. Long before the commercials began to appear, the Rockefeller and Tinker people had worked out a schedule based on a detailed analysis of the voters' market.

They had found, for example, that 86.7 percent of the registered vote lives in 22 of the 62 counties. Conclusion from that: Saturate the television markets serving those 22 counties. Thus, the 60-second commercials were scheduled for the six stations in New York City and for television stations serving Albany, Binghamton, Buffalo, Rochester, and Syracuse.

The television campaign was divided into three phases. Phase 1 covered the period July 5 to September 12. In that period, the schedule called for running 37 Rockefeller 60-second commercials every week in New York City and 18 every week in each of the five upstate markets.

The result was that the Rockefeller commercials, stressing the administration's accomplishments but never the candidate himself, were shown 700 times before the state convention even began.

That, of course, was only part of the pre-convention strategy. The governor himself quietly toured the state all during August, shaking hands and trying to make friends. Personal emissaries—men like George Hinman, who had done so much for Mr. Rockefeller in his Presidential efforts—toured the state, talking to "opinion makers." An indication of the success of this effort may be in the fact that only two daily newspapers in the state—the Adirondack Enterprise and the Syracuse Herald-Journal—ultimately decided to support a candidate opposed to Mr. Rockefeller. In New York City, both the liberal *Post* and the conservative *Daily News*, which rarely agree about anything, endorsed Mr. Rockefeller.

Dr. Ronan and his Substantive Issues Group were busy with other things too. One of these projects was campaign literature. "We had long felt most of it is not very valid," Dr. Ronan says. "There's a picture of a guy and it says, 'Vote for Joe Smith.' Now, here we had Nelson Rockefeller, one of the most visible of people. He'd run twice in the state and tried for the President twice. He was ubiquitous. There was no need to try to produce a recognition factor. Just what we didn't want people saying was, 'Aha, there's Nelson Rockefeller.' "

And so the Rockefeller literature turned out to be as strikingly original, in concept and design, as the Rockefeller television.

"OUT OF THIS WORLD"

"First," says Dr. Ronan, "we wanted to reach the opinion makers, for we were afraid we had lost them. They just weren't articulate for us and I mean the legislators, the newspaper people, the leaders of various special groups. So we decided to approach them on a clientele basis. We prepared eye-getting stuff in each category—a brochure for the people in the field of mental retardation, another for labor, another for the fine arts." Salty Bill Pfeiffer puts it in somewhat different terms. "It was out of this world," he says. "We had something for every group except the Times Square prostitutes."

Preparing the literature is one thing; distributing it is another. In most campaigns, thousands of brochures are still lying around headquarters the day after election. This time, a paid worker was assigned to each kind of brochure with instructions to make sure the literature got to the people it was written for. Thus, if there was a meeting anywhere in the state of people interested in higher education, there was a Rockefeller staffer there to make sure everyone got a brochure dealing entirely with what the governor had done for higher education in New York.

Another Ronan innovation was the preparation of a series of brochures aimed at individual regions in the state. Every major region had a Rockefeller brochure, and the text in each told precisely what the Rockefeller administration had done for that part of the state. Getting the facts out of the bureaucracy was the tough part of that job; it was accomplished only because the factgathering had begun months earlier.

DETAILED DATA SHEETS

Beyond this, the Ronan group prepared immense research reports for each of the 62 counties in the state. These data sheets showed how many miles of highways had been built, and where; the number of new bridges; the number of state scholarships awarded to county students; even specific examples showing how high property taxes would be if it weren't for increased state aid. All of the candidates used these data sheets in their personal appearances.

A bulkier document was called "The Massive Record." It was an account of the accomplishments of the Rockefeller administration and it was distributed to all of the campaign workers. A shorter version was prepared for the general voter.

Because they had started so early, the Rockefeller people had the time—and, to be sure, the cash—to anticipate the issues. Polls were taken regularly. They showed that one of the major criticisms of the governor was that he was arrogant. "So," says Dr. Ronan, "we flipped that over to the positive. The positive of arrogance is leadership. So we said, 'This is leadership and let's keep it in Albany.' It came through again and again in what we did. It was summed up by the phrase, 'He Cares.'"

The polls had also shown the voters were angry about high taxes. The answer to that was to show where the money had gone. All the Rockefeller material emphasized the amount of money that had been returned to local jurisdictions in the form of state aid.

ANTICIPATING THE OPPONENT

The Rockefeller people also tried to anticipate their opponent. The guessed right that Frank D. O'Connor, president of the New York City Council, would be the Democrats' choice. He was chosen at the Democratic State Convention in Buffalo on September 7–8. By then, the Republicans had a fat file on his career and almost everything he had ever said.

Thus, after both conventions were over, the Rockefeller campaign moved into a new—and tougher—phase. Gradually, radio and TV commercials (radio was used to supplement television) began to zero in on Mr. O'Connor. Finally, Mr. Rockefeller appeared full-face, using his own voice, to attack with extraordinary ruthlessness his gentle and bumbling Democratic opponent.

Mr. O'Connor had no meaningful reply. The Democrats, up to the time of their convention, had done almost nothing about preparing a campaign. They had no literature, no television, hardly any organization. The entirely predictable result was chaos in their camp. Worse, they were constantly on the defense. Troubling the waters, too, were the additional candidacies of Franklin D. Roosevelt, Jr., on the Liberal ticket, and Paul L. Adams, on the Conservative.

The Tinker agency returned to the battle, preparing 10- and 20-second commercials attacking Mr. O'Connor and his record. Typical was this script: "Frank O'Connor, the man who led the fight against the New York State Thruway, is running for governor. Get in your car. Drive down to the polls, and vote."

DISTORTING THE ISSUES

Of necessity, all spot commercials are oversimplifications. After all, no one can say very much even in 60 seconds. In the first phase, though, most of the Rockefeller commercials were reasonably truthful. Now, however, in the second and third phases, they became distortions. Take the thruway commercial. Mr. O'Connor, as a state legislator, didn't actually oppose a thruway. What he did oppose—taking his own party's position—was a toll road. He and the Democrats wanted a free road. That refinement, naturally enough, never was explained.

Or take this Rockefeller 20-second commercial. The script reads: "Frank O'Connor from New York City is running for governor. He says the New York subways should be free. Guess who he thinks should pay for them?"

It is interesting that this commercial was only run in *upstate* New York; never in New York City. Moreover Mr. O'Connor never meant to say that he wanted the New York subways free now or even at any time in the next few years. He had been musing about long-term goals when he made his proposal, and he had been thinking about subways in all cities. Again, Mr. O'Connor never was able to explain the refinements involved.

In every campaign, smart politicians look for the "gut issue," an emotional, supercharged issue that can be battered home to almost every voter. The Rockefeller people, months before the campaign began, anticipated just such a gut issue. When it came time, they were ready.

THE NARCOTICS ISSUES

The issue was, specifically, narcotics; more broadly, crime. Mr. Rockefeller, a governor, had proposed a sweeping narcotics program. It involved getting all of the addicts off the street—mandatory treatment, in other words—and jailing all of the pushers. It was strong stuff, so strong that it worried many civil libertarians. Yet, for voters generally, it was popular enough, for every poll taken in New York State recently rates crime as the leading concern of the citizenry.

The Rockefeller people expected that Mr. O'Connor would take a position against the Rockefeller narcotics program. Mr. O'Connor did take such a position, perhaps to win back dissident liberals to the Democratic line (many of them were flocking to the Liberal Party and its candidate, Mr. Roosevelt). Or perhaps Mr. O'Connor, as his aides suggest, just thought the program, as outlined by Mr. Rockefeller, was unworkable.

Whatever the reason, Mr. O'Connor was vulnerable, and he was clobbered by every device available to his opposition. The television commercials were eerie, frightening. A police car, lights flashing, cruises down a dark street. There's the sound of footsteps in the background. A disembodied voice begins talking: "If you walk home at night or if there's a teen-ager in your family, you should be worried. Governor Rockefeller's worried. As much as half the crime in New York is caused by addicts. That's why the governor has sponsored a tough new law that can get addicts off the street for up to three years . . ."

ROCKEFELLER SPEAKS OUT

At first, the commercials made no mention of Mr. O'Connor. Then they noted that, as district attorney of Queens, he had been alone among all prosecutors in the state in opposing a tough narcotics law. Finally,

Mr. Rockefeller himself—speaking into a battery of microphones in a television studio—took the fight directly to his opponent. "If you want to keep crime rates high," he concluded, "O'Connor is your man."

It was devastating. Its effect was heightened by a local issue in New York City—the police civilian-review board. The Conservative Party and the police themselves had managed to get a referendum on the ballot challenging Mayor John Lindsay's review board. It was, by itself, the most emotional issue in the city. And the narcotics issue dovetailed neatly with it.

In the final weeks of the campaign, the Rockefeller people simply overwhelmed the opposition. And television was the battering ram.

Consider these figures.

On television station WNBC, in New York City, the Rockefeller forces ran 208 commercials. They paid $237,000 to do it. The O'Connor forces ran on this same station 23 commercials. They paid $41,000. On WCBS, Rockefeller outspent O'Connor $231,105 to $35,920. On WABC, the third network station in the city, it was $137,000 for Rockefeller and $25,100 for O'Connor.

The disparity upstate was sometimes even more remarkable. On WBEN in Buffalo, Rockefeller spent $27,762; O'Connor, $2,465. Little WWNY in Watertown ran 99 Rockefeller commercials, at $3,067.50, against 18 O'Connor commercials, at $1,307.50.

Rockefeller strategists hasten to point out that they began their television campaign way back in July. They're right, of course—but they had to start that early to make a campaign. That early spending was just as crucial as the final spending. It was, in fact, one campaign. And when it was all over Rockefeller outspent O'Connor by almost 10 to 1.

What were the actual figures? It's hard to say. Democrats and even some Republicans insist that Rockefeller spent as much as $10,000,000. The National Observer's sampling of campaign costs would indicate a lower figure, perhaps something over $6,000,000. The official figure filed by Mr. Rockefeller and his people is $4,800,000. Hardly anyone doubts, however, that the O'Connor people are reasonably accurate when they say they spent $600,000. It just couldn't have been much more.

Even with this lopsided spending, Mr. Rockefeller didn't win by very much. The final count was: Rockefeller, 2,690,626; O'Connor, 2,298,363; Adams, 510,023; Roosevelt, 507,234. Almost surely, Mr. Rockefeller could have been beaten. He won because he had the money and the talent to wage a brilliant campaign. And, to be sure, he had luck on his side—luck in having the Democrats pick the bumbling Mr. O'Connor, luck in having Mr. Roosevelt and Mr. Adams splintering the vote.

A PERSONAL VICTORY

Then, too, it was a personal victory. New York Republicans failed to win back any of those Congressional seats they lost in 1964. They failed to win control of the State Assembly. They just barely held their margin in the State Senate.

It was a personal victory because almost everything was directed to the top of the ticket. That's where the action was, and that's where the money was. In point of fact, there hardly was a state committee operating in New York in 1966. Its function was taken over by the Rockefeller organization. Even now, weeks after the election, there is no real functioning state organization in New York. It remains a Rockefeller operation.

The lessons?

1. Money and more money. Money wisely, even ruthlessly spent. A candidate or a party must have it early and spend it often.
2. Television. It's the premier instrument for political campaigning. It penetrates into almost every home; it sways and angers and converts. Item: During the week of Oct. 18, Rockefeller ran 74 television commercials in New York City. They were seen in 91 per cent of all television homes in the city (and 5,600,000 of 6,000,000 New York homes have television). Not seen just once—but seen an average of 9.8 times in each home.
3. Experts. No one wins any more with amateurs. Good television means people like Dr. Ronan and the copywriters and art directors at Jack Tinker. Good organization requires innovators like Bill Pfeiffer.
4. Time. It takes time to put together a campaign. Mr. Rockefeller had the time, Mr. O'Connor didn't. It was as simple as that.

But what about candidates? Is there a lesson in New York that almost anyone can be elected, given money, television, experts, and time? Perhaps not. Mr. Rockefeller, after all, is a great campaigner, and he has been, many people think, a strong and effective governor. There was, in all the confusion and bitterness, a product to be sold, albeit in a battered and dusty package.

Yet a note of doubt remains. These new techniques are so overwhelming, so terribly effective. Some day, maybe they will elect a truly dangerous and sinister man to high public office.

The preventive, perhaps, is a general understanding of what it's all about.

23 *Daniel A. Dye*

Maximum Feasible
Participation: An Irony
of the "War on Poverty"

"Maximum feasible participation" (MFP) is a popular term which seems to have been designed to promote political ambiguity instead of academic clarity. Its lack of an accepted meaning provides the administrator, the politician, and the political evaluator with a diplomatic "out" of a potentially explosive situation in which he might find himself. It is also a member of that class of terms, such as "benign neglect," which is difficult to conceptualize adequately and seemingly impossible to test. Hence, both its usefulness and its disadvantages become apparent: it means only what the reader or listener wants it to mean.

Maximum feasible participation was incorporated in the Economic Opportunity Act in 1964 as one measure of the overall effectiveness of the local community action programs for which the act provided. Yet, the Congress failed to define adequately, among other terms, "community action" and "maximum feasible participation." It said only that the estimated forty million poor in this country should be systematically involved in the planning and decision-making phases to the "maximum feasible extent" in the local antipoverty programs.

This selection was written expressly for this volume.

In the absence of specific guidelines, the Director of the Office of Economic Opportunity (OEO) was charged with the responsibility of establishing an acceptable range of recipient participation. As one might suspect, memos flowed from Washington not unlike a babbling brook. MFP requirements were changed with the weather, and the embryonic libraries of the local community action programs (CAPs) were soon bulging at the seams with "superceded policy" on MFP. To compound the confusion and the uncertainty, OEO state and federal field directors and evaluators frequently substituted their own interpretations of what the Congress had meant by MFP. As a result, the local CAPs often did not resemble in structure or function the type of agency that the Congress had created.

Field interpretation had significantly modified Congressional intention, thereby contributing to the mass confusion which surrounds most new federal programs. In one rural county in southwest Virginia, for example, the executive director of the local CAP was fired by the local governing board of the CAP because he had succeeded in motivating and mobilizing the local "poor" citizens against the county's welfare policy. The "field supervisors and evaluators" from OEO either stood by and watched hopelessly or tucked-tail and ran back to Washington. Almost simultaneously, these same "field supervisors and evaluators" recommended to the local CAP board in an adjacent county that their executive director should be fired because he had failed to unite and mobilize the poor against, among others, the local "establishment."

MFP at first suffered the ambiguities, and later events made it somehow *much* less important what the interpretations were. At first, when a significant issue was involved, it seems MFP often was interpreted by OEO representatives to mean "minimum acceptable interference with the status quo." Hence, the CAPs and the poor people suffered because of legal and political ambiguities. Ironically, later, the Congress which created OEO and demanded "maximum feasible participation" by the poor subsequently relinquished control of the CAPs to local politicians. CAP programs ultimately became political rewards. Despite this, however, one cannot definitively say that the CAPs were significantly worse off as puppets of petty politicians than they were as clearing houses for the confusion of OEO's policy.

Generally, MFP was accomplished in most CAP agencies as described below. Although the basic plan for MFP appears to be sound, it nonetheless suffered from the many tactical and substantive errors which plagued most CAP agencies during the sixties. In addition, MFP constantly had to struggle against the mass lethargy which enveloped the entire "war on poverty." Moreover, frequent changes in supervisory personnel resulted in almost constant policy changes. The average "job tenure expectancy" of OEO officials in its formative years was approximately seven months.

Theoretically, most CAP agencies were private, nonprofit corporations chartered by their respective states for the purpose of receiving and expending federal funds as they related to the eradication of poverty, or of engaging in any charitable endeavour for which public funds might be received and expended. These corporations were ostensibly responsible only under the laws of the state in which they were incorporated. Hence, they were not responsible to OEO, HEW, or any other federal or state agency. Although the CAPs had to meet certain OEO requirements in order to receive funding, they were not creatures of Washington bureaucrats. At the same time, state and local governments were bypassed in order to fund certain federally approved local CAPs. Hence, local CAP agencies represented an added dimension to our age-old concept of federalism.

The organization of local CAPs was relatively simple and straightforward prior to the adoption of the Green Amendment in 1967, as depicted below. The Green Amendment made local CAPs responsible to direct control of local politicians.

A cursory examination of the chart indicates that the local CAP agencies deal with state and federal OEO offices, but they are independent entities which are governed by a board of directors comprised of volunteers from the areas to be served by the CAP. The boards generally are comprised of one-third representation of public officials, elected and nonelected; and one-third representation of businesses, clergy, and various clubs. The boards are responsible for establishing local policy—so long as it is not inconsistent with OEO policy—and determining the type, scope, and magnitude of local antipoverty programs. (Because of its limited resources, among other reasons, OEO generally funded only those programs which it had previously determined to have "national priority.") Finally, the boards are responsible for employing and supervising a paid staff sufficient to operate their programs. All salaried employees, however, must be budgeted and approved by OEO, which pays their salary and provides up to 100 percent funding for all program expenditures. Also, each employee is subject to all federal regulations concerning federal employment but he does not receive the benefits that other federal employees receive.

The board of directors of each CAP is assisted by "policy advisory committees" which are established to determine local "target areas." The committees are comprised of volunteers who have an interest in their communities and/or who are eligible to participate in the poverty pro-

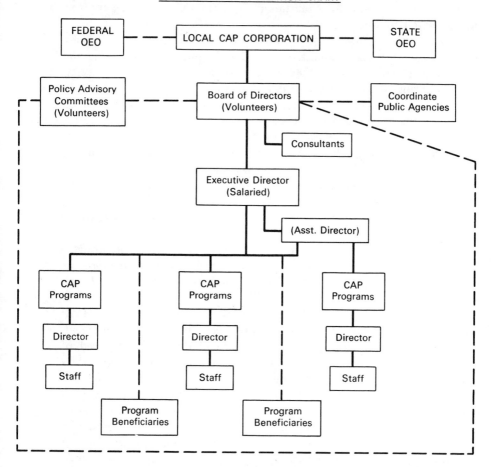

TYPICAL CAP ORGANIZATION CHART

grams. The latter are those who fall below the "poverty level" and are eligible to receive the benefits of the programs. Generally, a policy advisory committee exists for each local program; however, at least in the early history of OEO, the ideas for most programs originated with the local executive director and his paid staff.

The chart above also suggests the precarious relationship of the local CAP with other public programs. The existing public agencies are separate from the CAP and coordinate their endeavours only through mutual agreement, which often is lacking. That is, the CAP did not take one approach to the problem of poverty: the integration of all existing state, local, and federal programs directed toward that end. The Economic Opportunity Act, indeed, acknowledged the inability of piecemeal programs to cope with the problem of "hard core" poverty. In short, the existing public programs were not reaching the economically deprived, and primarily because there was no single agency to coordinate their individual activities. The creation of local CAPs, however, did not appreciably improve this situation as many of the existing agencies were either too defensive or too apprehensive to seek a common direction.

Despite vagueness and policy changes, each CAP had its day of reckoning. In order to justify the continuation of the local CAPs, OEO dispatched "review teams" or "evaluation teams" into each CAP agency in an effort to determine its effectiveness. The teams generally consisted of three OEO field representatives and two technical assistants from the state OEO who spent from one to three days in the CAP area, depending upon its geographical size, discussing the CAP agency with the local citizenry. Quite frequently, however, these discussions with the local citizenry became little more than brief chitchats with a few local public officials. Somehow, perhaps via that "ole black magic," the evaluators apparently were able to determine the effectiveness of the CAP and the degree of its MFP through these brief discussions. Ultimately, these evaluators determined the life or death of the CAPs they evaluated.

Finally, MFP all but disappeared from OEO after the enactment of the Green Amendment in 1967. Thenceforth, the complexion, scope, magnitude, and direction of all CAPs came under the scrutiny of the local governing authorities in the areas served by the CAPs. In short, the "war on poverty" became a "political plum" for local politicians, the courthouse gang, city hall, etc. Today, while OEO appears to be rapidly approaching its political demise, the primary beneficiaries of its few remaining programs appear to be the local politicians who, incidentally, were the first to demand its dismembering.

part four

Participation by the Rank and File

Who Turns Out?
Who Tunes Out?

Psychological and sociological characteristics of the rank and file are as crucial to an understanding of political participation as are institutional aids and obstacles to participation by political leaders. It is in this sense that the present chapter provides counterpoint to the preceding one.

The more specific thrust of this chapter may be sketched. The readings in this chapter examine the psychological and sociological differences between rank-and-file participants and nonparticipants, both individuals and groups. Political attitudes and their sources will be examined to provide insight about two key questions: Who turns out? and Who tunes out? In addition, part four seeks to provide a rough map of the direction of the politics of the near future.

Lester W. Milbrath provides an overall perspective on these key issues in his "Political Participation and Constitutional Democracy." Milbrath charts a kind of participative media via a middle road. Too little participation by too many of the rank and file can mean the decay of representative or democratic institutions, he notes. Intense participation by large numbers of the citizenry, oppositely, could heat up our social and political institutions to uncomfortable degrees. "Moderate levels of participation help societies find [a] type of balance," Milbrath observes, "that is between consensus and cleavage." As in other areas of complex life, he sees the division of labor as the vehicle for preserving this moderate level of participation. Some few will intensely participate in politics, while keeping the door more rather than less open for episodic participation by others, when they are somehow aroused.

The total sense of Milbrath's argument is that political elites are stewards of the common interests. The stewardship will be held accountable, loosely or strictly, as conditions vary. The dual goals are: to avoid ham-stringing political elites, while discouraging elitist overresponsiveness to its own needs.

A huge volume of research suggests that the overwhelming bulk of American citizens are well suited to the kind of moderately political role sketched by Milbrath. Fred I. Greenstein details some of this evidence in "The Citizen Base of the American Political System."

Greenstein's treatment has two specific thrusts. First, as a whole, American citizens only imperfectly meet a set of requirements that are ideal supports for the existence of a stable and popular government. These requirements include such factors as knowledge about politics, appropriate skills and values for political participation, and so on. Second, again on the whole, American institutions are such that they relate the fallible politician and his imperfect public in ways that in fact do result in a stable and popularly responsible and responsive system.

A conclusion seems appropriate. Viewed from the perspective of a direct-democracy or a majoritarian system, American citizens do not rate high on the scale of "ideal participants." Viewed from the perspective of a republican and representative form, however, the total effect does not distress Greenstein. The controls between elite and rank-and-file participants are imperfect and complex. Yet they trend toward outcomes that, on balance, are clearly those that Greenstein associates with a broadly representative and noncoercive form of government.

There are those who deny the representative and noncoercive character of American institutions, of course. For example, much evidence has been marshalled to establish the underrepresentation of the young, the poor, and the black. A number of selections arguing just such a point, the reader will recall, were introduced in part one. And those selections also show how some of the new participants variously reject the moderately participative style of American politics sketched by Milbrath and Greenstein. Intense and constant participation is their goal.

There seems no question that much of today's ferment in participation involves a conflict over the basic style of American politics. Is it to be politics as usual? Or politics of a new intensity, by a larger range of participants? Or somewhere in between? There is some evidence that changes in the direction of a mutual adjustment are occurring, that American politics will find its new level somewhere in between. But it also seems plausible that issues still in doubt—such as the management of our economy, inflation, wages, and prices—will play a critical role in determining whether it is mutual adjustment, or everyone for himself. Consequently, it is now only clear that the major alternatives to mutual adjustment imply major challenges, at the very least. These alternatives include a growing polarization of poli ipants–black against white, rich against poor, and so on–that cc of hand, or that might lead to some new synthesis.

Whatever the near future will bring, it is at least clear that there is something real behind the especial character of American political institutions and ideas. That "something real" is the composite American voter. That portrait is drawn in detail by Richard M. Scammon and Ben J. Wattenberg in "Demography Is Destiny."

There is no mistaking the clear outline of the composite Scammon and Wattenberg develop from a variety of research about who votes, and about their characteristics. The American voter is middle-everything: with a middle-income figure of $8,622 for the family median; middle-aged at about 47; middle-educated with at least some high school; and a member of the largest American categoric groups, that is, white and Protestant. Moreover, that profile does not change easily. Despite the unprecedentedly large numbers of people in college nowadays, for example, the voters will remain middle-educated and "uncollege." As Scammon and Wattenberg conclude:

> . . . because most of the electorate is middle-aged, the percentage of once-went-to-college among the electorate in the 1970's will not rise sharply. In 1968 about a quarter, 26%, had some college education. By 1972 this will have climbed to about 29%, and in 1976 to 31%.

The cry of "Power to the people" seems to need some modification, consequently. That is, on balance, power has been in the hands of "the people" represented by the composite American voter. That composite person may not be appreciated; he may even be despised for the policies he seeks and attains. But he is there, and his numbers are legion. There is no possible way to disregard that composite voter, except by violating or threatening major principles of both majoritarian and representative government.

The real slogan for the young, poor, and black—more appropriately—is "More power to different and larger numbers of people." With 18-year-olds now having the vote in national elections, it may be easier to achieve that modified slogan through that traditional vehicle for participation in politics—elections. But only time will tell.

Given the imponderables, a major activity of political scientists will be the development of models that attempt to describe what has happened and that hopefully will provide some glimmer of what may happen. George A. Taylor provides one insight into tomorrow's politics in "Toward a Theory of Revolution." Using concepts from two social sciences, he attempts to develop a model that describes what exists and what may come to pass. Taylor's goal is to describe major conditions that define active participation in a stable but evolving society. His model implies that much of today's political ferment—as among blacks—is a movement of hope, leaving behind a state of despair, and trending toward an enhanced participation in politics by a traditionally deprived group of citizens.

24 *Lester W. Milbrath*

Political Participation
and
Constitutional Democracy

Most Americans have been told, and have come to believe by the time they reach adulthood, that in order for democracy to flourish, it is essential for citizens to be interested in, informed about, and active in politics. If democracy is going to be rule "of the people, by the people, and for the people," the people, by definition, must be interested and active. Many citizens believe that a decision made by all the people is better than a decision made by only part of the people. When only part of the people participate, the government is likely to be directed so as to violate the interests of the nonparticipators. Disinterest and apathy are not approved because, should they become widespread, power could easily be usurped and the quality of government seriously decline. An important preventive is to have a societal norm proclaiming a duty for all citizens to be interested, informed, and active.

It should be obvious from reading the foregoing pages that very few United States citizens measure up to that prescription. Although the data are not quite so good for other countries, those we do have suggest that very few persons living in Western democracies measure up to it either. Is there reason, then, to fear for the future of democracy? This question has received a good deal of attention by some eminent political scientists in recent years. Although these scholars are not in total agreement in their analyses, none expresses great concern about the future of democracy. One reason for this lack of intense concern is that these scholars are confronted by evidence from many societies, accumulated over a considerable period of time, that, despite the low level of political interest and activity, democratic governments continue to flourish and provide reasonably satisfactory governance for their citizens.

In reconciling the fact of low participation with the fact of adequately functioning democracies, political scientists have enlarged their understanding of the political process and of the role of the average citizen in that process. The role of the citizen has evolved into something different from that envisaged by classical democratic theorists such as John Locke. He had in mind a small homogeneous society where most persons were engaged in primary economic activities (agriculture, forestry, fishing, and the like) and where any average man was considered qualified to hold public office and to resolve public issues (which usually were much simpler than those confronting society today). Each man was expected to take an active role in public affairs.

Modern society, in contrast, has evolved a very high division of labor, not only in the economic sector but also in politics and government. Political roles have become highly differentiated and specialized. This enables some men (elected and appointed officials) to devote their full attention to the complex public issues facing modern society. This division of labor allows other men (most of the citizens) to pay relatively little attention to public affairs. Politics and government are a peripheral rather than a central concern in the lives of most citizens in modern Western societies. As long as public officials perform their tasks well, most citizens seem content not to become involved in politics.

The fact of indifference to politics by many citizens should not be taken to mean that government would function well if citizens ignored it completely. In order to keep public actions responsive to the wishes and desires of the people, citizens must at least participate in the choice of their public officials. The institutions of modern democracies have so evolved that policy leadership is left in the hands of elected officials who at periodic intervals go before the people at an election to see which of two or more competing elites will have policy leadership in the next ensuing period. Both the leaders and the public acknowledge the essentiality of this electoral link between the public and its governing elite.

The burden upon the citizen is much less if he is called upon only to select who his rulers will be than if he is asked to decide the pros and cons of an abstract policy. Furthermore, choices of public officials confront the citizen only at periodic elections, thus taking very little of his time. Society has evolved helpful mechanisms, called political parties, to simplify further the choice between alternative sets of public officials. Instead of having to become informed about a number of individual candidates, the citizen can manage simply by knowing the record and reputation of the political parties under whose labels the candidates run. Parties also are helpful in calling the voter's attention to the failures of the opposition party and to their own successes. The citizen does not need to dig for information, it is literally thrust at him.

Another device for keeping public officials responsive to the people is to require and insure open channels of communication, so that citizens who so wish can be heard or consulted when public officials are making policy decisions. In part, this is achieved by constitutional provisions for freedom of speech, press, assembly, and petition. Society also has evolved social institutions, such as interest groups and the mass media, which keep citizens informed of what public officials are doing and public officials informed of what citizens want. The fact that top officials are placed there by election is very significant in insuring that channels of communication stay open between the public and their leaders. If an official should refuse to listen (thus closing the channel), he would probably pay for his folly by losing his position at the next election.

As we think about the role of the average citizen, then, we should not expect him to give a lot of attention to, and be active in resolving, issues of public policy. Nor should we expect him to stand up and be counted on every issue that comes along. The most we can expect is that he will participate in the choice of decision-makers and that he will ask to be heard if an issue comes along that greatly concerns him or on which he can make some special contribution. Many citizens do not even vote or speak up on issues, yet their passive role has the consequence of accepting things as they are. Indeed, it is impossible to escape at least a passive role in the choice of decision-makers. The choice process can proceed and government can continue to function even if many citizens choose to be so inactive as to fail to vote.

In evaluating citizen roles, we should keep in mind that citizens play two roles at once. At the same time that they try to make the government respond to their wishes, citizens also must play the role of obedient subjects of the regime under which they live. The participant and subject roles pull in opposite directions, and it is important that they be kept in balance. It is difficult for a compliant subject also to question the performance of his rulers and to try to influence their policy decisions. Similarly, it is difficult for a very active and intense participant in politics to subject himself readily to every policy and law decided on by the government. Most citizens work out a balance between the two roles in their daily lives, although there are individual differences in emphasis; some lean more toward the subject role, and others lean more toward the participant role. The moderately active, rather than the highly active person is more likely to achieve satisfaction in balancing the two roles.

A similar type of balance needs to be achieved at the system level, too. We want a government that is responsive to the wishes of the people but, at the same time, we want an effective government that is able to carry policies through to completion. There is a high probability of conflict between these two objectives. A government overly responsive to every whim of the public cannot pursue a consistent policy. The Fourth French Republic, which saw twenty changes of government in the twelve years following World War II, is a good example of a government made ineffective by responding too readily to every fluctuation in public opinion. Conversely, a government which pursued a given program without paying any attention to the wishes and desires of the public would be thought of as autocratic and unsatisfactory. Most dictatorships are in this latter category. In maintaining a balance between responsiveness and the power to act, the system is aided by the efforts of individual citizens to balance their participant and subject roles. As subjects, they tend to allow a government to develop and pursue a policy for a certain period before passing judgment. As participants, they scrutinize the actions of officials, communicate their policy desires to the officials, and prepare to replace them with other officials if they do not perform adequately. The system balance is further aided by the fact that some individuals prefer to emphasize the role of subject, while others prefer to emphasize the role of participant. If everyone were highly active in politics, or if everyone were passively obedient, it would be more difficult to maintain system balance between responsiveness and power to act.

Moderate levels of participation help societies find another type of balance, that between consensus and cleavage. It is in the very nature of politics that disputes will arise concerning issues and candidates, thus producing cleavages in the society. These must be bridged in some manner, however, if the society is to cohere and function adequately. Agreement on some larger principle, even though it is vague and platitudinous, often helps to bridge a cleavage. Resolution of a conflict by peaceful means, such as an election, facilitates movement toward consensus. The important point here is that societies having large numbers

of people who are intensely interested and active in politics (it is virtually impossible to have high activity without intense interest) tend to
have wide and deep cleavages that are very difficult to bridge. A current
example is the controversy over civil rights in the American South. The
intense feelings on both sides of that issue have assuredly stimulated active participation in politics by many who were formerly apathetic, but
their political activities have also served to deepen the cleavage between
the contending forces, making consensus increasingly remote. It is much
easier to forget about past disputes or to take a broad perspective on
present ones if those disputes are not considered vital by the participants.
It is paradoxical that the kind of issue that stimulates widespread participation in politics is also the kind of issue likely to create wide cleavages in society.

Although it must be conceded that governments continue to function adequately with moderate to low levels of participation in politics,
would they function even better if many more people became highly
active? Although it can be argued that participation in politics develops
character, there is doubt that the society as a whole would benefit if intense interest and active involvement in politics became widespread
throughout the population.

We would expect to find, in a society where most adults are intensely interested and involved in politics, that political concerns have
moved from the periphery to the center of life interests for most persons.
Probably most social relationships, in such a society, would become
politicized. Some of the new African one-party states, Ghana, for example, are characterized by high politicization of social relationships. In a
highly politicized society, political considerations determine a person's
opportunities for education, for a job, for advancement on the job, for a
place to live, for goods to enjoy. Furthermore, politics determines the
thoughts a citizen can express, the religion he follows, his chances for
justice. Such a permeation of politics into all aspects of life is antithetical
to the basic principle of limited government in a constitutional democracy. There is a consensus in limited constitutional democracies that
all the relationships (areas of life) mentioned above are out of bounds
to politics.

If societies could be arrayed along a continuum according to the
level of politicization of relationships, at the one extreme all social relationships in the society would be politicized; at the opposite extreme,
none of them would be. It is difficult to imagine societies being on either
extreme, but some examples come to mind that lean strongly toward extremes. Life in medieval Europe, with its fixed class divisions, hereditary

rulers, and prescriptive norms for every aspect of social relationships, is an example of a society close to the nonpoliticized extreme. Some politics-like choices were made in the governing hierarchy of the Roman Catholic Church and also within the courts of princes and kings, but so many human relationships were prescribed by customs, norms, and rules that only a small area of life was left open to political choice-making.

Approaching the highly politicized extreme are several new one-party states in Africa and the one-party Communist states of eastern Europe. A few areas of life are not politicized in these societies, especially relationships governed by tradition, but even these are under assault by forces bent on sweeping away the old order and using political passions as a weapon. Limited constitutional democracies, on the other hand, tend to be only moderately politicized. Citizens in these societies expect politicization of some aspects of life, such as decisions about land, resources, goods, and services held in common. By mutual consent, however, other areas are outside politics. In the five-nation study, about 90 percent of respondents in Great Britain and the United States said it would make no difference if their child married a supporter of the opposition party. They are "saying, in effect, that personal relationships ought to be governed by values other than political ones. The family ought not to be allowed to be divided by partisan considerations" (Almond & Verba, 1963, p. 297). Sometimes the boundaries between political and nonpolitical areas are spelled out in written constitutions (e.g., the freedom of speech and freedom of religion guarantees in the Bill of Rights); sometimes they are arrived at by common consent and tradition (e.g., parents have the primary right and responsibility in the bringing up of their children).

Knowing the boundaries of politics is basic to the ability of citizens to discriminate legitimate from illegitimate actions by their rulers. Being able to discriminate legitimate from illegitimate actions is, in turn basic to the ability of a body politic to act in concert to forestall tyrannous actions by their rulers. The social wisdom which enables a body politic to discriminate areas rightfully governed by politics from areas rightfully outside politics has evolved slowly and painfully over many centuries in Western society. Such boundaries would be difficult to maintain if a high percentage of citizens should become intensely interested and involved in politics. A study of participation rates and of the factors stimulating participation suggests that there is little likelihood that intense political interest and involvement will develop so long as government functions adequately, enabling citizens to keep politics as a peripheral concern in their lives.

The point that high levels of political interest and participation may not be beneficial to constitutional democracy should not be taken to mean that moderate levels of participation automatically guarantee the maintenance of constitutional democracy. A special burden of responsibility for the maintenance of the system rests on the shoulders of the political elites. If these elites are to perform their roles adequately, it is important that they array themselves into two or more competing groups (usually called political parties). As these elites compete for the support of the voters, they perform functions of vigil and criticism *vis-à-vis* their opponents that moderately interested and active citizens might not perform for themselves. Partisan criticism functions best if it is tempered by the realization that after the next election the elite currently in the role of critic may be called upon to govern. This tempered criticism not only gives the party in power a chance to carry a program through to completion and stand responsible for it, but it also enables bridging of cleavages and helps maintain over-all coherence of the society.

Several conditions are critical to the adequate functioning of a system of competitive elites in a constitutional democracy. It is important that the elites be committed to democratic values and believe in the rules of the game. It must be taken for granted, for example, that the elites will compete for mass support and that expression of that support in an election will determine which elite will rule for the ensuing period. Several bits of research suggest that participation in politics builds a commitment to democratic values and that elites are much more likely to understand and adhere to specific applications of general democratic principles than are average citizens. . . . An elite in power must have a live-and-let-live policy *vis-à-vis* its opponents out of power; elite political actors should be gladiators but not revolutionaries. Property rights may be important to insure that opponents out of power have some way to support themselves until they can regain power. From another perspective, no elite will readily relinquish power, should it be defeated in an election, if it has no alternative base of economic support. That base might be income-earning property, practice of a profession, jobs in industry not controlled by the government, and so forth. An elite also will be reluctant to relinquish power if it is convinced that its opponents will destroy the group, perhaps by imprisonment or other harassment, once the opponents have been given power.

In order that the interests of all sectors of society be adequately taken care of by the government, it is important that each elite recruit from many sectors of society. An elite from a single class or group would have difficulty gaining the confidence of the people, and competitive elites would be reluctant to entrust it with the reins of power. New recruits should have easy access to the center of power in the elite to prevent the inner group from getting out of touch with the people. It is vital that the recruits be socialized to elite norms and customs, especially basic democratic principles and the rules of the political game.

The system demands much less from the political beliefs and behavior of the mass of the citizens than from the elites. To perform its role, the attentive public must believe in the right of the public to watch and to criticize the behavior of the elites. It also needs a minimal sense of involvement in public matters and a sense of loyalty to the whole community rather than to only a segment of the society. It must perform the minimal chore of selecting among the elites at election time. This low level of attention and control by the mass of the public leaves a wide latitude to the elected elite for creative leadership.

Although we expect only this minimal surveillance by the public and their participation in the choice of elites, is even this effort too much to expect? What is to prevent a society from becoming widely apathetic and allowing an unscrupulous elite to destroy the chances for an opposing group to compete fairly? In the final analysis, there is no ironclad guarantee that this will not happen; eternal vigilance is still the price of liberty. Careful training of elite members in the norms and rules of democratic politics is one insurance against such an eventuality. Another is the outcry from the opposing group against the tactics of the party in power. This outcry has meaning, however, only if the public is listening, understands, and responds decisively.

In order for the public to respond adequately to dangers to their political system, it is essential that the system be kept open. There are two aspects to this openness. First, the communications network which provides the major linkage between actors in the political system must be kept open. Further, this network should carry a fairly high level of political content so that actors can, with minimum effort, find out what is going on in politics and government at any time. Lack of an open communications network would make it easier for an unscrupulous elite to subvert democracy. Almost the first act of elites seizing power by *coup d'état* is to grasp control of the communications system.

Secondly, the system should be kept open so that any citizen who so chooses can readily become active in politics at any time. Conversely, gladiators should be able to retire from politics readily and gracefully whenever they choose. This is important not only in circulating and replenishing elite memberships but also to the proper role behavior of gladiators, spectators, and apathetics. The potentiality that apathetics may become spectators and that spectators may become gladiators is an important property of the system confining and controlling the behavior of political elites.

> A good deal of citizen influence over governmental elites may entail no activity or even conscious intent of citizens. On the contrary, elites may anticipate possible demands and activities and act in response to what they anticipate. They act responsively, not because citizens are actively making demands, but in order to keep them from becoming active (Almond & Verba, 1963, p. 487).

In this respect, it is important to continue moral admonishment for citizens to become active in politics, not because we want or expect great masses of them to become active, but rather because the admonishment helps keep the system open and sustains a belief in the right of all to participate, which is an important norm governing the behavior of political elites.

> The democratic myth of citizen competence. . . has significant consequences. For one thing, it is not pure myth: the belief in the influence potential of the average man has some truth to it and does indicate real behavioral potential. And whether true or not, the myth is believed (Almond & Verba, 1963, p. 487).

It is a curious social fact that a norm, such as that which says citizens should be interested and active in politics, which is violated wholesale, still can be an important ingredient in the functioning of the political system. Should that norm wither or vanish, it would be much easier for unscrupulous elites to seize power and tyrannize ordinary citizens. Elites believing in that norm are more likely to welcome new recruits, are more likely to relinquish office easily when defeated in an election, are more likely to try to inform and educate their followers, are more likely to keep communication channels open and listen to the desires of the people, than are elites not believing in that norm. Perhaps one of the reasons the norm remains viable is that elites realize a decline of the norm could spell their own doom as they compete for the power to govern.

SUMMARY

Recapitulation of the foregoing argument, in brief form, may help the reader to see where it is leading. (1) Most citizens in any political society do not live up to the classical democratic prescription to be interested in, informed about, and active in politics. (2) Yet, democratic governments and societies continue to function adequately. (3) It is a fact that high participation is not required for successful democracy. (4) However, to insure responsiveness of officials, it is essential that a sizable percentage of citizens participate in choosing their public officials. (5) Maintaining open channels of communication in the society also helps to insure responsiveness of officials to public demands. (6) Moderate levels of participation by the mass of citizens help to balance citizen roles as participants and as obedient subjects. (7) Moderate levels of participation also help balance political systems which must be both responsive and powerful enough to act. (8) Furthermore, moderate participation levels are helpful in maintaining a balance between consensus and cleavage in society. (9) High participation levels would actually be detrimental to society if they tended to politicize a large percentage of social relationships. (10) Constitutional democracy is most likely to flourish if only a moderate proportion of social relationships (areas of life) are governed by political considerations. (11) Moderate or low participation levels by the general public place a special burden or responsibility on political elites for the successful functioning of constitutional democracy. (12) Elites must adhere to democratic norms and rules of the game and have a live-and-let-live attitude toward their opponents. (13) A society with widespread apathy could easily be dominated by an unscrupulous elite; only continuous vigilance by at least a few concerned citizens can prevent tyranny. (14) Elite recruitment and training is an especially important function. (15) To help insure final control of the political system by the public, it is essential to maintain an open communications system, to keep gladiator ranks open to make it easy for citizens to become active should they so choose, to continue moral admonishment for citizens to become active, and to keep alive the democratic myth of citizen competence.

It would be difficult to prove the validity of the above argument with research findings. For lack of evidence, many of the asserted relationships must remain hypothetical for the time being. Certain norms or preferred states for society have had to be posited (e.g., that governments should be both responsive and effective); others might disagree with those preferences. The points were put forward with the hope that they will stimulate discussion leading all of us to a clearer understanding of the dynamics of democracy. If this analysis is correct, present levels and patterns of participation in politics do not constitute a threat to democracy; they seem, in fact, to be a realistic adjustment to the nature of modern society. The political processes of that democracy may not be close to the ideal of the classical theorists, but they may well be the best possible approximation to popular control of government that can be achieved in modern, industrialized, mobile, mass society.

25 *Fred I. Greenstein*

The Citizen Base
of the
American Political System

There is more to a political system than meets the eye. Some observers attempt to understand government and politics by concentrating exclusively on the readily visible peaks of the body politic—public officials, party leaders, interest groups, and other widely publicized participants. But at least since the time of Plato, the more searching political theorists have acknowledged the necessity of also understanding the base on which the leaders rest—the citizenry whose countless acts of acquiescence, indifference, and defiance empower or weaken leaders.

Because of their belief in the importance of the citizen base of political systems, Plato and Aristotle would not have been surprised at the failure of democracy to take root in many of the former ,colonial nations which have entered the world community in recent decades. Noting the high illiteracy rates of these countries, their overpopulation, and the bare subsistence levels at which their citizens exist, they would surely have argued that in these nations the raw material is not present for anything but an autocratic—or anarchic—mode of politics.

From Fred I. Greenstein, *The American Party System and the American People.* Reprinted by permission of Prentice-Hall, Inc., Englewood Cliffs, New Jersey.

There are doubtless many requirements, some of them as yet unknown, which must be met by the electorate if a nation is to function as a stable democracy. At the very least, most theorists probably would assume that the following pair of broad prerequisites must be met:

1. *Citizen commitment to democratic rules of the game.* If a democratic constitution were grafted on a society in which all members strongly favored one-man rule, the constitution clearly would stand little chance of success. Perhaps it only is necessary for citizens not to "disbelieve" in democracy for a democratic system to work. This, however, seems unlikely: one would assume that some fraction of the citizens of a democracy must positively favor democracy if that form of government is to endure. Furthermore, this belief presumably must entail more than lip service to an abstract symbol. It must involve a commitment to concrete democratic procedures, such as those providing for the free expression of competing political viewpoints.

2. *Citizen competence at the game of democratic politics.* Democracy—that is, control of leaders by followers—also presumably would be impossible if the followers were totally inert. Therefore, it is obvious that some minimum level of citizen political activity is necessary in a democracy. Moreover, citizens cannot control their leaders by activity alone—to be effective, their activity must meet certain standards of rationality. One would assume that the activity of democratic citizens must be guided by information about government and its leadership and that the citizens must have at their disposal some reasonable criteria for evaluating the leadership's performance.

What kind of base do American citizens provide for government and politics? To what degree do Americans meet the seemingly self-evident requirements of democratic citizenship outlined above? The perhaps jarring thesis of this and the following chapter is that, as a whole, the American people meet these requirements quite imperfectly, but that because of other factors, important among them being the institutions which relate public and politician to one another, a political system which most of us would consider both democratic and stable persists in the United States.

With the development of modern public-opinion polling techniques, rather precise statements can be made about the citizen base of our political system. By various sampling procedures it is possible for interviewers to ask representative cross-sections of the population questions about their political activities, opinions, and information. If the sampling procedures are properly followed, the findings are almost always quite close to what would have been established if the entire population had been so interviewed.[1]

There are two general tacks we may take in using public-opinion poll data to assess the American citizenry. We can present an overall "photograph"—or rather a series of "photographs"—of the degree to which the public meets democratic citizenship requirements. This essentially is what is done in the present chapter, where we show the proportion of the public which supports democratic ground-rules and the proportion which shows political competence, as indicated by taking part in politics, acquiring political information, and forming political opinions.

We also can go beyond the photograph to what might be called the "X ray" and the "motion picture."

• • •

HOW COMMITTED ARE THE AMERICAN PEOPLE TO DEMOCRATIC RULES OF THE GAME?

The photograph of citizen adherence to the democratic rules of the game in the United States is scarcely encouraging. When questions are phrased in generalities, Americans are all for the democratic ground-rules. But when we get down to specifics the picture changes. Consider, for example, the matter of freedom of speech—particularly, freedom of speech for those groups to which most Americans are unsympathetic.

Table 1 reports the results of a 1940 survey in which a cross-section of the national population was asked, "Do you believe in freedom of speech?"[2] The 1940 finding neatly exemplifies the pattern of findings in a variety of surveys on this topic conducted over the years. Ninety-seven

[1]On sampling and public-opinion research and its findings see Mildred Parten, *Surveys, Polls, and Samples* (New York: Harper, 1950); Frederick F. Stephan and Philip J. McCarthy, *Sampling Opinions* (New York: Wiley, 1958); Herbert Hyman, *Survey Design and Analysis* (Glencoe, Ill.: The Free Press, 1955); Robert E. Lane and David O. Sears, *Public Opinion* (Englewood Cliffs, N.J.: Prentice-Hall, 1964).

[2]No single reference work provides a complete compilation of the numerous public-opinion polls taken over the years that provide insight into public political awareness and commitment to democratic ground-rules. Virtually all of the findings of the first decade of public-opinion research have been assembled in a single compendium: Hadley Cantril and Mildred Strunk, eds., *Public Opinion: 1935–1946* (Princeton: Princeton University Press, 1951). For recent data see the "Quarter's Polls" of *Public Opinion Quarterly*, the regular reports in the periodicals *Gallup Opinion Index* and *Polls*, and John P. Robinson et al., *Measures of Political Attitudes* (Ann Arbor: Survey Research Center—Institute for Social Research, 1968).

TABLE 1   Degree of Public Commitment to Democratic Rules of the Game: General vs. Specific

---

Do you believe in freedom of speech?

Yes	97%
No	1
Don't know	2

Do you believe in it to the extent of allowing fascists and communists to hold meetings and express their views in this community? (Asked of the 97 percent who answered "Yes.")

Yes	22%	(4 percent feel strongly that they should be allowed to hold meetings; 18 percent not very strongly)
No	70	(48 percent feel strongly that they should not be allowed to hold meetings; 22 percent not very strongly)
Don't know	5	

Source: American Institute of Public Opinion (AIPO) survey, November 19, 1940, reported in Hadley Cantril and Mildred Strunk, eds., *Public Opinion, 1935–1946 (Princeton: Princeton University Press, 1951), p. 245. The AIPO is popularly known as the Gallup Poll.

percent of the sample stoutly averred approval of free speech, and only 1 percent took the negative. But when the proponents of free speech were asked whether this right should be extended to two especially unpopular groups—fascists and communists—well over two-thirds of them answered that it should not. Moreover, those Americans who opposed granting free expression to these two groups were considerably stronger in their feelings than those who favored free speech for everyone "to the extent of allowing fascists and communists to hold meetings and express their views in this community."

Numerous instances of more recent similar findings can be shown:

1. A study in the late 1950's of two university towns of Ann Arbor, Michigan, and Tallahassee, Florida, showed that between 95 and 98 percent of the registered voters agreed with such general assertions as "Democracy is the best form of government"; "Public officials should be chosen by majority vote"; "Every citizen should have an equal chance to influence government policy"; and "People in the minority should be free to try to win majority support for their opinions." But about four-fifths of the voters in each of the two cities saw nothing wrong with the assertion "In a city referendum deciding on a tax-supported undertaking, only taxpayers should be allowed to vote." About a third were unwilling to permit an anti-religious speech to be given in their community, and

a fifth of the Ann Arbor voters and two-fifths of the Tallahassee voters raised no objection to the statement "A Negro should not be allowed to run for mayor of this city."[3]

2. A national survey conducted in 1957 and 1958 by Herbert Mc-Closky revealed, among other things, that while only about a tenth of the respondents failed to agree with the statement "I believe in free speech for all no matter what their views might be," one-half of them were at the same time able to accept the assertion "A book that contains wrong Political views cannot be a good book and does not deserve to be published."[4]

3. Eighty-seven percent of a 1962 sample of voting-age residents of the state of Minnesota agreed that "no matter what a person's political views are, he is entitled to the same rights in this country as anyone else." Yet 56 percent of the same sample also agreed that "the government should not allow people to make speeches which contain dangerous ideas."[5]

Some idea of where Americans draw the line when the question of the desirability of the democratic rules of the game is put in terms of specifics may be gained from Table 2, which is based on an extensive national survey on these problems. Very few Americans were willing to let communists or atheists speak in their communities. A majority, but not a very substantial majority, would extend this privilege to a socialist. Many more were in favor of free expression for the man accused of communism who denies the truth of the accusation. Even in this case, a fifth of the sample were opposed to freedom of expression.

Thus the findings of public-opinion research converge in suggesting that there is remarkably weak commitment to what seem to be fundamental democratic ground-rules.

HOW COMPETENT IS THE AMERICAN CITIZENRY AT THE GAME OF POLITICS?

A portrait of the American people in terms of the effectiveness of their political participation reveals a similarly puzzling departure from the apparent requirements of democratic citizenship.

Level of Political Participation.   First let us consider the public's

---

3James W. Prothro and Charles M. Grigg, "Fundamental Principles of Democracy: Bases of Agreement and Disagreement," *Journal of Politics*, Vol. 22 (May, 1960), pp. 276–294.
4Herbert McClosky, "Consensus and Ideology in American Politics," *American Political Science Review*, Vol. 58 (June, 1964), pp. 361–382.
5Minnesota Poll Release, *Minneapolis Sunday Tribune*, April 8, 1962.

level of political activity. One indication of the degree to which Americans are politically active is available without even turning to public-opinion surveys: the number of voters who actually vote can be compared with the potential electorate (the voting-age population). Such a comparison confirms the well-known observation that numerous Americans fail to perform even the rather undemanding act of voting.

In the 5 presidential elections between 1952 and 1968, close to 4 out of 10 adults were non-voters—and these elections were marked by

TABLE 2   Freedom of Speech for Whom? More Evidence on Public Commitment to Democratic Rules of the Game

	Yes	*No*	*Don't Know*
1. Consider a man whose loyalty has been questioned before a congressional committee, but who swears under oath he has never been a communist. Should he be allowed to make a speech in your community, or not?	70%	21%	9%
2. If a person wanted to make a speech in your community favoring government ownership of all the railroads and big industries, should he be allowed to speak or not?	58	31	11
3. If a person wanted to make a speech in your community against churches and religion, should he be allowed to speak, or not?	37	60	3
4. Suppose an admitted communist wants to make a speech in your community. Should he be allowed to speak, or not?	27	68	5

Source: Samuel A. Stouffer, *Communism, Conformity, and Civil Liberties* (Garden City, N.Y.: Doubleday, 1955), pp. 29–42. Based on a national sample of 4,933 respondents, surveyed in the early 1950's.

the *highest* turnout of any consecutive presidential elections since the advent of female suffrage. During the less dramatic off-year congressional elections, participation is always considerably lower—less than half the adult population goes to the polls (see Figure 1).

Of course, it is possible that turnout statistics underestimate citizen political activity. It occasionally has been argued that there are many Americans who are deeply interested in politics but who fail to vote simply because of the similarity of the two major parties and their candidates. Moreover, some citizens are kept home on election day because of illness, are unable to fulfill state residency requirements or are prevented by other mechanical impediments from voting. Therefore, a more detailed characterization of public political participation would be useful.

Table 3, which summarizes citizens' responses to inquiries regarding their political activity during the four presidential campaigns from 1952 through 1964, makes it clear that if turnout statistics are at all misleading it is because they *over*estimate public political involvement. While a majority of voters surveyed reported that they had gone to the polls in the current year's presidential election,[6] half admit that they have missed a presidential vote at one time or another. And while anywhere from 70 to 80 percent report having read something about the present campaign in the newspapers, less than half report following it assiduously or being "very much interested" in it. Moving on to some-

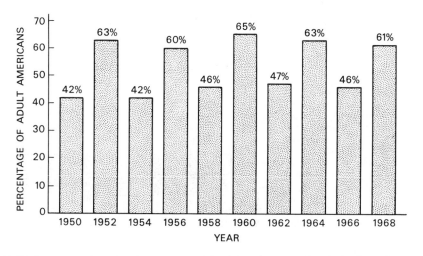

FIGURE 1   Participation in recent presidential and congressional elections. Source: *Statistical Abstract of the United States, 1967* (88th ed.). I am indebted to Richard M. Scammon of the Elections Research Center for providing me with the 1968 data.

what more demanding citizen endeavors, we find that a third or fewer Americans practice the indoor sport of attempting to persuade some fellow citizen how to vote; less than a fifth wear a button or sport bumper stickers; a tenth claim to have made a financial contribution or attended a meeting; and a twentieth or fewer work for the parties or candidates, belong to political clubs or organizations, or attend more than a single meeting. As far as registering a political opinion via some means other than the ballot box, somewhat fewer than a fifth have *ever* written a public official, and a mere 3 percent have ever sought expression through the letters-to-the-editor columns.

[6]But see the note to Table 3 for an explanation of why the rolls do show a somewhat higher percentage of turnout for any particular election than the election results would seem to indicate.

Level of Political Information.   Turning from the quantity of public political participation to its quality, we find more that clashes with

TABLE 3   Proportion of Adult Americans Engaging in Varying Kinds of Political Activities

	1952	1956	1960	1964
Voting				
Reports having voted in current year's presidential election[a]	73%	73%	74%	78%
Registered to vote (those who are certain they are)	NA[b]	75	78	82
Reports having voted in all elections for president since old enough to vote	43	42	46	50
News attention				
Read something in the newspaper about year's presidential campaign	79	69	80	79
Read regularly (1952: "quite a lot") about the campaign	39	NA	43	40
Very much interested in campaign	37	30	38	38
Campaign activity				
Talked with someone and tried to persuade him how to vote	27	28	33	31
Wore a campaign button or put sticker on car	NA	16	21	16
Contributed funds to a candidate or party	4	10	12	11
Worked for one of the parties or candidates	3	3	6	5
Belongs to political club or organization	2	3	3	4
Attended a political meeting, rally, or dinner during campaign	7	10	8	9
Attended two or more meetings, etc.	NA	NA	3	4
Political communication				
Has written a public official, expressing an opinion	NA	NA	NA	17
Has written a letter to the editor, expressing a political opinion	NA	NA	NA	3

[a]Note that for each of the presidential elections about 10 percent more of the survey respondents report having voted than the aggregate election-data statistic in Figure 1 shows. The aggregate statistic is computed with the total vote as the numerator and the voting-age population as the denominator. A number of categories of voting-age individuals are underrepresented or left out in public-opinion polls, and these are groups that tend not to vote (for example, the institutionalized and non-citizens). Furthermore, some small percentage of the non-voting population bends the truth when answering survey interviewers and claims to have voted. See Aage R. Clausen, "Response Validity: Vote Report," *Public Opinion Quarterly*, Vol. 32 (Winter 1968–69), pp. 588–606.
[b]Not asked.
Source: Regular election-year polls of the Survey Research Center, University of Michigan. These and other findings are summarized in John P. Robinson et al., *Measures of Political Attitudes*, pp. 591–625.

the evident requirements of democratic citizenship. No one today—least of all the student of public opinion—would argue, as did the civics textbooks of a generation ago, that every voter must have a well-considered viewpoint on all the diverse problems which governments face: "city problems, national problems, international problems, labor problems, transportation problems, banking problems, rural problems, agricultural problems, and so on *ad infinitum.*"[7] Nor would it be argued that each citizen must be his own political expert—a walking guide to the political system. Nevertheless, even hardened pollsters sometimes are unable to conceal their wonder at the assiduousness with which many Americans insulate themselves from the massive flow of political news and commentary.

To begin with, much crucial factual information about the basic structure of the political system is not widely shared. Polls have shown that somewhat more than half of the population does not know the number (not to speak of the names) of the Senators sent by their state to Washington. Slightly less than half know the length of the terms of Senators and Representatives—a piece of information of no small consequence if one conceives of the voter as responsible for rewarding and punishing elected officials at the polls. Consistent with what we have seen about support for the rules of democratic politics, one survey found that only 23 percent of a national cross-section could name any provision of the Bill of Rights.[8]

It is conceivable, of course, that knowledge of the structure of government is a mere "civics book matter," and is not vital to effective citizenship. Let us, therefore, look at one further aspect of public political information—awareness of the names and duties of the nation's leaders. It would be difficult to maintain that citizens can control their leaders without knowing who these individuals are. In fact, however, the occasional systematic efforts to assess public awareness of leaders have consistently shown that very large numbers of Americans are unaware of very large numbers of their leaders.

[7] Walter Lippmann, *The Phantom Public* (New York: Harcourt, Brace, 1925), pp. 23–24.
[8] The findings in this paragraph are from AIPO polls of the mid-1940's, reported in Cantril and Strunk, *op. cit.*, pp. 41, 134, 790, and 936 of that volume. That there has been little if any change can be seen from various more recent surveys. A 1962 survey of the educationally advanced state of Minnesota, for example, showed that while most voters correctly agreed with the assertion that the United States Constitution guarantees the freedoms of religion and speech, a very substantial number also agreed with such wholly erroneous notions as that the Constitution guarantees the right to a college education (60 per cent agreed) and the right to a job (49 per cent agreed). And only 70 percent correctly recognized the Constitutional guarantee of free assembly. Minnesota Poll Release, April 15, 1962, *Minneapolis Sunday Tribune.*

TABLE 4   Proportion of Americans Able to Identify Correctly Various Political and Non-political Figures

Figure to Be Identified	Percentage Correct
1945 survey	
Harry S. Truman, President of the United States	95
Joe Louis	94
Bop Hope	88
Thomas Dewey, presidential candidate in previous election; Governor of New York	86
Charlie McCarthy	85
Dick Tracy	78
Henry Wallace, former Vice-President; controversial cabinet official	66
James F. Byrnes, former Supreme Court Justice; wartime "Assistant President"; just appointed Secretary of State	51
Robert Taft, Senator from Ohio; leading spokesman of conservative Republicanism; aspirant to Republican presidential nomination	46
Arthur Vandenberg, Senator from Michigan; leading Republican foreign policy spokesman	41
James Forrestal, Secretary of the Navy	38
1963 survey	
Elizabeth Taylor	91
Richard Nixon, 1960 presidential candidate; 1962 California gubernatorial candidate	88
Nelson Rockefeller, Governor of New York; contender for Republican presidential nomination	88
Barry Goldwater, well-known Senator; the following year's Republican presidential candidate	72
George Romney, Governor of Michigan; contender for Republican presidential nomination	37
William Scranton, Governor of Pennsylvania; still another Republican contender	32
Mark Hatfield, Governor of Oregon; also frequently mentioned in the press as a potential Republican nominee	10

Source: 1945 survey, AIPO, reported in Cantril and Strunk, *op. cit.*, pp. 563–564; 1963 survey also by AIPO (Number 676). I am indebted to Philip Hastings of the Roper Public Opinion Research Center, Williamstown, Mass., for the 1963 data.

Table 4 reports two surveys, one from 1945 and one from 1963. The 1945 survey showed that while nearly everyone was able to recognize the President of the United States, a professional boxer (Joe Louis) and a comedian (Bob Hope) were better known than the defeated presidential candidate of the previous year, and a comic-strip detective (Dick Tracy) and a ventriloquist's dummy (Charlie McCarthy) were better known than leading members of Congress and various Cabinet officials.

The 1963 survey placed a film actress (Elizabeth Taylor) ahead of an entire field of politicians. A fourth of the population apparently had not yet heard of the man whom the Republican party was to nominate for the Presidency the following year; and other Republican politicians who were regularly presented in the news media as potential Republican presidential or vice-presidential candidates were known only to rather small minorities of Americans (George Romney, 37 percent; William Scranton, 32 percent; Mark Hatfield, 10 percent).

Focusing more closely on the citizen's *own* Representative in Congress, Table 5 shows that only about 2 out of every 5 Americans can name their Congressmen, and less than 1 out of 5 know of *any* of his congressional votes or actions for the district. Moreover, as in other studies, there was evidence of the absence of information about the rudimentary fact of the length of the congressional term, with only slightly less than a third able to tell when their Congressman would next come up for re-election.

The Holding of Political Opinions. When information about government and politics is lacking, opinion on these matters is likely also to be lacking—or at least to be ill-informed. Few citizens are apt to have clear criteria for assessing public policy-making. Most Americans will obligingly express an off-the-cuff "opinion" about the questions asked of them by the pollster—"the 'no opinion' vote . . . seldom exceeds 15 percent, and is often much lower"[9]—but further exploration invariably shows that many such expressions are based on almost no prior thought, and some on total unfamiliarity with the issue at hand.

TABLE 5 Proportion of Americans Knowing Their Congressman and Various Things about Him

	Percentage Correct
1. Do you happen to know the name of the present Representative in Congress from your district?	43
2. Do you happen to know when he comes up for election next?	30
3. Do you know how he voted on any major bill this year?	19
4. Has he done anything for the district that you definitely know about?	14

Source: 1965 AIPO survey, reported in November 1965 *Gallup Opinion Index.*

[9]Herbert Hyman and Paul Sheatsley, "The Current Status of American Public Opinion," *National Council for the Social Studies Yearbook,* Vol. 21 (1950), reprinted in Daniel Katz et al., *Public Opinion and Propaganda* (New York: Dryden, 1954), reference on p. 37.

This becomes especially evident in responses to surveys using open-ended polling techniques in which the respondent is asked to come up with his own formulations of the problems of the day. Under these circumstances the proportion of people expressing opinions plummets. For example, in May, 1958, while a "Battle of the Budget" was being fought in Washington and on the front pages of the nation's newspapers, and a Republican President and a Democratic Congress were warmly debating the magnitude of the nation's expenditures, only half the respondents, in one survey, were able to think of "anything for which the government should be spending less than it is at present." Of these the largest proportion (17 percent of the sample) advocated cutting foreign aid, a policy favored by neither the President nor the Democratic majority. Others referred vaguely to a reduction in the number of government personnel. On the question of defense spending, which most agitated the disputants, a "mandate" could be found both for the President's view that military expenditures were adequate and for the congressional claim that they sorely needed to be expanded. Nine percent of the sample offered each of these views.[10]

Lest our photograph of the state of public opinion become a caricature, we should add that the public is not totally devoid of opinions. At least a few members of the electorate are close observers of and commentators on public affairs. For many other voters the fine points of governmental policy are not clear, but the general outlines of what the individual prefers are: "I don't know much about government, but I know what I like." Thus, since its inception, nation-wide polling has regularly shown that certain kinds of public attitudes are firmly established and consistently held. These, in general, are attitudes which bear on broad values, on overall policy *directions*. It was totally evident, for example, from the polls conducted during the several years before the United States entered World War II that the sympathies of most Ameri-

---

[10]AIPO release, May 1, 1958. It should not be assumed, incidentally, that because few citizens could think of ways to cut expenditures, many were in favor of increasing government activity. Only a third of the respondents could think of anything "for which the government should be spending more money than at present." A striking example of the absence of widespread opinion-holding on hotly contested issues occurred a decade later in connection with the Nixon Administration's proposal of an anti-ballistic missile (ABM) program. In early 1969 only 69 per cent of a national sample had heard of this widely discussed issue and a mere 40 percent *of the 69 per cent* had formed an opinion. The opinion-holders were slightly (5-to-3) in favor of the program. *Gallup Opinion Index,* April 1969. For a general discussion of voters' awareness of current issues, see Angus Campbell et al., *The American Voter* (New York: Wiley, 1960), pp. 171–176. The classic statement on these matters has come to be Philip E. Converse's "The Nature of Belief Systems in Mass Publics," in David Apter, ed., *Ideology and Discontent* (New York: The Free Press, 1964), pp. 206–261.

cans were with the Allied, not the Axis, cause. After Pearl Harbor, devotion to winning the war was intense and widespread.[11] In subsequent years there has been consistent further documentation of broad consistencies in public assessments of many domestic and international issues.

It has been just as regularly shown, on the other hand, that public assessments of *specific* government policies and programs are often ill-formed and weakly held. This was well illustrated in some of the early experiments in questionnaire wording by the pollsters. These experiments showed that it often was possible to get people to endorse totally contradictory policies by slanting the phrasing of questionnaire items one way or another. One group might agree with the proposition that "all able-bodied men should be called into the Armed Forces immediately in order to hasten the end of the war." A second comparable group—or perhaps even the same individuals questioned a few weeks later—would be just as certain that "civilian workers in essential war industries should be deferred from the draft." Or, as in the experiment in question-wording summarized in Table 6, it might be possible to get virtually everyone to agree with the desirability of "planning the peace" —but if this was phrased so as to be seen in contrast to "winning the war," the percentage approval would contract radically. This did not mean, of course, that public attitudes were merely a shapeless mush. In every case the *general* principle of winning the war was fully accepted. But the inconsistency in assessments of concrete policies showed that ability to move from the general to the specific was at best defective.

IS DEMOCRACY IN PERIL?

In spite of the reassurance that public attitudes are not totally amorphous, our photograph of the American electorate provides the discouraging image of a citizenry ill-equipped to control its leaders effectively and undevoted to fundamental democratic principles. Nevertheless, the reader is correct if he suspects that these findings tell only part of the story.

The survey findings reported in this chapter are, after all, curiously discontinuous with the common-sense impression that the United States is a nation ranking high in democracy and stability. Election of public officials up to and including the President has continued uninterrupted from the early days of the republic. Many of the choices made by the electorate have—by anyone's standards—been meaningful. Who, for ex-

11 Jerome Bruner, *Mandate from the People* (New York: Duell, Sloan, 1944).

TABLE 6   How Wording Affects Public's Response to a Question: Views of Two Comparable Wartime Samples about Peace Planning

	In Favor of Planning for Peace	Opposed to Planning for Peace	No Opinion
1. Do you think we ought to start thinking now about the kind of peace we want after the war?	81% (yes)	15% (no)	4%
2. Which of these seems better to you: for us to win the war first and then think about the peace, or to start thinking now about the kind of peace we want after the war?	41% (start thinking about the peace)	55% (win the war first)	4%

Source: National Opinion Research Center (NORC), September 1942, reported in Hadley Cantril, *Gauging Public Opinion* (Princeton: Princeton University Press, 1944), p. 37.

ample, would argue that governmental policy would have been the same if Bryan had defeated McKinley in 1896, or if Hoover had defeated Roosevelt in 1932, or if Goldwater had triumphed in 1964? In 1968 the unpopularity of an Administration policy in the realm of greatest presidential autonomy—foreign affairs and military policy—contributed to President Johnson's decision not to run for re-election and to a variety of changes in military strategies in Vietnam (decisions to stop bombing the North, to join in negotiations with the enemy forces in the South, etc.). And, especially important, after each presidential election (with the exception of that of 1860) the defeated parties have readily acceded to the decision of the voters. Even in 1968, when the recurrent strand of violence in American society stood in especially clear relief, there was no sign whatsoever that American political leaders had come to consider violence an acceptable means of managing political change. And, although minor party dissidents cannot be said to have been completely free from harassment in the United States, the American Independent Party of former Alabama Governor Wallace was able to find a place on the ballot in every state in 1968, and, in general, restraints on free expression do not remotely approximate those in the many nations that bar electoral competition and enforce a single political orthodoxy.

26 *Richard M. Scammon and Ben J. Wattenberg*

Demography Is Destiny: Middle-Age, Middle-Class Whites

If young, poor, and black are what most voters aren't, let us consider the electorate for what it largely is: white; median family income of $8,622; median age of about forty-seven. In short: middle-aged, middle-class whites.

This middle constituency can also be described as middle-educated. Typically, the middleman in America is a high school graduate, no more, no less:

Voters, by Years of School Completed, 1968

Years of School Completed	% of Electorate
Elementary School or less	22%
High School:	
1–3 years	16%
4 years	36%
College:	
1–3 years	13%
4 years or more	13%
	(U.S. Census Bureau)

In other words:

1. Almost three in four voters have never set foot in a college classroom (74%).
2. Only one in eight voters has been graduated from college—any college —with major fields of study including animal husbandry and physical education (13%).

Looking into the future, these figures will change, because larger proportions of young Americans are now going on to college. Yet because most of the electorate is middle-aged, the percentage of once-went-to-college among the electorate in the 1970's will not rise sharply. In 1968 about a quarter, 26%, had *some* college education. By 1972 this will have climbed to about 29%, and in 1976 to 31%. This will mean, still, that the greatest number of the electorate will have, at most, only the "middle" high school diploma. Accordingly, if we are to add to our categories of unyoung, unpoor, and unblack, we may say that the typical voter is, and will be through the seventies, "uncollege."

The typical voter is no "intellectual," if we assume that an intellectual has at least a college degree, but that not all college graduates are necessarily intellectual. If we move up the qualification a bit and apply the term only to those with *advanced* college degrees (MA, PhD, and the like) the weight of the oft-discussed "intellectual vote" is ridiculously minuscule.

But if the electorate is not "intellectual," it is most certainly not composed of ignoramuses. For a candidate to treat the voters largely as jerks (62% are at least high school graduates) would be as disastrous as considering them largely as intellectuals. Indeed, it might be impressionistically noted here that it is the authors' opinion that the inherent wisdom of the American voter is substantial. This point will be elaborated upon later. For now, let us observe rashly that the corporate wisdom of voters is often greater than that of politicians. For a truly shocking statement, it can be said that voters are even wiser than political theorists. Others have shared this view of voter wisdom. It was the distinguished political scientist V. O. Key in his esteemed work *The Responsible Electorate* who said:

> The perverse and unorthodox argument of this little book is that voters are not fools. To be sure, many individual voters act in odd ways indeed; yet in the large the electorate behaves about as rationally and responsibly as we should expect, given the clarity of the alternatives presented to it and the character of the information available to it. In American presidential campaigns of recent decades the portrait of the American electorate that develops from the data is not one of an electorate straitjacketed

by social determinants or moved by subconscious urges triggered by devil-ishly skillful propagandists. It is rather one of an electorate moved by con-cern about central and relevant questions of public policy, or govern-mental performance, and of executive personality.

Middle-income, middle-aged, middle-educated, and white, the voters in the middle can also be viewed vocationally as men and women pri-marily "at work with their hands, and not exclusively their minds."

Voters by Occupational Status, 1968

	% *of Total Electorate*
High Level White Collar Workers*	19
Manual, Service, Clerical & Sales Workers	42
Farm Workers	3
Unemployed	1
Not in Labor Force	
Women (mostly housewives)	28
Men over 65 (mostly retired)	5
Other men	2
	(*U.S. Census Bureau*)

*Professional, technical, managerial, officials and proprietors.

Some of the numbers need further explanations:

The number of high-level white-collar workers is climbing. In the 1964 election the percentage was 16% compared to the 19% in 1968. If one allocates a proportionate share of the "housewives" and considers them as the spouses of these high-level white-collar workers, we might estimate that about 27% of the voters are in the *families* of those white-collar workers.

Of course, that leaves about 73% who are *not* in such families, still the vast majority; all *those* voters are in families where the earners are working with their hands. When one realizes that fact, the rhetoric of George Wallace can be fully savored, at least for its demographic accuracy:

> Now what are the real issues that exist today in these United States? It is the trend of pseudo-intellectual government, where a select, elite group have written guidelines in bureaus and court decisions, have spoken from some pulpits, some college campuses, some newspaper offices, looking down their noses at the average man on the street, *the glassworker, the steel-worker, the autoworker, and the textile worker, the farmer, the policeman, the beautician and the barber, and the little businessman,* saying to him that you do not know how to get up in the morning or go to bed at night unless we write you a guideline. . . .

Furthermore, consider for a moment that "policeman" falls into the "work with hands" category. When the "cops" clashed with the "kids" at the 1968 Democratic Convention in Chicago, the journalists and many liberal politicians (high-level white-collars both), picked up the cry, "They're beating up our children." This was accurate: Most of the "kids" came from high-level white-collar homes. On the other hand, the other 73% of the voters could say, "Those student punks are beating up our children, or *our* husbands, or *our* fathers." That, too, would be accurate if one considers the policeman as a respected part of the nonelite.

After the convention, the opinion pollsters asked the public what they thought about the Chicago confrontation, and about two of every three Americans said they thought the police acted correctly, which coincides rather well with the occupational categorizations above. The old political axiom applies: "It depends on whose ox is being gored," or, in other words, "It depends on who is the clobberer and who the clobberee."

The confrontation at Chicago probably etched the lines of social class as sharply as they have ever been drawn in America. The fight in the streets was not between hawks and doves. For many it was perceived as between "elitists" and "plain people." There are more plain people than elitists in America.

Finally, and paradoxically, how do these "high-level" families vote? Despite all the recent comment about elitist Democratic intellectuals, the cold fact remains that the elite in America has a Republican majority. They are the doctors, bankers, and businessmen, with a good proportion of the lawyers and scientists as well. Only the vocal minority of the high-level voters are generally Democratic leaners. In the 1968 election the "professional and business" group went 56–34% for Nixon over Humphrey. The Democrats, despite the Agnew hoopla about the Democratic elitist establishmentarians, are those "plain people who work with their hands." Manual workers went 50–35% for Humphrey over Nixon.

That the Democrats have held the allegiance of most of the "plain people" has been the critical fact in American Presidential politics for more than a third of a century. That is why Democrats have won so often. Now, upon the shoals of the Social Issue, there seems to be the possibility of a rupture in that pattern. If it happens, it will be bad news for Democrats. If it can be prevented from happening, if it can be reversed, it will be happy days again for Democrats.

Next, don't forget the farmer. Although, numerically, there are many more voting blacks than voting farmers, this is somewhat misleading. While the numbers of farmers has decreased strikingly in recent years, there remains a substantial part of the population whose work is directly related to farming.* A rural town in the Midwest may have few "farmers," but the townsfolk sell and repair tractors and reapers, store grain, work as agricultural extension agents, publish weekly newspapers for farmers, and give loans to farmers or all the people whose work is related to farming. The analogy might be to a "mining town." Perhaps no more than 20 to 30% of the population work as "miners," but close down the mine, and you've rather effectively closed down the town. In short, the "farm vote," in its broad sense, is still with us, particularly in the states of the Midwest and South.

Next item: More than half the voters are women—51.9% to be precise. They show up in the preceding table not only as housewives, but as substantial parts of both the large employed groups: clerks, secretaries, teachers, etc. In America today, 43% of the women are working.

Since the advent of woman suffrage, no candidate for President has been solidly identified as a "woman's candidate." Women vote pretty much as their men do, or vice versa. In the last five Presidential elections, the largest margin of variance between men and women voters was 6% in the 1956 election—with women more likely to vote for General Eisenhower than Adlai Stevenson. Curiously, despite the legend building that has gone on about John Kennedy's "appeal to women voters," he would have lost the 1960 election had only women voted. In 1960, men voted 52–48% for JFK; women voted 51–49% for Nixon. As solace to Mr. Nixon, had only women voted in 1968, Hubert Humphrey would have won the popular vote, but the differentials aren't great in either case.

Middle-income, middle-aged, middle-educated, white, and what else?

Protestant, mostly:

Voters, by Religion

	Percentage
Protestant	68%
Catholic	25
Jewish	4

Catholics in America are substantially more likely than Protestants to be first- and second-generation Americans (Italians, Poles, Mexicans, Puerto Ricans) and are more likely to be residents of big cities. Residents

*Compared to the 3% farmers in 1968, in the election of 1900 the percentage of farmers in the population was 38.

of big cities and so-called ethnic Americans have traditionally been more likely to vote Democratic. Accordingly, Catholics are somewhat more likely to vote Democratic than are Protestants, but with the single exception of 1960, when Catholicism itself became an issue, there is little recent evidence that Catholics vote heavily *as* Catholics. Catholics will usually vote a few extra points for a Catholic candidate, but not always:

McCarthy vs Humphrey, July, 1968

	McCarthy	*Humphrey*
National	48%	40%
Catholics	47	41
Protestants	49	39
	(Gallup)	

It is interesting to note how fast an issue can be laid to rest in American politics. Such results—Protestants outvoting Catholics for a Catholic candidate—would have been wholly inconceivable in the years between the defeat of Al Smith in 1928 and the victory of John F. Kennedy in 1960. In November, 1928, a Midwestern newspaper reported the defeat of Al Smith, a Catholic, under the banner headline THANK GOD, AMERICA IS SAVED. Today Catholicism seems thoroughly dead as a political issue. An interesting parlor game to demonstrate this is to ask: "Is Spiro Agnew a Catholic?" (He is Episcopalian.)

Two of every three voters are Protestant. Less likely to be big-city urban, less likely to be first- or second-generation Americans, Protestants are somewhat more likely than Catholics to vote Republican in Presidential races. But with the apparent disappearance of Catholicism as an issue, no national candidate has been able to figure out a way to be the Protestant candidate.

Will religion be an issue if a Jew runs for President in the 1970's? Perhaps less so than we might imagine. A Gallup Poll in 1969 showed that only 8% would not vote for a candidate *because* he was Jewish. Gallup data from 1937 showed 46% would not vote for a candidate because he was Jewish. Of course, Barry Goldwater was born of a Jewish father, but as Harry Golden said ruefully: "I always knew the first Jewish President would be an Episcopalian."

With the exceptions of blacks and Latin Americans, the Jews in the United States are the most solidly liberal-Democratic bloc in the entire electorate. Thus, in 1968, Jews voted 81% for Humphrey. During the years of Franklin Roosevelt the proportion was even higher, according to the studies of Lawrence H. Fuchs in *The Political Behavior of American Jews*. Jewish voting patterns are generally unique in that the vote is usually a liberal and Democratic one even among the wealthy and well educated. Among the non-Jewish well-to-do the trend among the wealthy and well educated goes the other way: Republican.

The so-called ethnic vote is hard to calculate. For how many generations does an Italian-American family remain under the influence of the first half of the hyphenation? How does one classify the children of a Polish father and an Italian mother who moved recently from an in-city "Little Italy" to a suburban neighborhood called Piney Grove? Or, as the late Joseph P. Kennedy, Sr., said, "How long do I have to live here to be an American?"

Yet the ethnics exist, or at least there are many precincts where 70% or 80% of the voters are of Italian, or Slavic, or Mexican origin. For the most part, ethnics have tended to vote Democratic:

Ethnic Groups, Vote for President, 1968

	Humphrey %	Nixon %	Wallace %
Latin Americans			
East (mostly Puerto Ricans)	81	16	3
South (mostly Mexican Americans)	92	7	1
West (mostly Mexican Americans)	81	17	2
Slavic	65	24	11
Italian	51	39	10
		(NBC data)	

The "solid" Democratic-liberal group is clearly the "Latin-American" one.

Of more than passing psephological interest is the fact that ethnics are dying out in America and becoming a smaller percentage of the total population. In 1940, Americans of foreign stock (*i.e.*, first- or second-generation) constituted 26% of the population. Twenty years later, in 1960, the foreign stock constituted 18% of the population. An estimate for 1970 shows the foreign stock at 15%, and in ethnic neighborhoods all over America the remark one hears is the same: "All the kids are moving out to the suburbs."

On the surface of it, at least, this data would tend to say that as the masses of immigrants and their children breed and die out, then it may be said that ethnicism in American political life may be dying out also. A first-generation Polish stevedore from Brooklyn via Krakow may feel "Polish." His grandson, the electrician who lives in Hempstead, Long

Island, may feel more like an "electrician from Hempstead" than like a "Pole." But even this is too simple. As Nathan Glazer and Daniel Moynihan have pointed out in *Beyond the Melting Pot*, the ethnic feelings may last for far longer than the point when, after two generations, the Census stops classifying people as "foreign stock." Surely, tens of millions of Americans still feel deep ties and ethnic, racial, or religious allegiance as Poles, Hungarians, Jews, blacks, Italians, Mexicans—as well as "just plain Americans." And frequently they still vote along these ethnic lines, and politicians can still attempt all the ethnic appeals with some success. In certain areas, a politician can do worse than to be found with his mouth full of blintzes and knishes, or kielbasa, or soul food.

A middle-aged, middle-income, high-school-educated, white Protestant, who works with his hands, decreasingly ethnic—our portrait of the Middle Voter is beginning to emerge. What else? Generally metropolitan, and increasingly suburban, following the pattern of the American postwar hegira: from farms to cities, from cities to suburbs.

U.S. Population Distribution

	1950	1960	1968	Gain in Population, 1950–68
	%	%	%	
Central cities	35%	32%	29%	6 million
Suburb	24	31	35	32 million (!)
Small cities, towns and rural	41	37	36	9 million

Those are population figures: the *voting* figures are about the same, but give the suburbanite a one-point bonus for a higher participation rate:

Voters by Place of Residence, 1968

	% of Electorate
Central cities	29.6%
Suburbs	35.6%
Small cities, towns and farms	34.8%

Among many of the biggest, and oldest, metropolitan areas the voting figures etch in sharp relief this demographic movement from city to suburb. Comparing the 1948 election to the 1968 election, one finds that New York City *lost* more than half a million voters, while the suburbs around New York City (Westchester, Nassau, and Suffolk counties) gained 750,000 voters. The City of Chicago *lost* 400,000 voters; the Chicago suburbs *gained* 500,000. The city of Minneapolis: down 40,000; the Minneapolis suburbs: up 160,000. The term "central cities" refers to cities with populations of 50,000 or more. Accordingly, 2 of every 3 American voters live in or near (suburb) a large city. About an additional 15% live in cities of between 10,000 and 50,000. Accordingly, it is fair to view most of the American electorate as metropolitan or, alternately, as urban.

And where are these metropolitan areas? Following is a map that shows where Americans live:

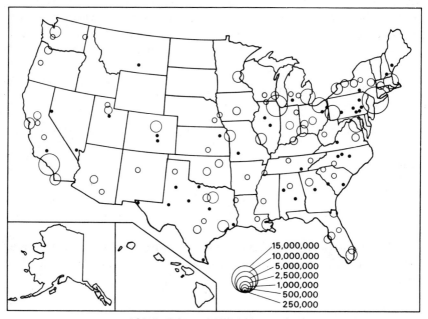

POPULATION DISTRIBUTION: 1960

Because, at least through 1968, the state has been the basic unit of Presidential politics, it is very important to note in which *states* these metropolitan areas lie. And unless a national popular vote replaces the electoral college,* then the *state* will remain of vital importance to political strategists.

*Which is doubtful for 1972, possible for 1976.

There has been much talk of a Southern Strategy, a Border State Strategy, a Sun State Strategy, each supposedly designed to corral enough states to win an election for Republicans. Those are excellent strategies to convince your opponents to use. As for the authors, our geographic strategy is an elementary one called Quadcali. It is the essence of simplicity. If one draws a *quad*rangle from Massachusetts to Washington, D.C., to Illinois, to Wisconsin, and then adds in *Cali*fornia, it includes a majority of Americans. Where Americans live, they vote. Where a majority of them live and vote is where Presidents are elected.

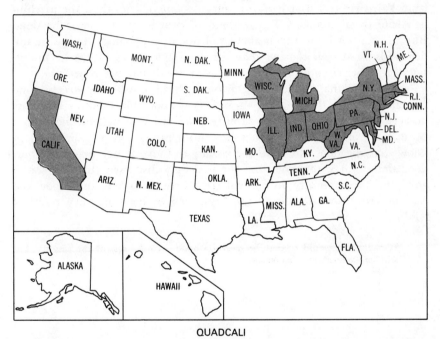

QUADCALI

In all, 266 electoral votes are needed to win. It is estimated that Quadcali will comprise about 300 electoral votes after the 1970 census.

Of the sixteen states in Quadcali, all but one (Indiana*) are either Democratic or close—the Republican margin of victory being no higher than 4.5% and usually slimmer than that. In a tidal year, all those close states can drop like a row of falling dominoes—a familiar image. Carry Quadcali—win the election. Lose Quadcali—lose the election. Split Quadcali close—and it will be a close election that no book can tell you about in advance.

*Which is more than balanced by Minnesota, Maine, Hawaii, Texas, and the state of Washington, all non-Quadcalian states that voted Democratic.

So there you have it: Middle Voter. A metropolitan Quadcalian, middle-aged, middle-income, middle-educated, Protestant,* in a family whose working members work more likely with hands than abstractly with head.

Think about that picture when you consider the American power structure. Middle Voter is a forty-seven-year-old housewife from the outskirts of Dayton, Ohio, whose husband is a machinist. She very likely has a somewhat different view of life and politics from that of a twenty-four-year-old instructor of political science at Yale. Now the young man from Yale may feel that he *knows* more about politics than the machinist's wife from suburban Dayton, and of course, in one sense he does. But he does not know much about politics, or psephology, unless he understands what is bothering that lady in Dayton and unless he understands that her circumstances in large measure dictate her concerns.

To know that the lady in Dayton is afraid to walk the streets alone at night, to know that she has a mixed view about blacks and civil rights because before moving to the suburbs she lived in a neighborhood that became all black, to know that her brother-in-law is a policeman, to know that she does not have the money to move if her new neighborhood deteriorates, to know that she is deeply distressed that her son is going to a community junior college where LSD was found on the campus—to know all this is the beginning of contemporary political wisdom.

*Quadcalians would tend to be more Catholic than the rest of the country, but still predominantly Protestant.

27

George A. Taylor

Toward a
Theory of Revolution

Investigators have variously concerned themselves with racial tensions and the problems of blacks in the United States during the 1960s. With W. E. B. Dubois, Gunnar Myrdal, *Brown vs. Board of Education*, and Michael Harrington as a background, blacks in America and their problems suddenly sprang forth in the literature of the early 1960s. Further inspired by the "War on Poverty," literally hundreds of articles, reports, and books have been published on this same topic.

Although the facts and visible efforts of discrimination and deprivation have been listed many times over, relatively few studies have attempted to formulate theories concerning the causes or effects of such conditions. This article is an exception. It will bring together two existing theories (one from social psychology; the other from political science) in an attempt to formulate a theoretical scheme which can be utilized in understanding some of the effects of racial discrimination.

One of the most interesting concepts in social psychology related to race relations, especially in light of the violence and turmoil experienced in the late 1960s, is that of relative deprivation. Its application is

This selection was written expressly for this volume.

direct. An example of a relatively deprived individual is a black who states that there has been too little change and that he deserves more. At least neglectful of the concept is the white who says: "You're better off than you used to be, let's slow down and take stock of the entire situation."

First conceived by Stouffer[1] and later developed by Spector,[2] Davis,[3] Patchen,[4] Blau,[5] and others, relative deprivation occurs when "an individual or class of individuals feels deprived . . . in comparison to relevant reference groups and individuals. Thus, comparison with a non-deprived referent leads to high expectations that, if unfulfilled, lead in turn to severe feelings of deprivation and unfairness."[6] Pettigrew's treatment of Davies' theory of revolution relies on the concept "relative deprivation." Pettigrew posits four revolution-stirring conditions and says that "all four of these conditions set off by improving objective standards are present for Negroes in America of the 1960's."[7]

Establishing the point above requires brief review of revolution,[8] of Davies' theory. By revolution we mean the attempted displacement of one ruling group by another group which resorts to civil violence in order to attain this end. Davies, according to Pettigrew:

> carefully analyzes the involvement of rising expectations in a number of revolutions . . . [and] finds the best fit from a model characterized by a relatively lengthy cycle of objective economic and social development followed by a short period of sharp reversal. Presumably relative deprivation accumulates during the long period of improvement; and then it dramatically rises to what is commonly perceived to be intolerable levels when the abrupt regression intervenes.[9]

[1]Samuel Stouffer, *et al.*, *The American Soldier*, Vols. I and II (Princeton, N.J.: Princeton University Press, 1949).

[2]A. J. Spector, "Expectations, Fulfillments, and Morale," *Journal of Abnormal Sociometry*, 52 (1956), 51–56.

[3]J. A. Davis, "A Formal Interpretation of the Theory of Relative Deprivation," *Psychology*, 22 (1959), 281–84; "Structure Balance, Mechanical Solidarity and Interpersonal Relations," *American Journal of Sociology*, 68 (1963), 442–62.

[4]M. A. Patchen, "A Conceptual Framework and Some Empirical Data Regarding Comparisons of Social Rewards," *Sociometry*, 24 (1961), 136–56.

[5]Peter M. Blau, *Exchange and Power in Social Life* (New York: Wiley, 1964), pp. 157–60.

[6]Thomas F. Pettigrew, "Social Evaluation Theory: Convergences and Applications," in *Nebraska Symposium on Motivation: 1967*, ed. David Levine (Lincoln: University of Nebraska Press, 1967), p. 262. (Hereinafter referred to as "Social Evaluation Theory").

[7]Ibid., p. 294.

[8]James C. Davies, "Toward a Theory of Revolution," *American Sociological Review*, 27 (1962), 5–12.

[9]Pettigrew, "Social Evaluation Theory," pp. 267–68.

Drawing upon this idea, Pettigrew posits four conditions of relative deprivation which will lead to revolution or revolt: (1) when blacks' expectations have climbed faster than actual changes, (2) when living conditions for the dominant group in a number of realms improve more rapidly than for blacks, (3) when there has been an increase in status inconsistency among blacks when compared to whites,[10] and (4) when there is a broadening of comparative reference groups.[11] In other words, as the black increasingly views his socioeconomic position in terms of the white man's position, he sees that although he is investing more and more time and effort into himself, the black man's rewards are not commensurate with his investments relative to those of the whites.

The theories and concepts concerning relative deprivation and revolution are interesting and useful as far as they go. There would seem to be little doubt that the conditions posited above for revolt must be fulfilled in order for revolution or revolt to occur. However, these conditions alone do not appear to be enough to create such a situation, at least not in this country.[12] While sociological and psychological theories are extremely pertinent to this problem, the area of political theory apparently has been overlooked. In fact, one student on blacks in America flatly contends that the revolution in race relations is actually the study of change in political power.[13] Professor Blalock has also noted that within the American social structure, race relations are power relations.[14] With this in mind, let us now turn to Easton's description of the political system and the concept of diffuse support.

The political system is a set of structures and processes through which demands of the population are converted into binding decisions and related actions.[15] These conversion processes persist as long as some type of system is able to generate support from its members. Conceptually, therefore, it is helpful to interpret the political system as a conversion process in which the inputs of demand and support are converted

[10]G. E. Lenski, "Status Crystalization: A Non-vertical Dimension of Social Status," *American Sociological Review*, 19 (1954), 405–13; 'Social Participation and Status Crystalization," *American Sociological Review*, 21 (1956), 458–64.

[11]Pettigrew, "Social Evaluation Theory," pp. 294–302.

[12]George A. Taylor, "Diffuse Support and the Conditions of Revolution: A Social Psychological Approach to Easton's Hypothesis" (unpublished Master's Thesis, University of Georgia, 1970).

[13]Everett Carl Ladd, Jr., *Negro Political Leadership in the South* (New York: Atheneum, 1969).

[14]Hubert M. Blalock, Jr., "A Power Analysis of Racial Discrimination," *Social Forces*, 39 (October 1960), 53–59.

[15]David Easton, *A Framework for Political Analysis* (Englewood Cliffs, N.J.: Prentice-Hall, 1965); *A Systems Analysis of Political Life* (New York: Wiley, 1965).

into outputs—"into authoritative decisions and actions."[16] (See Figure 1.)

The inputs of demand call for action on the part of the political system, i.e., goods or services. This type of input constitutes a significant part of the material upon which the system operates. Most of the research dealing with inputs of demand on the micro level have been conducted in the area of voting behavior. From these studies we have found that inputs of demand are also one of the sources of change in the political system, since as the environment fluctuates it generates new types of demand inputs for the system.[17]

Inputs of support—which are defined as the attitudes and behaviors that provide stability for the political system—can be divided into two different types, specific and diffuse. Specific support consists of favorable attitudes produced by system outputs. These attitudes are developed as individuals perceive their demands being met by the outputs. Diffuse support is composed of the good will which a system may generate. Patriotism and loyalty to the system are examples of diffuse support.

Diffuse support is defined by Easton as relatively independent of day-to-day outputs. He further states that diffuse support is the product of political socialization and feels that if a system is to persist, "one of its major tasks is to provide for the input of at least a minimal level of support."[18]

Support for the political system may be either overt or covert. Overt support involves action in the form of observable behavior. This type of support may consist of speaking in behalf of a governmental proposal at a meeting or hearing, carrying signs supporting a governmental act, and many other actions that require some physical output. Covert support consists of attitudes, sentiments, and predispositions or frames of mind. This type of support is not always observable. To tap covert support, one must probe into a person's thoughts or attitudes.

Support for the political system is, at best, a vague and ambiguous concept. Thus support may be different for the different elements of the political system, for example, it typically does so only for certain of the basic aspects of the system and not for others.[19] The input of support

[16]David Easton and Jack Dennis, *Children in the Political System: Origins of Political Legitimacy* (New York: McGraw-Hill, 1969), p. 48. (Hereinafter referred to as *Children in the Political System*).

[17]Angus Campbell, *et al., The American Voter* (New York: Wiley, 1964).

[18]David Easton and Jack Dennis, "The Child's Acquisition of Regime Norms: Political Efficacy," *American Political Science Review*, 61 (March 1967), 25.

[19]Easton and Dennis, *Children in the Political System*, p. 65.

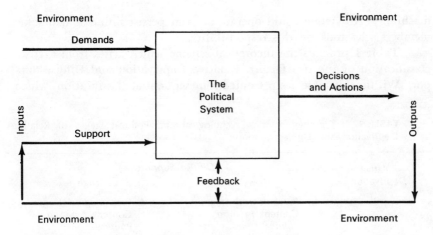

FIGURE 1   A Simplified Model of a Political System.

is better understood if we identify the basic components of the system for which support is relevant.

The political system can be divided into three basic objects of support: the political community, the regime, and the authorities. The political community is not concerned either with constitutional order, or whether a government exists at all. Rather, we should ask if the members of the groups are sufficiently oriented toward each other to want to contribute "their collective energies toward specific settlement of their varying demands . . ." (National unity.)

"The political regime is the underlying goals that the members of the system pursue."[20] The definition also includes the rules or norms of the game through which the political business is carried out and refers to the formal as well as the informal structures of authority in the political system. One of the assumptions in this area is that these "norms" are "expectations about the way people will behave. They may be embodied in laws or in constitutional codes; they may be simply customary expectations founded in experience with the system."[21] No political system could hope to persist if it did not provide for the input of support for these regime norms.

The last object of support defined by Easton are the "authorities": the members of the political system who make the primary day-to-day political decisions. These are the elected or appointed officials and their staffs who actually go about the business of operating the governmental

[20]Ibid., p. 66.
[21]Ibid., p. 65.

machinery. No system could operate or even persist unless it had some members who took on this responsibility.

Table 1 presents the theoretical scheme which arises from a cross-classification of the two factors, Relative Deprivation and Diffuse Support. Within this table are presented four sequential classifications which

TABLE 1 Typology of the Psychological and Political Stages of Relative Deprivation and Diffuse Support

Relative Deprivation	Diffuse Support	
	Low	*High*
Low	1. *Psychological Stage:* Content Fatalism *Political:* Traditional	4. *Psychological Stage:* Content Activism *Political:* Stable
High	2. *Psychological Stage:* Discontent Fatalism *Political:* Unstable	3. *Psychological Stage:* Discontent Activism *Political:* Transitional

The initial concept of this typology is presented by Thomas Crawford and Murry Nadith, "Relative Deprivation, Powerlessness, and Militancy," *Psychiatry* (Special Issue), 33 (May 1970), 203–23. This elaboration of their typology introduces the concept of diffuse support.

are the product of the interaction of relative deprivation with support for the political system. While these ideal types are presented as four distinct classifications, they can also be thought of as a continuum.

Each of the four combinations of low or high level of relative deprivation and low or high diffuse support has been labeled at each of two levels: psychological and political. Those persons who perceive little deprivation and also have little diffuse support for the political system are characterized as being in a psychological stage of content fatalism. We can assume that the political stage would be traditional.

The second condition, which is high relative deprivation and low diffuse support, is the most explosive of this typology. The individuals at this stage perceive wide gaps between desires and accomplishments and at the same time have very little diffuse support for the political system. Consequently, this is the stage when revolution can occur.

Moving across to the third cell, a large gap exists between desires and accomplishments. Therefore, we also find discontent as in cell 2. However, because of the high diffuse support for the political system, the political stage is transitional and the psychological stage becomes discontent activism. In cell 4, the optimum of the typology, we find the psychological stage at content activism; the political stage is stable.

If we were to position the majority of the black population in the United States in this typology, it would be in cell 3. The reasons seem obvious. The *political* stage is in a transitional phase now. For example, there are black mayors of large cities; black legislators in southern state houses; and blacks have become increasingly important in elections.

The *psychological* stage is discontent activism. For example, blacks have for some time shown this discontent through sit-ins, and so on.

part five

Games Students Can Play

Four Simulations

The final part of this book seeks a transition from emphasis on the contemplation of ideas to their expression in action. Four simulations have been designed and pretested with large populations of undergraduates to facilitate this transition. The rationale is direct. It is well and good to read about the dilemmas of participation, and to discuss them to seek greater understanding. It is perhaps even better to experience those dilemmas. This experience offers the possible excitement of resolving those dilemmas in life; the potential cost is the frustration of demonstrating the gap between what we desire and what we can help make happen.

The four simulations below seek to expose the student to the dilemmas of participation in action, as a complement to the readings above which are intended to highlight major issues and dilemmas of participation. Those simulations are literally the student's, to fill with whatever content he or she deems appropriate. This content includes the student's estimate of what the political world should be. Simulation also provides an opportunity for the simulator to make ideas and values come alive, or to experience how difficult that is.

Every set of political ideas implies a set of skills to make appropriate things happen, in sum. And the earlier a person begins realistically testing those skills and insights, the sooner will it be possible to get down to the serious business of developing or changing aspects of the political self that he or she may lack or may not like. Directly, the simulations provide a variety of opportunities to act on the student's concept of an ideal degree of participation, to experience in life the dilemmas that are variously suggested in the readings above, and to work toward that synthesis of ideas and action skills that will shape a person's unique and distinctive approach to politics.

28

Beyond a
Reasonable Doubt

Supplies

Name tag;
Note pad or slips of paper;
Pencil or pen.

In this simulation or game you play the role of juror, a role which you as a citizen can anticipate performing in the near future. Your tasks as a juror are framed by both the facts of the case and the law which applies to those facts. The facts in this murder case are fictitious, but they are not beyond the realm of possibility. The instructions on the law, which will be given you by the judge (your teacher) are typical of the law in cases such as this. The general discussion of your tasks is followed by (1) the schedule for the game, which orders your tasks, and (2) a description of the specific mechanics of performing as a juror.

Tasks

Your initial task is to determine whether or not the accused is guilty beyond a reasonable doubt of murder or of some lesser included offense. If you find him guilty beyond a reasonable doubt, you have the additional task of setting his sentence. Since murder is a capital offense, the death penalty may be imposed. A personal belief opposing capital punishment is no longer a sufficient reason for you to be barred from a jury in a trial for murder, under the Supreme Court's ruling in the case of *Witherspoon v. Illinois, et al.*, 391 U.S. 510 (1968).

In order to accomplish your tasks, you will need both the facts and the law which applies to those facts. These will be given to you orally by your instructor. As is true for actual jurors in most jurisdictions, you are not permitted to take notes on either the facts or the law. Your alertness and your recall will aid or retard your sense of justice.

Before he dons his role and "robes" of judge, your teacher will read to you the facts in *State v. John Brown*. This procedure introduces into the game an artificiality which has at least one redeeming feature. Although you are denied an opportunity to judge the demeanor, manner, and truthfulness of witnesses, you will not be misled by the seemingly sincere and articulate answers of a practiced liar or by the nonresponsive answers of a truthful but inarticulate witness.

The *facts* (what happened) in *State v. John Brown* are not in dispute. The State's Attorney and the defense counsel do disagree, however, over several questions of law: Does what occurred constitute (1) first degree murder? (2) second degree murder? (3) voluntary manslaughter? (4) self-defense? These are proper questions for a jury—your jury. The judge will instruct you on the law and how you are to accomplish your tasks by applying the law to the facts before you. Listen carefully and follow strictly his detailed instructions as to what constitutes (1) guilt for each offense, (2) self-defense, and (3) reasonable doubt.

You will serve as one of about twelve jurors on the particular jury to which you are assigned. (The number may vary slightly depending upon the size of your class.) As is true for any trial, members of each jury will reach their verdict independently of any other jury. The verdict must be unanimous, that is, each and every juror on a jury must agree that the accused is (1) guilty beyond a reasonable doubt of a particular offense, or (2) not guilty beyond a reasonable doubt of any and all offenses.

Note well: You will have before you the facts generated by both the prosecuting attorney and the defense counsel. The burden is upon the prosecution to put into evidence enough proof to convince you of the defendant's guilt beyond a reasonable doubt. It is not necessary for the defense to show that the defendant is innocent beyond a reasonable doubt. He is to be acquitted if the State's evidence does not convince you that he is guilty beyond a reasonable doubt or if the defendant's plea of self-defense raises a reasonable doubt of guilt. "Not guilty beyond a reasonable doubt" does not mean "innocent beyond a reasonable doubt." If a juror or jurors have a reasonable doubt as to the guilt of the accused, they must seek his acquittal. It is not necessary that they be without reasonable doubt that he is innocent. They can have reasonable doubt as to his innocence and still be just as forceful in seeking his acquittal because of their reasonable doubt as to guilt. The law requires no less and no more.

Schedule

1. Convene in main meeting room at the appointed time.
   a. Discuss the instructions and be assigned to juries.
   b. Teacher-judge reads the facts in the case and instructs jurors on the law. No jury member is permitted to take notes.
2. Jurors go to their assigned jury rooms.
   a. Jurors discuss whether or not the accused is guilty (20 minutes).
   b. Jurors vote by secret ballot whether or not the accused is guilty of first degree murder. If "not guilty" of first degree murder, then vote on second degree murder. And if "not guilty" of second degree murder, vote on voluntary manslaughter.
      (1) If vote is unanimously "guilty" for one of the offenses above, consult the chart listing verdicts and sentences and determine unanimously by secret ballot the sentence you feel appropriate. When this step is completed, notify the judge.
      (2) If vote is unanimously "not guilty" for each and every offense listed above, notify the judge.
3. All jurors return to main meeting room at the call of the judge where the foremen of the juries will announce the verdicts and sentences.
4. Rap session.

Jurors' Decisions

Before jurors go to their jury rooms, the judge will assign one member of each jury the role of *jury foreman*. The foreman's tasks are not difficult, but they are important:

1. Obtain paper clips and/or envelopes from your judge if he wants you to keep separated the ballots on each offense.
2. See that all members of your jury have affixed their name tags so that discussions can proceed smoothly.
3. Choose someone to help tabulate and record individual ballots.
4. Lead, but do not dominate, discussions and recognize jurors who want to speak.
5. Announce (1) when balloting is to begin, (2) the specific offense for which ballot is being taken, and (3) the results of the balloting.

Except for the first item in this list, everything can be accomplished in the jury room. Jurors should spend about 20 minutes discussing the facts and the law in *State v. John Brown*. The discussion will be more orderly if each of the possible verdicts is discussed in turn and possible punishments are ignored until the question of guilt is settled one way or the other.

Whether the discussion is orderly or rambles, it is absolutely essential that the foreman specify the offense for which each guilty/not guilty ballot is cast. Each ballot must be both written and secret. The jury foreman should designate a fellow juror to record the specific offense which is being balloted upon (for example, first vote: first degree murder) and to record the results of each ballot. This juror should keep the ballots from each vote separate from each other, fasten them with a paper clip, and give them to the teacher in the Rap session.

(Note that saving jury ballots for analysis is not usual, indeed it may be prohibited in some courts. Your teacher may not use the ballots. However, those of you and your teachers who are interested in decision making generally or jury decisions specifically may find your endeavors informative. Access to actual juries is denied by law, and simulations are one of the few ways you can gain insights into what takes place.)

The most serious offense, first degree murder, should be considered first; then second degree murder; and finally voluntary manslaughter. However, anytime that all jurors' ballots show a guilty verdict, there is no need to ballot on lesser offenses. This is not true for a unanimous vote of "not guilty of first degree murder," for example. It may be that there is total agreement that the accused is not guilty of first degree murder and equal agreement that he is guilty of either second degree murder or voluntary manslaughter. If, and only if, members of the jury vote unanimously that the defendant is "not guilty" of (1) first degree murder, (2) second degree murder, and (3) voluntary manslaughter, then, and only then, is he acquitted.

Deadlocks should be avoided. Only after the foreman is convinced that the jurors are hopelessly deadlocked should he notify the judge of this fact and obtain his instructions. In addition, if the jurors need any further clarification as to a *point of law*, the foreman may send a message to the judge requesting such clarification. The judge probably will not reopen a *point of fact*.

When members of a jury find the defendant guilty they must also unanimously (by secret ballot) set his sentence, within the ranges shown in the chart below. The question of leniency in respect to a first degree murder conviction is properly considered here rather than during considerations of whether or not the accused is guilty.

Verdict	*Sentence*
Guilty:	
First degree (premeditated)	
murder: a. no leniency	a. death
b. leniency	b. life in prison
Second degree (not premeditated)	
murder	10 to 20 years in prison
Voluntary manslaughter	5 to 10 years in prison
Not guilty: self-defense	None: defendant is acquitted

After completing your tasks notify the judge.

29

University Grades:
To "B" or not to "B"

STUDENT'S INSTRUCTIONS

Supplies

Name tag showing committee number and role;
Note pad or slips of paper;
Pencil or pen.

This simulation or game involves you in the resolution of a crisis which has a great university in turmoil. The crisis, as explained in the *Background*, began with a controversy over the grading system used at the university and grew into a confrontation in which a student was killed. Your task is to participate on a committee charged with selecting a grading system which might calm the campus. Within your committee you will play an assigned role as an administrator, faculty member, or student. The roles, schedule, and specific procedures provide the framework within which you and the other committee members attempt to remove the crisis atmosphere.

328

Background

Five weeks ago, radical and moderate students and faculty members staged a demonstration in front of the administration building in favor of the abolition of all grades and the university's grading system of A, B, C, D, and F. About 500 of the university's 15,000 students and 1,350 faculty members were involved in the demonstration. The demonstrators broke into the administration building and staged a sit-in. The local police and the National Guard were called in by the university president, on orders from the governor. In quelling the disorder and evicting the demonstrators, one student was killed, several were injured, and 125 were arrested. Three policemen and guardsmen suffered cuts and bruises.

Due to the death of the student, John Marks, a university-wide boycott of classes was called for by the student government and by radical student groups. For three days class attendance was reduced to 40 percent of normal. The situation prompted an emergency meeting of the University Board of Regents, whose members issued an ultimatum to the striking students to either return to classes or risk expulsion. The Regents' ultimatum prompted the faculty senate to vote in favor of a teachers' strike in support of the students, although only about 25 percent of the faculty actually participated in this vote.

After three weeks of turmoil, when attendance and class meetings were sporadic, the student government called for a referendum to poll faculty and student opinion on the issue. Multiple voting was permitted, and the only question on the ballot which received a majority vote was the recommendation that a committee of students, faculty members, and administrators be formed to seek a resolution to the situation. The results of the referendum are shown in Table 1.

TABLE 1   Referendum Results

Alternative (You may vote for more than one)	Percentage of Total Vote
Continuation of current grading system	12
Pass-Fail for only those courses outside the major	22
Pass-Fail for all courses	19
Essay evaluations by teachers of students' performances	4
No grades	27
Form a committee of students, faculty members, and administrators to attempt to settle the issue	61

Total number of ballots cast: 6,083

Task

Your task is to select an alternative, if any, to the current grading system. This task will be accomplished in committees of about twelve members, each committee working independently in separate committee rooms.

Roles

Your task is limited by the role you are assigned and by whatever special instructions you might receive to define your individual role and tactics. If there are special instructions for your individual role, they must be followed closely and disclosed to no one. This may force you to advocate a position for which you have no sympathy; however, if the game is to succeed, you must play your role.

These roles are not meant to imply that all people fall neatly into the few types characterized here. In one game, as in any particular situation, it is not possible to represent the multitude of varied and complex human personalities. These roles, therefore, sketch but a few of the many types of people, with different ideas, commitments, and vested interests, who might confront each other over an issue such as this.

Table 2 shows the composition of each committee and the number of votes which each member casts. Following Table 2 are the *Schedule* and the *Procedures* which you need as you accomplish your task.

TABLE 2   Committee Members: Roles and Votes

Roles	Number of Votes
Administrators:	
Vice President for Academic Affairs	2
Vice President for Student Affairs	2
Dean of Students	2
Faculty Members:	
1 Radical Faculty Member	2
2 Moderate to Uncommitted Faculty Members	2 each
Students:	
2 Radical Students	1 each
Moderate Students (regardless of the number of Moderate Students on the committee, they have only 4 votes to divide equally among them)	4 total
	18 total

Schedule

1. Convene in main meeting room at the appointed time.
2. Discuss instructions and role assignments.
3. Committees go to separate conference rooms assigned to them (45 minutes).
   a. Subcommittee Strategy Period (15 minutes). Student Subcommittee, Faculty Subcommittee, and Administration Subcommittee meet separately, within the same room, to plan strategy for the meeting of the whole committee.
   b. Committee Meeting (30 minutes). Subcommittees combine into the whole committee to seek a grading system which will end the turmoil.
   c. Notify the teacher when a decision is reached or if a deadlock occurs.
4. All participants reconvene in main meeting room at the call of the teacher to announce decisions.
5. Rap session.

Procedures

Subcommittee strategy period (15 minutes). In each committee room the three subcommittees (Student, Faculty, Administration) meet separately to plan their strategies for the meeting of the whole committee. Individuals may communicate with other members of their own subcommittee and with members of the other subcommittees. Also, all members of a subcommittee may communicate with all members of another subcommittee. These communications may be either verbal or written; however, demands, proposed deals, proposed compromises, and counterproposals must be exchanged in writing. So that notes can be delivered to the proper person, it is important that you wear your name tag and that it bear your committee number and role assignment.

Committee Meeting (30 minutes). The Vice President for Academic Affairs calls the full committee into session and presides over the meeting; the Dean of Students acts as recording secretary. *By a majority of the votes,* members of the committee are to choose a specific alternative to the current grading system or they may decide to retain that grading system.

In the voting each of the three administrators has two votes; each of the three faculty members has two votes; each of the two radical students has one vote; and the moderate students have a pool of four votes to be divided equally among them. Thus, a majority of the *voters* may not be enough to gain a majority of the *votes*. An individual may cast his vote(s) regardless of how other individuals within his subcommittee vote, but an individual may not split his votes (that is, an administrator need not vote for the same alternative as other administrators, but he must cast both of his votes for the same alternative).

Votes are taken by a show of hands, and the Dean of Students records each vote. This record should include which individuals supported which alternative. When the committee has reached a decision, notify your teacher.

In the event that a majority (ten votes or more) is not obtained, a five-minute bargaining session will take place. A vote may be bypassed if after five minutes it is apparent that a majority vote still cannot be reached. After three successive votes with no majority vote, consider yourselves deadlocked and notify the teacher (treat a bypassed vote as an unsuccessful vote).

30

Desegregate Now!

STUDENT'S INSTRUCTIONS

Supplies

Name tag showing committee number, high school PTA, and role;
Note pad or slips of paper;
Pencil or pen.

This simulation or game confronts you with one of the most disruptive issues of the day: school desegregation and the assignment of pupils —black and white, rich and poor, white-collar and blue-collar—to three high schools which traditionally have not done an equal job of preparing students. As explained fully in the *Background*, members of the local school board clashed over an appropriate response to the Court's order to desegregate now. Time is short, and the school board members have passed the buck to members of the three PTA's to find an acceptable desegregation plan. Playing the role of a representative from one of the PTA's, you serve on a committee where the task is to recommend a solution that will defuse a potentially explosive situation. As you and your fellow committee members strive toward an acceptable desegregation plan, the schedule and specific procedures serve as the boundaries for your efforts.

Background

A three-judge federal panel has rejected the petition of your school district to allow its "freedom of choice" plan to continue in operation. The Court ruled that desegregation must take place at once and that the school board must come back to the Court in three weeks with an acceptable plan for fully integrating the three high schools located within the school district.

The high schools and their current pupil composition are as follows:

High School	Composition	Enrollment
Martin Luther King	All blacks	1,000
Samuel Gompers	All blue-collar whites	1,200
George Washington	Upper- and middle-class whites and 8 blacks	900

Martin Luther King High has the highest drop-out rate in the school district; few graduates go to college, and those who do are usually athletes. Many students at Samuel Gompers High also drop out; some go to vocational schools. Most male graduates from Gompers go directly into apprenticeships for the skilled trades; few nonathletes go to college. In contrast, almost all students at George Washington High graduate, and most of them go to college.

Each of the three high schools is centrally located within the neighborhood it serves (that is, King is in the black neighborhood; Gompers is in the blue-collar, white neighborhood; and Washington is in the upper- and middle-class, white neighborhood). The school district currently owns no school buses, but there is a public bus system throughout the school district.

The members of the district school board have been unable to reach a decision as to the composition of the high schools. At a recent board meeting, Board Chairman T. M. Brice proposed that a fixed ratio of blacks to whites for each school be approved. The ratio which he suggested was one black student for every two white students in *each* high school.

Joe Sims, the only black member of the board, agreed that the ratio of blacks to whites should be one to two, but proposed further (1) that Gompers High—the oldest school in the district and a fire trap—be closed, (2) that King and Washington Highs absorb the extra students, and (3) that the students be put on a split-shift schedule. In this way, Sims explained, the better facilities at King and Washington Highs could be utilized for the benefit of all the students in the district.

Board member Tim O'Reilly agreed that Gompers should be closed but proposed (1) that the composition of King High remain 100 percent black, (2) that the students from Gompers be transferred to Washington High only, and (3) that Washington High go on a split shift to accommodate the new students.

Board member James Bentley Anderson proposed as a fourth alternative that the composition of the three high schools be as follows:

King	*Gompers*	*Washington*
60% from King	65% from Gompers	75% from Washington
25% from Gompers	25% from King	15% from King
15% from Washington	10% from Washington	10% from Gompers

The assignment of students under the Anderson proposal would be made by lottery.

The final proposal was presented to the Board by its fifth member, Mrs. James Otis Smith: (1) that Gompers be extensively repaired and become the school for all tenth graders, (2) that King become the school for all eleventh graders, and (3) that Washington become the school for all twelfth graders in the school district.

Chairman Brice then called for a vote on the various proposals made that evening. Each proposal received one vote. The board members, after taking five identical votes, decided to adjourn. Called into session three days later, the members were still deadlocked. Mrs. Smith, at this point, argued that the parents of the youngsters would have to bear the greatest burden, no matter which proposal is adopted. Therefore, she proposed that representatives from the PTAs of the three high schools meet jointly to decide on a desegregation plan to recommend to the school board. The deadlock was broken by the members unanimously adopting Mrs. Smith's new proposal.

Two of the three weeks permitted by the Court to adopt a resolution have elapsed. The PTA's must meet at once.

Task

Your task is to draft a proposal to desegregate the three high schools in the school district (1) that the parents of the district can tolerate, (2) that the school board can adopt, and (3) that the U.S. District Court will approve. Your task will be accomplished in a committee of about 12 members, each of whom has been assigned an individual role to play. The schedule and specific procedures impose upon your committee time restrictions which are almost the only way to simulate time and other pressures which exist in actual decision-making situations.

Committees

In other localities, mass PTA meetings have proved chaotic; when everyone wants to speak, a consensus is impossible to reach. In order to avoid such confusion, representative PTA spokesmen from each high school are to form a committee. The committee is to recommend an acceptable solution to the school board. You and about three others are the spokesmen for the PTA of your child's high school. Approximately the same number of spokesmen are to represent each of the other two PTAs, for a total committee membership of about 12. You will receive your (1) committee assignment, (2) high school PTA to represent, and (3) individual role to play in representing that PTA. You have *one vote* regardless of the number of members on the committee.

Roles

Every member of your committee has an assigned role to play. All roles are important; therefore, it is crucial to the success of the game that you participate vigorously. Your individual role instructions roughly define your role and tactics. Even though your actual views may differ from those imposed by your role, follow your individual role instructions. Disclose them to no one except through your behavior as you play the role.

These roles are not meant to imply that all people fall neatly into the few types characterized here. In one game, as in any particular situation, it is not possible to represent the multitude of varied and complex human personalities. These roles, therefore, sketch but a few of the many types of people, with different ideas, commitments, and vested interests, who might confront each other over an issue such as this.

The various roles represented on each committee are shown in the following list.

PTAs	Roles	Votes
Martin Luther King	1 civil rights leader, middle-class black	1
	1 militant, middle-class black	1
	2 uncommitteds, blue-collar blacks	1 each
Samuel Gompers	1 social climber, blue-collar white	1
	1 segregationist, blue-collar white	1
	2 uncommitteds, blue-collar whites	1 each

George Washington	1 civil rights advocate,	
	upper-middle-class white	1
	1 constitutional conservative,	
	middle-class white	1
	2 *nouveaux riches,*	
	upper-class whites	1 each
		12 total

Schedule

1. Convene in main meeting room at the appointed time.
2. Discuss instructions and role assignments.
3. Members of each committee go to the committee room assigned to them (45 minutes).
   a. Individual PTA Strategy Session (15 minutes). Representatives of Washington PTA, Gompers PTA, and King PTA meet separately, within the same room, to plan strategy for the Joint PTA Committee Meeting.
   b. Joint PTA Meeting (30 minutes). Representatives of the three PTAs combine as the Joint Committee to draft a proposal to the school board that will be acceptable to parents, the school board, and the Court.
   c. Notify your teacher when your proposal to the school board is ready or if the members of your committee are deadlocked.
4. All participants reconvene in main meeting room when called by the teacher to announce decisions.
5. Rap session.

Procedures

Individual PTA Strategy Sessions (15 minutes). In the room assigned to your Joint PTA Committee your initial 15 minutes are allotted for representatives from each PTA to meet separately to map their strategy for the Joint Meeting with representatives from the other two PTAs. Individuals may communicate with other members of their own PTA and with members of the other PTAs. Also, all representatives of a PTA may communicate with all representatives of another PTA. These communications may be either verbal or written; however, demands, proposed deals, proposed compromises, and counter proposals must be exchanged in writing. So that notes can be delivered to the proper person, it is important that you wear your name tag and that it bear your PTA and role assignment.

Joint PTA Meeting (30 minutes). During this 30-minute period, representatives of the three PTAs combine as the Joint Committee with the task of drafting a desegregation proposal which will be acceptable to the parents in the school district, to the district school board, and to the U.S. District Court.

The representative from the Washington High PTA who has the role of civil rights advocate will serve as moderator for the Joint PTA Meeting. His responsibilities are important, but they give him neither a stronger nor a weaker voice within the committee than his role warrants. All of the moderator's tasks are performed during the Joint PTA Meeting.

The moderator will call the Joint PTA Meeting to order. The first 20 minutes will be devoted to the recommendation and discussion of proposals for desegregating the schools. At the conclusion of the discussion period, the moderator will call for a vote by a show of hands and will count and record the votes. Each representative has one vote to cast and may cast it as he chooses, regardless of how other members of his own PTA vote. A majority vote of the committee members is necessary for a proposal to be adopted.

The teacher should be notified by the moderator either (1) when a majority of the members of the committee have reached agreement on a proposal to present to the school board, or (2) if at the end of 30 minutes a majority of the committee members do not support any one proposal and the comittee is deadlocked. (Your teacher may give you an extension of time.)

31

Presidential
Nominating Convention

Supplies

Name tag showing state and member number;
Note pad or slips of paper;
Pencil or pen.

Through this simulation you are involved in power politics. First, you serve as a member of your political party's state caucus. Then you serve as a delegate to your party's national convention.

In Part One, members of the caucus from each state choose one of their number who will be their state party's "favorite son" for the national party's presidential nomination. Your objective in Part One is to become (1) your caucus' candidate for the presidential nomination, or (2) a "king maker" so that you can expect to be rewarded, if Part Two is played.

In Part Two, caucuses become delegations and meet together in the presidential nominating convention to choose their party's nominee for the presidency. Members of each delegation put forward the favorite son they have chosen to support. From among the favorite sons—or a "darkhorse," if delegates to the convention become deadlocked—they select a presidential nominee.

Your party's nominee for the presidency has an almost certain chance of winning the office in the general election. Whoever becomes the nominee in Part Two, therefore, probably will be the next president of the United States.

The president has the authority to appoint more than fifteen hundred personnel to fill public offices of great policy-making importance. Among the more influential offices are those contained in the partial listing at the conclusion of these instructions. These are the offices which you may promise or use to strike bargains with members of your caucus in Part One and with delegates from other states in Part Two. Although no one obtains a position or office at the conclusion of Part One, the winner of Part Two can dispense the offices listed. (Your instructor may and probably will limit the number of listed jobs which you are to use as you play this game, particularly if Part Two is not played.)

PART ONE

You are confronted with several restraints as you and other members of your caucus choose the favorite son candidate for your party's presidential nomination. Every member of the caucus wields a different number of votes, which simulates the different impacts exerted by heavy financial contributors to the party and the various pressure groups aligned with it. Pressures of time and of relatively blind negotiations are rampant in the presidential candidate selection process in the U.S. These pressures are simulated by the limitations upon time, bargaining, and information which are noted in the *Schedule* and explained under *Procedures*. Be conscious of these restraints!

Task

In each caucus, the task is to select from among caucus members a candidate for the party's presidential nomination. The task for each caucus member is either to become that candidate or to have the greatest possible voice in determining who the candidate is.

You have been assigned as a numbered member of a state party caucus where you and your fellow caucus members are to choose your state's "favorite son" candidate for your party's presidential nomination.

Member Number 4 in each caucus is the temporary caucus chairman. If Part Two is being played, the chairman's first task is to list the caucus rooms assigned to other caucuses so that negotiations in Part Two are not delayed.

As a member of the caucus you have an opportunity to vote for the favorite son (including voting for yourself); however, each member of the caucus does not have an equal number of votes. Votes are weighted as follows:

Member Number	Massylvania	Bamasippi	Illibraska	Calihoma
1	1 vote	1 vote	1 vote	1 vote
2	2 votes	2 votes	2 votes	2 votes
3	3	3	3	3
4 (Chairman)	4	4	4	4
5	5	5	5	5
6	6	6	6	6
7	7	7	7	7
8	8	8	8	8
9	9	9	9	9
10	10	10	10	10
11	11	11	11	
12	12	12	12	
13	13	13	13	
14	14	14	14	
15	15	15	15	

Calihoma's caucus will be about two-thirds the size of the larger caucuses, and the larger caucuses will be roughly equal in size. Lowest member numbers will be assigned first.

Schedule

1. Convene in main meeting room at the appointed time.
2. Discuss instructions and receive caucus and member number assignments.
3. Caucus chairmen (Members Number 4) list rooms where other caucuses meet (unless Part Two is not to follow immediately).
4. State caucuses go to their individual caucus rooms.
   a. First note-writing period, with notes not to be read until the end of the period (20 minutes).
   b. Second note-writing period, during which notes may be read when received (15 minutes).
   c. Verbal negotiating period (15 minutes).
   d. Test vote on readiness to select favorite son—a majority of caucus members must agree that they are ready to select the favorite son before the next step is taken. If after two votes a majority are

still "not ready" consider yourselves deadlocked and notify the instructor.

e. Selection of favorite son by a majority of the (weighted) votes (or, alternatively, an additional 15-minute verbal negotiating period and second vote). After a favorite son has been selected notify the teacher. If no candidate has a majority of weighted votes after two votes are taken, select a favorite son by a majority of members, one vote per member. In the event that no candidate receives a majority of votes following this procedure, consider yourselves deadlocked and notify the teacher.

5. Rap session in main meeting room, if Part Two is not to be played.

Procedures

Before a state's candidate for the presidential nomination can claim favorite son status, he must surmount two hurdles. First, a majority[1] of all caucus members (*not* just those caucus members voting) must be ready and willing at that point in time to make their choice for favorite son. Second, after a majority of the caucus shows it is ready to select its favorite son, the successful candidate needs only a majority of the (weighted) votes,[2] whether or not those who cast the majority of the votes constitute a majority of the members.

This selection process is preceded by two periods during which negotiations are written only, plus a negotiating period during which communications may be either written or verbal.

First note-writing period (20 minutes). At the outset, make certain that your name tag, showing your state and member number, can be read from across the room.

The positions listed at the conclusion of these instructions may be used to bargain for support for yourself or your preferred candidate for favorite son. Remember that the president and vice president cannot be from the same state.

During this 20-minute period, communications are to be conducted solely by notes, which are to be written and delivered *but not read* until the end of the 20 minutes. *Verbal communications during note-writing periods violate the rules of the game.*

Any caucus member can write as many notes as he chooses to any other members of the caucus. It the sender needs to identify himself, he should do so on the inside fold of the note. In every instance, the name

---

[1]More than 50 percent, i.e., 7 of 12, 6 of 11, 6 of 10, etc.

[2]For example, if there are 12 members of the caucus, 40 of the 78 votes; if 11 members, 34 of the 66 votes; if 10 members, 28 of the 55 votes, etc.

of the caucus member to whom the note is addressed should appear on the outside fold.

At the end of 20 minutes, about 5 minutes will be allowed for notes to be read and new individual strategies to be developed.

Second note-writing period (15 minutes). With the first set of notes read, the simulation proceeds into the second note-writing period. Here, again, you may write as many notes as you wish to anyone in your caucus. In this period, however, *notes may be read immediately upon receiving them.* This note-writing period will last for 15 minutes. Again no verbal communications are permitted.

During the verbal negotiating period which follows you may meet with members of your caucus face to face; therefore, your notes in this second note-writing period need to contain the details as to where you should meet (either in the room or outside of it) and what you would like to discuss.

Verbal negotiating period (15 to 20 minutes). The verbal negotiating period comes immediately after the second note-writing session and lasts from 15 to 20 minutes. Here caucus members, having arranged meetings by note in the second note-writing session, consult with each other, make plans, construct coalitions, strike bargains, etc. More than two caucus members are permitted to meet together.

Test vote on readiness to select favorite son. Following the verbal negotiating period, a hand vote will be taken by the temporary caucus chairman (Member Number 4) to determine whether or not members of the caucus are ready to select their favorite son candidate for the presidential nomination. Each member has *one* vote, and if he is ready to select a favorite son he should vote "ready." If a member prefers further negotiating, he should vote "not ready."

If a majority of the caucus is "not ready," members of the caucus repeat the previous step, that is, they engage in 15 more minutes of verbal negotiations. If the majority is still "not ready" at the end of the second verbal negotiating period, the temporary caucus chairman should notify the teacher of the deadlock.

Selection of the Favorite Son. When a majority of the caucus is ready to vote (or when your instructor breaks your deadlock), select your favorite son. Your *weighted votes* are the ones you cast in this part of the game, and they can be split. They need not be cast as a bloc. (Split voting simulates characteristic behavior by leaders of political interest groups who support different candidates so that their group has access, regardless of who wins.)

The temporary caucus chairman simply (1) asks each member for whom he casts his votes, (2) records the votes, and (3) announces the results.

If no one receives a majority of the (weighted) votes, the temporary caucus chairman declares a 10-minute verbal negotiating period. If no one receives a majority of the votes after this second verbal negotiating period, elect a favorite son by a majority of the members, one vote per member.

After a favorite son has been selected, notify your teacher. It neither of the procedures above breaks the deadlock, notify your teacher.

After the teacher has been notified that members of each caucus have selected their favorite son he will either (1) reconvene all participants in the main meeting room for the rap session, if Part Two is not to be played, or (2) instruct you to begin Part Two. It is important that all states wait to begin Part Two at the same time!

PART TWO

Part Two is an extension of Part One; it is in Part Two that the national party's presidential nominee is selected from among the favorite sons from the various states.

You have already chosen your state's favorite son who is now your spokesman and strategist in negotiating with spokesmen from other states. Your caucus becomes a delegation to the convention and continues to operate in and from the caucus room which you utilized in Part One; Member Number 4 has a list of the headquarters (rooms) for the other delegations.

Your objective in this part of the game is to support the candidate (1) who can win your party's presidential nomination, and (2) who will give you the most and best patronage appointments after he wins the general election. Your favorite son, with or without your helpful insights, may or may not decide that the way to accomplish this objective is to form a coalition (combine) with another state or states and support their favorite son, dropping his own candidacy. Such coalitions are necessary because states have different numbers of votes:

State	Votes
Massylvania	30
Bamasippi	19
Illibraska	40
Calihoma	11
Total	100

The differences here are artificial, but similar ones exist in actual convention situations due to differences in (1) population, (2) which party's candidate carried the state in the last presidential election, (3) how many U.S. House and Senate seats are held by state party members, etc.

The favorite son who receives a majority of the convention votes becomes the national party's presidential nominee. Each state's delegation must cast its votes as a bloc; votes from a state cannot be split. (Bloc voting is becoming increasingly artificial, as Democrats limit the practice in the U.S. In this game, however, there is no simple way to divide these votes by the number of delegates from each state. An additional consideration is that bloc voting here reduces considerably the amount of time required to play the game.)

The *Schedule* and *Procedures* specify the time and procedural boundaries for your efforts.

Schedule

1. Remain in your caucus room from Part One; it is now the headquarters for your state party's delegation to the convention. Discuss instructions for Part Two.
2. Note-writing period (20 minutes).
   a. Seek or offer support and/or offices.
   b. Arrange for face-to-face negotiations between representatives from various delegations.
3. Negotiations between delegation spokesmen at the time and place arranged during the previous period (15 minutes).
   a. With no more than two negotiators present.
   b. For no longer than three minutes per meeting.
   c. With only one meeting between negotiators representing any two delegations.
4. Members of delegations deliberate and decide whom they will support for the presidential nomination; a simple majority—one vote per delegate—determines for whom the delegation's bloc of votes will be cast (15 minutes). After two votes, if no candidate has received a majority, consider yourselves deadlocked and notify your teacher.
5. A messenger from each delegation notifies the teacher when its members are ready for the convention to begin.
6. Teacher reconvenes all delegations in the main meeting room to select the presidential nominee. The nominee is selected by *a majority of the weighted votes cast as blocs* by members of state delegations.
7. Press conference by the presidential nominee.
8. Rap session.

Procedures

Before the delegations from each state go to the floor of the convention (main meeting room) to choose a presidential nominee, there are three separate but related deliberation/negotiation periods. The first is a negotiation period during which written negotiations are conducted between and among delegations. The second is a verbal negotiation period conducted by delegation spokesmen, and the third is the period during which delegates from each state deliberate and decide for whom their bloc of votes will be cast.

Note-writing period (20 minutes). Each state's favorite son and/or those he designates utilize the 20-minute note-writing period to bargain for support and to arrange meetings (for the subsequent 15-minute verbal negotiating period) with negotiators from other delegations. Each state delegation needs a messenger(s) (a volunteer or an appointee of the favorite son). All notes must be written by or with the approval of the favorite son. Notes may be read upon receipt.

Notes arranging meetings should include time and place (outside the delegation rooms) where delegation spokesmen are to meet to bargain and negotiate for support and appointments to high office. Only two delegations may be represented at any one meeting, and only one negotiator may represent his delegation at a meeting. This means that no more than two negotiators are to meet together at the same time during the 15-minute verbal negotiating period which is to follow. (Of course, delegates from the same state who are neither a negotiator nor a messenger remain in their delegation room.)

Verbal negotiating period (15 minutes). The time and site of meetings conducted during this 15-minute verbal negotiating period may have been arranged by note during the note-writing period or they may be arranged during this period. Only note-bearing messengers, who must remain silent, are permitted to enter another delegation's room.

Favorite sons or their designated negotiators may meet and bargain with their counterparts from other state delegations in an effort to create a winning coalition. A spokesman from any delegation may meet with a spokesman from any other delegation *only once* and then for no more than three minutes.

Delegation deliberation (15 minutes). Negotiators, having concluded their meetings with other negotiators, report back to their delegations.

During this 15-minute period members of each delegation decide whom to support on the floor of the convention. The favorite son presides over his delegation's decision, which is reached by a simple majority, *one vote per delegate.* As soon as members of a delegation have reached their decision, their messenger should notify the teacher. After two votes, if no candidate has received a majority, notify the teacher that the members of your delegation are deadlocked.

Choosing a presidential nominee. All delegates will be called back to the convention hall (main meeting room) by the teacher after he has been notified that each delegation is ready to choose the party's presidential nominee. Members of each delegation should sit grouped together in the convention hall.

The teacher will act as the convention chairman and the favorite sons will act as the spokesmen for their state delegations in the voting.

The chairman will call the meeting to order and ask for nominations for president of the United States. The favorite sons will be recognized by the chairman to nominate candidates and later to cast their votes. (Candidates for the presidential nomination, by custom, do not attend convention sessions, but in the simulation, it is important that everyone participate in all phases of the game. When favorite sons are delegation spokesmen, it insures that members of other delegations know each favorite son, at least by sight.)

States are *not* allowed to split their votes; they must vote in a bloc for one candidate. Thus, in voting for the nomination, the favorite son casts his delegation's *weighted votes as a bloc* for the candidate chosen by a majority of the delegates from his state. A simple majority of the total number of votes is needed to select a presidential nominee for your party.

If on the first ballot no candidate has a majority, delegates will negotiate and deliberate for ten minutes within the convention hall. The favorite sons may consult with favorite sons from other states. In addition, the members of each delegation will be able to take a re-vote as to whom to support for president. Moreover, in this period members of one state delegation may consult with members of other state delegations to try to arrange for another candidate besides the favorite sons. Prior to the second ballot, one of the members of any new coalition formed by members from different states should gain the attention of the chairman to make a nomination. However, you must remember that, even though you decide on a different (darkhorse) candidate for the presidential nomination and make an agreement with members of another delegation, delegates from each state always vote their total number of votes as a bloc—no split voting is permitted during any balloting.

Convention balloting will continue until a presidential nominee is selected. If no one receives a majority on the second ballot, another negotiating period takes place, then another ballot, *ad infinitum*.

Press conference. After a presidential nominee has been selected by the party he will hold a press conference in the main meeting room. Here he announces whom he will appoint to the different positions which will come under his authority after the November election. He may do this since his party has an almost unbeatable lead over any other party.

Patronage Appointments which the President will be Able to Make when he Takes Office*

Vice President of the United States

Department Heads

Secretary of State
Secretary of the Treasury
Secretary of Defense
Attorney General
Secretary of the Interior
Secretary of Agriculture

Secretary of Commerce
Secretary of Labor
Secretary of Health, Education, and Welfare
Secretary of Housing and Urban Development
Secretary of Transportation

Judgeships

Chief Justice of the U.S. Supreme Court
2 Associate Justices of the Supreme Court
12 Circuit Court judges
17 District Court judges

Ambassadors

21 Ambassadors, including the U.N., England, France, the Soviet Union, Japan, Thailand, India, Mexico, Canada, Norway, and Israel.

Positions in the Executive Office of the President

3 members of the President's Council of Economic Advisors, including the Chairman
Director of the Office of Management and Budget
Director of the Office of Emergency Planning
White House Staff, including Press Secretary, Appointments Secretary, Chief of Legislative Liaison, plus 6 Counsels

*These positions are either currently vacant or will be vacant by the time the new president takes office.

Other Federal Positions to Become Vacant

Director of the Federal Bureau of Investigation (F.B.I.)
Director of the Secret Service
Secretaries of the Army, the Navy, and the Air Force
Director of the Selective Service System
Chairman of the Federal Reserve Board
3 vacancies on the Federal Communications Commission, including the Chairman
3 vacancies on the Interstate Commerce Commission
1 vacancy on the National Labor Relations Board
2 vacancies on the Federal Aviation Authority
2 vacancies on the Tennessee Valley Authority Board of Directors

Author Index

Subject Index